IT'S OVER

BY

R. KEITH MARTIN

Copyright ©2010 Ron Martin

ISBN-13: 978-0-615-37762-9
ISBN-10: 0-6153776-2-9

All rights reserved. No part of this publication may be reproduced, stored in a retrieval system or transmitted in any form or by any means, electronic, mechanical, photocopying, recording or otherwise, without prior written permission of the publisher.

Published by R. Keith Martin
Suches, Georgia

Web Site: its-over.info

I dedicate this book as I have dedicated my earthly life, to my "everything girl," my wife, Dianne

Contents

RULES OF ENGAGEMENT (PROLOGUE)	6
FATAL SEQUENCE	11
BONDAGE, FAITH, COURAGE & FREEDOM	13
ABUNDANCE TO COMPLACENCY	16
COMPLACENCY TO APATHY	23
ABORTION	25
NANNY STATE	28
HOMOSEXUALS	32
POLITICS OF THE DARKSIDE	38
LIBERALS AND CONSERVATIVES	46
EDUCATION	52
APATHY TO FEAR	60
FEAR TO DEPENDENCY	66
TERRISOM	72
MILITARY	103
DEPENDENCY TO BONDAGE	117
THE BLACK IMBROGLIO	118
WHITE SLAVERY	119
BLACK SLAVERY	123
RECONSTRUCTION	130
THE SECOND RECONSTRUCTION	152
WHITE GUILT	168
DIVERSITY, AFFIRMATIVE ACTION AND EQUALITY	182
INCONVENIENT TRUTHS	189
WHITE RACISM IS RARE, BLACK RACISM IS RAGING	193
SUICIDAL WHITES	203

VERY MERRY BARRY	208
THE PERFECT STORM	222
THE MADHI COMETH	225
OBAMA MANIFESTO	228
OBAMA'S ROGUES	232
OBAMA'S DEMONS	247
USEFUL IDIOTS	256
BODY COUNT THUS FAR	264
THE FASCIST MEDIA	274
NATIONALIZED INTERNET	278
PRAVDA REBIRTH	280
CLOWARD-PIVENS MEETS THE DARKSIDE	284
NATIONALIZED HEALTH CARE	302
CAP AND TRADE	306
ILLEGAL ALIENS	308
NATIONALIZING OUR ECONOMY	321
CRIMINAL SUFFRAGE	324
BIGGER BROTHER	329
LAMENTABLE AMERICA	332
PERSONAL LAMENTATIONS	337
THE FINAL SOLUTION	340
DIGGING AMERICA'S GRAVE	342
AMERICA'S HARDENED HEARTS	346
AMERICA'S ROAD TO SERFDOM	349
THE COMING DEMICIDE	363
WHY OBAMA MUST MURDER YOU	391
SUM	395
POSTSCRIPT	426

RULES OF ENGAGEMENT (PROLOGUE)

Allow me to be the first author to give you the ending at the beginning. Simply put, **IT'S OVER!** By that I mean that the America of your father is gone, and the America now enjoyed by you will soon be gone forever. More importantly, your hopes and dreams for your children and their children shall remain just that, a dream. Your daily mundane routines and thoughts of 401K's, retirement, growing old together, Caribbean cruises and a cabin in the mountains are not in the cards. All that you have taken for granted since birth will change and disappear before your very eyes. Happiness will turn to tragedy. If you survive, your life will be like the walking dead, a serf among many serfs.

America is terminal and its demise is not the result of Algore's global warming or Michael Moore's phantom conspiracies. Neither is it Iran's nuke(s), Putin's reconstituted USSR or China rising. It's an "in house job" by people whose names you have come to know, but really don't know at all. For the past 100 years or so they have been called liberals, progressives, statists, communists, Nazis, fascists, socialists, leftists and, most recently, Democrats. Regardless of how Webster defines each of these belief systems they all share the same dream: dismantling our 234 year old democratic republic and replacing it with a serfdom ruled by oligarchic elitists. For simplicity, I will combine all nine of these evils into one and simply call it the "Darkside", as in Star Wars. Unlike the movie, there is no Darth Vader coming after you, and no Luke Skywalker to save you, and sadly, the good guys don't win in the end.

Fortunately for the Darkside, most Americans are the products of 50 years of intentional numbing and dumbing down. Like a boiling frog, they are unaware of being slowly boiled to death. These Americans perceive that we're having a few problems lately, but so what, America has always bounced back, right? They've seen Democrats and Republicans shouting at each other for years. The pendulum has always swung back, yes? Even now, with insane spending and a Chicago mob running the White House they think our system of checks and balances will arrest the downward spiral starting with the 2010 elections, and will bring in a new crew to right the ship of state. We may have a few bumps and bruises but, like AIG, America is too big to fail. Surprise! Even before the messiah came to save us, the United States was imploding thanks to the criminal spending spree by both political parties. With the arrival of Obama, the fall will go from linear to light speed.

Thank God for optimists, especially the conservative ones. They keep pointing to Obama's declining poll numbers in the hopes of taking back Congress in 2010, and gutting some of Obama's worst attacks on our freedoms, like Obamacare. They should temper their euphoria by simply recalling that an unknown community organizer who never worked a day in his life, birthplace unknown, grade transcripts from four colleges unavailable, a question mark for a background, who was begat by an atheist and an alcoholic, raised $668 million from mystery donors, beat unbeatable Hillary Clinton, easily won against a war hero, and went on to become the President of the only superpower on planet earth.

This book was written for those good Americans who have been working and living their lives, but have not had the time to read between the lines of a media that now does the bidding of the Darkside. I have tried to compress a year of diligent research into a few hundred pages to bring you up to speed on our grave danger and how we got here. After this book, I encourage you to read the writings of Friedrich von Hayek, Edmund Burke, Rudolph J. Rummel, Michelle Malkin, Rufus Choate, Mark Levin, Ann Coulter, Dore Gold, Brigitte Gabriel, and others like them. This is just a short list. To grasp the depth of the extreme peril faced by Americans you must take advantage not only of the facts and evidence compiled over years of effort by these and many more great conservatives, both living and dead, but you must also keep abreast of current events because the Darkside is moving swiftly.

I have used the "fatal sequence" format to take you through America's history from our colonial founding to today. Although the teaching of American exceptionalism to our children was sacrificed to political correctness long ago, it is still an unquestionable axiom of truth. There has never been created by man a more perfect union of balanced opportunity, fairness, freedom and faith. The more I study our founding fathers and their wisdom, the more I am amazed at their almost superhuman foresight and intellect. But even their knowledge of the ages could not prevent the eventual seepage of evil into our almost perfect system of governance. Simple, seemingly innocent acts of government charity actually start a democracy on the path to incremental progressivism which becomes socialism. Socialism always produces a single ruler that tastes the forbidden fruit of power. And, as you'll see later, power corrupts and absolute power corrupts absolutely.

There are many great conservative thinkers and authors and I hardly have the credentials to criticize them. But I will. Not even one contemporary author of conservative thought has honestly addressed the issue of white and black race relations without the usual pandering arising out of fear of being accused of racial insensitivity or outright racism. To me, replacing truth with pander either means the author feels superior to the black race and treats them like children, or the author feels he is inferior to the black race. I think all conservative authors feel neither of these motives, but they appear to be such. In my "Black Imbroglio" section I have tried to give you a history of slavery that our political correctness has erased from our history books, and a perspective of which even most conservatives are ignorant. I am a Yankee who moved to the segregated South in 1958. I saw the court-ordered end of segregation only to see it re-imposed later, not by the process of law, but by the very people who wanted it to end. I argue that the re-introduction of segregation by the black elite is really a control technique to keep the elite in perpetual power, which it has done. My real ultimate destination in bringing you the "Black Imbroglio" is Obama. Were it not for the inculcated guilt of whites, absorbed from a society dripping with it, and the black elitists institutionalizing black dependency, Obama would never have progressed beyond community organizer.

But, Obama did progress, and he is President. If he was just another black liberal pushing welfare programs or other liberal causes like all black politicians I would not have spent the last year cloistered with my computer. Obama is dangerous - crash and burn dangerous. The deeper and deeper I dug into the Obama machine, and the Darkside, the greater I realized just how much trouble America is in. We have simply never faced such an array of problems, or had to depend for our rescue from the precipice, on someone that is pulling the lifeline away from us as we reach for it. What is even more amazing is that is seems that nobody, or at least very few, really believe that we are very near the point of collapse. What Obama is doing routinely on a daily basis, no other President would have even attempted. Bill Clinton came closest to this chronic criminality with the FBI files scandal, White House Travel Office, Vince Foster, and numerous others, but nothing compared to what Obama and the Darkside are doing every day in every part of his administration.

More amazing still is the realization of just how powerful a President can be if they use the powers enumerated to them plus powers not enumerated to them. Part of this power comes from the fact that the Democrats control both houses of Congress. Another, perhaps even more exacerbating aspect giving Obama unlimited power, is that, for the first time in our history, we have no media watching the President's every move, and grilling him constantly as they did Bush. I wrote a section on what I call "hardened hearts" because that term is the closest I can come to in defining the nonchalance of all but a few Washington observers of Obama's eccentric behavior. It's almost as if Obama moves at a superhero speed while the rest of us are locked in slow motion. By the time we recognize and comment on a particular action, he has moved on to another issue, and ignores our questions about the former.

The election of a President from a 13% black minority group is earth shaking when you recall that blacks were chattel property just 145 years ago. What an amazingly fair society we must be, right? Wrong. The "race card" is being played more than ever, and black racism is alive and well in post-Obama America. This should be a wake-up call to Americans that appeasement only whets the appetite for more appeasement. Whites do not treat blacks with equality. They treat them as if they are inferior wards of the state who must receive special dispensation from cradle to grave. After 60 years of this coddling, the majority of the black race is in a dreadful condition, both morally and fiscally bankrupt. The race divide is wide, it is increasing, and the Hispanics are joining the blacks. It will explode soon and there is probably nothing we can do about it.

In the Final Solution and Sum sections, I tell you of the unavoidable collision approaching soon between the Darkside and the only force capable of stopping them before they bury us all. This collision is coming as assuredly as the sun will rise tomorrow. The time to have prevented this clash is long past. You can run like a deer and hide like an ostrich, but you can't escape what's coming. Contrary to my opening paragraph there is hope, but it does not come from the political arena like all other conservative writers expound. It must pour forth from the hearts of what's left of America's remnant or, **"It's Over."**

FATAL SEQUENCE

It has been 234 years since the Continental Congress appointed a "Committee of Five", Thomas Jefferson, Ben Franklin, John Adams, Robert R. Livingston and Roger Sherman, to draft our Declaration of Independence. Our Constitution came along 12 years later and was ratified on June 21, 1788. It was the greatest governance document ever authored by the hand of man. How have we traveled from a near perfect blueprint for a democratic republic to the consternation swirling about us in 2010?

Most of you have heard of Scottish history professor Alexander Tyler's words written in 1788 regarding his study of the Athenian Republic some 2000 years earlier. You may have first encountered Tyler's prediction in an email chain letter that made the rounds in 2008. He said:

"A democracy is always temporary in nature; it simply cannot exist as a permanent form of government. A democracy will continue to exist up until the time that voters discover they can vote themselves generous gifts from the public treasury. From that moment on, the majority always vote for the candidates who promise the most benefits from the public treasury, with the result that every democracy will finally collapse due to loose fiscal policy which is always followed by a dictatorship. The average age of the world's greatest civilizations from the beginning of history, has been about 200 years. During those 200 years, those nations always progressed through the following sequence:

1. *From bondage to spiritual faith;*
2. *From spiritual faith to great courage*
3. *From courage to liberty*
4. *From liberty to abundance*
5. *From abundance to complacency*
6. *From complacency to apathy*
7. *From apathy to dependence*
8. *From dependence back to bondage"*

Although Tyler is widely reported as the author of both the paragraph and the "fatal sequence" listing the 8 stages of a democracy, he actually wrote neither according to my research. The author of the paragraph remains unknown, but the 8 steps of the "fatal sequence" first appeared in a speech given by Henning Webb Prentis, Jr. on March 18, 1943, at the Waldorf Astoria in New York. Regardless of authorship, the truth of both is self-evident if you have studied the rise and fall of democracies, generally, and the internal decline of the United States, specifically. Also, students of government will argue that we are a democratic republic, not a democracy. But, the way Obama is totally dependent on opinion polls and continues to campaign rather than govern means we now resemble more a populist democracy than a republic.

In 1946, three years after Mr. Prentis gave us the above "fatal sequence", he modified the list slightly, but significantly, as follows:

> *"1. Bondage to spiritual faith;*
> *2. Spiritual faith to courage;*
> *3. Courage to freedom;*
> *4. Freedom to abundance;*
> *5. Abundance to selfishness;*
> *6. Selfishness to complacency;*
> *7. Complacency to apathy;*
> *8. Apathy to fear;*
> *9. Fear to dependency;*
> *10. Dependency to bondage."*

Being a student of history, and concerned for the survival of our unique republic, I prefer the latter list with the addition of selfishness and fear. Given our present economic problems, our autocratic, progressive, elitist, leaders, and unemployment numbers, who can deny that these two additions to the list are needed? At what stage in this fatal sequence do we find the United States in 2010? Let's proceed down the list and see where we stop.

BONDAGE, FAITH, COURAGE & FREEDOM

I've combined the first four steps of the sequence because I hope you do not need a detailed lesson in early American history. Also, while I believe Mr. Prentis's hypothesis to be beyond doubt, the steps do not have precise chronological beginning and ending dates, but rather overlap and parallel each other.

Thanks to the voyages of Columbus and others in the 15th and 16th centuries, the mass of land we now call the United States was discovered and the race was on to colonize it. England, France, Spain and Holland all vied for a piece of the pie. Shiploads of immigrants poured in from these four countries plus many others, mostly from Europe. Ownership of the Atlantic coastal settlements was not a settled issue by any means. England and France were the primary combatants after Spain was finally driven to the south and west and no longer claimed any part of the original thirteen colonies. At the conclusion of the French and Indian War (also called the Seven Year's War) in 1763 the thirteen colonies were in bondage to the victor, England. Officially, the colonists were in subjugation, but really enjoyed more freedoms than existed in the mother country. Religious denomination, like ethnicity, language, and country of origin, was an important determinate of where the earlier colonists settled. Faith in a Christian God was the common thread that united the individual colonies and the glue that held the divergent peoples within each colony together. Although there were many sects, freedom of religion was practiced long before it was codified in our Constitution. Struggling against the elements, trying to establish a new life in a new land, and fighting Indians, makes you closer to God, so you don't have time to be agnostic or atheist. Those silly ideas would come later when humans thought they <u>were</u> God. Since shared belief systems outweighed differences, their religion acted to bring them together when united action was needed. Imagine the chaos and divisiveness had our original colonists been composed of Muslims, Hindi, Atheists, Satanists, Catholics, Protestants, Voodoo, Jews, Shamans, Moonies, Mythologists, Christian Scientists, Scientologists, Universal Unitarians and all our other present day alphabet religions and cults. Like the Tower of Babel, the colonists would never have united on anything, let alone fighting Indians, fighting a seven year rebellion, or drafting our unique Constitution. As it happened, our Christian-based religion was one of the important ingredients that gave the colonists the courage to weather the disease, starvation and dangers of the frontier life, and the perseverance to stay the course while suffering the increasing privations of the British Empire.

Actually, the thirteen colonies were very, very slow to anger. It took about 150 years from the time the Pilgrims first settled in New England until the "shot heard round the world" was fired at Concord, Massachusetts on April 19, 1775. Of course, that was just the beginning of the American Revolution. It would not really end until the Paris Peace Treaty was signed on September 3, 1783, even though Cornwallis had surrendered at Yorktown on October 19, 1781. Anyone who has not read and appreciated the all-or-nothing, life and death personal sacrifice of our known and unknown founders does not deserve to be called an American, or deserve to share in America's wealth and freedom. Few today realize that George Washington and the other patriots could count on only about one-third of the population for support. One-third was loyal to King George III of England, and the final third didn't give a damn who won or lost. Before each battle Washington and his officers had to count heads to make sure the expiring terms of the militia left enough men to fight. For example, the famous battle of Trenton, where George crossed the Delaware River through ice and freezing sleet (the famous painting shows him standing in the bow of the boat), was purposely timed just one week before most of his army was due to head home because their terms of enlistment had expired. Unless you have studied and know our early history in great detail you can never understand or appreciate how nip and tuck was our long seven year war of revolution. In today's political climate, I really hate to give the French credit for anything. But, had not the Comte de Rochambeau joined Washington with his 5500 French troops at Yorktown, and, had not the Comte de Grasse blocked Cornwallis's escape by sea with his French fleet, we would probably still be speaking the Queen's English. Just as important to our cause was the $25 million loaned (never repaid) to us by King Louis XIV, largely, through the influence of the 19 year old general Marquis de Lafayette and Ben Franklin.

George Washington had been selected by the Continental Congress as Commander-In-Chief and agreed to serve for the duration without pay. His ragtag combo of militia and continental troops lacked suitable clothing, food, or equipment. All of the initial funding had to come from each of the thirteen colonies. They, in turn, had to depend on individual citizens to cough-up the money voluntarily since there was no system for collecting taxes for the common defense. In 1777, when four of the colonies failed to contribute funds to the war, and Washington needed money just for the next battle, Robert Morris gave Washington $10,000 from his personal funds. After Morris's own fortune was depleted he borrowed heavily to finance the war and build ships for the privateers like John Paul Jones. As repayment for his sacrifice, Morris was imprisoned after the war for failure to repay his debts. How sad that most people that call themselves Americans today have never heard of Morris or Francis Marion, Nathaniel Greene, Lafayette, Daniel Morgan, Lighthorse Harry Lee, Thaddeus Kosciuszko or Kazimierz Pulaski.

So, after six years of combat and two more years of dickering in Paris, the 13 states won their independence from King George III. Now that the fighting was over, the farmers went back to farming and the rest took up where they had left off when they became soldiers. In September 1786, five of the colonies met in Annapolis to discuss changes to the Articles of Confederation to improve commerce. It soon became apparent that they needed a more comprehensive agreement, so work was begun at the Philadelphia Convention in mid-June to replace the Articles of Confederation with a Constitution. The new Constitution was completed on September 17, 1787, and, in accordance with Article 13 of the Articles of Confederation, it had to be ratified by at least 9 of the 13 states. New Hampshire became the ninth state to ratify the document by a vote of 57 yeas to 47 nays on June 21, 1788. The new government began on March 4, 1789, and the electors voted George Washington to begin his first term as President on April 16, 1789 in the nation's capitol of New York City.

ABUNDANCE TO COMPLACENCY

The United States, with its new Constitution, system of laws, freedom to move about, and with unsettled lands to the west, began to expand and prosper. There were a few early bumps in the road like the Whiskey Rebellion in the early 1790's when Pennsylvania farmers refused to pay taxes on whiskey, and the War of 1812 to stop England from impressing our sailors on the high seas, but no real threats to our existence. The United States doubled its size when President Thomas Jefferson signed the Louisiana Purchase on April 1, 1803. We then expanded to the Pacific Ocean by acquiring California, Arizona, Nevada, Utah and parts of Colorado, New Mexico and Wyoming after war with Mexico and the signing of the treaty of Guadalupe Hidalgo on May 30, 1848, accompanied by a required payment of $18 million. The Oregon Treaty with Britain settling the boundaries of Oregon and Washington states had already been signed in 1846. On June 8, 1854, the Gadsden Purchase was signed by the U.S. and Mexico whereby 30,000 square miles of land was added to Arizona and New Mexico to provide a southern route for construction of a railroad. In 1867 Alaska was purchased from Russia for $7.2 million. In short, the United States now comprised the land which became the 48 contiguous states plus Alaska. All we had to do now was stay together as one big happy family of states and not get in a spat with each other.

Then, along came the Civil War. I am not going to get into a pis....g contest of what caused the conflict. Most say it was either slavery or states' rights. Guess what, slavery _was_ a states' right in the 1860's South. So, it was both of these causes plus a lot of long-term seething hatred and festering resentment. Having read the 2500 books currently in my library on the subject, and not having been brainwashed by the history revisionists of the last 50 years, I sympathize with the South even though I am a Yankee by birth and against slavery. Actually, the northeast U.S. in 1860 was very similar to the northeast today, politically speaking. Namely, they were liberal/leftist/progressives _and_ hypocrites. They started off in the early 18th century buying, selling, and working slaves on their farms. As the population moved south and found more flat, fertile, and larger parcels of land, it became less profitable in the northeast to employ slaves. So, they turned to other endeavors or packed-up their slaves and moved south. It seemed as if the religious fervor of northeastern abolitionists increased inversely proportionately to the number of slaves they owned. Soon, the South was raising tobacco, cotton, and rice more efficiently, and the North turned to textiles and industry while trying to control the South with high taxes and tariffs. In 1831 the South balked at the tariffs and a civil war was avoided only by political compromise. By 1860 the abolitionists in the North and the fire-eaters in the South would no longer compromise and the election of Lincoln tipped the scale. After four years of war and 618,000 white soldiers had been killed, the war ended and northern occupation of the South began. Reconstruction lasted another 12 years. Only 3% of the Southerners had owned slaves, but the North also wanted to force co-habitation with freed slaves on the 97% that were small farmers, mechanics, lawyers, and merchants. Most of the Northern efforts and military occupation of the South was done out of retribution, greed, and revenge, rather than reconciliation. As a result, their efforts slowly petered out as all colonial autocracies eventually do.

By the mid-1870's over 90% of the freed slaves had gone back to work for the planters as either hired labor or share-croppers. This actually benefited the larger planters because the plantations had never been a profitable enterprise. Contrary to liberal history revisionists, the planters were almost universally bankrupt before the Civil War even started. Slaves were already treated like hired labor, and when they were too old to work in the fields they were still provided the necessities of life even though they were no longer productive. After the war it was now possible to pay a black worker a day's wages for a day's labor and no longer have to provide room, board, clothing, and medical care for life. Also, unlike today's revised history, most planters in the South despised the "peculiar institution" of slavery and wanted it to just go away. But how? How do you suddenly release 4 million ignorant, uneducated blacks with a foreign, strange culture, upon a highly educated, refined, white citizenry without destroying the society? Even though importation of new slaves from Africa had ceased in 1808, and many freedmen were living in both the North and South, the two races were still too divergent to comingle in either area.

Actually, the New England shipping industry had thrived on the slave trade for a century after they took over this cruel business from England. They began by picking up black slaves in Africa that had been captured by warring tribes and sold to the slavers. These slaves would be delivered to the West Indies where they would off-load the slaves and on-load rum, sugar, and spices for delivery to the New England merchants. As tobacco became a cash crop in the colonies, the Yankee ships simply bypassed the West Indies and delivered slaves directly to the states where they picked-up tobacco and dropped it off in England on the way back to Africa. As mentioned above, when agriculture moved south, so did the Yankee slavers move their delivery destinations south.

While the liberals in the northeast gave only loud lip-service to the abolitionist's cause, the Southerners actually tried to do something about the problem. Repatriation back to Africa was about the only viable solution acceptable to both North and South since both sides were against mingling of the races. Many thousands of blacks were sent back to Africa. So many in fact, that the freed slaves founded their own nation of Liberia and named their capital Monrovia after President Monroe. Thomas Jefferson's nephew, Randolph, used his own funds to repatriate over 400 of his slaves back to Africa.

But, the rabid abolitionists were impatient and would not help fund the repatriation, work out a solution, or give the South time to resolve this issue that they had inherited from the North. They, along with the fire-eaters in the South like Yancey, Rhett, and Ruffin, were itching for a fight. So, the blood flowed freely for four years from April 1861 to April 1865.

After reconstruction, the South prospered right along with the North. Immigrants poured in, primarily from Europe, and there was room and work for all of them because everything was booming. Cities sprang up, railroads tripled their mileage of tracks, farms blossomed in the western and prairie states, and new inventions and industry exploded the wealth of the nation. Being surrounded by two oceans gave the United States the isolation it needed to develop our infrastructure and support the burgeoning economy without encroachment and interference of near-neighbors as was the case with European nations. Thankfully, wars were something that always happened "over there" in Europe or elsewhere, not in America. The Spanish-American War of 1898 was a newspaper war exacerbated by Hearst's "yellow journalism", and the Boxer Rebellion in 1900 was 10,000 miles away in China and largely ignored. Abundance was abundant and anybody that wanted to work and apply himself could thrive in this land of opportunity.

Then, the Archduke Franz Ferdinand of Austria got himself killed and the rest of Europe took sides. Germany sank a few of our ships, so we also took sides with the allies, England and France. We sent "Blackjack" Pershing over with an expeditionary force of Americans and helped win WW1, "the war to end all wars." German corporal Adolph Hitler would refute that claim 20 years later.

But, during the next 20 years America boomed. They went through the gay 90's and a few financial crises, but kept right on trucking. Henry Ford pumped-out 15 million Model T's and America continued prospering until October 29th, 1929, when the bottom of the stock market fell out. The stock market crash was a symptom of a sick economy, not the cause of the depression. They blamed the depression on Hoover and elected FDR to put the country back together again. FDR tried the CCC (Civilian Conservation Corps), the WPA (Worker's Progress Administration), NRA (National Recovery Act) and many other programs, and spent billions of government funds. FDR took the United States off the gold standard so that he could keep the Treasury Department printing dollars without the worry of backing-up dollars with real gold bullion in Fort Knox. But the unemployment stayed astronomically high. At least FDR made an attempt to spend the created deficits directly on jobs. Today, Obama treats the trillions of dollars in deficit spending as his own private slush fund to pay-off unions, ACORN, liberal special interests, Democrat politicians, and even some has found its way to his relatives in the Luo tribe in Kenya! Anyway, after all of FDR's programs failed, our economic savior came in the form of a war, WWII.

Within a short time after Japan attacked Pearl Harbor on December 7, 1941, the unemployment dropped to around zero. We churned out more planes, trucks, ships, jeeps, ammo, and materiel than any nation had ever produced.

Since blacks were largely prohibited from military service, they replaced white soldiers at the factories and contributed to the war effort while greatly improving their quality of life. Again, unlike both the Allies and Axis powers, we were blessed with oceans on both sides of our borders, so we could prepare and produce without molestation. Of course, that did not stop our loss of over 400,000 brave young men. In less than a year after landing on the beaches of Normandy we were in Berlin and Hitler was dead.

Now we trained our attention on the Japs. After years of island hopping we were set to invade the imperial island of Japan. We ordered a half-million body bags, but knew we would need twice that many. Truman made the decision to drop "Little Boy" on Hiroshima and "Fat Man" on Nagasaki, and forego the pleasure of splashing ashore on the beautiful but hostile beaches of homeland Japan. Major Paul Tibbets, piloting the Enola Gay, dropped the first bomb and until his death on November 1, 2007, said he never regretted his decision. Neither do I.

As we do after every war, the U.S. immediately downsized the military and all the boys came home. You would think that turning a million young men loose on a nation that had been producing only war materiel and no consumer goods for the last four years would cause immediate chaos and unemployment. But the opposite was true. The victors were in high spirits. There was a pent-up demand for all the pleasures of life denied to them due to war production, and the boys wanted to make babies, not war. With enabling legislation that made college more than a pipe-dream (GI Bill), affordable housing made possible with government-backed loans, and assembly lines turning out affordable cars, the economy boomed, and so did the population. More babies were born from 1946 to 1960 than any other time in U.S. history, over 59 million. Fortunately for these little ones, Planned Parenthood had not yet set-up their abortion factories and killing children was not yet the "choice of a new generation."

Roosevelt and Churchill had necessarily functioned in a symbiotic partnership with Russia during WWII to keep the fighting limited to foreign soil, and to use Russian soldiers in a war of attrition rather than sacrifice American and British lives. This was true even though both of the Allied leaders knew Stalin was a ruthless dictator who had murdered millions of his own people, notably in the Ukraine. Also, he was initially Hitler's ally in invading and slaughtering thousands of Poles in 1939. Only in 1989 did Russia finally admit that in 1940 their NKVD (secret police) had executed 21,768 Polish military officers by shooting them in the head and dumping their bodies in a mass grave in the Katyn Forest. It was only when Hitler turned on Stalin in Operation Barbarossa that Stalin pleaded for America's help. Some of Truman's generals, like George Patton, wanted to continue on through to the Russian border after reaching Berlin because he hated the Russians. Had Truman followed Patton's advice there would never have been a Communist East Germany or a Berlin Airlift. But, Truman and everybody else were sick of war even though they knew they would hear from Stalin again in the near future.

Sure enough, Stalin had not only been observing America's atom bomb development, but had spies inside our Manhattan Project, and soon had the bomb himself. Simultaneously, he invaded the surrounding countries and absorbed them into his new Union of Soviet Socialist Republic (USSR). Thus, the cold war began. We both aimed thousands of nuclear warheads at each other. It was a chess game called MAD (mutual assured destruction). We constantly sent our surveillance aircraft into Soviet airspace to test their response time and alertness. We took turns building ever better nuclear submarines like the Ohio and Los Angeles class attack subs, intercontinental ballistic missiles (ICBM's), and long range bombers. They would provide arms to our enemies and we would provide arms to theirs. The closest we came to total war was the Cuban Missile Crisis in October 1962. I remember it well because I was sent to the Dry Tortugas by a CIA subcontractor to erect and operate a 100,000 watt propaganda radio station and radar jammer. From only 55 miles away we beamed 55 millivolts of power to downtown Havana. We fired the only live rounds expended during the crises when a shrimp trawler named the "Bahama Mama" unknowingly tried to dock at the Dry Tortugas. A black Navy corpsman named Jordan gave the "Mama" a burst from a BAR (30.06 Browning Automatic Rifle) across the bow and they quickly chose to visit Fort Jefferson during a less-volatile period.

It is my contention that the United States entered into a period of complacency around 1963 after enjoying 182 years of almost undisturbed abundance. Not once in over one and three-quarters centuries had we been seriously invaded by a foreign power. How many nations have been so blessed? Our complacency had no specific starting date. It was more like a cataract, slowly clouding our vision and blurring the very real dangers that we knew existed, but were not yet on our immediate horizon.

Domestically, the generation fathered by the WWII vets had reached maturity. Their parents had sworn that their children would not suffer a depression or fight in a war like they had. They raised them according to Dr. Spock and spoiled them rotten. The intersection of Haight and Ashbury Streets in San Francisco became "Main Street" to the free-loving flower children, and the only god they worshiped was at the altar of self-gratification. Madelyn Murray O'Hare was proof to them that there was no God looking over their shoulder to chastise their behavior. The dangerous "reefer" of black and white movies had become the acceptable "pot" or "mary jane" to fuzzy brains and weakened inhibitions. The cold war was still out there, but the new "hippies" were tired of hearing about the Russians and left that worry to the "old man" or the "old lady." Dresses got shorter and sex was no longer sacred or requiring of love. Universities became the centers of dissent rather than centers for learning. If complacency meant caring about nothing then this "beat" generation was in full-blown complacency.

The saving grace during this period of the sixties was that the parents of the drop-outs were still in their 40's and 50's, and those that had not adopted the liberality of their offspring were still vigilant of foreign dangers, and still thanked God for the blessings of America. This shrinking majority passed this philosophy on to their sons who answered the call when Kennedy and Johnson fired-up our involvement in Viet Nam. This undeclared war split our boomer generation right down the middle; half supporting the war and half anti-war. Some of this anti-war group served in uniform anyway, thanks to the draft, and joined the volunteers that were already there to stop the "domino theory." Jane Fonda, Joan Baez, and other traitors donned NVA uniforms, did photo-ops sitting on North Vietnamese artillery, and became the Tokyo Rose's of the conflict. Although impossible to calculate, Jane Fonda's prolongation of the war probably indirectly caused the deaths of 5000

American soldiers. She should be tried by military court martial and shot. But, we don't do those kinds of things anymore in our kinder and gentler country, do we? And, if we did, Clinton or Obama would just pardon them anyway.

COMPLACENCY TO APATHY

Sometime during the mid-sixties to the mid-seventies we crept from being merely complacent to being apathetic. I stated above that the U.S. became complacent in the early 60's, and here I am saying they are already apathetic in a few short years. With the advent of drugs, loose morals, and Viet Nam I believe we underwent a sea-change in those few short years. Keep in mind that "apathetic" does not mean that most Americans cared about nothing. It really means that they ceased caring about issues important to the survival of the United States, and preserving our way of life as intended by our founders. They were not apathetic when it came to self-gratification. The Dr. Spock generation morphed into the self-esteem, love thyself, "me" generation. Instant gratification not only became the norm, but the entrepreneurs were soon scrambling to satisfy these instant needs as they realized the buying power of the boomers. The 59 million baby boomers were highly educated, wielded enormous buying power, and were really the engines driving all sectors of our economy.

Even the daily TV newscasts showing body counts, body bags, and planeloads of dead American boys at Dover Air Force Base became boring. Over 50,000 soldiers had been killed as of May 4, 1970, when 4 students at Ohio Kent State University were shot by National Guardsmen trying to keep order at one of the frequent anti-war demonstrations. These four deaths outweighed the thousands of dead soldiers who were seen simply as fodder for the hate-America- first crowd. Their deaths gave Ho Chi Minh a boost in his efforts to win the war at the Paris Peace Talks instead of on the battlefield. Even though polls consistently showed majority support for the war, the shootings at Kent State, the Watergate cover-up, and the Mai Lai incident hastened the pull-out of American troops. The most persuasive factor in public opinion was perhaps the press led by Walter Cronkite. Uncle Walter kept up the drumbeat to label American soldiers the invaders and losers, while the NVA was the winner and simply defending their homeland. Lyndon Johnson had opted out of a second term and Nixon was weighed down with Watergate. So, rather than fight a foreign and domestic war simultaneously, the U.S. troops left South Viet Nam and it came crashing down, surrendering to the communist North on April 30, 1975. So, after almost 15 years we wrote off 58,202 killed, 304,704 wounded, and 2338 still missing in action. Another 766 of our CIA and black ops guys disappeared, also. Imagine the heartbreak of American families behind these statistics. We are doing the same thing today in Iraq and Afghanistan; fighting wars of attrition against an enemy that has unending replacements while every one of our soldiers is irreplaceable.

Americans had already begun to turn inward before the Viet Nam War and this trend gained momentum after the war. We were still threatened by Russia's nukes, but the loud music, free-flowing drugs, casual sex, and epicurean outlook overshadowed all negative aspects of life in America.

In this stage of the fatal sequence, "complacency to apathy," so many forces were at work that a detailed discussion in a single book, or even a single library, is impossible. It was a few hundred agenda-driven despots mesmerizing millions of minions. These millions prided themselves as relativists and free-thinkers, when actually their brains were hollow cavities waiting to be filled by the first progressive elitist not requiring them to relinquish any of their base pleasures or illicit habits. Some of these changes were born after the mid-sixties, while others had been latent or festering, and emerged later as the Darkside gained followers. A short list of these issues, movements, the forces behind them, and the evil effect upon our nation follows below. Afterwards, we will continue scrolling down the fatal sequence list and see how close our precious nation is to the edge of the precipice.

ABORTION

The best recent example of the unadulterated divisiveness of abortion is Scott Brown. No pundits could have imagined a Republican winning Ted Kennedy's Senate seat. And, he would not have won that seat in abortion-loving Massachusetts had he been pro-life. Another example is Tim Tebow's simple 30 second ad during the Super Bowl telling people he was glad his mom allowed him to be born. Abortion wasn't even mentioned, but the feminazis and the baby killing industry went crazy, as they often do when their cash cow is threatened.

Everybody knows that Roe V. Wade was the Supreme Court decision that ushered in legal abortion. But, few know the details. Norma McCorvey was a young lady in Dallas who said she was raped and wanted permission to get an abortion. She was blocked in her attempt by District Attorney Henry B. Wade because abortions were illegal. Two feminist lawyers, Sarah Weddington and Linda Coffee, heard about the case and joined forces with Planned Parenthood and others hoping to change the law, and cash-in on the lucrative abortion business. McCorvey was given the pseudonym "Jane Roe" to hide her identity. The case first entered the Texas courts in 1969, but the Supreme Court ruling was not made until January 22, 1973. During this time the baby arrived alive, but this did not deter the pro-death cabal.

A few years after the ruling, McCorvey admitted she had not been raped. Then, after a few more years of working in the baby-killing business, she had an epiphany when she saw women killing their children simply because they were the wrong sex. She had routinely witnessed late term abortions which were supposedly illegal. She and the daughter who had been slated to be chemically fried in the womb became outspoken Pro-life advocates as they are to this day. Of course, Pandora's Box had been opened and baby-killing mills sprang up all over the country to meet the demand of the inconvenient consequences of our free-loving society.

Abortion is the ultimate defining issue between conservatives and the Darkside. It is truly a life and death matter. Real conservatives are 100% pro-life. So-called "fiscal conservatives" are not conservatives at all. But, they can't quite bring themselves to join the radical left which has become increasingly radicalized under Obama. The Darkside's thirst for abortion has two components. One is money. With an average of 4,500 abortions per day at a typical fee of $700 means that about $11 billion is made annually from the slaughter of children. The second component of abortion is the dehumanizing effect that humans killing their young has on an already sedated, relativistic society. Dehumanizing the masses until they resemble a herd of cattle, or a mindless mob, is a control technique used for thousands of years. Before the advent of the progressives in the 20th century, dehumanizing techniques were used to discipline armies and control captive populations. Once people are inured to the killing of their own offspring, other atrocities offer few obstacles. The genocides of Hitler, Pol Pot, and Stalin show that once killing becomes the norm, the horror continues unabated and society eventually self-destructs.

Abortion is simply one step in the progression of infanticide and euthanasia. This is indisputable. Infanticide is already practiced in the United States. When Obama was serving in the Illinois Senate he supported legislation to simply allow infants that survived abortion to be removed to a separate location and allowed to die a slow death. Could open, unlimited infanticide be far behind? Euthanasia is already practiced in Europe, Asia, and legal in five of our states. It is included in Obamacare and don't dare believe otherwise. With the passage of Obamacare your tax dollars will now flow directly to Planned Parenthood. If you doubt that Obamacare will fund abortions with your tax dollars, or that "death panels" will decide who lives and who dies, then you need to lay this book down, and go watch Oprah because you have not been watching and listening lately.

Scott Brown's replacing Ted Kennedy means nothing to genuine "social" conservatives. Massachusetts is too far gone to ever change their view on the grisly trade of disposing of their unwanted children. Former Massachusetts Republican governors, Weld and Romney, won only because they were pro-death. The latter only switched sides to run for President in 2008. Like Obama saying he sat in Wright's church for 20 years but didn't _really_ listen to the sermons, I suppose Romney wants us to believe he thought the 90 million abortions to date were performed to save the life of the mother. Or, perhaps he had a vision from God that made him run for President?

What is it that makes pro-aborts foam at the mouth and spew obscenities at an elderly Catholic woman quietly wanting to counsel a pregnant teenager outside an abortion mill? An even more baffling question is why are animal rights wackos, tree-huggers, global warming nuts, green freaks and feminazis universally bent on killing all babies without reservation? After all, they don't all profit directly from the gruesome trade. The answer must lie in either personal guilt from actual experience, or the need to dehumanize the unborn to facilitate their other mother-earth based, pseudo-religious belief systems. Some of these weirdos actually yearn for an earth free of humans and their resultant pollution. Others associate pro-life with Christians even though Muslims share this sanctity of life view. Muslims do acquire an affinity for killing people once they escape the womb, though. Imagine the combination of 2 billion Christians and Muslims battling the pro-death forces! That's a fight I would want to be a part of. Of course, after winning the battle, the Muslims would turn on us infidels, and we Christians would have to fight a second war.

Other than racism, abortion is the most oft repeated issue in Obama's books. He does not merely defend the killing, but has <u>promoted</u> it since his days in the Illinois legislature. His detailed familiarity with the issue makes him well aware that it is not just the suctioning out of a perfectly formed miniature child weighing an ounce or two. But, increasingly, it involves knifing through the brain of an eight-pound, fully-formed, lip-quivering, wriggling baby, and vacuuming out the shredded body parts. Paradoxically, the founder of one of Obama's largest supporters, Planned Parenthood, was Margaret Sanger whose central theme in starting Planned Parenthood was the killing of black babies because she considered them inferior. Today, there are 838 Planned Parenthood killing centers and most are located in black neighborhoods. But, what the hell; when it comes to the aggressive pursuit of raw power Obama disregards race, both his white side and his black side.

If you doubt Obama's absolute lust to make sure every unborn child is killed that can be killed in the entire world, consider that he has even found a way to spend at least $10 million of our tax dollars to make sure Kenya includes abortion in their Constitution. And, he thought killing children in Kenya was important enough that he violated our federal laws besides spending our money in another country. Kenya is drafting a new constitution which will be voted on in August. Millions of our tax dollars were provided to Obama's U.S. Ambassador to Kenya, Michael Ranneberger to lobby and spend wherever necessary to get the pro-abortion language included in the new constitution. It was only through investigation and a Freedom of Information Request that House member, Republican Chris Smith of the House Africa Global Health Subcommittee, discovered this expenditure by Obama tucked away in mountains of files that are rarely examined by house members. Smith and fellow Republican House members, Ileana Ros-Lehtinen and Darrell Issa sent a letter on May 6 to the Inspectors General at the State Department and the U.S. Agency for International Development seeking a probe to see how many more millions and billions of our tax dollars have been dumped down black holes to avoid scrutiny. With Obama accustomed to a Chicago mob mentality and answerable to no higher authority, it is unlikely Obama's spending of our money on anything he wants can be curtailed, controlled or even disclosed to the public. The power of the U.S. President has always been available for misuse since 1789, but few of our Presidents have taken advantage of the power, and when they did, it was not so flagrant as Obama. Before, there were checks and balances and a free press. Now, Obama is virtually free to nationalize private companies and spend hundreds of billions on his personal consolidation of power and no one can stop him.

NANNY STATE

"Nanny state" was a term coined by conservatives to identify those things that a government imposes on its citizens because they don't think the citizen can do it as well on their own. It is also a form of paternalism, or parentalism, and state control of the individual is often the goal. It is state-mandated protectionism. Identifying nanny state practices is subjective depending on your age, ambition, and self-confidence. What a young person considers a right that has always been provided to him, an older person may see as an unnecessary government-provided luxury. People that are ambitious and confident would rather earn their way in life than receive windfalls or help from a government which seems to be incapable of doing anything correctly.

I am 66 years old and grew-up in an environment of work and self-improvement. I began by picking cabbage at local farms, and walking "hot" horses just off the exercise track at Fairmont Park near Collinsville, Illinois. I was able to attend college only because of the GI Bill, unloading trucks at a cargo terminal, and working as a professor's assistant. The nanny state was not overwhelming in my day. It did come around in time to help Obama though. Nanny paid his way to Occidental, Columbia, and Harvard while he consumed beer and booze, savored varieties of pot, snorted coke, and sat around cursing whitey for the persecution of poor blacks like him.

I've never heard the connection made before, but I think the nanny state was created by politicians who work at a job for 12 months that could easily be done in only 12 weeks. To justify their pay they sit around and dream-up bills to pass. Let me give you a few examples of nanny statism:

1. Handicap Parking Spaces-When is the last time you saw a person park in one of these and not <u>run</u> or walk fast into the supermarket or Wal-Mart? Most of these spaces are vacant. Many are used by ambulatory relatives of permit holders. Doctors hand out these permits like candy. I won't even discuss the silliness of "Expectant Mother" parking spaces, or "Mothers with Children." My wife's doctor told her to walk regularly for an easier delivery, and walking off some of that excess fat after having a baby (while carrying your new baby) won't hurt you, either!
2. Military Disability Payments-Don't doubt me on this one. I personally know hundreds of guys, many never in combat, who get 100% disability which equals about $3000 a month. And, there is <u>absolutely nothing wrong with them.</u> Some of them have told me to just see a shrink at a VA hospital, act a little crazy, and when he asks you what your thoughts are tell him you would like to "<u>cut off his head and s...t down his neck.</u>" They guarantee I'll get 100% for PTSD shortly thereafter. The problem with Military Disability Payments is that no politician will dare touch them for two reasons. First,

almost none of the politicians today served in the military, and they don't want to be seen as anti-military. Second, malingering vets on fake disability payments protect their welfare and carry a lot of political clout. Just like Social Security, military disability payments are sacred, and politicians will let us go bankrupt before even considering cutting back on these hallowed stipends.
3. Unemployment Comp-I own a store and I have employees. Like all employers, I pay Unemployment Compensation on all my workers. Some work a while, leave their job for any reason at all, and then sit at home and collect 24 months, or more, of UC from the state. Every time I call to see if they want to come back to work they have a new excuse. I know for a fact that UC costs could be halved if the fraud was eliminated. With Obama's planned destruction of our economy the unemployed will be exceeding 20 million soon, and they will all get perpetual unemployment compensation checks paid for by our printing presses at the Treasury.
4. Supplemental Security Income (SSI), Social Security Disability (SSD), Aid to Dependent Children, and the multitudes of other government programs are fraught with fraud. Many recipients are not really disabled, the kids live on pizza and pot, and many work at jobs where their pay is under-the-table and spent on booze and drugs. Probably half of all Americans getting these payments cheat. But, like fake vet payments, politicians won't touch these benefits with a 10 foot pole.
5. Food Stamps-This program has now greatly expanded and is re-named EBT (Electronic Benefit Transfer) and SNAP (Nutrition Assistance Program). These are just two of the many, many more alphabet giveaway programs. You probably don't need a lesson on these, but there are currently over 44 million recipients just on EBT and SNAP costing $75 billion and rising. Many recipients sell or give away the products provided by these welfare programs, and others trade them for drugs or cigarettes. This is unnecessary, unearned, and un-American.
6. In 2000, the Consumer Product Safety Commission proposed banning a type of bath seat for infants; not because the product wasn't safe, but because it was *too* safe and might lull the parents into a false sense of

security. This is just one example, among many, of government stupidity.
7. Motorized Grocery Carts-You've seen these people either creeping or speeding through the aisles in supermarkets. Ninety percent of them use the carts rather than walk like the rest of us for one simple reason-they are battleship fat, I mean FAT! Their bodies ooze over both sides of the carts. They all weigh 600 pounds and you can see why if you look in their carts. Most are on food stamps, yet they pile in the candy, pizza, chips, and beer. Make these slobs walk and work-off some of the fat. They will be better off, and our taxes can be spent more wisely, too.
8. The ultimate Nanny soon to enslave us is Obamacare. It is more a spike through America's heart than a mere nail in our coffin. I owned a business and a second home in Newfoundland, Canada, and saw first-hand how our friends up there suffered under universal healthcare. Canada's healthcare system began with the same promises that Obama made to us, but both nations will end up killing people. One of my employees in Canada was told that it would be 11 months before he could schedule an appointment for an MRI unless it was an emergency, in which case they might be able to squeeze him in on a special visit in only 8 months.
9. Government Paperwork-I recently closed on a home loan. My wife and I signed our name or initialed 63 documents. When I bought my first home 45 years ago, I signed my name 5 times. Nobody sees these documents, they exist only to increase lawyer fees, and they do not serve any purpose.

Nanny state laws of cities, counties, states, and federal government now number in the hundreds of thousands and <u>growing</u>! Nanny state laws provide fodder for American humor and late night talk shows, but they do have a serious side. Besides costing billions of our tax dollars, they numb us to the statist takeover of every facet of our lives. The more nannys put in place, and the longer they stay around, the more people demand them. It's the old "privilege once granted becomes a right" argument. Obama is the ultimate nanny who will beg you to take government money until you are dependent and owe your very existence to his "benevolence." Later, after we have all become addicted to

Nanny, he and the Darkside will take it all away because it is "economically unsustainable." Then, the elimination process will begin as it always has during the transition from socialism to totalitarianism.

HOMOSEXUALS

Other than the contrived liberal textbooks of today, homosexuals have been absented from our written history. We all know they've been around forever. So why did we pretend they didn't exist before about 1960? This is because America was born of Judeo-Christian principles, and believed God's Bible when He said that sodomy was an abomination. So, we suffered their presence, avoided contact, were grossed out just imagining what they did to each other, and hoped they would keep to themselves. Even an agnostic or atheist can see from our anatomical structure that there are only two sexes, and that they fit together like a puzzle. And, given the absence of either of our two sexes, the species will cease to exist. But, of course, that kind of thinking approaches too close to common sense, and who uses common sense anymore?

Until the 20th century, homosexuals stayed in the shadows and were ignored like the aberration they are. Conflict with normal people was rare because they mostly sought out their own kind to do whatever they do to each other. Occasionally they would cross-over and attempt to infect young boys (favorite targets) with their illness. Three personal instances come to my mind in the early '50's.

Every year my Boy Scout troop would go to summer camp at Camp Sunnen in the Missouri Ozarks. One of our scouts was a boy named Frankovich, who would visit various tents at night and perform fellatio (we didn't call it that in those days). No, I didn't partake. Another local homosexual was a 40'ish man named George, who was the grounds manager of a nearby horse-racing track. Our neighborhood was kind of poor, and one of my casual acquaintances seemed to always have more spending money than the rest of us. It turned out that George was paying him $2 to perform some acts, which I don't recall, and wouldn't describe them if I did. Another time, some other boys and I were trying to launch an oval shaped galvanized tub in Canteen Creek when George and one of his limp-wristed friends started coming down the creek bank toward us. I was carrying a sawed-off lever-action 22 caliber rifle that I had altered (without my dad's knowledge) to look like Steve McQueen's rifle in "Wanted: Dead or Alive," our most popular TV show in those days. George said something like, "hi boys, what have you got there, a BB gun?" About then I aimed from the hip at the muddy water and racked off about 20 rapid rounds like Chuck Conners in the "Rifle Man," cocking the lever as fast as I could. George and his friend scampered back up the bank. That's the last time I remember seeing old George. The third and last type of contact with homos from memory was fairly common. When I was playing high school football we often had to hitchhike home after practice because most of us didn't own a car. Every once-in-a-while we would get picked-up by some guy who would start to scoot nearer to one of us, or let his right hand wander too close to our leg. We would just move over or say, "watch it budd." I don't remember any case where it went farther than that. Of course, nowadays there are many more aggressive homosexuals and many more violent attacks, especially on young boys. But, the liberal media only reports the occasional good old hetero boy who beats up a "gay" guy.

Homosexuals have never been the objects of wholesale discrimination in the United States. They have never been forced to have a tattooed red "H" on their forehead, or hunted down and shot. Life for them has been like the current (soon to be former) "don't ask, don't tell" in the military. But, "separate but equal" prevents them from achieving their real goal, which is molestation of young boys of heterosexual families. That's why they have had a running battle with the Boy Scouts and the military. That is why they sued eHarmony and won tons of money, and the right to force their way into this moral dating service. They go wherever they are not wanted, and sue or legislate their way into the lives of good people.

Homosexuals are like chicken snakes trying to get into your chicken cage. Night after night they will keep slithering from one side to the other, and from top to bottom, looking for an opening large enough for them to enter. Usually, they eventually find a tiny opening which they squeeze through and start wrapping their unhinged jaws around your birds. The policy of the Boy Scouts of America has always been to exclude homosexuals because of the simple fact that homosexuals like to have sex with little innocent boys. San Francisco has always been the hot bed of sodomites, and is also the hometown of Levi Strauss, the makers of Levi jeans since the 1849 gold rush. When the Boy Scouts refused to allow queers to become scoutmasters back in the 1980's, Levi stopped contributing money to the Scouts. When I read this in the newspaper I stopped buying Levi's and switched to Wranglers, which is still my policy to this day. But, like the chicken snake, a few homosexuals slithered in amongst the normal scout leaders and violated the trust that young boys have for adult male leaders who are supposed to set examples in all things, including morality. In April, a former Boy Scout molested in the 1980's by one of these perverts, was awarded $18.5 million by a Portland, Oregon jury. There are at least 7 more former Boy Scouts that have filed sex abuse cases against the Boy Scouts in Oregon, and probably a lot more in other states. Like the chicken snake, homosexuals, with the help of the in-your-face ACLU, have found a way to exact retribution from the BSA for their unmitigated gall in refusing to open their membership to pedophiles.

Homosexuals are abnormal and dangerous to the survival of our nation, but it may already be too late to stop these deviates. I remember reading stories about the bathes in San Francisco where hundreds would meet at darkened swimming pools, and have their brand of sex 20 or more times without ever seeing the face of any of their multiple "partners." Is that normal for any heterosexual? If so, I've sure missed out on a lot of fun. The 11,000 or so Catholic Priests prosecuted for sex with altar boys, and other male children, are still riddled with euphemisms. Have you ever heard of these priests molesting little girls? I haven't. No, only little boy's lives have been ruined forever. If there are only young boys involved, then have you ever heard of these priests being called homosexuals? I don't think so. The media, at worst, labels them pedophiles. If these 11,000 priests molested only little boys, then what's the problem with calling them H-O-M-O-S-E-X-U-A-L-S? Apparently the media suffers from the same amnesia they had when looking into Barney Franks' homosexual whorehouse operating out of his House of Representative's office, or another of his boyfriends' ripping-off the taxpayers at Fannie Mae and

Freddie Mac. The media reporters must be suffering from terminal homophobia.

The homosexuals have waged a long campaign to gain acceptance into our "straight" society. This has been made easier since the 60's by the declining morals and relativism of our silly, sick society. Like the progressive statists, homosexuals have organized for the long journey to full integration into society, which will open up sexual opportunities they could only dream of just a few years ago. Unlike normal heterosexuals, they cannot multiply, so they must constantly recruit from without.

One of their first hurdles was name change. Sodomite, queer, homosexual, rump ranger, fudge packer, or fag, just wouldn't do. They hijacked our word "gay", which I didn't appreciate because my father-in-law, Roy Gilbert, was a POW in WWII and held at Sanbostel, a sub-camp of Belsen death camp; and he used to say, "Hell, we were all gay back then." Of course, his "gay" meant "happy" back in 1945.

In the 1980's AIDS came along and gave gay guys a big boost. They marched, threw blood on cops, had their gaudy parades in San Francisco, and still got sympathy because AIDS was knocking them off like dominos. The police started wearing latex gloves and made fewer arrests for fear of the dreaded disease. The mortality rate would have been less, but medics couldn't trace back the origin of infections because homosexuals hid the identities of their "boyfriends". Not wanting to be stingy with their new disease, homosexuals traveled to faraway places like Thailand, Haiti and Sao Paolo, rented young boys from destitute families, and infected them with the slow death. The North American Man-Boy Love Association (NAMBLA) is just one of the worldwide efforts by homosexuals to reach the goal that they have been striving for from the beginning: uninhibited and unlimited sex with very young little boys. But, they want to come out of the shadows and change our laws to make sex with little boys not just fair game, but legal. As anyone with a basic knowledge of behavioral science knows, young boys are especially vulnerable at ages 10 through puberty. The goal of homosexuals is to make contact with these boys during this period of their lives when they are most vulnerable in order to recruit them into their sickness. If they can be stopped from recruiting these youngsters, their numbers will stabilize at a lower figure, and they will recede back to the closet where they belong.

While normal Americans feel sex is a blessing from God, sodomites embrace their nasty, deviant behavior as if it were God. Historically, they were barred from the military, CIA, and other jobs requiring integrity and secrecy because they are susceptible to abandoning their mission, or divulge state secrets in exchange for sex. They would sell their mother, brother, or lover for a half-hour tryst against an alley wall behind a dumpster.

Homosexuals gained numbers throughout the 90's using AIDS as a crutch, and the liberal Democrats as their mouthpieces in Washington. Like Hitler's brown shirts, they alternated violence with passivity. Like the IRA (Irish Republican Army), they simultaneously attacked with their storm troops (ACTUP) in the streets, and with their soft-spoken political action committees in Washington and the state capitols. Presently, they are a protected species like the blind and handicapped, and are busy in every state passing civil union and marriage laws. Even Secretary of Defense Gates has commissioned a study to allow them to have sex with our young soldiers in uniform; just what we need with two hot wars, worldwide terrorism, and a crumbling economy! With 100% support from Obama, and perverts like Barney Frank, how can they lose?

The tactics of homosexuals are similar to those of the Jackson-Sharpton extortion duo. The Parents, Families and Friends of Lesbians and Gays, Inc. (PFLAG) put pressure on PepsiCo last year to donate money and fund some of their causes, or, just maybe, they would buy less of their products like soft drinks, Gatorade, Frito-Lay, and Quaker Oats. Like most profit-oriented, morally bankrupt companies, PepsiCo responded with donations of money, and things like sponsoring a float in the 35th annual Lesbian and Gay Pride Parade in New York. In fact, they became the leading corporate sponsor of homosexual groups. An alternative group, Parents and Friends of Ex-homosexuals, and current homosexuals (PFOX), uses a faith-based approach to help people break away from the sodomy lifestyle and become normal. PFLAG uses part of the donations from PepsiCo to personally attack the efforts of PFOX, and tells everyone to protest their religious conferences that have former homosexuals as speakers.

PepsiCo's homosexual advocacy doesn't stop at just sending a big check to the deviants. Their website brags about their perfect rating on the 2009 Corporate Equality Index which is a scale created by the Human Rights Campaign to measure a company's pro-homosexual advocacy. The nice sounding so-called Human Rights Campaign is not for human rights at all, but rather for universal sodomy for all. All homosexual activists advocate extreme measures to protect their subhuman habits, and fight any groups like PFOX from peacefully diminishing their numbers. And, you unknowingly finance the radical homosexuality that is invading our society every time you partake of the products of companies that pump millions into their coffers.

The only obstacles faced by homosexuals while their Deviant-in-Chief, Obama, is President, will come from the individual states. If it were solely up to Obama he would assign each of your young sons to a "Big Brother" for instruction in the art of "fisting." Obama will meet most of the sodomite demands by simple memos to his agencies, or verbal instructions when no paper trail is desirable. Of course, with the Obama-salivating media, he has no fear of them reporting anything negative about his "boys." The media has always covered-up rapes and murders of young boys by homos. In April, Obama simply told Kathleen Sebelius of HHS to give queers all rights of normal patients at all hospitals that receive Medicare or Medicaid. Show me even one hospital in the U.S. that does not participate in these two giant health monsters. So, now your aged mother or father, through no fault of theirs, may be suffering from Alzheimer's, and be forced to share a hospital room with a homosexual who got their disease by one too many trips to the bathes in San Francisco.

Like all Christians, I believe in co-existing with homosexuals because we are all part of the human family. Besides, we need the extraordinary talent of people like Elton John, who is, in my opinion, the greatest solo performing artist and the next door neighbor of my wife's cousin, Betsy. Also, my favorite song of all time is "Rhapsodia Bohemia" by Queen. Even though the lyrics are sick I very much appreciate the instrumentation and vocals.

POLITICS OF THE DARKSIDE

I am going to tell you about a couple of my early brushes with politics before delving into a more serious discussion. I lived and worked in Freeport, Grand Bahama Island, for a few years in the early '70's. I even had dinner a few times with the Bahama's first black Prime Minister, Lynden Pindling, and his wife, Marquerite. He had just assumed power from the white "Bay Street Boys," who had ruled the Bahama Islands since the days of slavery. I was there in that first year of black rule, and even then kickbacks and pay-offs were the rule, not the exception. To be fair, the new black government was no more corrupt than the "Boys". When I had my 1963 Pontiac Bonneville convertible shipped over from Miami, I had to slip $150 to the customs officer to get it out of the bonded compound. Later, when I attended an auction for a 30 ft. sailing sloop, I was outbid by the same customs officer. I knew the pay scale of the government, so this guy was raking in the bucks to the tune of $1000, in "1970's dollars," per day. A short time later, I discovered that our Royal Bank of Canada account was missing large sums of cash. The theft was traced to three attractive young black ladies all with the same last name of Sanders, who were all tellers in the bank. The white president of the bank, a Mr. Reynolds, made good our funds, but didn't fire the girls to avoid "disturbing our good race relations" with the Bahamians. Then, when the very first Kentucky Fried Chicken was about to open in Freeport, I heard an explosion one morning and the KFC had disappeared into dust. They started rebuilding and just before it was about to open for the second time, "BOOM" sounded again. It turned out that Pindling's brother owned the competing chicken joint, the "Boss Bird," and didn't want the competition. KFC didn't try a third time. After living in the Bahamas for a few years and knowing almost everybody in the islands, I don't think I ever met even one employee of the government during that time, from cops to the prime minister, who was not on the take.

A while later, my wife and I were married in North Little Rock, Arkansas, and lived on Greers Ferry Lake near Heber Springs. Bill and Hillary had married the year before in Fayetteville. Arkansas added a whole new dimension to my concept of corruption. I met Senator Dale Bumpers, Governor David Pryor, and Attorney General Jim Guy Tucker (later Governor) all shortly after we moved to Arkansas. My wife and I had a restaurant on the lake with a landing strip for small aircraft, and it became the place for the Little Rock solons to escape from the heat of political shenanigans and the scrutiny of their constituents. They would land at our strip and exit the aircraft arm-in-arm with their women. I soon learned that these women were almost never their wives. I swear, every damn politician, staffer, lobbyist, office clerk, judge, and the moneyed people that hung around them, cheated on their wives. They called themselves "players." We were often invited out to Don Tyson's (who owned a small chicken business at that time) for his frequent parties. But, since my wife was so good looking, I passed on taking the risk of becoming a "player." One of these players went down in his single-engine Beechcraft Buccaneer over East Texas. We went to the funeral and met his wife for the first time. He had never brought her to our restaurant. His girlfriend was there, too, grieving in her own alcove in the rear of the church. My wife and I met Attorney General Jim Guy Tucker and gave him our $1500 check under-the-table for a license to have a bottle club so that we could serve liquor at our restaurant. As in the Bahamas, everybody was on the take, and everybody was on the make. Little Rock made Peyton Place look like a church.

Years later, in the mid-80's, I often traveled to Mexico City where my partners in a U.S. housing development lived. They resided in the wealthier part of the city up in the hills. It seemed all their neighbors had guards walking around with submachine guns. From their home I could see the compounds of past Mexican presidents with their high walls, gardens, and more machine guns. The more I visited Mexico City, the more I could see that the Bahamian corruption was small potatoes compared to Mexico. Whereas Lynden Pindling stole perhaps a few million, the Mexican presidents were leaving office with billions, and lower-level government officials were mere paupers who only skimmed a few million for their old age retirement. Everywhere I looked, it was easy to contrast their life with that of the 27 million peasants in the city who got their half kilo of subsidized tortillas for 11 centavo, and were happy. Back then, I felt proud that at least America was great because America was not corrupt (except Little Rock) like these banana republics.

That was at least partially true back then. A level of corruption has always been present in America. I know that. Growing-up in rural southern Illinois I remember being awakened twice by loud explosions in the early 50's. Buster Workman and other micro-mafioso's were always blowing-up each other's bars and nightclubs, or fixing horse races. But, usually when crime got out of hand or affected non-combatants, a countervailing force arose to oppose it. Often, a crusader politician (after a few years he, too, turned into a crook) would come along or the media (remember when we had one) would expose corruption, and public outcry would lead to correction. Things started to change when Bill Clinton got elected. The media finally had helped elect one of their own. Most of the media wanted and tried to look the other way whenever Bill's zipper got stuck, or when "bimbos erupted." Too bad for Bill though, because enough of the press liked a good scandal, and not all of his eruptions could be hidden. To the media, Lewinski was Clinton's badge of honor, proof that he just did what the boys and girls in the press were doing. They reported on it, not out of malice, but rather because it was easier to report on frivolous things, and less harmful to Bubba than it was to report on important things like letting Bin Laden escape, or getting 18 Rangers killed in Somalia. (See "Black Hawk Down" and you'll see my cousin, Jimmy Martin, as one of the 18 Rangers. Jimmy took out 70 of the bastards before they got him). The press even pitied poor Hillary when she acted shocked that Bill cheated on her, even though Little Rock had been Bill's whoredom for twelve long years prior, and she had not minded a bit as long as Bill didn't bring any STD's home with him. Bill and Hillary tried to force socialized medicine on us, but failed. Bill did pass a few bills to help his homosexual friends. He also signed the "Motor-Voter" bill so that dead people and dumpster dwellers could keep exercising their right to vote. He was prevented from helping Cloward and Pevin bring down the country with their welfare scheme when the Republicans took over in 1994. When Newt Gingrich used his "Contract with America" to take over Congress in 1994 it severely limited the damage Clinton could inflict on the country.

When Clinton left office and Bush took over in January 2000, the honeymoon with the press was immediately over, and they went on the attack again. Unlike Clinton, this guy

Bush not only attended church, but believed in God, and didn't screw around on his wife! But, before he took office, and even during the campaign, the media didn't give him a rest. They joined the Democrats in the "hanging chad" war in Florida where they championed Algore. Luckily, Bush's brother, Jeb, was governor of Florida, so George at least got a fair hearing and the Supreme Court ruled him the winner. The Darkside had poured millions in their clandestine voter fraud in Florida, and just could not understand how they could possibly lose. Clinton left Bush with a sick economy which he struggled with for 8 months. The media kept on his trail right up until 9/11 when the Twin Towers came down. For one or two days they gave him a break.

In less than a month after the attacks, Bush had pieced together a coalition and invaded Afghanistan on October 7, 2001. Then, against Democrat wishes, he invaded Iraq on March 20, 2003. On August 29, 2005, hurricane Katrina hit New Orleans. Despite two wars and a natural disaster, Bush managed to pass important legislation limiting the killing of children nearing birth, stem cell harvesting, The Patriot Act, and No Child Left Behind. Bush had to deal with the 2001 Anthrax scare, the 2002 Bali bombing, the 2004 Madrid train bombing, the 2005 London bombing, the 2008 Mumbai attack, and a thousand other large and small crises. It's easy to see why his hair turned gray. Imagine wimpy liberals like Clinton or Obama facing one crisis after another. Clinton was too busy chasing women, and Obama is too busy trying to tear down what he perceives as a racist nation and rebuild it in his own image. He also wants to make sure our soldiers have to sleep with one eye open to keep sodomites at bay.

Beginning in December 2007, the economy of the U.S. started seriously crashing. The root cause was the downward spiraling housing market that was a direct result of Barney Frank's, Chris Dodd's, and Obama's legislation giving loans to unqualified borrowers. Three of their unspeakably vile friends were criminal executives working for Freddie Mac and Fannie Mae that collectively stole over $137 million dollars, and left Americans with the worst economy since the Great Depression. The three crooks and the money they stole are: Franklin Raines - $90 million, James Johnson - $21 million, and Jamie Gorelick - $26 million. Herb Moses, Barney's "spouse", also worked for Freddie Mac while boyfriend Barney's committee oversaw the lender. These people were all appointed by Clinton. To show their appreciation to the politicians, Fanny Mae and Freddie Mac employees gave $165,400 to Dodd, $126,349 to Barack Hussien Obama, and $40,000 to Barney Frank as campaign contributions. It would take 10 of these books to explain Obama's den of thieves' culpability. But suffice it to say, Obama intentionally created the very crisis he is telling you he is going to save you from.

Corruption and philandering has been around since the creation of Adam and Eve. Like homosexuality, if these vices remain on the fringes and do not pollute large segments of the normal society, then they can be tolerated. But, when the cadre and infrastructure of the entire ruling elite is corrupt, the society is doomed. It can no longer self-correct. It would be like Robin Hood finding himself surrounded with only poor people. There would be nobody left to rob.

The present coterie of Democrat political whores led by Obama's Chicago pimps, and buttressed by legions of symbiotic sycophants and the adoring media, are bringing us ever closer to the precipice. Democrats are no longer the "loyal opposition" as were Scoop Jackson and Tip O'Neill when Richard Nixon and Ronald Reagan were in office. These two Democrat icons would spar like pit bulls with Republicans while never losing sight that America's survival as a constitutional republic was paramount. Today's brand of Democrats is hell-bent on destroying every brick and mortar joint of our 234 year old foundation. The sheer number of attacks on every aspect of our culture, society, and established principles are overwhelming us. With Obama's effective control of all three branches of government, 3 million federal employees, all government agencies, 37 mysterious unvetted czardoms, virtually all the media, thousands of bloggers, millions of special interest radicals and now the health and insurance industries, our voices of protest are getting more faint, and soon will be totally silenced.

Let me give you just a few examples of the literally thousands of "below the radar" operations that Obama's Chicago mob are using to influence, confuse, and corrupt our political system. Before I stopped reading newspapers, my favorite section was "Letters to the Editor." Sometimes I would send in my own opinion if the issue caught my attention. I found out recently that you can no longer assume the contributors to this public opinion section are your fellow citizens. An alert editor with the Cleveland Plain Dealer apparently peruses other newspapers from around the country to stay on top of his trade. His eye caught something unusual in the "letters to the editors" sections. His newspaper and a few others were getting letters vehemently supporting Obama's stand on various issues from someone named "Ellie Light." This tweaked his interest so he really started digging into these phenomena. He found that Ellie Light letters were popping up in 68 U.S. newspapers in 31 states from Alabama to California and in Washington D.C. He also found Ellie Light letters in two foreign newspapers and three national publications: Politico, The Washington Times, and USA Today. When the editors of the Gannett Wisconsin Media heard of this story, they acted on their suspicions and called Ellie Light at the number listed on the letters. Each time a call was made the person responding gave false information and a series of different hometowns. How many thousands of Democrat operatives, or their surrogates, are out there writing letters to newspapers that we think are from concerned citizens? How many letters are right out of Obama's army of "opinion benders"? I'm sure most of them are not as stupid as Ellie Light and use a different "nom de guerre" for every letter they write.

Another example of Obama's sea of covert activities is "TheTeaPartyisOver.org" website. The website proclaims that it is strictly a grassroots organization formed to fight the "radical" and "divisive" practices of the Tea Parties. Joseph Abrams of Foxnews.com did a little digging. Instead of coming from a groundswell of concerned citizens, the group was established by the American Public Policy Center (APPC), a Washington D.C. Democrat political operation run by two Democrat Party strategists, Craig Veroga and George Rakis. When Abrams dug deeper he found that these Obama Democrats own a consulting firm called Independent Strategies in Maryland. That firm has an office at Suite 1102, 300 M Street in Washington D.C. From that single office they run shell operations such as The American Public Policy Committee, Patriot Majority, Citizens for Progress, Oklahoma Freedom Fund, Mid Atlantic Leadership Fund, Public Security Fund, Public Security Now, Pioneer Majority, Bluegrass Freedom Fund, and more. These nice sounding organizations swap money among themselves in confusing transactions, but the money to operate them all originates from large unions like SEIU, Change to Win, the Communications Workers of America, the National Education Association, the Teamsters Union, the United Food and Commercial Workers Union, and others. The idea is to have groups in every area in every state plant stories supporting Obama, and also to attack Obama's detractors, but, at the same time, appear to be grassroots groups of concerned citizens. These groups also funnel millions to Democrat candidates, but the donors are listed as locals to give the impression that funds are not coming from outsiders.

Literally, not virtually, every Democrat in Washington is a thief and a scoundrel. The inner-circle Democrats are full-blown traitors. We hear "respect the office, not the person" regarding Obama. If Obama is the President, then how can we respect the office of a person who is literally anti-American, racist, hates all that we stand for and is trying his best to destroy our homeland? Obama is like the 9/11 hijackers and we are the unsuspecting passengers. Only a very few passengers like Todd Beamer and Jeremy Glick grasped the horror that United flight 93 was not being hijacked to Cuba. But, by then it was already too late. If the declining numbers of rational, truly unbiased Americans will read Obama's books, and examine his life and actions from Hawaii to the present day, they too will fear for their lives. Not only is he an angry black racist, but his pure hate will not be satiated until America mutates into something resembling the retrograded residue of South Africa or Zimbabwe.

Obama's spendathon tenure since taking office, and the Tea Parties, have finally awakened America to the fact that we are now one of the most corrupt and broke nations on earth. Washington politicians are voluntarily or involuntarily leaving in droves. They have spent us into bankruptcy and are leaving us with the debt, while they retire to a life of comfort and big retirement checks and benefits provided by your taxes till the day of their death. We first knew that something was happening when Scott Brown took "Turd" Kennedy's seat in Massachusetts, and Christy won in New Jersey. Then Utah kicked-out Republican Senator Bob Bennett and now, John McCain is scared of J.D. Hayworth. I Hope J.D. wins since McCain has had his chance to fight.

Instead of spending his time fighting the Darkside, he has worked with Russ Feingold and Kennedy on leftist legislation. Rand Paul beat Trey Grayson even though the latter was the choice of Senator Mitch McConnell of Kentucky. The most common reason for leaving office is represented by West Virginia Democrat House member Alan Mollohan. He has occupied his seat for 30 years, and his father was in the same seat for 14 years before that. Just in the past 10 years Mollohan brought $369 million in pork back to his district. Of that amount $250 million went to five not-for-profit companies formed by Mollohan and run by his close friends. Over the same 10 years these same friends repaid Mollohan's "kindness" by giving him $400,000 in contributions. So, Mollahan will receive the same punishment that all multi-millionaire Congressmen receive when leaving office; a perpetual lavish lifestyle, while we struggle with the legacy of debt that we can never, ever repay caused by these gangster politicians. Term limits and even an old-time independent press would perhaps have prevented criminals like Mollohan, but all we will ever do about term limits is bring the subject up every so often. If justice was swift and blind Mollohan would be executed or get life in prison, but that also will never happen. When I ran for Congress back in 1988 one of my often repeated warnings was "Get serious or get used to it." Alexis de Tocqueville said, "America is great because America is good." Well, we are not good anymore, are we?

Nearly 100% of Democrat congressmen and almost that many Republican congressmen are millionaires. The majority didn't enter political office with that kind of wealth. Most of these mortal men simply could not resist the temptations and power of high office. I ran for Congress in 1988 (and lost) and I can't be certain that I could have resisted the temptation of money and power either. The longer they stay in Washington, the more corrupt they become. Using their power to accumulate wealth is morally wrong, but not near the equal of the damage they are wreaking by following lockstep with Obama's intentional race to fascism. If you have not followed the corruption of Reid, Pelosi, Rangel, Dodd, Frank, Jefferson, Hastings, ad infinitum, then you are the problem, and not part of the shrinking minority that could have locked arms and helped stop the gathering momentum of the Obama malignancy. The light of truth is still shining every day from Fox, Rush, blogs, Malkin, Beck, Steyn and many others <u>for awhile</u>. At least they are trying to get the word out. Maybe you are just not listening.

LIBERALS AND CONSERVATIVES

I was listening to Rush on February 11, 2010, and a caller asked him why he didn't use the more up-to-date term "progressive" rather than "liberal." Rush replied that progressive implies progress or movement forward in small steps, and that is not what liberals do. "Besides," Rush went on, "the main reason I call them liberals is that it just makes them mad as hell!"

A prerequisite to a meaningful discussion of conservatives and liberals is first to define these two polar opposites. You can't trust the dictionary definition because a conservative is defined as someone who wants to retain the status quo, and a liberal as someone who seeks change. Both are much more complicated.

First, we can exclude from conservatism the group euphemistically labeled "fiscal conservatives." These people do not meet my strict criteria of conservatism. The prefix "fiscal" when used with conservatism is simply an oxymoron meaning pro-abortion. Abortion is synonymous with morality, and you can't be a conservative unless you are moral. These people want to promote themselves, not save lives or advance society with conservative principles. Examples are Mitt Romney, Scott Brown, Rudolph Giuliani, etal.

Retaining the status quo is an important part of conservatism, but it doesn't mean keeping things the way they are now. It means first removing the corruption wrought by the liberals over the last 100 years. Once that is accomplished the task would then become one of guarding the constitutional principles promulgated by our founding fathers, and preventing further liberal erosion. Liberals have never respected or appreciated the inspired foresight of our founders; the intricate web they wove to prevent the very bastardization of the Constitution that has, and is, still occurring.

The most reliably consistent factor in distinguishing conservatives from liberals is that the former believes in an active, watchful, supernatural God while the latter, at best, are existentialists. Many liberals say they believe in God, too, so I think it best to just narrow down what a heartfelt belief in God really entails. Remember, I'm not trying to show empirical proof of God's existence. That would be like liberals proving global warming, or how Obamacare will lower the deficit. All that I am claiming is that the Judeo-Christian God that the majority of Americans profess to believe in does not exist in the hearts of liberals. Since we have no device to reliably measure the feelings of the heart or peer inside the brains of people, then we are left to depend only on words and actions.

Does church attendance attest to a belief in God? Bill Clinton attended his Baptist church regularly while staining blue dresses, and pardoning a criminal political contributor while having sex with that contributor's wife. Ted Kennedy went to his Catholic mass regularly before leaving his young playmate to drown and then joking about it. Ted Kennedy's confessions, rosary and hail Marys did not prevent him and Chris Dodd from playing "sandwich" back in 1984. These two scions of the United States Senate played the roles of two slices of bread, and forced a waitress to become the meat. I spoke to a Capitol Police officer that was present during this senatorial performance. Obama sat for 20 years in Wright's den of iniquity, and magically never once heard the racist preacher spew out his hatred. These are three examples of Democrat "churchers" who do not believe in God. I'm sure there are a few Republican hypocrites too, but I think the point is made.

If not church attendance, then how about religious titles to indicate a belief in God? Let's discuss four of these "reverends." Sorry to say, but the four are all black. It is increasingly hard to find a black personage these days whose name is not preceded with "reverend." Chubby Al Sharpton earned his initial fame when he became the spokesman for Tawana Brawley, a young black girl who had smeared her body with doggie doo-doo, wrapped herself in plastic, and claimed she had been raped by no less than six white guys. It turned out Tawana was raped only in her dreams, but Al still got his 15 seconds of fame. But, Al didn't stop there. Even though Tawana had lied, Al sued the prosecuting attorney, Steven Pagones, charging him with racism (the old stand-by). Pagones turned the tables on Sharpton and was awarded damages of $345,000. Al had a lot of bluff, but no bucks, so he talked some local black business leaders into coughing-up the money to pay Pagones. Al went around calling himself "reverend" even though he had never attended any theological school. Al soon found that extorting money from white-owned businesses, under threat of boycott, paid better than the doggie-doo-doo business. All that was required was for Al to show up, flash the race card, and pocket the cash. He also has a radio show nobody listens to, and magically appears anywhere in the United States where there is racial strife coupled with a chance to pick-up a buck. All of the TV networks, including FOX, keep giving him guest appearances which fool the public into perceiving him as somebody with credibility when he is really a simplistic charlatan.

The second "reverend," Jesse Jackson, actually preceded Fat Al in the extortion business. In fact, Jackson makes Sharpton look like a cheap street corner pimp. One of Jesse's many front (read fencing) operations is called "Rainbow Push," and he uses it to push around Toyota, BP Oil, Coca Cola, Anheiser-Busch, and others to extort millions or else face black boycott of their products. Among the charities of Rainbow Push is Karin Stanford who Jackson knocked-up and was/is paid a few hundred thousand for Jackson's few minutes of romp. Since Stanford is black I guess you could say Jackson and Rainbow Push are helping blacks...one black at a time.

Louis Farrakhan is my third "reverend" and at least he looks the part in his flowing robes and zoot-suits. Louis is no dumb guy. He quickly deduced that Jesse and Al had the Christian money spigot all to themselves, so he established his fiefdom in black Islam-land. He even had the foresight to ban hard drink, cigarettes, and wild women so that his loyal congregationalists would have more money to drop into his collection coffers.

Our fourth and last "reverend" comes complete with a biblical name, Jeremiah Wright. Just as Edmund Ruffin could not wait to pull the lanyard on the first cannon to fire on Fort Sumter to open the Civil War, Jeremiah can't wait to press a magical button to kill all "whities," if ever such a button were invented. Jeremiah is a "Black Liberation Theologian" which is a nice way of saying that, even though Christ forms a part of the name of his church, his real god is anything black, and the real Satan is anything white. In short, he is an unrepentant racist. Unlike Christ, Jeremiah has not sworn off riches. He recently retired to a multi-million dollar mansion with a healthy income from his megachurch. Retirement has not prevented him from firing a few salvos at whities every chance he gets.

So, if we can't judge whether a person sincerely believes in God by his godly title or his presence in the house of God, then how? Why not just look in God's word, the Bible, and see which qualities He wants His people to exemplify. The one most often referred to is meekness or humility. It is the most obvious, observable, and provable difference between conservatives and liberals. It is the honorable quality of self-introspection and honest confession of a person's errors and omissions admitted of his own free will. Again, I could give you a definition of humility, but I think examples are better since we can associate them with real people.

After leaving Mount Vernon and fighting the British for seven long years without receiving a cent as compensation, George Washington finally came home to his wife, Martha, to spend his remaining years at his farm, Mount Vernon. A courier came knocking soon afterward, and gave him word that he had been chosen as the first President of the United States. He had not campaigned or sought the job. In two weeks he climbed back on his horse and went to New York. Recall there was no Air Force One or White House or any of the perks of today. There were no established precedents to tell him what Presidents are supposed to do. He started from scratch. After four really trying years, he had started a new country on its way, and wanted to go home. His countrymen begged him to stay for four more years. The United States was still shaky, and war with France seemed likely, so he agreed to another four years. When his second term ended they begged again, and he said no. Would liberals like Clinton, Obama, Pelosi, or Reid turn down four more years at the most powerful job in America?

George Washington patterned his life after the Roman dictator, Lucius Quinctius Cincinnatus, who had the title of dictator, but was really no dictator at all. When his son got into political trouble, Cincinnatus, who was a nobleman, was banished to live on a small farm outside of Rome. Later, when the Aequians trapped the Roman army in the Alban Hills and threatened them with annihilation, Senate Consul, Horatius Pulvillus, sent a group of Senators to Cincinnatus's farm and begged him to become Rome's dictator. Cincinnatus went to Rome, gathered all military-aged men at the Field of Mars, organized the infantry and cavalry, attacked the Aequians, killed or captured them all, resigned as dictator, and returned to his small farm; ALL IN 16 DAYS! He could have stayed and ruled Rome as it's dictator, but he chose not to do that. That's humility. And that is why George Washington formed the Order of the Cincinnatus for his officers after the war. It lasted until the death of the last man, then was disbanded.

Washington's great grandson-in-law, Robert E. Lee, declined the job of General-In-Chief of all Union forces in 1861 when the job was offered by Winfield Scott. Lee had fought for Scott in the Mexican War and Scott knew the valor, strength and integrity of Lee. Lee was a Union man and hated slavery, but had pledged his loyalty to his home state of Virginia. After the bloody repulse of Picketts Charge at Gettesburg on July 3, 1863, Robert E. Lee didn't blame his generals for the thousands of soldiers lost, and did not even say he lost because he was greatly outnumbered. He simply said, "It is all my fault" and offered Jefferson Davis his resignation. Could you imagine "massa" Obama or the real first black President, Bill Clinton, ever admitting an error? These two leftists, and most blacks and liberals today, think of Lee as a slave-holding racist. None of them deserve to even shine the shoes of Robert E. Lee.

On D-Day, June 6, 1944, Supreme Allied Commander Dwight D. Eisenhower was not sure that the thousands of men set to storm ashore on Normandy that day would succeed. If defeated by the Nazis, he could have blamed it on the Canadians or the British or even the weather. Instead, he prepared a letter of resignation to President Truman admitting that he personally took all the blame. He never had to send that letter. Could you ever hope to see Obama possessing even a fraction of this kind of selfless humility? Instead, Obama never admits to guilt for anything, and finds a scapegoat for every one of his disasters. For his first year in office, he had George Bush to blame everything on. When his stupid friend, Henry Gates, had to break into his own house, and was questioned by an alert cop, Obama called the cop, "stupid." When the "Deepwater Horizon" rig blew-up in the Gulf, it took Obama 5 days to even pay attention to the disaster. Then, all he did was talk about "kicking ass," appointed three commissions to study the problem, told how he would make BP pay through the nose, and forced the resignation of his man in charge of offshore drilling.

Why is humility so important in the Bible and such a necessity in the character of a leader of men? In its essence, humility tells us that we are mere humans, ultimately answerable to a higher power. How can you believe in a higher power if you think you <u>are</u> that higher power? If this trait is lacking in liberals, then they must not hold God as omnipotent as do conservatives. Without this self-truth, this self-confession of imperfection, the liberal is free to practice relativism, to do as he pleases to others, and constricted only by the bounds of society which he tries to circumvent. And, all without fear of the wrath of God.

Thus far, we see that going to church and calling yourself "reverend" does not a conservative make. But, humility is a step in the right direction. I will briefly describe four other differences between conservatives and liberals.

The first is abortion, which was covered earlier. No conservative agrees with killing children, and every liberal believes in unlimited killing of the unborn. The super-liberals even believe in killing the after-born babies. This is infanticide, and Obama is the pace-setter in this perversion.

Conservatives believe that we are the stewards of the planet until God chooses the time to take over. This means using and conserving the natural resources of the earth, but not worshiping the earth itself. This means living with black, white, brown, red, and yellow people in harmony, fighting only when threatened. Liberals use the differences in race, religion, wealth, ethnicity, and gender to divide, conquer, and take power and control over the conquered masses.

Conservatives are proud that America is exceptional and unique among all nations ever existing. Liberals are ashamed of that success, and want to destroy it with the one stipulation - that they and their ilk are around afterwards to rise like the Phoenix from the destruction and control what is left.

Both conservatives and liberals are selfish in that both desire to accumulate personal wealth. But, it is how they acquire and spend that wealth that makes Conservatives unique. Conservatives work, create their own wealth, and use it for family, capital, job creation, and charity. Liberals take money from other people in the form of taxes and outright confiscation and use it to control the folks they took it from.

EDUCATION

Again, I will start off with my personal experiences and observations. The first 14 years of my life were spent on Jesse Street in southern Illinois in an unincorporated neighborhood called "State Park," which was named after the Cahokia Mounds State Park nearby. The other unpaved streets in the neighborhood were named Joe, John, Pearl, Bernice, and Black Lane (paved, sort of). Most of us lived in small houses with water wells and outhouses.

Our school was about two miles distant across Route 40 and we got there by walking. The grade levels at the school were 1st through 7th. When we got to the 8th grade, and then high school, we had to travel about 12 miles to Collinsville. I remember every teacher in every grade because they all gave me reasons to remember them. In 2nd grade Mrs. Foster's punishment was to make me hold out my hand and she would whack it with the flat side of a ruler. In 5th grade I had Mrs. Shiebal who was almost bald. She took away my school patrol sash and badge, and refused to return it until I improved my grades. I will not bore you with tales about Mrs. Bear, Mrs. Bromelick, or Mrs. Sanders. Our principal was Mr. Krost who sat me down and talked glowingly about my Uncle Sherman's war record at the Chosin Reservoir in Korea before telling me to bend over and be wacked ten times by his homemade paddle as punishment for something long ago forgotten.

All of my teachers were older women until the 7th grade. Most were plump with rouge on their cheeks. They were probably paid about $1500 a year in the late 40's and early 50's. Some, we hated, and some, we loved, but all of them taught us, and we learned, or else. We had gangs back in those days, too. I was the leader of the "Jet Brothers" because we were all enamored with the F-86 Saber Jets of the U.S. Air Force. My gang never merely walked around the school grounds. To get from point A to point B we would all hold out our arms like wings and run as fast as we could. One time, Jerry Balcom made fun of my gang, so I gave him a roundhouse right punch, and then ran and hid behind the school. I lived in fear for a day or two, but Jerry never made fun of us again. Our school was full of bullies. We found ways to handle them and nobody ever got seriously hurt. We didn't have sensitivity classes or counselors counseling the counselors who counsel the students, like nowadays.

When I made it to the 7th grade I got my first male teacher, Mr. John Ball. I was not a good student because I always looked at classroom studies as an extension of recess. One time Mr. Ball took me by the ear and we both headed for the principal's office. About halfway there, Mr. Ball stopped and told me I was the smartest kid in the class, but "you need to apply that intelligence" to succeed in life. To this day I love that man. All of our teachers cared for all of us back in those long ago days.

Jesse Street was an unpaved wide path that was a dust-bowl when it was dry, and covered with about four feet of water when nearby Canteen Creek overflowed and flooded our neighborhood. There were about 30 homes and mobile homes on our street. If my memory serves me, there were about 100 kids living in those homes. Fully half graduated from college and 14 earned their doctorates. My brother, Sanford, graduated from John Marshall Law School in Chicago and became a lawyer. I graduated from the University of South Florida and became a Certified Public Accountant. Not a single one of the families in our neighborhood could afford full tuition, so we all had to earn scholarships, work, or go into the military to get the GI Bill. My brother was in ROTC, cleaned out barges on the Mississippi, worked at Fairmont Park horse track, and earned scholarships to get his Doctor of Jurisprudence. I had goofed around so much in high school that when I returned from overseas service, and applied to college on the GI Bill, I was admitted subject to a "final academic warning" which meant that if I got even one failing grade, out I went. They allowed me in only because I was a returning vet. I graduated two and half years later with honors. Have you ever wondered how Obama got into Occidental, Columbia, or Harvard with such lousy grades, and how he paid for his tuition and expenses? Poor little black kid! Tell ya what, I'll produce my grade transcripts showing my 3.88 GPA, if Obama will produce his.

Now, some will read this and say, "That is ancient history. Today's world is much more complex." No, it isn't. We are still flesh and blood, kids still need an education, and discipline still works when tried. We have simply allowed the NEA, NTO, and all their state teachers unions and political mouthpieces to take over our schools and destroy our children. Teachers unions are the very best examples of why unions quickly outstrip their reasons to exist. At least the UAW and most other unions produce products that are superior to what was made years ago. The NEA has ruined so many lives that if justice prevailed many educators today would be imprisoned or executed. Glenn Beck suggested a bumper sticker that reads "If you can read this thank a teacher; If you can't read this thank a teacher's union." Recently the NEA and New York Teacher's Union successfully prevented the firing of a teacher for fondling a female student, and then was retired and given a lifetime salary of $108,000 annually, plus full benefits. New York City has 14 "rubber rooms" where over 600 teachers can be found spending 8 hours a day, 5 days a week, making an average salary of $100,000, and playing checkers, watching TV or sleeping. Each has been assigned to a rubber room for reasons ranging from molesting students to showing up for class drunk. Some teachers stay in the rubber rooms for many years until eligible for retirement. The union will not allow them to be fired. After retirement, they receive full benefits. The rubber room teachers are paid over $40,000,000 per year for doing absolutely nothing to earn it. Alan Rosenfeld of Queens has been in a rubber room since 2001 for improper sexual advances to a student. He draws $100,000 salary while looking over his $7.8 million dollar stock portfolio, and practicing law on the side. Francisco Alevere, a math teacher who allegedly married one of his 16 year old students, and sexually molested two 12 years olds, also sits in a rubber room drawing a salary of $94,124 plus benefits.

If you follow the history of public education, you will see it began as home schooling. Then it moved to the county, then the state, and now the education of our children is under federal control. Hard work and determination to pursue higher learning by our original colonists is what made us exceptionalists. We remained exceptional until unions and the liberal federal government got involved. The only concerns of the unions are pay increases and tenure. The government's goals are more numerous and destructive. Where schools formerly had the single purpose of educating people, they are now used to inculcate social doctrine of liberal interest groups representing homosexuals, abortionists, feminists, animal rights freaks, greens, socialism, diversity, racism, and social engineering.

The late night talk shows find humor using street interviews of students who don't know who Vice-President Biden is or where Missouri is on the map. If the dumbing down doesn't stop, we will lose our country without an external shot being fired. Walter E. Williams writes about black education in Detroit and Washington D.C., two districts that have the highest per student expenditures, the highest teachers' salaries, the highest drop-out rate, and the lowest student scores. Black academia in Philadelphia, Chicago, New York and Los Angeles is almost as bad. Washington D.C. spends $15,000 per student, has smaller class sizes than the norm, and the average teacher pay is $61,195. Yet, the students score the lowest on National Assessment of Educational Progress (NAEP) tests, score only 925 average on SAT's and 19.1 on ACT's compared to national averages of 1017 and 21.1. Washington D.C. ranks 51st out of 51 districts, which means they are dead last. There was one bright light for the academic future of black students, called the Opportunity Scholarship Program, which allows qualified low-income families (almost all black) to claim up to $7500 per student toward a private education of their choice. Obama and his Democrat Congress killed the program, and the 1700 students are now on their own to find a decent education. Meanwhile, Obama sends his kids to Sidwell Friends School for $28,000 per kid, and 37% of the members of the House and 45% of the Senators send their offspring to private schools, too. These politicians are merely mimicking the public school teachers of which an average of 40% send their kids to private schools. Williams concludes his article by saying that for the people in power to do this to children is despicable, and for Obama, with all his lofty claims of love for blacks, it is downright betrayal.

One aim in writing this book was to avoid statistics and numbers, because people get dizzy with too many numbers and can't concentrate or remember them. There are plenty of sources where you can read the depressing statistics of our education terrorists, or, better yet, just look around you. Educators should be ashamed of themselves, especially where black kids are involved. Williams cites the psychobabble that asserts that black students respond to black teachers more positively. He calls that nonsense. Black performance is the worst in the very cities where large percentages of teachers and administrators are black, the school superintendent is black, the mayor is black, most of the city council is black, and very often the chief of police is black. The Congressional Black Caucus could probably improve black education in Washington if they cared as much about these black students as they did milking the government tit for more black victimization money and disguised reparations for past fabricated injustices.

We've discussed black student education, and the criminal blacks and liberal whites who are intentionally, and purposefully, wasting young minds. Now, let's talk about the average 65% of the dummies that somehow graduate high school and make it to college.

Dr. Richard Brake wrote an article describing the results of the fourth annual Civic Literacy Report released by The Intercollegiate Studies Institute (ISI). This test measures the graduate's fundamental knowledge of American history, government, foreign affairs and economics. I meet dumb people every day, but, I still cracked-up reading this. Less than 60% of college graduates can identify on a multiple-choice test the three branches of our government. They cannot quote seminal passages from our Declaration of Independence or even the short Gettysburg Address. Neither can they relate the basic events from the Revolutionary War, Civil War, and Vietnam War. Nor, can they recite the primary features of our free enterprise system. Now, we're not talking about Podunk University in Oil Trough, Arkansas, here. These are graduates of Yale, Princeton, Duke, and Georgetown. And, the seniors did worse than the freshmen, so this indicates a phenomenon called "negative learning." This means that students graduating college have "de-learned" since the time those same students entered college. The radical left professors that now dominate all universities have perfected their art of "de-education" into a science.

As often happens, the results of ISI's Civic Literacy Report raised a slew more questions than it answered. If graduates of some of the best colleges in the U.S. were learning nothing of our American history, our capitalist system, our American heroes, wars, and founding events, then just what were they learning, and does it contribute to maintaining America's position in the world? Was the college experience strengthening their American values of freedom and justice, or indoctrinating them with socialist/leftist views? What were they being taught about abortion, the Bible and Ten Commandments, our founding documents, same-sex marriage; and, are the students being pushed more toward leftist Democrats than conservative Republicans?

The 1999 North American Academic Study Survey (NAASS) was the first sophisticated quantitative analysis done to provide empirical proof that the colleges in general, and the professors in particular, are spewing out leftist propaganda in addition to purposely ignoring the instruction of American values. The 1999 NAASS survey showed in terms of partisanship and ideology that the humanities faculty broke down as follows: 62% Democrat and 6% Republican and 77% liberal and 8% conservative. Social science's breakdown was 55% Democrat and 7% Republican and 66% liberal and 8% conservative. The English faculty led the way in ideological imbalance with 69% Democrat, 2% Republican and 85% liberal and just 3% conservative. But, they were followed closely by historians which were 70% Democrat and 4% Republican and 79% liberal and 7% conservatives; and political scientists were 58% Democrats and 8% Republican and 79% liberal and only 2% conservative. Only the economics professors came anywhere near equity with 36% Democrat and 17% Republican and 43% liberal and 27% conservative.

My favorite conservative, William F. Buckley, wrote "God and Man at Yale" in 1951, and in it, he intimated that college professors were far more liberal than the American public and the students they teach. Even though anyone with eyes that see, and ears that hear, knew the answer, it always seemed that conservatives demanded empirical proof, while lefties draw their conclusions out of thin air. Finally, after 48 years, the NAASS report came along and proved what Buckley already knew to be true.

So, now that we know professors are all flaming leftists, does that translate into flaming leftist students? Dr. Brake looked at the Intercollegiate Studies Institute (ISI) report to see if the student's ideology shifted left after four years of propaganda expounded by the professors. ISI held all variables constant in the study of the student's background such as age, race, income, gender, religion, and physical attributes. They did their scientific best to look only at the independent impact that college alone had on their view of world issues and our American values system. They found in all cases that from the time a student entered college, to the time they left college, the shift leftward was dramatic. This was especially true on polarizing issues like abortion and same-sex marriage. When a new student comes to college either pro-life or neutral, and the pro-death harangues of his peers are drummed into him for four years, it is easier on both academic and social life to relent than to keep disagreeing.

Besides shifting left on abortion and same-sex marriages, the professor's propaganda also made students less likely to support prayer in school, and less apt to believe that hard work led to prosperity and success. One of the more obvious conclusions was that the students were more likely to call themselves liberal than conservatives. The final conclusion of the report was also obvious to me. It said that if a student entered college with a sound understanding and appreciation of our American founders and documents, and the sweat and blood that was shed by thousands of our countrymen, then they are much less likely to be influenced by the poisonous words of leftist professors. Dr. Brake said, "Apparently, greater familiarity with America, instead of breeding contempt, actually fostered more respect for key elements of America's free society."

I sincerely appreciate studies like the ones conducted by Dr. Brake and ISI, but their earth-shaking and nation-ending conclusions are written in such drab, boring rhetoric that no good ever comes of them. He comments on the studies by saying, "This peculiar combination of collegiate civic ignorance on the one hand, and collegiate liberalism on the other, suggests a wholly different story, one featuring academic neglect at best and political indoctrination at worst." Perhaps I'm just too impulsive, but am I the only one that would like to take these tenured, leftist idiot professors and ship them to Cuba so they can quit sucking-up our tax money and turning our kids into little Joseph Stalins? Dr. Brake goes on to say, "It will be hard for the wizards of academia to escape the growing perception that all they are producing are a cadre of intellectual munchkins who share the wizards' political views." I don't know who paid for Dr. Brake's studies or who funds ISI, but conservatives need to do more than conduct studies and issue results on subjects we already know all about. To blithely report that there is a "growing perception" that we are turning out a "cadre of munchkins" sounds like we should maybe do another study in 10 or 20 years, and see if we still have any conservatives left. We just went through eight years of George Bush. Why did we just allow the Darkside to keep right on indoctrinating our kids as if this was North Korea instead of the United States of America? The Darkside's grip on our education system is almost total. Professor Bill Ayers and Professor Obama, with the help of the NEA have won. We conservatives commission studies, get the depressing results, and then file it all away as if it is not killing us slowly. We are paying tenured professors our tax money to teach our kids to hate the system that pays the money to pay the professors. Virtually all of our colleges and universities have been taken over by the Darkside. Is it any wonder that they voted for their socialist-in-chief?

The Soviet Socialist State of Illinois saw fit to hire an admitted, indicted terrorist like Bill Ayers, and give him a lifetime, tenured professorship at a tax supported college. And now, somebody, no, a lot of somebody's, elected Bill Ayers' fellow professor, neighbor, friend, confidant, and homeboy, Barack Hussein Obama, to the office of Terrorist-in-Chief. If you believe the above percentages then somehow our nation still holds together with most of our kid's professors being socialists. There is a big difference between the indoctrination of college kids by teachers, and the brainwashing of 300 million Americans. Obama will take over where the professors left off. Education of your children, **and** you, is about to jump to light speed.

APATHY TO FEAR

I have given you a brief history of the United States, starting with the first colonists that landed on the Atlantic coast, and covering our experiences through about the mid-1970's. I then elaborated on seven issues that have impacted, or are still impacting our lives. <u>Abortion</u> came in 1973 and is the single most divisive social issue. <u>Nanny statism</u> began before the 70's and is still expanding today. <u>Homosexuals</u> have come out of the closet and now they want to be in your son's closet. <u>Politics of the Darkside</u> simply tells a little of the criminal mob now in charge of D.C. <u>Liberals and Conservatives</u> gave you some criteria on recognizing differences between the two. <u>Education</u> shows you how it should be renamed "indoctrination." We continued our state of apathy which had begun shortly after WWII and would not, in my opinion, morph into fear until September 11, 2001. We have some more ground to cover before this happens.

As mentioned, the 60's ushered in the greatest social upheaval in our history. Drugs, Vietnam, relativism, and the counter-culture changed America forever. The real beginnings of the Darkside developed in this period with the likes of Bill and Hillary Clinton, Obama, and thousands of deluded, self-styled, radical precursors to domestic terrorism. For public consumption these elitist leaders professed a belief in God, but their actions were more inclined to reflect their belief that man could solve the world's problems through social and economic control of people's lives by the liberal-statist Darkside.

The 1970's brought us the oil embargo, end of the Vietnam War, and the slow, gradual and continued infiltration of all our lives by the Darkside. Unlike previous generations of Americans who eventually grew-out of their adolescent ideas, the 60's had produced a crop of dreamers with a disconnected, twisted sense of reality. Maybe it was drug-induced or Dr. Spock or an overdose of self-esteem. Whatever it was, they shelved the lessons learned from 6000 years of history and boldly started cramming their New Age, one-world, earth-based ideas down our collective throats. Their tentacles slithered into all nooks and crannies of our lives. They entered politics, education at all levels, the media, music, religion, entertainment, our government, and even the military. Like the movie, "The Matrix," it was as if all these divergent aspects of our life were being attacked by a single command and control center. They all had as their strategy the anesthetizing and domination of the entire population of the United States.

The Darkside made great strides in the 1970's, but hit a speed-bump when Reagan was elected in 1980. They had worked hand-in-hand with the apologist, "hate-America-first" crowd in the "Jimma" Carter administration, and looked forward to another four years to work their magic, until Ronnie Reagan spoiled their party. Reagan bypassed the Democrat Congress and the media, and appealed directly to the American people. He took one look at the downsized military that Ford and Carter had decimated and started a concerted effort to rebuild it to its former greatness. He saw the stagflation and melancholy economy and went into action. When the air traffic controllers went on strike, he fired them all. He lowered taxes and thereby increased tax revenue. He created 25 million new jobs. In 1984 he was reelected in a landslide, taking 49 of the 50 states. He wanted to end the stranglehold of the NEA, but that monster union was too much even for Reagan. Ted Kennedy tried to defeat Reagan's Strategic Defense Initiative by calling it "Star Wars," but it didn't work. Not being content with "Détente" or the cold war, Reagan brought down the whole Soviet Union. The Democrat Congress fought Reagan tooth-and-nail all the way. They did their best to aid the communist take-over of Nicaragua by Daniel Ortega, so Reagan just did an end-run and had the CIA fly in the military supplies for the Contra rebels. Also, he used the CIA to supply the Mujahideen in Afghanistan with stinger shoulder-held missiles to knock the Soviet Hind helicopters out of the sky.

Unlike later hate-America-first Presidents, like Clinton and Obama, President Ronald Reagan did not believe in natural selection when it came to weak nations, because he knew the Soviets and other Communist powers were always working behind the scenes to gain advantage. When Marxist-Leninist Bernard Coard overthrew the government of Grenada, Reagan initiated Operation Urgent Fury, surreptitiously to rescue U.S. medical students. When Colonel Muammar al-Gaddafi sent agents to bomb a German discotheque frequented by U.S. servicemen, Reagan sent a squadron of F-111's to hit selected targets in Libya. He used covert means to supply El Salvador, Honduras, Guatemala, and Nicaragua with needed arms that had been denied by "Jimma" Carter. Ronaldo Maximus worked with and through South Africa to help the RENAMO and UNITA rebels to topple Marxist regimes in Mozambique and Angola, respectively. He also aided the KPNLF and royalist Funcinpec insurgents fighting the communist regime of Hun Sen in Cambodia. Unlike today, where Obama and Hillary Clinton think talking to Mahmoud Ahmadinejad and Kim Jong Il will make them forget nuking us, Reagan knew that evil embedded in the hearts of men was not so easily dispersed.

Even though Reagan had been governor of California for eight years, he was not a machine politician in the mold of Daley of Chicago or Obama. He took one look at the UN and didn't like what he saw. He pulled the U.S. out of UNESCO and deliberately withheld our UN dues. The Democrat doves begged him not to put cruise missiles in Europe because it would "upset" the Soviets. Too bad! When Mikhail Gorbachev offered him concessions if he would end the SDI anti-missile program, Reagan said no again. When all of Reagan's advisors told him not to rock the boat while in Berlin, Reagan ended his speech there with "tear down this wall." Unlike his predecessors or successors Reagan was not a hawk or a dove, but simply an American who studied everything he did in light of whether it benefited his country. The signing of the Intermediate-Range Nuclear Forces Treaty (INF) in 1987 is a good example of this "good cop/bad cop" attitude.

George H.W. Bush became the 41st President by defeating Democrat Michael Dukakis in 1988. Bush had a hard job filling the shoes of a popular President like Reagan, but I think he did a pretty good job. He ordered 24,000 troops to Panama in the December 1989 "Operation Just Cause" and removed Manuel Noriega, and installed Guillermo Endara as the democratically elected president. Bush's real test came in August 1990 when Saddam Hussein invaded Kuwait and threatened Saudi Arabia. He put together a coalition starting in September and the UN forces, spearheaded by the U.S., launched an air attack on January 17, 1991. Bombing continued for four weeks until the ground assault began on February 24. It was all over in 100 hours. After this short war Bush had a voter approval rating of 89%.

In the 1992 elections Bush received 38% of the popular vote while Perot got 19%, and Bill Clinton won with 43%. Like Obama, two of the first issues Clinton broached were sodomites in the military and socialized healthcare. Clinton and Obama made these moves to repay homosexuals, and grasp the power that comes with controlling the healthcare industry and the people that depend on it. After Clinton's first two nominees for Attorney General were rejected, his third, lesbian Janet Reno, made it. His other picks for high office were a mixture of misfits, socialists, incompetents, and pay-backs. He made Joycelyn Elders Surgeon General because she had helped cover-up one of his illegal activities (murder) back in Arkansas. Her only claim to fame while in Washington was affixing condoms to a tree in her office. He appointed Ruth Bader Ginsburg to the Supreme Court to assure that the court would continue moving toward Marx. Leftist-statist Madeleine Albright was made Secretary of State.

The Gennifer Flowers affair, Whitewater, Hillary's 1000% stock trading windfall profit, White House Travel Office firings, FBI files and too many "bimbo eruptions" to mention, caused the voters to give the Republicans both houses of Congress in 1994 for the first time in 40 years. The full 8 years of Clinton's two terms were consumed by one scandal after another; although he did manage to sneak-in the "Motor-Voter" bill to relegate our sacred right to vote to the trash heap. He successfully reinstalled the ousted socialist President Jean-Bertrand Aristide of Haiti because socialists have to stick together. He was also hailed for bringing together Israeli Prime Minister Yitzhak Rabin and Palestine Liberation Organization chairman, Yasir Arafat, to sign a historic agreement which was trash the second it was signed because it resulted in nothing. Clinton's Deputy White House Council Vince Foster was found dead in a small parking lot on the Potomac, obviously murdered, but covered-up well by Clinton's gang from Little Rock. I visited the small park along the Potomac where Clinton's people placed his body neatly with his arms folded. Vince Foster was one of the "players" in Little Rock society until he became a threat to Billybob. No less than 52 unsolved murders have been linked to Clinton and his gang in Arkansas, but, of course, nothing stuck.

Clinton did manage to tick-off pro-2nd Amendment voters in 1994 when he and the outgoing Democrat Congress passed the Assault Weapons Ban which banned simple semi-automatic guns, and not the full-auto weapons that the Brady bunch and press had fooled the public into believing was being banned. Ignorance must be bliss.

Modern day Clintonista propagandists will point to the Clinton years and say that millions of jobs were created, we had the first surplus since 1969, and unemployment dropped dramatically. All true, but none of it was due to Mr. Clinton. The Republican Senate and the Republican House originated and passed all the bills that revitalized the economy, while Bill was playing house with a different "housemate" every other day. He did manage to launch 20 Tomahawk missiles at a pharmaceutical factory in Khartoum, Sudan, to distract attention from his Lewinski "bimbo eruption." It was later discovered that this plant produced antibiotics without which over 20,000 Sudanese died. Looking back, maybe it's a good thing Clinton spent all his time chasing women. Like Obama, he brought all his hometown boys to staff the White House, but they were mostly interested in stealing napkins, cheating on their travel expense accounts, and helping the other Arkansas "players" like Tyson, Wal-Mart, and Worthen Bank get rich. While the Clintons did have a socialist agenda, for example the Hillary Healthcare initiative, they were kept too occupied by things like the continuous Kenneth Star investigations, the bimbo eruptions, and the missing FBI file fiasco to accomplish much. So far, Obama has not had a zipper problem. He has not only brought along his Chicago Mob, but has hand-selected the most anti-American, racist, socialist den of inequity ever assembled in the United States.

In 2000 George W. Bush beat Algore, chads and all, to become the 43st President of the United States. If you Google George Bush you'll see that he is the most despised President in history, and the hatred has not abated merely because he is out of office. Much of this vehemence came from the rapid-fire courtroom drama and hanging-chad controversy following the 2000 election. Liberals prefer their leaders to be really stupid, and Algore fit the bill to a "T". To come so close, and yet not quite manage to get this dummy in the White House was more than most liberals could handle. As you will discover much later in this book, the Democrats thought they had rigged the election, and took it for granted that all of their efforts over the years were about to prove their invulnerability. They didn't count on Karl Rove or Florida Secretary of State Katherine Harris to actually try and run an honest election. It set the stage for everything else Bush did for the next 8 years. Even simple, innocuous actions that passed unnoticed by previous Presidents were roundly attacked by the media and their Darkside puppeteers.

George W. Bush graduated from Yale University and Harvard Business School. He ran the family-owned Zapata Petroleum business, owned the Texas Rangers baseball team, served two terms as governor of Texas, and flew the F-102 Delta Dagger in the Texas Air National Guard. Yet, to hear liberal sore-losers, you would think he was Satan's surrogate, born with a cranial lobotomy, and represented evil incarnate. Liberals are not too bright, but they do know how to use their state-run media bedmates to repeat the lies eternally, until all but the most astute Republicans doubt the truth. Even the leftists rarely went after his lovely, intelligent wife, Laura. Unlike "Lurch" Obama, Laura was the perfect First Lady and the first one to give class to the White House since her mother-in-law, Barbara, left in 1993.

After finally convincing Algore to clear out of the White House, finding new "W's" for White House computer keyboards, and after replacing all the silverware and presidential place-mats stolen by Clinton, Bush staffed his cabinet and agencies with a mix of experienced people from former administrations along with new blood. He was a delegator, so he picked people that could think out of the box. Eight months into his presidency 19 Muslims crashed jetliners into the Twin Towers, Pentagon, and a field in Pennsylvania. Our world would never be the same again. Fear had arrived.

FEAR TO DEPENDENCY

On September 11, 2001, my wife and I were in Newfoundland, Canada, hunting caribou and moose at Sharon Valley with Ironbound Outfitters. It was in a remote area accessible only by helicopter. I had just shot my first caribou, and it was so hot at camp that I was walking around in combat boots and my underwear. All we had for communications was a radiotelephone that never worked, and a small 110 volt radio that picked-up only one Canadian radio station from the mainland. Our guide, Max Payne, told us that something had happened in the states so we cranked-up the 2500 watt gas generator and Max, my wife, and I all went up in the attic of the small cabin, and rigged the antenna to receive the weak signal the best we could. The other four hunters and guide waited below as we relayed what little was known about the drama that was unfolding a thousand miles away. All we could think about was our three kids and grandkids back in the states.

Then the radiotelephone rang and it was our daughter, Jennifer, calling us from Georgia. She said that up to 50,000 people had been killed, all aircraft in the states were grounded, and our military Combat Air Patrols (CAP) were in the skies with orders to shoot. We told her to contact our other kids and get to our isolated cabin in the mountains. I had always been prepared for the end of the world anyway, and my cabin was equipped for survival. For the next few days we would sit outside and look for contrails of aircraft over Newfoundland. We saw none. Even the helicopters normally ferrying hunters back and forth to the remote hunt camps were grounded. Finally, after four long wearisome days, we heard the wash of a distant chopper and ran outside. The pilot hovered and screamed to us that he couldn't land on the slope because his blades might dip down, hit the hillside, and disintegrate. So, we rushed around, cut some small logs and built a 15 ft. X 15 ft. landing deck held together with nails and rope. As the weight of the skids settled down the logs moved a little, but held long enough to allow us to throw our guns, equipment, and ourselves onboard and get out of there.

We landed at Peter Strides base camp and went immediately to the only place with a satellite TV and tuned to Fox. After getting up-to-date on the latest news, we drove to

Port au Basque and took the ferry across the Cabot Strait. We then drove across Nova Scotia and took the Cat Ferry to Bar Harbor where my brother lived. We had been the first ones to bring weapons from Canada into the U.S., but encountered no problems. Everybody we met on the long drive back to Georgia had changed. America had awakened from its long period of complacency and had entered into an era of fear.

Getting back to George Bush; he was in a Florida elementary classroom when notified of the attacks on 9/11 and was onboard Air Force One within 30 minutes on his way to Washington. He addressed the nation from the Oval Office that very night and told them that we were Americans, we would grieve together for the dead and injured, and that the perpetrators of this terrorism would not for long go unpunished. Three days later he was standing beside Mayor Rudy Giuliani at Ground Zero with firefighters, police officers, and volunteers addressing the crowd with a megaphone with the words, "I can hear you. The rest of the world hears you. And the people who knocked these buildings down will hear all of us soon." On September 20th his competent security professionals had identified the monsters behind 9/11, so Bush gave the Taliban an ultimatum to "hand over the terrorists, or...share in their fate." Had Obama been President, I truly think he would have sent Hillary Clinton to sit down with the Taliban to inquire as to why they were angry with us, and what could we do to ameliorate our differences.

On October 7th, less than a month after 9/11, our military launched operation "Enduring Freedom" in Afghanistan, quickly wiped-out the Taliban in Kabul, and replaced it with the Hamid Karzai government as an interim measure. Later, Karzai was popularly elected by the Afghan people. To this day we are still fighting the Taliban and still looking for Bin Laden. As usual, the spineless United Nations, with its cabal of communists and Muslims, refused to authorize any retaliation against Afghanistan. So, Bush formed a coalition with the British, Canadians, Afghan Northern Alliance, and Australians to form the International Security Assistance Force (ISAF). Later, NATO and other nations took over control of ISAF, but were mostly involved in non-combat operations.

In his 2002 State of the Union address, Bush began to push for action against Iraq. He labeled Iraq with its leader, Saddam Hussein, as part of the "Axis of Evil" along with North Korea and Iran, and accused them of possessing weapons of mass destruction. After many frustrating attempts to get the UN to enforce disarmament mandates, Bush put together a "coalition of the willing" and commenced the invasion of Iraq on March 20, 2003. Baghdad fell on April 9 and Bush declared the end of major combat operations on May 1. But, with sectarian violence, insurgency, improvised explosive devices (IED's), the Kurds, the Mahdi Army, beheadings, and strife between the Sunni's and Shia, the American dead and wounded kept mounting. Saddam Hussein was finally discovered hiding in a hole and executed on December 30, 2006.

During the 2004 elections Bush pushed for a continued commitment to the wars in Iraq and Afghanistan, support for the Patriot Act, constitutional amendments to ban abortion and same-sex marriages, income tax credits, social security savings accounts, and implementation of a worker program for immigrants. John Kerry was his opponent and made the mistake of mentioning his Vietnam service, which was a well-known fake, and this fact was hammered home by the Swiftboat Vets for Bush. These real combat vets put together their own TV ads and put out a book showing Kerry to have lied about everything he ever did. Bush won 31 of the 50 states and got 286 Electoral College votes compared to Kerry's 249. To this day, the Darkside still refers to Kerry as a "war hero." They and the media think that if they repeat something often enough the public will accept it as fact. The election of Obama proved this to be correct.

Bush had pushed for increased regulation of Fannie Mae and Freddie Mac starting in early 2003. Finally, in 2005 the new regulations passed the House, but died in the Senate. Bush and his economic advisors could see that the loose lending practices were building up for a crash in the near future and were unsustainable. John McCain led the fight to curtail and control these mortgage monsters before the unfolding disaster struck. Congressman Barney Frank and his "boyfriend" at Freddie Mac, along with Jamie Gorlick and other leftover lefties from the Clinton era, were pocketing millions while the two mortgage giants were being flooded with red ink. In December 2007 the housing market started a downturn. Adding to this problem, the price of oil started rising in late 2007 and reached a peak of $145.29 per barrel on July 4, 2008. Bush had tried to get Congress to allow drilling in the Alaska National Wildlife Refuge (ANWR), and offshore drilling on the east and west coast, but the coalition of tree-huggers, green-nuts and earth-worshippers pulled their usual "snail-darter" tricks, so oil kept climbing. Actually, the environmental wackos used caribou as their crutch for not drilling in ANWAR. As the only American big game outfitter in Canada, I know more about caribou habitat that all the fools in Washington and the Sierra Club combined, and believe me, caribou love heated oil pipelines. This was a pure ruse by the Democrats to destroy the economy following the guidelines of Cloward-Piven which we'll discuss later. Of course, the housing and energy crises caused rippling effects throughout the economy. Unemployment climbed, median household income fell, trade deficits rose, GDP fell, and the stock market crashed. Like dominos, Lehman Brothers collapsed, Fannie Mae and Freddie Mac were taken over by the government, and American International Group (AIG) was bailed out for a cost of $85 billion. Over 2.5 million jobs were lost in 2008. Of course, the Democrat state-run media made it clear 24/7 that Bush alone was to blame. All of these catastrophes were intentionally precipitated by the Darkside in preparation for their coming messiah, Obama.

In other non-war, non-economic matters, Bush vetoed the State Children's Health Insurance Program which was an attempt by the liberal Democrats to incrementally socialize healthcare. They had tried to sneak it through by piggy-backing it on a military funding bill. Bush signed the Medicare Act of 2003 to help the elderly with prescription drugs. He held town hall meetings all over the nation to try and pass legislation for Social Security reform to save it from insolvency, but the Democrats killed it after they took control of both houses of Congress in the 2006 elections. Bush signed legislation creating the Papahanaumokuakea Marine National Monument which, at 84 million acres, is the largest marine conservation area in the U.S. Unlike Clinton and Obama, he did not remove lands here on the U.S. mainland from the public domain and render them unusable by Americans. Like Stalin and Mao, Clinton and Obama want to herd Americans like cattle into specific areas for better control. Bush also signed the Clear Skies Act of 2003, and committed $2 billion to promote clean energy technology. He authored and signed legislation for AIDS research that exceeded anything the Democrats had ever even attempted. Of course, Democrats, greens, and homosexuals are never satiated, so the relentless barrage of media attacks never ceased, regardless of Bush's attempts to promote social and environment issues.

Bush used his veto for the first time to kill the Stem Cell Research Enhancement Act which would have repealed the 1995 Dickey Amendment preventing the use of embryonic stem cells, but allowing the use of adult stem cells. He, like Planned Parenthood and other killers of children in the womb, knew that if he signed the bill it would mean eventually that babies would be aborted simply for the harvesting of stem cells, just like any other farm crop. It mattered not to the liberals that adult stem cells had led to at least a score of important discoveries, while embryonic stem cells had not been helpful in even one scientific advancement, nor were they a useful tool in disease prevention research. Obama has reversed this policy, so look for the marketing, selling, and killing of babies for money. Obama is indeed afflicted with the same maniacal hatred of babies as Hitler had for the Jews.

The greatest windfall gift came to the Democrat Darkside and their black supporters on August 29, 2005, when Hurricane Katrina hit New Orleans. Even though it was only a category 3 storm, the levees broke and flooded the "City in a bathtub." The black mayor, Ray Nagin, was picking his nose, or doing one of his other mayoral duties, and was held blameless. Democrat Governor Blanco was getting her hair done and out of touch. As usual, in a national disaster, Katrina was the signal for blacks to loot, carjack, murder, and rape, so all these crimes immediately surged. In response to the 46,838 National Guard Troops who gave their time, left their own families, and risked their lives to help bring order out of the chaos, the blacks shot and sniped at them until the Guard locked and loaded and fired back. Texas opened their homes to 300,000 of the black refugees. When they ran background checks they found that 45% had criminal records, and 22% were for violent crimes. The crime rate in Houston alone rose 23% in a 6 month period relative to the same period a year earlier. They found that 29 of the

170 murders were due just to blacks from New Orleans. All cities accepting black refugees from New Orleans had the same or worse experience. When FEMA issued $2000 per month credit cards to the blacks they found that it was used for prostitutes, gambling, and alcoholic beverages. My wife and I visited Dallas in 2008 and stayed at a La Quinta Inn. The manager told us that after the blacks left his hotel not one towel or wash cloth was not stolen and that the hotel had to be closed for two months just to repair the damage done by these "victims." Over 11,000 free, brand-new mobile homes were rejected by blacks because of the smell from the interior paneling, which is not unusual. It is the same paneling used in every mobile home sold in the U.S. The "smell" is simply the curing process of the interior paneling and fades away in a few months. I know this for a fact because I've owned ten RV's, and my family of five have all survived this horror and lived to tell about it.

Never before in human history has so much disinformation, lies, half-truths, and false propaganda been rained down upon the head of a single individual than that which befell George Walker Bush. I don't see why his own mother, Barbara, didn't hate his guts. You would, of course, expect the liberal media to attack his pro-life or pro-God beliefs, but there was no issue too miniscule, no personal attribute too minor, and no fault too far in the past to dredge-up and dissect in minute detail. The hatred of "all things Bush" was monumental and historical. In the Huffington/Puffington blog, the attacks ran the gamut from plain vile and bile, to death wishes for Bush and his family. Had this happened to our present self-proclaimed messiah, Obama, the Secret Service would be knocking on doors, and the Jackson/Sharpton "justice brothers" would be screaming racism.

The anti-Bush hysteria was not limited to the poisoned-pens and words of the Darkside here in the U.S. With the AP, Rueters, internet BLOGS, and other tag-a-longs, all the media in the world piled-on Bush. Neither was the vitriol limited to only Bush-The-Younger. Scooter Libby, Karl Rove, Donald Rumsfeld, Dick Cheney, and even George's dog, Buddy, were open game for the frothing media. After eight long years of Bush-bashing, the Darkside's state-run media campaign had won, and proved that "a lie repeated often enough becomes truth." The "peopleofwalmart.com"

American voting public was now skinned, hung-up by the hind-leg tendons, and ready to be sliced-and-diced by the mob from Chicago, promising "Hope and Change". It had taken us 234 years to go from bondage to somewhere in the "unknown zone" between fear and dependency. Just as the Biblical Satan is to be given 1000 years to have a free-hand in converting God's chosen ones, so too will Barack Hussein Obama be given 4 to 8 years to convert the majority of Americans from dependency back to bondage.

Before examining the "Dependency to Bondage" period of the fatal sequence, I want to discuss terrorism since it forced us into the fear sequence, and after that, our military, since it is our ultimate defense against terrorism.

TERRISOM

The entire population of the United States is only 14% of the world Muslim population. Muslims claim over two billion members. All two billion aim their faces toward Mecca and bow and pray five times a day. They are brought up on the teachings of the Koran. Muslims wish death to all infidels. If you are not Muslim then you are an infidel. All Muslims view Israel as the little Satan and the United States as the big Satan. The only reason Muslims do not kill absolutely every American is that they do not yet have the capability. They are working on it.

For those of you who say that the majority of Muslims are not Jihadist, please save your breath. And please don't tell me about your Muslim friend or neighbor who would not hurt a fly. That's what good Americans said about Colleen "JihadJane" LaRose, Jamie "Jihad Jamie" Paulin-Ramirez, Ramy Zamzam, Sharif Mobley, Daniel Boyd, Najibullah Zazi, and Nidal Hasan. They are all American citizens. The two women are blond-haired and blue-eyed. Zamzam was a Howard University dental student. Mobley worked for a power plant in New Jersey. Zazi was employed as a shuttle service employee at the Denver Airport. Hasan, as you know, was a major in the Army with 13 years in service. Boyd is the "nicest terrorist I ever met" said one of his neighbors in Willow Springs, North Carolina. Aasiya Hassan even trusted her husband before he cut her head off for acting too much like an American. How many Methodist or Catholic husbands in your neighborhood have cut-off their wife's head after a spat? A Muslim's loyalty is not to you or any other infidel.

Am I picking on Muslims specifically? Yes. Ask yourself if there would be terrorism in the world if it weren't for the fanatic behavior of Muslims; no. The only people that consider Christians a greater threat to the world than Muslims are the Muslims themselves, and Obama, Napolitano, Holder, and the rest of the White House gang of criminals. They are more concerned about a group of idiots in Michigan driving around country roads, espousing anti-government rhetoric with an FBI informer egging them on, than they are about stopping real terrorists. Napolitano lives in absolute fear of the Second Amendment because it is really the only way to protect the First Amendment. Obama has done all he can to help the Muslims and damage the Christians without showing his hand too much. He doesn't attend any church and is itching to get down on his knees at a Mosque, but the time for that has not yet arrived. So, he is working in other ways to help out his many Muslim friends, but wants to avoid being too controversial right now. His most significant early move was to appoint Janet Reno, oops, I mean Janet Napolitano to be Homeland Security Secretary. An important qualification demanded by Obama for the job was that the applicant display no particular skill or knowledge concerning terrorism, and no desire to catch any terrorist unless they are from one of the 50 known terrorist states of the United States. Additional qualifications were anti-Christian, pro-homosexual, and be a devotee of late-term abortion. Once those formalities were out of the way, Barry and Janet quickly moved to avoid offending terrorists by renaming them "Man-caused disasters." Just the name change alone probably caused suicide bombers to change occupations because who would want to go down in history as a "man-caused disaster"? Next, since New York still seems to be the most popular terrorist vacation destination, Janet and Barry wanted to make the terrorist's one-way trip less a hassle by cutting $54 million out of those pesky security thingamajigs, like the New York Transit Security Grant program, Port Security Grant program, and others, so that Muslims wouldn't black-list New York on their travel itinerary. Sure enough, the new Obama "man-caused disaster" tourist program soon attracted Muslim, Faisal Shahzad. He drove all the way over from his adopted homeland of Bridgeport, Connecticut, on May 1, and brought his own fireworks, alarm clocks, and propane tanks to liven-up an otherwise boring day at Times Square. Having failed Fuse-Lighting 101 in his Madrasah school, Faisal decided to catch a quick flight to Dubai. Unfortunately for him, Obama and Janet did not provide fast enough cover for his exit from the "Big Satan," and the New York authorities nabbed him. But, just hang-in there Faisal. Eric "The Red" Holder has you now and he has never met a "man-caused disaster" he didn't like.

Being deadly serious about Faisal Shahzad, he had been placed on the Homeland Security watch list by George Bush and was still on the list when Bush left office. But, he was removed from the list by Obama, or his stalwart defender against "man-caused disasters," Eric "The Red" Holder, sometime after Obama took office. Shahzad had been placed on the list because of his ongoing contacts with the Taliban, and the Yemeni-American terrorist, Imam Anwar al Awlaki. He had also made at least 12 round trips to Pakistan since his initial arrival in the United States, and bought a one-way ticket for cash, which is supposed to be a tip-off to our ever vigilant TSA guard dogs of freedom. Walid Phares, whom I think would make a great director of Homeland Security, said the fireworks bomber had been blogging and posting on the radical Muslim website, Salafist, since 2006. Of course, when Shahzad was arrested for the Times Square fiasco he was mirandized, and is expected to be charged for parking in front of a water hydrant by our pro-terrorist Attorney General, Eric "the Red" Holder. What really pointed up the stupidity, or complicity, of the media in the Shahzad fiasco was their strident attempts to blame his motivation for bombing Times Square on the foreclosure action filed against him for failure to make his house payments. Michael Bloomberg, the blooming idiot Mayor of New York, said he thought he might be a member of the Tea Party. Is the media and the Mayor really this stupid, or do they have an agenda?

There was a lot of finger-pointing surrounding the Shahzad case and why the so-called watch list or no-fly list did not stop him from boarding the airliner back to Pakistan. It seems every time a terrorist is caught with explosives in his shoes, underwear or bottled drink we have a new revelation that every bomb doesn't have a cylindrical shape with tail fins. The same epiphany has yet to occur with the no-fly and other terrorist lists. Any terrorist worth his salt that suspects his name is on the list can find many Islamic counterfeiters and even just plain crooks in every city in the U.S. that can obtain a fake driver's license and other forms of ID with bogus names for a couple hundred bucks. These foolish lists should give no comfort to American airline passengers.

President Bush initiated our "War on Terrorism" right after the attacks on the Twin Towers. He did a great job in quickly pursuing the Taliban, and establishing the new cabinet post of "Homeland Security." Unfortunately, this agency is too riddled with political correctness and politics to be effective. Even more ominous is the election of our new "Terrorist-in-Chief," Obama. Most Americans identify with a particular religion. Obama says he is a Christian. A Christian he is not. Obama is most likely agnostic or atheistic like his mother, and he finds it difficult to worship anyone other than himself. But, he recited the Koran in "Mangaji" classes in Indonesia and worshiped in mosques regularly. He was aided in getting admitted to Harvard by a Muslim, and his first home in Chicago was made possible by another Muslim. Just because he is not a practicing Muslim does not mean he will not at least do anything in his power to further their Jihad or spread their influence. Never forget that it is permitted in the Muslim religion to lie about being a Muslim if it advances the goals of Allah.

Murderers usually succeed in killing their intended victims because they know who, when, and where to kill them, while this information remains unknown to the victim. The terrorist has this same advantage. They make all the plans and preparations, and we try to find them out before their plans are executed. We have done poorly at this task and our success rate will only get worse. Muslims reside in 195 countries, including the United States, and we are their number one target. The terrorists killed 2973 Americans on 9/11. Over 6000 of our soldiers have been killed in Iraq and Afghanistan. Terrorist Army Major Nidal Hasan killed 13 at Fort Hood in December 2009. Abdulhakim Mujahid Muhammad killed Pvt. Willian Long and wounded Pvt. Quinton Ezeagwula at a military recruiting office in Little Rock, Ark. on June 1, 2009. Five Muslims of the Arabic Translation Program were arrested in Columbia, South Carolina, for trying to poison the food supply at Fort Jackson

Army Base. There are a minimum of 35 known Jihadist terrorist training camps within the U.S. Muslims are ready to strap on suicide vests and pull the pin. These people are all like Manchurian Candidates, programmed from birth, and just concentrating on those 72 virgins. I have no idea what the female suicide bombers are looking forward to. They certainly are not looking forward to sex since Islam is the only religion that specifically forbids this pleasure to females by sniping-off the clitoris. Heartfelt Christians are ready to die for their Savior, but blowing-up innocents to facilitate sex with six dozen virgins seems like a really stupid idea. Stupid or not, we have to face the fact that there are 2 billion of these fanatics out to kill us, and we either have to separate ourselves from them, or kill them first. Obama is doing everything he can to make the United States a Muslim nation, and for that idea to succeed, the Christians must be subdued, converted, or exterminated.

What are we doing to stop the terrorists before they blow us up? Well, we have the TSA screeners at the airport. They are mostly stupid, fat, have weird corn-row or dreadlock funky hairdos, and can usually be found flirting with the other sex. But, at least we will have a lot of them hanging around because Obama's intention is to unionize thousands of them to repay his debts to his union benefactors. We have Obama's envoy to the Organization of Islamic Conference, Rashad Hussain, who defended the actions of Sami al-Arian who spent four years in prison for conspiring to aid a terrorist camp. I refused to send a contribution to my alma mater, University of South Florida, when I found out Sami al-Arian was a professor there. I guess terrorists can always earn walking-around cash by moonlighting at some university while planning their next attack. After the 13 people were killed at Fort Hood the Army appointed a committee to investigate. Two of their conclusions were that it was not a terrorist act, and that the military needed to watch all religions for unusual activity to prevent mass shootings. So, we really need to watch those Baptists, Jehovah Witnesses, and Catholics, right? Gotta watch that profiling or the PC cops will be upset.

Obama's goal of using the Cloward-Pivens strategy to further immerse the country in chaos, while simultaneously staffing his administration with people competent enough to fool Congress, yet, unquestioning of his directives, is proving difficult for the messiah. Knowing Janet Napolitano could not find the executive bathroom, let alone run the Homeland Security job, he postponed the selection of someone to run the Transportation Security Administration for the first 8 months of his administration to give the terrorists time to get their act together. After Republicans started to badger him about the need for a TSA chief, he finally picked Erroll Southers in late 2009. Southers withdrew his name in January after he found out that Congress was going to question him about his reprimand from the Los Angeles police for running background checks on his estranged wife's boyfriend, and lies he had already told Congress. Too bad for Southers. He would have fit right in at the TSA which, according to their own employees, stands for "Thousands Standing Around."

Obama waited a few more weeks and nominated retired Army Major General Robert Harding for the TSA post. It has become a trademark of Obama to make unsavory announcements very close to 5PM on Fridays, and the White House's withdrawal of Harding's name for the TSA nomination on March 26, was no different. Harding had formed his own consulting company after he retired in 2001 to provide the government with interrogators in Iraq. After the contract ended in 2004, Harding Security Associates claimed more money from termination of the contract than the Defense Department's Inspector General said it was entitled to receive. Harding refunded $1.8 million of the funds in a 2008 settlement with the Defense Intelligence Agency. If you delve deep enough into the backgrounds of Obama's chosen ones in the military establishment, you will find a fairly small group of the most liberal, wishy-washy officers from which he chooses for jobs requiring some military experience. Harding was friends with and worked for both General Barry McCaffrey and General Wesley Clark in the U.S. Southern Command as their J2 in the Intelligence Directorate. These two are perhaps the most anti-American leftists ever in our military, and just being in the same room with them should have disqualified Harding from consideration for any job in government. But, when you have an anti-American President in power, then I suppose Harding's nomination should be expected. There is probably much more to the story, but we'll never find out because he wrote out a quick statement withdrawing his name, and departed the scene. Meanwhile, your TSA has no leader, and Janet Napolitano is still looking for the executive bathroom.

The agents of the FBI, ATF, U.S. Marshalls Service, Homeland Security, TSA, and other agencies tasked to protect Americans from terrorists, seem very adept at catching home-grown bubbas that are not Muslims, who just like to blow-up cardboard boxes in their backyard. A recent case involved infiltrating, arresting, and indicting three homeboys from Alabama who had an ounce of black powder and a couple of pipes bought from their local Ace Hardware. They were tape-recorded saying they hated blacks and Jews. The FBI spent months eavesdropping and observing these idiots. Normally, if you find over three of these locals together, at least one of them is an FBI informant. I suggest that the FBI keep a skeleton crew pursuing these skinheads or KKK members, but concentrate on the real danger posed by Muslims.

The United States has always been a prime breeding ground for far-out wackos. We've had 900 people drink poisoned Kool-Aid for Jim Jones, 39 people cut-off their genitals for Heaven's Gate while waiting for the Hale-Bopp Comet, and numerous groups scaling hills to await pick-up by aliens. We can expect an uptick in this behavior from alienated and disaffected people resulting from Obama's planned increase in unemployment. Blacks are especially vulnerable for conversion to Islam because they have a head-start due to their ingrained hatred of the United States and all it stands for. We can't assume that all black Muslims are as stupid as Louis Farrahkhan. He and his soul mate, Jeremiah, can be counted on to incite hatred and racism. But, they make too much money from their victim-cults to cause any real serious trouble. It's the little black guys that sit in the rear pews, and believe their BS, that you have to worry about. It also seems that more whites are being seduced by the Muslims. John Walker Lindh, Colleen LaRose, Daniel Boyd, and a slew of other white Americans are being converted to this sick religion every day under Obama's encouragement.

Muslims use our charity and anti-discrimination laws against us to infiltrate and take over our communities and institutions. Recently, Lancaster, California Councilwoman, Sherry Marquez, placed her comments on Facebook concerning the beheading of Aasiva Hassan by her husband.

She said, "This is what the Muslim religion is all about." Kamal Al-Khatib, of the American Islamic Institute of Antelope Valley, denounced Marquez's remarks as bigoted and divisive to the community. This is the problem with winning the terrorist war. Anti-American, pro-Sharia Muslims are already among us. In the U.S., we not only have an increasing Muslim population, but Islamic watchdog organizations, with peace-loving names, are monitoring every word written or spoken by Americans. Just as white Americans have been beaten down by white guilt in relation to blacks, so have they been conditioned to watch what they say and do in public. Muslims are tracking their every movement, and listening to their every comment to box them in and keep them contained. Muslims are assuming an ever-increasing role in American society until the day when they can start heading this nation toward Sharia law. And, this scenario does not require a majority of the population. When Saddam Hussein ruled Iraq, his tribe was the minority Sunni. Being a minority doesn't really matter when you have all the bullets and deadly gas canisters to wipe out all your competition. In America, Muslims will use our liberal laws on profiling and anti-Christian policies to prevent any criticism of Muslims until they have effectively silenced all dissent. Then they can proceed with their take-over, unencumbered.

Shortly after the above Muslim anti-Christian group went after the councilwoman, another Muslim group attacked the mayor of Lancaster. On February 5, 2010, Mayor R. Rex Parris gave his "State of the City" speech in which he said simply that he was "growing a Christian Community." Right away, Hussam Ayloush of the Council on American-Islamic Relations (CAIR) filed a civil rights complaint with the U.S. Justice Department stating Parris had violated the civil rights of non-Christians, and shouldn't have used his official capacity at a city event to advance a particular religion. He demanded an investigation. He used the same old "wall of separation" crap that is not in any law of the U.S. or any state. Parris said he made the comment in a speech to Christian ministers at an event he paid for, and thought it was appropriate. He said, "All of us get to express our opinion, wherever, whenever we want to, including opinions of faith, and that is what I did and that is what I will continue to do." I hope Americans are paying attention to what is happening before their eyes. As soon as Muslims are able to do so, they will establish Sharia law. They will not be filing complaints or removing Christian displays. They will be killing and beheading infidels to make-up for lost time.

Sarah and Amina Said were 17 and 18 year old sisters who lived with their father and mother in Lewisville, Texas. The girls were both very attractive, honor students, and athletes. Sarah had already earned a $20,000 scholarship and planned to attend college in the fall of 2009. Their mother was American, but their father was an Egyptian-born Muslim. They were good girls by anyone's standards, and well-liked by everyone in Lewisville. Their father, Yaser Said, was like all Muslims, controlling and violent with his wife and children. On Christmas week, 2008, Yaser's wife, Patricia, took the girls to a nearby town because she had decided to leave after years of seeing Yaser violently mistreat Sarah and Amina. On December 27th, Patricia had remorse and told the girls they were going back to Lewisville to put flowers on her mother's grave. Instead, she took them to their home. There, Yasar talked nicely to the girls and suggested they go out to dinner, just the three of them to "patch things up." At 7:30 PM New Years Day, the Irving police dispatcher received a call on 911 that said, "I'm dying, I'm dying, I'm dying." About an hour later a man walked up to an orange cab parked at the Omni Mandalay Hotel in Irving. He discovered the bullet-shredded bodies of Sarah and Amina in the back seat. To this day, Yasar has never been found. Police are sure he fled to Egypt. Killing daughters or sons or wives or infidels or anyone is okay in the world of the Muslim.

Rifga Bary is a 17 year old girl whose parents, Aysha and Mohamed Bary, are immigrants from Sri Lanka. They are Muslims. Rifga was interested in studying the Christian religion with a view to convert from Islam. When her parents discovered this, she appealed for help on Facebook. She claimed she could be harmed or killed for converting to Christianity. Minister Brian Williams heard of her appeal, and bought her a Greyhound bus ticket to Orlando, Florida. There, Rifga was met by Pastor Blake Lorenz and his wife. They provided a place for her to stay, and contacted the Florida Department of Children and Family Services three times to inform them exactly where she was, and why they were helping her. Now, both Williams and Lorenz have hired attorneys under threats from Muslim-financed lawyers and groups outraged that a Muslim might consider becoming an infidel. Why is it that Muslims go around recruiting people of all religions to become Jihadists and blow themselves up, and one little girl can't become part of a real religion, especially after the two little girls in Texas got blown away by their own father? Wake-up America, the Muslims know where you are and they know how to get you. They all want to install Sharia Law, but will use our system of protective laws to achieve their devious ends.

    I saw a headline recently that read "Child Bride Dies After Sex Organs Rupture." It was about a 13 year old girl named Ilham Mahdi al Assi who was forced into marriage on March 29th by the Islamic customs of Yemen. She died on April 2, 2010, only five days after her so-called marriage. Her 23 year-old husband, Al-Hikmi had taken sex-enhancement drugs, tied Ilham up, and raped her repeatedly, tearing her extensively around the vagina and rectum. She died the next day. Stories like this are a daily occurrence in Yemen. Another young girl of 12 died in September during childbirth. Yet another girl of 8 was forced to marry a man in his 30s. She went to court and demanded a divorce, and luckily got it. When a law banning pre-puberty marriages was proposed, thousands of women demonstrated outside the parliament building against the proposed law. I'm sure most of them were in favor of the change, but when a Muslim husband tells his wife to demonstrate, she demonstrates, because Islamic law also permits the lawful beheading of a wife for disobedience. I realize that this is an example from Yemen and not the United States, but I mention it to point out the extreme differences between our Christian traditions, and Sharia-governed Muslims. Muslims, Sharia Law, and the Koran are inseparable. Sharia law is rigid, inflexible, and based on power, deceit, murder, sex, and intolerance. Conflict between Muslims and other religions can be avoided only by separation. Put the two in close proximity and they become explosive. A free and open society envisioned and established by our patriot founders cannot be endured by Muslims. Let them stay in their native lands and fight among the different sects, but prohibit them from importing their cruel, debasing beliefs to a land that they abhor, with a greatness they did not help create, and do not appreciate.

    A good illustration of how Americans are bowing and accommodating to every wish of Muslims is the action of the

American Association of Pediatricians (AAP) regarding their stand on female genital mutilation (FGM). FGM is practiced only in Muslim countries, and is a surgical procedure to remove a girl's or woman's clitoris (clitoridectomy), so she does not become aroused in sex or have an orgasm. Only Muslim men are supposed to enjoy sex, according to the Koran. It seems that the growing Muslim population in the U.S. is shipping their daughters to Islamic countries to have clitoridectomies instead of having them performed here in the U.S. Always valuing a buck over the Hippocratic Oath, or the Golden Rule, or civilized behavior, the AAP agreed to relax their opposition to clitoridectomies, and are now lobbying to have state and federal laws allowing the surgical procedure on girls here in the United States. So, we stalwart Americans are now in the young girl genital mutilation business to avoid being called anti-Muslim, and to assure that we cash-in on the female genital mutilation market. What a sick religion is Islam, and what a bunch of panty-waists Americans have become since this great country was left in our care by George Washington and the gang.

There is open season on Christians and Christianity 365 days a year in the United States. These are the same Christians that founded the original 13 colonies, fought all the wars, and established a superpower that allows dissent and freedom of expression. They have been repaid by being forced to remove the Ten Commandments from public buildings, stop prayer in schools, and have Jesus Christ depicted in a glass of piss. But, if anything, Christians are law abiding. So, after exhausting their legal arguments they obey the laws as interpreted by the ACLU and their leftist judges, and comply. That's what Christians do. They can take the heat, so they stay in the kitchen. Can Muslims stand the heat of ridicule and criticism like Christians? Back in April, the cartoon show "South Park," depicted Muhammad, the Muslim's prophet, as a character in a bear suit on the Comedy Central TV show. A few days later, a warning was posted by Abu Talhah al Amridee on the website, "revolutionmuslim.com," that read, "We have to warn Matt and Trey that what they are doing is stupid, and they will probably wind up like Theo Van Gogh for airing this show." Trey Parker and Matt Stone are the show's owners. The website posting included a graphic photo of Van Gogh, who was a Dutch filmmaker murdered in 2004 for making a documentary on violence against Muslim women. Amridee also said, "This is not a small thing. We should do whatever we can to make sure it does not happen again." The posting on Revolutionmuslim.com also included an audio of a sermon by Anwar al-Awlaki, a radical U.S. born Muslim preacher, now believed to be hiding in Yemen, who discusses assassinating individuals who defame the prophet Muhammad. It also included a link to a 2009 story in the Huffington Post that gave details of Stone and Parker's mansion in Colorado to make sure that any Muslim crazies wanting to assassinate Stone and Parker could find them. Stone and Parker apologized for the cartoon character and removed it from the series. Had the character depicted Jesus Christ would they have removed it after criticism? Hell, no! The hunting season for Christians is open all year long and there is no bag limit.

Since terrorism will be with us forever, the most we can hope for is to kill or catch them before they blow us up. If we capture them, then they must be held securely until tried, preferably in a military court. I couldn't imagine a more perfect detention center than on a flat spit of sand surrounded by ocean, and not on the U.S. mainland, but nearby, so we can keep an eye on them. Hey, don't we have a military base in Cuba called Guantanamo? Gitmo is the perfect location. That's why Bush spent millions constructing a secure, well-designed facility. There has never been an escape or even a serious attempt to escape. The terrorists there pose no threat to U.S. citizens. Why on earth would Obama and his Chicago mob want to close it down and move all terrorist to our mainland? The only way to explain Obama's desire to move the terrorists here is that he is trying to help his brother Muslims while still not quite crossing the line and appearing to be on the other side.

You will not only see an increase in home-grown Jihadists, but you will see an upsurge in their success rate at blowing things up or killing people. One reason for this is that terrorists are learning from our captures how to avoid detection. Another reason is that our sad excuse for an Attorney General, Eric "The Red" Holder, is a closet terrorist who has staffed his office with terrorist-loving lawyers to thwart the efforts of sincere law enforcement officers. At a November 2009 hearing before the Senate Justice Department Oversight Committee, Senator Charles Grassley of Iowa asked Holder for a list of the attorneys who may have conflicts of interest with detainee issues. This had resulted from Obama and Holder's insistence that Gitmo be closed, and the terrorists held there be tried, similar to shoplifters in the United States. Holder responded to Grassley's request by saying he would, "consider" it. Three months later Grassley got a letter from Ronald Weich, of the Justice Department, stating that nine of their lawyers had represented terrorists. One of the lawyers, Neal Katyal, principal Deputy Solicitor General, had defended Usama Bin Laden's driver who was detained at Gitmo. Another one, Jennifer Daskal, of the National Security Division, represented detainees as a lawyer for Human Rights Watch, which is a radical leftist group like the ACLU.

Of course, Grassley and Rep. Peter King of New York, got the same evasive answers they always get from Obama's pro-terrorist Justice Department, but Grassley is persistent. Grassley said, "We're not talking about a murderer or bank robber; we're talking about the defense of our country." Grassley noted that the suspects being tried in federal court will have more constitutional rights than members of the U.S. military do in military commissions.

At least one of the Justice Department lawyers had to recuse himself. Associate Attorney General Thomas J. Perrelli, the number 3 official in the Justice Department, had to recuse himself on at least 13 active detainee cases, and at least 26 cases listed as closed or mooted.

The response to Grassley was predictable. When the Attorney General responds to a U.S. Senator's simple request that he will "consider" giving him an answer, and then casually sends it over three months later, you know the idiot has a chip on his shoulder. Holder's terrorist-loving lawyers had stock replies like, "All department appointees understand that their client is the United States," and "This familiarity with and experience in the relevant area of law redounds to the government's benefit." Don't even try to figure out why a President, Attorney General and all government cabinet officers would actually want to aid terrorists trying to destroy our country. Just accept it as fact and act accordingly.

From a Mark Steyn article in May, I read the following exchange between Congressman Lamar Smith and Eric "The Red" Holder at a May 13th hearing before the House Judiciary

Committee. Smith was asking if Holder thought the Fort Hood massacre, Christmas Pantybomber, and the Times Square Bomber were connected by a common thread, radical Islam.

Smith: "In the case of all three attempts in the last year, the terrorist attempts, one of which was successful, those individuals have had ties to radical Islam. Do you feel that these individuals might have been incited to take the actions that they did because of radical Islam?"
Holder: "Because of...?"
Smith: "Radical Islam"
Holder: "There are a variety of reasons why I think people have taken these actions. I think you have to look at each individual case."
Smith: "Yes, but radical Islam could have been one of the reasons?"
Holder: "There are a variety of reasons why people..."
Smith: "But was radical Islam one of them?"
Holder: "There are a variety of reasons why people do things. Some of them are potentially religious."
Smith: "Okay, but all I'm asking is if you think among these varieties of reasons radical Islam might have been one of the reasons that the individuals took the steps that they did."
Holder: "You see, you say radical Islam...I mean, I think people who espouse a...a version of Islam that is not..."
Smith: "Are you uncomfortable attributing any actions to radical Islam? It sounds like it."

Eric "The Red" never did answer the question. He and Obama will never question anything Muslims do or say. Obama is a closet Muslim and hates Christians. Steyn went on to describe how Muslims were also busy at the UN Human Rights Council (UNHRC). The Organization of the Islamic Conference (OIC) succeeded in getting the Islamic nations of Mauritania, Malaysia, Qatar, Maldives, and Libya on the UNHRC with 80% of the UN's vote. The OIC is pushing a proposal to forbid public discussion of Islam or its practices because they consider Islam above reproach, and regard any questions of their actions blasphemous. Imagine a Christian organization attempting this in the UN.

Obama and Holder may not have to wait too long for their friends, Hezbollah, to strike at targets in the U.S. Four indictments were handed down in Philadelphia last November for four men charged with trying to export 1200 Colt machineguns and other material to Syria financed from the sale of fake passports and counterfeit dollars. One was a U.S. citizen. Another four were charged in Miami for exporting electronics to Paraguay to generate funds for Hezbollah. According to New York's Deputy Police Commissioner, David Cohen, Hezbollah is the most disciplined and capable terrorist group in the world because it has unlimited funds directly from the Iranian intelligence services. Although Hezbollah killed 241 Americans in Beirut in 1983, and 19 more in Saudi Arabia, there is no doubt they are capable of hitting targets inside America anytime they want. There is positive proof that Hezbollah is now entering South America, making their way to Mexico, and crossing into the United States with other Mexican illegal aliens by the thousands.

Steve Emerson, of the "Investigative Project on Terrorism," said the arrests in Philadelphia and Miami are "just the tip of the proverbial iceberg." According to him there are cells all over the U.S., in-place, and just awaiting the order to strike. Professor Omar Ashour, of the Middle Eastern studies program at Exeter University in England, said there are sympathizers, supporters, and members of Hezbollah throughout the Americas. Walid Phares, of the Foundation for Defense of Democracies, has stated that well-trained forces of Hezbollah have been inserted in the major cities of the U.S., and are just awaiting instructions to wreak havoc inside this country. Phares says the really scary part is that our Homeland Security Agency is failing to recognize Hezbollah's recruitment process in a timely manner, and fears if, and when, they attack here it will be on a national scale, and not just a single act of violence as they've done in the past.

The new wave of Jihadists will come in all sizes, sexes, and colors. They won't wear blankets or sandals or head scarves. They will speak perfect English, and smile while they cut your head off or shoot you between the eyes. The unexpected, unexplainable deaths will strike fear in every American, but nothing will be done about it. Obama's response will be to curtail, limit, and deny innocent Americans the instruments and materials they need for self-defense. And don't tell me they will have to pry your weapons from your cold dead hands because that's no problem at all when the greater good of mankind is at stake. To give you an idea of how many terrorists that Americans have to look forward to in the future, just think back to high school science class and remember studying kinetic energy and potential energy. Now, think of Muslims as potential energy, and suicide bombers as kinetic energy. There may be only 1000 active Muslim suicide bombers with C-4 strapped to their bellies at any given time, but there are millions whose potential energy can be activated to kinetic with the promise of 72 virgins. Samuel Jackson's character in the movie Jurassic Park gave us good advice when he said "Hang on to your butts."

We've been discussing domestic terrorism so far. How are our foreign efforts against terrorism progressing? The Americans, British, UN and NATO are busy appealing to the Taliban to sit down and discuss sharing power with the government in Afghanistan. They want to give the terrorists jobs, cash, and representation in the Karzai government as a bribe for peace. Do the allies really think that these jihadists, who used to round up hundreds of people and machine gun them in the soccer stadium, are going to suddenly become parliamentarians? I'm sure that people who cut-off the heads, hands, and feet of loyal followers for minor offenses against Sharia Law, and stick-whip women who bare a centimeter of ankle skin, will make reasonable government bureaucrats and citizens who will become Republicans in a short time. They differ from Al Qaida in name only. Rather than operate in the hills outside Kabul and other cities, and plant bombs and set-up ambushes, they can now live within the metro areas and not have to drive so far to kill people. Hamid Karzai was really ticked-off when Pakistan captured Mullah Abdul Ghani Baradar, the Taliban's number 2 guy in March. Other than being responsible for killing hundreds of people, Baradar is really a reasonable guy. His opening demands are that the U.S. get out, they stop calling the terrorists "terrorists," and let all their buddies out of jail. Sounds good to me. Next thing you know, the Taliban will host the Olympics and win the Nobel Peace Prize. In April, Hamid Karzai threatened to join the Taliban because of the United States' meddling in the last election. Karzai said we withheld sending the 30,000 troop surge in the hope that his opponent would win. When the U.S. pulls out of Afghanistan how long do you think it will take the Taliban to take-over the country? How do you think the parents of the six or seven thousand dead soldiers will feel when they realize their sons died for nothing?

Rather than applaud the FBI or Homeland Security for their efforts to stop terrorists from blowing up our commercial jets, you'd better cheer the real hero of this so-called war, and he is named "luck." First, we had the ding-dong, Richard Reid, who was refused a boarding pass because he looked like such a slob. So, he went home, took a shower, and came back the next day. This time the French let him board the aircraft. When a stewardess caught him lighting a match she told him there was no smoking allowed. He apologized and she left. Later, she saw him trying to light a fuse sticking out of his shoe in his lap and asked, "What are you doing"? He pushed her to the floor and she got up and ran to get some water. Another stewardess came and Reid bit her on the thumb. Meanwhile, the first stewardess came back and threw water on Reid and his shoes. Then, she and some passenger wrestled him to the floor and tied him up with phone cords and seatbelts. The luck this time was delivered in the form of this idiot's sweat. When he was refused a boarding pass the first time, he went home for a full day. He returned the next day and was allowed to board the plane. Being 6' 4", weighing a chunky 230 pounds, and being out of shape, he sweated profusely on the fuse sticking out of his shoe. This caused the fuse to be too damp to light when the dumb-dumb tried to light it.

All of the airlines in the world immediately started making passengers remove their shoes for inspection before boarding. I can understand most people not realizing that plastic explosives can be put into shoes. But, how about "experts" like the FBI and TSA? I was a medic in the Army, and like all recruits, we spent a few days training on shape charges and mines in basic training. Plastic explosives and C-4 can take almost any form. It is just silly-putty with a bang.

In 2006 the British agency MI5 secretly searched Ahmed Ali's luggage on his return trip from Pakistan. They found a bottle of powdered Tang soft-drink and batteries, which made them begin the largest surveillance operation ever in the UK. For three months they dug through dumpsters, and bugged every location used by a hundred suspects and their contacts. Finally, on August 10, they locked-down and searched 69 residences, businesses, vehicles, and open spaces, and arrested 25 Muslims and the few white British subjects with them. After the trials, seventeen were sentenced, eight were released, and seven were arrested in Pakistan. The Keystone Cops (Homeland Security) again swung into action. They banned water bottles. What an epiphany. Liquid explosives could actually be put into containers and detonated aboard airliners! Homeland Security, MI5, and all other super high-tech agencies could have saved a lot of time and money by just watching an old spaghetti western where a cowboy carries a vial of nitro glycerin very carefully lest it blow-up. Nitro is a clear liquid that is mixed with sawdust to make dynamite. Just one, full-time agency employee assigned to watch spaghetti westerns could have saved millions in time and effort. So, now we had to take our shoes off <u>and</u> leave our water and baby bottles at home.

The next wannabe bomber was a retard black guy named Umar Abdul Abdulmutallab. I'll call him the "Fruit of the Loom" bomber. Fruity Umar is one of 16 offspring of his Muslim father and one of his many wives. Those Muslims certainly like to sow their wild oats. As a child, Fruity liked to play Playstation, basketball, and criticize his banker father for charging interest because he considered interest a "Jewish" thing. I happen to agree on the interest thing since I could save a lot if those damn banks would quit charging me interest. Anyway, after going to 20 different schools, sucking in all the Koran nonsense, and meeting with Jihadist idiots, Fruity goes to Amsterdam and books Northwest Airlines flight 243 Airbus, A330, to Detroit on Christmas Day 2009. After spending 20 minutes in the crapper, Fruity took his seat and covered himself with a blanket. The next thing passengers noticed was loud popping noises, a foul-smelling odor, and Fruity's pants on fire. The flames soon spread to the walls. A stewardess soon doused the fire and a Dutch passenger jumped on Fruity. Fruity was taken to the front of the aircraft, minus his pants, and plus a few burns on his legs. He and his al Qaeda buddies had stuffed his stinky underwear with a mixture of PETN and TAPN. When mixed together they surpass TNT in brisance. PETN is the ignition for the propellant in 22 rifle cartridges. Fruity had first and second degree burns on his hands, thigh, and cojones. If we're lucky, the last injury may prevent more little Fruity's from using underwear for anything more dangerous than cojones. The scarier part of this drama came later as HS Secretary Janet Napolitano said our security systems "worked" before she said they "failed." Chaulk-up one more near miss to luck. Obama jumped into the fray and said something stupid as usual. He made sure Fruity was read his Miranda rights so his African relatives and Muslim Jihadists would not order a Jihad against POTUS. A month after the underwear bomber screwed-up his suicide, Obama announced that 150 full-body scanners were planned for U.S. airports. The first three would be installed at Logan International Airport in Boston. The White House said that the scanners will cost $25 million and had been available for years, but that the underwear bomber had hastened the need to install them immediately. There is just one problem with Obama's rush to get the scanners to our airports - experts said they would not have picked-up the hidden explosives in the suspect's underwear.

So, our illustrious anti-terrorist agencies now know that shoes, baby bottles, and underwear can explode. The Jihadists must be shaking in their sandals. Starting from the basic assumption that Muslims are nut cases and will blow-up anything to get at those 72 virgins, let's try and guess what the up and coming jihadi's have planned for us next. When I was a developer and homebuilder in Kissimmee, Florida, I used to visit our Osceola Country Planning Deptartment quite often. On the desk of the department head was a silicone breast implant serving as a paper-weight. I used to pick it up and use it as a hand exerciser. It weighed about a half-pound, and I supposed it was a normal sized implant used for all but the largest of boob jobs. Do you have any idea how much damage two half-pound blobs of C-4 would cause? Imagine the damage done by a D-Cup! If a Muslim female couldn't be located to undergo a C-4 breast implant, then do you think a Muslim buck could be found to have a few pounds of flesh removed to make room for the silicone implants (C-4) in his thighs or buttocks?

The bottom line is that when the Muslims want to blow-up a commercial airliner, they will blow-up an airliner. If we stop all Muslims from flying then they will recruit one of the many white-westerners that are flocking to the Jihadist's idiots. But, keep in mind that there are two billion Muslims that want to kill you, so just keep a look-out for shoes, bottled water, underwear, and boobs the next time you fly. If you are an American female you should also watch out who you marry. Homeland Security officials cracked a vast illegal-alien Middle Eastern marriage-fraud ring in "Operation Broken Vows." Authorities were stunned by the scope of the operations, which stretched from Boston to South Carolina to California. Literally hundreds of American females were duped into marrying Muslim jihadist to facilitate their covert and subversive activities.

For those complacent Americans who think Sharia Law and Muslim domination of the United States is too far in the future to worry about should have attended the "Emerging World Order: The Khilafah Will Shape the World" conference held at the Chicago Marriott Oak Brook in July. The conference is hosted by Hizb ut-Tahrir America, an al Qaida linked radical Muslim group committed to establishing a caliphate, or international Islamic empire in the United States. The first conference was held last year at the same Marriott in Chicago and was entitled "Fall of Capitalism & Rise of Islam." It drew 500 attendees and blamed capitalism for both World Wars, Michael Jackson's decision "to shed his black skin" and every other problem in the world. Walid Phares, director of the Future of Terrorism Project at the Foundation for Defense of Democracies, said, "Hizb ut-Tahrir realized that U.S. laws, in this stage, allow them to work undetected as long as they use a narrative that fools the public and law enforcement." He said the group's vision of a worldwide caliphate "is identical to the Taliban regime but spanning on three continents, as a first stage."

Ishtiaq Hussain, former member of Hizb ut-Tahrir, stated, "They don't believe Israel should exist, some of their leaders have denied the Holocaust, and they believe that homosexuals should be thrown off the highest building." He went on to say, "It's actually a very dangerous group." Phares said former members of Hizb ut-Tahrir include confessed mastermind of 9/11, Khalid Sheikh Mohammed, and the Iraqi leader of al Qaida, Abu Musab al-Zarqawi. Phares concluded, "The bottom line here is that we are witnessing the emergence and the expansion of a jihadist recruitment factory in our midst, openly calling for jihad and for the establishment of a caliphate instead of many governments...and in its last stage, to what they call jihadism against America and its allies, that is, technically speaking, terrorism and massacre." Hizb ut-Tahrir is holding conferences regularly in most countries including Europe, England, India, and Canada to recruit members.

While Marriott of Chicago gladly re-booked the radical group for a second jihadist conference, the Marriott of Delray Beach, Florida, refused to host an event held by the Florida Security Council (FSC) to honor an anti-jihadist advocate. The stated purpose of the FSC is to raise awareness of security threats facing Florida and the U.S. by "radical supremacists, Muslims, and Latin American totalitarianism." FSC Director Tom Trento said, "You let lunatics come into your hotel, and then you have people trying to defend the United States of America and you throw them out."

So, America, if you think Muslims are just another religion that will meld into our society you are wrong. You have a choice: deport them all or buy yourself a kneeling rug, a Koran, practice beating your wife, and make an appointment for your daughter to get a clitorectomy.

Profiling is one of the subjects most often brought up by the so-called Muslim-American love-fest organizations. Council on Islamic-American Relations (CAIR) is the most vocal of the many make-believe, love, and harmony organizations. These groups exist to slither into the heart of American society and kill it from within. They are constantly bringing charges of profiling against cops and agencies claiming that Muslims are being singled out for discrimination. What's wrong with that? The average human would live about one day if they did not discriminate continuously. Try and pet a snake the next time you see one. If it bites you and you die, then you should have discriminated that rattle snake from a garter snake. If you go to the medicine cabinet and grab just any of the pill bottles and pop one in your mouth, and then fall over dead, you should have discriminated and taken the aspirin and not your husband's decongestant with your high blood pressure. Profiling or discrimination is vital to our existence and we must do it every day. If you live in a gated, upper-scale community shouldn't you be suspicious of a dread-locked, baggy-pants black guy sneaking along the hedges? You know that he doesn't belong there, just as a clean-cut, young white female teenager shouldn't be walking down a sidewalk on Mooreland Avenue in Atlanta at midnight on a Saturday night. Both should be stopped by the cops and checked out. More importantly, all Muslims should be suspect wherever they are encountered. Terrorism today is synonymous with Muslims. All white, western nations like those in Europe, Canada, and the U.S. confuse the issue with political correctness, but the truth is evident every time people are slaughtered or a car bomb explodes. Islam is a violent religion because its founder based it on a system of murder, sex, and power. All other religions attempt conversion through persuasion while Islam simply says convert or die. The reason Islam has grown to outnumber all other religions is that it is sort of like a prison. Once a child is born into its rigid dogma it is impossible to escape alive. There is no right or wrong, only Islam. It is a totalitarian form of control disguised as religion with world domination as its stated goal. This is why I treat Muslims interchangeably with terrorism.

We are not alone in our increasing problems with Muslims. In fact, Europe, Canada, and other countries are facing crises with Muslims earlier than we are. Muslims are intentionally multiplying like rabbits. In France approximately 25% of the population is Muslim. Most of them are young. Their problems have ranged from restaurants serving Muslim ethnic food, to burning 25,000 automobiles back in 2007, to protesting cuts in Muslim welfare. Their problems are just beginning.

A building permit has been applied for in Newham, England, for construction of the largest mosque in Europe. It will accommodate 12,000 Muslims. The most common birth name in England is already Mohammad. Through birth and immigration, Muslims hope to take control of England within 25 years. Let me give you just a few of the signs held-up at the recent Muslim "Religion of Peace Demonstration" held in London in 2009: "Slay those who insult Islam," "Behead those who insult Islam," "Europe you will pay-your extermination is on its way," "Europe is the cancer-Islam is the answer," "Exterminate those who slander Islam," "Islam will dominate the world," "Freedom go to hell," "Europe take some lessons from 9/11," "Europe you will pay-your 9/11 is on its way," "Be prepared for the real holocaust" and "Massacre those who insult Islam."

Germany is up to its ears in Muslims, too. Back in the 1960's and 70's German steel production was booming and they had a shortage of labor. So, thousands of Turks were brought in to work in the steel mills. Now, the mills are all shut down, but the Turks never left, and they are all Muslims. There are already 170 mosques in Germany and 200 more are under construction. They are spreading to the hinterland. Germans are only recently waking-up to the fact that Muslims are taking over their country.

Switzerland has taken the boldest step yet in combating the take-over of Europe by Muslims. Last November Swiss voters overwhelmingly approved a constitutional ban on minarets, effectively stopping construction of any more mosques in Switzerland. Muslims comprise about 6% of Switzerland's 7.5 million people. Switzerland has taken note of the rising Muslim influence across Europe, and decided to act before their nation was consumed like the rest of Europe. The reaction to the Swiss ban has been fast and threatening. Muslims, in Switzerland and abroad, have condemned the ban as biased and anti-Islamic. Business groups warned of damaged relations and the reduction of banking transactions, travel, and shopping. The most serious reaction has been from Muammar Qaddafi of Libya. Qaddafi not only has urged Muslims all over the world to boycott Swiss products, and bar Swiss planes and ships from airports and seaports, but has called on all Muslim nations for a holy war, a jihad, against Switzerland. Qaddafi has been ticked at the Swiss ever since his son, Hannibal, and his wife were arrested in Geneva in 2008 for beating their servants. It's just really hard for Muslims to understand why they can't just beat-up or kill whomever they choose. Qaddafi retaliated by recalling diplomats from Switzerland, taking his money out of Swiss banks, and disrupting oil shipments to the Swiss. When the Swiss responded by imposing a travel ban on Qaddafi, he banned citizens of 25 European countries from traveling to Libya. Take note America. When we infidels interfere with Muslim plans to take over the world they really get upset. I've always admired the Swiss. Wish they would take Obama off our hands and give us their president.

Common sense should tell us that we must take steps to avoid the Muslim take-over being experienced by every European country. But common sense has been a stranger to the United States for many years. Before 9/11 we had not even one Muslim in Congress. Now we have two. And, now that Muslims have killed 3000 New Yorkers in the Twin

Towers, they are building not one mosque next to Ground Zero, but two. The first is a 13 story super-mosque just 600 feet from Ground Zero. The cost of the mosque will be $150 million, and will be built by Muslim-owned Cordoba Initiative, but the land and existing structure was purchased for $4.85 million from Burlington Coat Factory by Soho Properties, which is run by Imam Rauf. Nobody can find out where the money is coming from, but if it was being raised from American Muslims it wouldn't be so hard to track down. Three American groups are fighting the construction of the mosques. The "9/11 Families for a Safe and Strong America" group, which was founded by members of 9/11 families, can't believe the Muslims would have the audacity to build next to where their Islamic religion killed 3000 people. Their spokesperson, Debra Burlingame, said, "The idea that you would establish a religious institution that embraces the very Sharia Law that terrorists point to as their justification for what they did is an obscenity to me." Pamela Geller of "Stop Islamization of America" calls the mosques "an insulting flag of conquest of Islamic supremacism." She asks, "How can you build a shrine to the very ideology that brought down the World Trade Center?" Of course, the politically correct Lower Manhattan Community Board, who must approve construction projects, had no problem approving the building plans. Madeline Brooks of "Act! For America Now" says the mosques are an act of Islamic fascism, and designed to co-opt the 9/11 narrative and transform it into a Muslim conquest.

The second mosque is called the Masjid Mosque and will be built just two blocks from Ground Zero. The ads requesting donations says it plans to "build the House of Allah" and "raise the flag of LA ILLAH ILLA ALLAH" in downtown Manhattan. The present Masjid Mosque is located about 4 blocks from Ground Zero, and the crowds of Muslims spill over into the streets during prayers. Their website says they are deeply involved in converting people to Islam and run a special program to convert those who are interested. The groups fighting the Muslim takeover of the U.S. are fighting a losing battle. Like Neville Chamberlain, the pre-WWII English Prime Minister, we have adopted a capitulation stance and use appeasement to avoid confrontation with evil. We will soon learn that evil returns over and over until it wins.

All people living on the American and European continents can visualize their Muslimized future by looking at a "civilized," developed, nuclear nation like our friend and ally, Pakistan, and see how non-Muslims are treated there today. Arshed Masih and his wife, Martha, lived in Rawalpindi, Pakistan, with their 3 children. They both worked for a powerful businessman named Sheik Mohammad Sultan. Arshed and Martha were both Christians. Sultan and some of his other employees aggressively tried to convert Arshed and Martha to Islam. It got so bad that they quit their jobs. A Muslim mob, which included the police, attacked Arshed and his wife last March at their home, and demanded they recant their religion. When Arshed refused they bound him, poured gas on his clothing, and lit him on fire. While he was burning, a policeman raped Martha in front of him and the three children. Arshed was the 10th Christian to be burned alive in a month. Earlier, 37 year old Asia Bibi was arrested and is still being held under section 295-C of the blasphemy law for saying, "Jesus is alive. Muhammad is dead." Pakistani law includes many laws against blasphemy, and makes no provision or tolerance for any belief outside Islam. Section 295-C of the blasphemy law reads, "Whoever by words, either spoken or written or by visible representation, or by any imputation, innuendo, or insinuation, directly or indirectly, defiles the sacred name of the Holy Prophet Mohammed (PBUH) shall be punished by death, or imprisonment for life, and shall also be liable for a fine." Another law includes penalties for anyone who says or writes anything against Muhammad's family members, associates, or successors. Christians are routinely arrested and charged with crimes under the blasphemy laws, and police participate willingly and avoid any semblance of protection of the non-Muslim minorities, like Christians. The Pakistani representatives at the United Nations are pressuring the organization to include its blasphemy laws in the U.N. Declaration of Human Rights. This will not only embolden the Muslim nations to step-up their attacks on Christians, but spread the violence to all nations of the world. Obama, Hillary Clinton, and every one of the Darkside oligarchy now running the United States, advocates our signing of the Declaration of Human Rights, and the protections it will afford all Muslims, and deny to all Christians.

Another so-called civilized Muslim nation is Saudi Arabia. In April there was a headline that read, "Saudi Girl 12, Wins Divorce From 80-Year-Old Husband." The girl had been married, and the marriage consummated to her father's 80 year-old cousin in return for a dowry payment of $23,000. In other words, if you have the money and want to have sex with a little girl, just take your pick. The basis of the Islamic laws allowing child marriages is that 14 centuries ago their so-called prophet married a 9 year old little girl. So, the reasoning is that if something is good enough for Muhammad, it must be okay for all Muslims. That's the root of the problem, isn't it? Muhammad was a murderer, philanderer, and pedophile. He wrote the Koran to tell his followers how to kill people and commit terrorism. And, if they obeyed his teachings they could have multiple wives, kill them on a whim, and then blow themselves up and earn 72 virgins in the process. Is that the kind of religion Americans need here to guarantee peace and tranquility? Saudi Arabia is also a very dangerous place if you happen to forget or misplace your Islamic headscarf. There were 15 young girls at a theatre enjoying themselves when a fire broke out. Like most humans wanting to avoid burning to death, they all rushed outside the building to escape the flames, leaving behind their headscarves in their mad dash. Once outside, the ever-alert Saudi firemen realized immediately that Allah would not approve of their uncovered heads, so they forced the girls back into the building where their charred bodies were later discovered. Examining the blackened corpses, the firemen noted that the girls were still without head scarves, and therefore, their actions were justified under Islamic law.

There has been much speculation about whether Obama is a closet Muslim. The question is not really important because he acts like one, and does all in his power to advance Islam. His Muslim sympathies are important for all of us because terrorism hit home to Americans on 9/11, has been a part of our lives ever since, and Muslims are synonymous with terrorism. But, imagine living in the tiny country of Israel, surrounded by hundreds of millions of Muslims, all wanting to kill you, all the time. Before Obama, the Israeli's could depend on their highly-trained military to defend them, and the backing of the U.S. in supplying arms and even military assistance if a conflict threatened Israel's existence. Under Obama's tutelage not only have we backed-away from helping Israel, but we are pro-actively helping Israel's enemies to equip and train to attack Israel.

Obama's Secretary of Defense, Robert Gates, appointed United States Lieutenant General Keith Dayton to educate, train, and equip Palestinian Authority Fatah forces in Jordan to attack Israel's Defense Forces (IDF) if Israel does not surrender Judea and Samaria within two years. Obama has spent $300 million already on this project and will spend more. With Hezbollah in Syria and Lebanon, Hamas controlling Palestine, Fatah being trained by us in Jordan, and Iran financing and pulling the strings of anti-Israel terrorism all over the region, Israel will soon be overwhelmed. Their IDF is good, but Israel cannot hope to stand against 100 to 1 odds in manpower and equipment, plus be denied help from its only ally in the world, the U.S. Obama has been openly snubbing Israel because of their refusal to give Jerusalem back to the Muslims. He, along with Russia, the United Nations, and the European Union has demanded that Israel surrender to all demands by the Palestinians within two years. General Dayton has said that if this is not done then the likelihood of the American-trained Palestinian Authority troops may attack Israel. If these troops attack as part of a combined Muslim force, then Israel has little hope of survival because Obama, and his Muslim-loving Darkside, dream of the day when all Jews are dead and gone, so that they will be free to eliminate the Christians next.

Helping Obama to bring about Israel's death is the Christian-hating, Islamist, terrorist state of Turkey. Turkey murdered over two million Christian Armenians starting before WWI, and has been killing Kurds every chance they get. Christians are imprisoned, or worse, for the mere possession of a Bible. Turkey's latest attempt to build a global jihad against Israel is the six ship armada supposedly sent to Gaza to bring needed supplies to the Palestinians. Israel warned them time and again that Hamas was bringing in weapons to Gaza, and that if countries wanted to send anything to the Palestinians it must go through an Israeli port of entry. Since Turkey's real purpose was to embarrass Israel, they made sure that the ships were staffed with Hamas and al Qaida terrorists. When the Israeli Seals boarded the ship, Marmara, they were attacked with knives, steel bars, bats, and clubs. The Seals were armed with paint-ball guns and service pistols to be used as a last resort. The terrorists immediately attacked the Seals with knives, and actually wrestled with the Seals until they took some of the guns from them and shot four of the Seals. When the Seals killed nine of them out of self-defense, the radical Islamists had their propaganda machine ready to go into action. Turkey and the rest of the Islamic whores immediately took their case to the UN (United Nuts) where Israel used to have one friend (us), but now has none. Predictably, the Islamic-controlled UN immediately passed a resolution condemning Israel. Our Islamic-controlled President joined his Islamic brothers, of course.

Getting building supplies to Gaza is definitely not the goal of Turkey. They have always wanted a global jihad against both the Israeli's and the United States. Now that the United States has a fellow Islamist in charge they figure Israel is an easy target. Turkey is uniting with Iran, Syria, Hamas, al Qaida, Hezbollah, and even Egypt and Muslim-dominated Europe in building hatred of little Israel. Make no mistake; this is just the beginning of the build-up of the world-wide push to kill Israel. There will be more contrived events, more condemnation of Israel, and eventually, an invasion of Israel to kill every last Jew, and give the little country to the worthless Palestinians who never populated the land in the first place, and have no right to it at all.

To me, the most immediately dangerous Muslim country on earth is Iran. Not only are they close to producing their first nuclear weapons, but they have the only state-sponsored, state-owned industries specifically designed to support and expand worldwide terrorist activity. The United States has specific intelligence on all of Iran's dirty operations, but has done nothing about them under Bush, and will actually help further their terrorism under our terrorist-in-chief, Obama.

I wish the press would just stop reporting on sanctions against Iran. Year after year the blather is simply filler for newspapers and websites. It is repetitious, it never changes, and it never works. Iran has wanted the bomb since 1980 and they are going to soon have it. Bush tried sanctions, but Russia and China didn't like them. Russia is paid billions for helping Iran build their nuclear power plants and infrastructure, and China depends on Iran for oil until they develop their own sources. Obama stupidly said he could just talk to Ahmadinejad and solve the problems. He is either dumb, or lying, or both. He and Hillary do not see the United States as a separate and distinct entity or a superpower, but rather just another member of the UN family of nations, no more important than Burundi or Ireland. The idea of unilateral action against Iran will not even be considered by these fools.

The daily articles and talking heads discussing sanctions on Iran would be laughable if they weren't so serious. The really funny ones are those that still ponder whether Iran is enriching uranium for nuclear power plants or weapons. Their pondering will end shortly because Iran's first bomb should be ready soon. Then the question will not be if they test it out on Israel, but <u>when</u> they test it out on Israel. We've lived under the nuclear umbrella now for 65 years and only two atomic bombs have been used in warfare. Mutually Assured Destruction (MAD) has prevented the use of atomic bombs being used between Russia and the United States. MAD isn't going to work with Ahmadinejad because he is literally MAD.

In a number of speeches, both in Iran and standing before the UN in New York, Mahmoud Ahmadinejad has invoked the name of the 12th Imam, or Mahdi. It's too complicated to explain succinctly, but it is a belief held only by the Shiite branch of Islam which is the dominate sect of Iran. Shiites believe that Muhammad decreed that all imams (anointed teachers/leaders) would be descendants of his son-in-law, Ali. Ali had two sons, Hasan and Hussein, who became the first Imams. This lineage worked fine until the eleventh Imam, Hasan ibn Ali al-Askari, died in 872 AD as a teenager without heirs. This supposedly ended the line of Imams at eleven. Shiites believe that Hasan Ali and his wife, Fatima, had a son (even though he was a teenager) and this son was hidden at age 5 from the caliphs for fear of being killed in a power struggle. The son was named Abu al-Qasim Muhammad or Muhammad al Mahdi, and supposedly went into "occultation" or absence for 70 years, but was in communication with some of his chosen deputies during this time. The last deputy died in 939AD, and since that time until the present, there has been no communication with him. Muhammad, this twelfth imam, is also called Imam al-Asr, "the imam of the age" or Sahib al-Zaman, "Lord of the Time." Even though he has not been seen for over 1070 years he is considered to be merely absent, not dead. He will return at a suitable time to lead in the final battles in the last days for the ultimate triumph of Islam. He is also sometimes called Imam Mahdi. Mahdi is similar to the Christian term Messiah which means savior or rescuer. He will not return until the world is in a state of chaos and subjugation because the Mahdi cannot bring peace unless there is first chaos from which to bring peace.

In the same way that our Christian God, Jehovah, made our Bible difficult to interpret, so is the Koran hard to figure out, and can mean different things to different people. Since the reader of this book is probably not a Muslim, it doesn't matter what they make of the above story, but it does matter how Ahmadinejad interprets it. From everything I read, hear, and see, this stunted twerp has studied the coming of the Mahdi and believes every word of it. Not only does he believe every word of it, but thinks it will occur in his lifetime, and that he must prepare the world for the coming of the Mahdi, personally. Ahmadinejad has claimed that he was "directed by Allah to pave the way for the glorious appearance of the Mahdi." To me, this means he is not going to wait for the natural progression of events to occur of their own volition. Rather, he seems to be saying that he is going to create the prophesied set of circumstances necessary for the Mahdi to return. Dictators like Hitler and Ahmadinejad are so consumed with declaring war on the world that they do not want to wait until they have the power to do so. Had Hitler waited a few years until he had the "bomb" things might have gone his way. But he could see the time ticking away and he was getting older. Ahmadinejad will not wait to have a large arsenal of nuclear weapons before he takes on Israel.

Ahmadinejad and his entire cabinet said they have a signed contract with al Mahdi in which they pledge themselves to his work. In this case, "work" means creating chaos. What would cause more chaos in the world than just one medium-sized plutonium bomb delivered by land or air into the heart of Israel? Israel is about two-and-one-half times as large as Rhode Island. I would expect Israel to either pre-empt or respond with devastating results for Iran and a few of its neighbors. Casualties would be in the millions. Gas prices would jump to $25 per gallon. Muslim Obama would side with his brothers, which would result in civil war in the United States since we would no longer be in doubt as to his loyalties. The chaos in the U.S. would be the signal for all nations to attack their weaker neighbors since they would no longer have us as the world's protector.

Whether you accept the above scenario or not, you should be prepared for something similar happening quite soon. Iran will have the bomb shortly and you can take that to the bank. Obama and Hillary know this and their silly sanctions prove it. The time when we could have stopped Ahmadinejad unilaterally has long past. Hitler told us exactly what he intended to do in "Mein Kampf." We didn't listen. The result was WWII and 60 million deaths. Ahmadinejad brags about what he has, and what he wants to do with it. We have been witnessing, since 9/11, Muslims strapping on suicide vests voluntarily without hesitation. With this fervor what would be the big deal for Ahmadinejad to hasten the Mahdi by killing millions of Jews and Arabs?

In the "Godfather" series of movies Michael Corleone told Tom Hagen, his consigliere, that it was time to go to the mattresses because the crime families were going to war. Michael then replaced Tom with a "wartime consigliere" because the requirements were different in wartime. What the United States needs right now is a wartime President. Instead, we have something called Barack Hussein Obama who has declared war on America.

There are over 2300 Islamic mosques in the United States. More are being built every day, two right next to Ground Zero. Very few Christian churches are being built. Strange as it may sound, jihadists are working with the Darkside in every country to make Sharia Law universal. It doesn't make sense because the Darkside has no belief in our God or Islam's Allah. But, if you will read Andrew McCarthy's "The Grand Jihad" you will see the extensive operations these two strange bedfellows share in the United States and worldwide. The ACLU works hand-in-glove with the Council on American Islamic Relations (CAIR) to use our own legal system to destroy the United States. Andrew McCarthy was the Special Federal Prosecutor who tried the Islamic terrorists for the first attempt to blow-up the Twin Towers. His first book, "Willful Blindness," is about the trial of the "Blind Sheikh," Omar Abdel Rahman, and his terrorists who killed 6 and injured over 1000 Americans in 1993. If all Muslims are not deported soon the United States will lose its Christianity and democracy in a short time.

MILITARY

While our troops were mopping-up after the Marja, Afghanistan offensive, General Stanley McChrystal and the military-loathing White House said that Kandahar was the next objective. Kandahar is the "capital of the Taliban movement" and the operation commences in May 2010. Marja had just been secured and was still in the early stages of the four-part strategy called "clear-hold-build-transfer." This sounds very similar to something we tried 45 years ago. Then, it was called "Vietnamization." The idea was to recon a hamlet and ascertain how many Viet Cong were present. The next step was to surround and kill or capture all the bad guys. Then a new crew came in with a mixture of MOS's (Military Occupation Specialties) and built or teach how to build dams, pumps, and shelters, crop planting, potable water supplies and first aid. After a few months we moved on to the next hamlet and did the same thing. More often than not, when we returned to the secured villages a few months later, we found carnage. After we left, the VC filtered back among the people, lined-up the brave ones who had taken a leadership role at our behest, executed them, cut-off their heads and placed them on high bamboo poles making it clear that if even one of the living cooperated with the Americans again the entire village would have their heads on poles. We simply did not have the manpower to station American soldiers at every hamlet and village. Sooner or later the troops must leave and the villages must maintain themselves, or all the lives and work that went into their perceived liberation was for naught. This is exactly what will happen with our "Afghanistanization" program. Haven't we learned anything in 45 years?

In Viet Nam we lost over 60,000 of America's best young men killed and over 300,000 of them maimed for life. It took us 15 long years of using our sophisticated, supersonic aircraft, mini-guns, "spookies," napalm, and "dusters" against skinny little guys in black pajamas with a rice-ball for rations, and 20 rounds in their bolt-action type 56 rifles, to find out we couldn't win. We were fighting a war of attrition against an enemy that cared not a whit about human life. We knew this back in 1954 when 50,000 Viet Cong and North Vietnamese attacked the French outpost at Dien Bien Phu. Only one-third of these Communist forces were issued rice balls and weapons, and the others were told to take their food and guns off of dead Frenchmen. There was only one doctor on hand to care for the 50,000 VC, and he was General Vo Nguyen Giap's personal physician. Communist, socialist, Nazi's, and fascists care only about the cause, not human life. Remember this when our own socialist president tells you "I care" about every American life.

Never, ever forget that Obama and the Darkside despise the military. To him and his legions of malcontents, racists, and radicals, they see the present military as the only possible force with the power to prevent their planned takeover of the United States. To them, the men in uniform stand for the morality, patriotism, and love for family that they detest and must subvert before victory can be achieved. Obama's jaundiced view of the military is similar to Clinton's leftist hordes when they took over Washington in January 1993. At Clinton's inauguration day festivities, actor Ron Silver looked up at the fighter jet flyover and remarked how much he disliked the military. Then, realizing that Clinton was now President, he changed his expression and said, "Oh, that's right, those are OUR planes now!" Even though Obama is Commander-In-Chief he knows he must tip-toe in making his planned radical changes to the armed forces before he can claim total control. He is making these changes using the same approach as he is using for the takeover of all other areas of our life: rapid fire, multiple attacks against every aspect and institution we as Americans hold dear to keep us confused and divided. While we were fighting healthcare, he was sneaking the government takeover of student loans, and consolidation of financial institutions under our radar.

Obama's intent is not to totally disband, weaken, or gut the military and be left with a skeleton force unable to do his bidding. No, he must have military strength to control both foreign and domestic enemies. One of his campaign promises to homosexuals was to get rid of any hurdles so they could get at our young soldiers whom they view as fresh meat. Secretary of Defense Gates is a lapdog to Obama, and the most pitiful leftover from the Bush administration. That's why Obama kept him around. Gates is supposedly studying the homosexual issue, but he is actually going to weed out the generals who are against it, and force their early retirement. Clinton opened the door a crack by instituting "don't ask, don't tell," but Obama will not be denied. Homosexuals and their supporters will be needed when election time comes around. Their inclusion among our soldiers will serve a double purpose for the Darkside. First, homosexuals will increase their political contributions to Democrats. Secondly, many soldiers still abhor the gross unnatural sex practiced by sodomites. They will leave the service rather than having to fight on the battlefield all day only to sleep with one eye open at night, unsure if their bunkmate will stay in his own sleeping bag. The following was taken from an article by Frank Turek entitled "Gay Rights: Don't Ask, Don't Think," and explains why homosexuals have no place in the military:

The central argument in favor of same-sex marriage or overturning "Don't ask don't tell" contains a fatal flaw. In fact, this is the flaw at the heart of the entire gay rights movement.
Joint Chief Chairman Adm. Michael Mullen dutifully proclaimed the flaw as truth the other day when speaking in favor of ending the "Don't Ask Don't Tell" policy. He said, "I cannot escape being troubled by the fact that we have in place a policy which forces young men and women to lie about who they are in order to defend their fellow citizens." Lie about who they are?
Sorry Admiral, but as a former ROTC instructor and legal officer in the United States Navy, I helped deny entrance to potential recruits and prosecuted existing service people for all sorts of behaviors that were incompatible with unit cohesion and military readiness. As you know, the Uniformed Code of Military Justice prohibits numerous behaviors that are not criminal offenses in civilian life (including adultery, fraternization and gambling with a subordinate), yet I never once saw anyone excused for their behavior by claiming that's who they are.
The military is essential to our survival as a nation. It's not a social experiment and serving in it is not a right. People have to qualify and then make sacrifices. Military people must subordinate many of their individual rights to advance the national interest. Recruits must agree to give up some of the freedoms that civilians enjoy, including certain sexual freedoms and even the freedom of speech! So even if homosexual behavior is permitted in society, that doesn't necessarily mean it should be permitted in the military.

Having served, I believe that the military needs as few sexual distractions as possible, be they from men and women serving together in combat or open homosexuality. The job is too difficult and critical to be complicating matters sexually.

More could be said, but I want to zero in on the fatal flaw in most gay-rights causes, and the one the Admiral repeated. It is the failure to distinguish between desires and behavior. Having certain sexual desires—whether you were "born" with them or acquired them sometime in life—does not mean that you are being discriminated against if the law doesn't allow the behavior you desire.

Take marriage as an example. Despite complaints by homosexual activists, every person in America already has equal marriage rights. We're all playing by the same rules—we all have the same right to marry any non-related adult of the opposite sex. Those rules do not deny anyone "equal protection of the laws" because the qualifications to enter a marriage apply equally to everyone—every adult person has the same right to marry.

"But what about homosexuals?" you ask. The question would better be stated "what about people with homosexual desires?" Put that way, you can see the flaw. If sexual desires alone are the criteria by which we change our marriage (or military) laws to give people "equal rights," then why not change them to include polygamy? After all, most men seem born with a desire for many women. How about those who desire their relatives? By the gay rights logic, such people don't have "equal rights" because our marriage laws have no provision for incest. And bisexuals don't have "equal rights" because existing marriage laws don't allow them to marry a man and a woman.

If desires alone guarantee someone special rights, why are there no special rights for pedophiles and gay bashers? The answer is obvious—because desires, even if you were "born" with them, do not justify behavior, do not make anyone a special class, and should have no impact on our laws. (See Born Gay or a Gay Basher: No Excuse.)

Laws encourage good behavior or prevent bad behavior. Desires are irrelevant. We enact all kinds of laws in the country and military that conflict with people's desires. In fact, that's why we need them! We wouldn't need any laws if people always desired to do good, which is why James

Madison wrote, "If men were angels, no government would be necessary."

In other words, there should be no legal class of "gay" or "straight," just a legal class called "person." And it doesn't matter whether persons desire sex with the same or opposite sex, or whether they desire sex with children, parents, or farm animals. What matters is whether the behavior desired is something the country or military should prohibit, permit or promote. Those are the only three choices we have when it comes to making law.

The standard comparisons to race and interracial marriage don't work either. Sexual behavior is always a choice, race never is. You'll find many former homosexuals, but you'll never find a former African American. And your race has no effect on your military readiness, but your sexual behavior often can. Likewise, race is irrelevant to marriage while gender is essential to it. Interracial couples can procreate and nurture the next generation (the overriding societal purpose of marriage), but homosexual couples cannot.

The truth is that our marriage and military laws do not discriminate against persons for "who they are"—they discriminate against the behaviors in which they engage. But so what? That's what most laws do. For example, the Thirteenth Amendment discriminates against the behavior of some businessmen who might like to improve their profits through slavery, but it does not discriminate against those businessmen as persons. And the First Amendment's freedom-of-religion protections discriminate against the behavior of some Muslims who want to impose Islamic law on the entire nation, but it does not discriminate against those Muslims as persons. Likewise, our marriage and military laws discriminate against the desired behaviors of homosexuals, polygamists, bigamists, and the incestuous, but they do not discriminate against them as persons. Now some may object to my comparison of homosexuality to polygamy, incest or pedophilia. I agree that the behaviors are not the same, but the point here is that the logic used to justify homosexuality is the same. "I was born with these desires" could also be used to justify polygamy, incest, pedophilia, and even gay bashing—"Don't blame me. I just have the anti-gay gene!"

That's the logic reduced to the absurd. And that's why people who want to make a case for same-sex marriage or homosexual practice in the military should use different *arguments. Claiming you "are" your sexual desires, is a case of don't ask don't think.*

Indoctrination or propaganda has been an increasing and detrimental part of military life since it became all-volunteer. It has been expanding since Clinton, but is going ballistic under Obama. Soldiers in Afghanistan and Iraq in combat scenarios cannot fire on the enemy until the enemy fires first. When they are in close quarter combat, such as urban environments, they have milliseconds to respond, and they usually lose. With Obama, Attorney General Eric Holder, and Gates looking over their shoulders at every move a soldier makes, the confused men either do nothing out of fear of a court martial, or just give up and get out of the service entirely. Like Rush Limbaugh says, soldiers have two jobs, "kill people and break things." When you load them down with politically correct directives they can no longer be soldiers.

Feminism has had a deleterious effect on our military since the late 1980's and is getting worse. American women in Viet Nam were welcome sights to soldiers as nurses and "Donut Dollies." Now, women are everywhere, including combat areas. They attain rank faster than men who put their lives on the line, and are a distraction to men who need all their faculties just to stay alive. The cost effectiveness of women is half that of men. A large part of the military budget is spent on women who have out-of-wedlock kids who receive allotments and housing allowances that should be spent on combat ready troops in the field. Blacks comprise more of this group than they do in the general population. Most of these women are overweight and out of shape; something that is not tolerated for the men. Unlike the men, these misfit women hold jobs that are akin to tenured positions at liberal colleges. They cannot be fired or scolded without charges of discrimination based on sex or race. If a white male sergeant reprimands a fat black female for inefficiency on duty, the sergeant must fear for his job and career advancement. So, nothing changes and the inefficiency remains systemic. Many of our best soldiers can just take so much of this frustration, and either leave the service early or retire after 20 years when they had intended to give their valuable experience for the full 30 years. The lazy, least productive women stay in the service because they are unaccountable and untouchable, and rank is awarded without effort.

One example of the moral and financial degradation of our service is the 70, 500 single parents on active duty. Nearly half of them are in the Army. One recent example is Alexis Hutchinson, a black woman who had a kid out of wedlock. All was okay until her unit, the 3rd Combat Aviation Brigade of the Army's 3rd Infantry Division, decided to deploy to Afghanistan. Since she was just a cook, it wasn't like they were asking her to get in a firefight. She decided to just not show up for the deployment flight because she claimed there was no baby-sitter handy. The Army said evidence indicated she had no intention of deploying regardless of the kid's babysitter problem, but discharged her without a court martial anyway because it was a waste of time. Our military today is only 25% as large as during Viet Nam, yet costs 4 times more, and has 3 times more useless dead-weight like this woman.

Obama, the anti-American, military-hating Commander-In-Chief, is also putting women on our last line of defense: nuclear subs, for the first time ever. Women have been allowed to serve co-ed on surface ships since 1993 and the pregnancy explosion on our Navy ships proves it. We are proving again that sex is a better route to defeating our American military than bullets. Our submariners are some of the most dedicated, close-knit groups in the service. I've never met one yet that didn't feel like they belonged to a unique, special branch of the Navy. I think women will destroy this men-only tradition, forever. Submarines are sometimes submerged for months and return to base many times after 6 to 9 months at sea. Pregnancies are certain to occur. The decision will be to carry the baby to term or kill it. Which do you think will be the standing order in Obama's Navy, given his past lust for going out of his way to promote the killing of babies, and even infanticide?

Another important area of the military that occupies Obama's attention is the staffing in the highest echelons, namely, general officers. While most of the PFC's and sergeants are ready and willing to serve their country in any capacity, there are many high level commanders with no such lofty motives. Like Colin Powell, they have achieved their rank for reasons other than bravery, and offer their lives only to themselves, not our country. These are the kind of people Obama will seek out and promote after they pledge their loyalty to him and his evil ends. Last year he hand-picked Wesley Clark and Togo West to look into the shooting at Fort Hood, knowing that they would produce a belated, watered-down report calling for increased scrutiny, but glossing over the Muslim-terrorist aspect. Wesley Clark is actually a hand-me-down from the Clinton era whom Obama can be confident will toe the leftist line. The same goes for Togo. The practice of choosing gutless, controllable military commanders started with Clinton's pick of General John Shalikashvili as Chairman of the Joint Chiefs of Staff, and General Barry McCaffrey as his drug czar. Shalikashvili's father was a Nazi with the SS-Waffengruppe. After his service with Clinton, Shalikashvili was an advisor to the fake soldier, John "3 purple hearts in 3 months" Kerry, and wrote an op-ed piece in the New York Times advocating homosexuals be allowed to have sex with combat soldiers. Like Wesley Clark, Togo West, and Colon Powell, Shalikashvili never had a bullet fired at him in anger. The only difference between these people and the other Darkside cowards is that they wear uniforms, and are in charge of men better than they.

Having non-combat, anti-American upper-echelon military commanders that eschew the glorious military traditions of the United States, destroys morale among the troops that must do the actual fighting, and, given the reduced size of our military, we need every soldier to be the very best they can be. Obama's hand-picked, medal-bedecked, pseudo-military elites have been instructed by the Commander-In-Chief to drastically increase the number of homosexuals, while simultaneously loading the enlisted men down with so many encumbrances that their effectiveness is halved. They emphasize diversity, political correctness, humane consideration of the enemy's feelings, and sensitivity training to bring the gentler, kinder elements of a soldier's personality to the surface, so that terrorists want to be their friends. Obama's new breed of commanders want to avoid a repeat of what transpired in Fallujah, Iraq, when Navy Seals were suspected of having the audacity to inflict a small cut on the inside of the mouth of a terrorist whom they suspected of masterminding the murder, hanging, and burning of 4 Americans in 2004. Navy Seals are the best trained, most fierce warriors in the world, but composed mostly of white guys, and that is reason enough for Obama to despise them. Julio Huertas, Kevin DeMartino, Jonathan Keefe, and Matthew McCabe were forced to endure a humiliating court martial, and defend their heroic actions against a single accusation of abuse by Ahmed Hashim Abed, an Iraqi terrorist. He had a small cut on the inside of his lip which indicated that he bit his own lip and blamed it on the Seals. Huertas said, "Compared to all the physical activity we go through, this has been mentally more challenging." Obama's Fascist subalterns know the detrimental effect that this court martial will have. It will reverberate throughout the branches of service and not only damage the careers of the four Seals, but cause other Seals to underperform the horrendous demands of their jobs, and discourage civilians from entering the special services for fear of prosecution. Like Rush says, "don't doubt me" when I say that the persecution of our troops is intentional and designed to "cleanse" our military of the bravado and patriotism we have always respected and expected in our troops. Don't think for a minute that this case, the new CIA interrogation limits, and the stupid claim by Congressman Murtha, another pseudo-vet, that Marines killed civilians in Haditha, are not planned by Obama's anti-American regime to weaken the morale of our servicemen. Our military is perhaps the only force that could stop Obama's march to Fascism, so he must move quickly to drain it of individualists and men of independent thought, and replace them with homosexuals and men of a kinder and gentler persuasion who owe their unquestionable loyalty to the messiah-in-chief.

Being a closet Muslim, and knowing that a freedom-loving American military has roots in Christianity, Obama must do everything he can to weaken their Christian zeal. To this end he will keep alive and growing the movement begun under Clinton to dilute the traditional Christian influence in our military. His first priority in this regard is to provide encouragement and opportunity for Muslims to worship equally with Christians and Jews. Gradually, they will have government financed mosques and imams, and authorized, mandatory times of prayer five times a day. Special Muslim menus will be published at all bases, military installations and aboard ships, specifying no pork. Later, as Muslims become dominate, Sharia law will be invoked for the growing number of Muslim troops. To make the acceptance of Muslims more palatable in the near future Obama will temporarily introduce distasteful, but necessary, cults and sects into the religious groups in the military. Recently, the Air Force Academy in Colorado Springs, Colorado, dedicated their first outdoor sanctuary as a Wiccan prayer circle. It is actually a number of very large boulders arranged in a circle similar to Stonehenge in England. Now, the witches, druids, and pagans share equal footing with the Protestant, Catholic, Jewish, Muslim, and Buddhist chapels on base. The Air Force now officially recognizes distinct forms of neo-paganism including Dianic Wicca, Seax Wicca, Gardnerian Wicca, shamanism, and Druidism. As with other radical changes in the military, the traditional Christian soldiers will suffer discrimination from these lowlifes, and feel like outcasts in what used to be a normal military.

Similar to the tactics of the civil rights movement, the "victimization" of the weird religions has already commenced. On January 17, 2010, self-described pagan, Tech Sergeant Brandon Longcrier, said he spotted a cross of railroad ties lying against a rock at the pagan worship center at the Air Force Academy. Longcrier has complained to the base that his group had been "thrown under the bus by the system we trusted," and that the cross was a "hate crime" against the earth-centered religions. Mikey Weinstein (I don't pay attention to anyone named "Mikey"), of the 16,000 member New Mexico based Military Religious Freedom Foundation, said the incident was clearly a hate crime, and any denial was preposterous. Like the blacks, feminists, and homosexuals these earth-worshiping fruitcakes will probably get with the ACLU and go all the way to the Supreme Court if they can find the heinous criminal who dared to place an inanimate wooden cross next to their most sacred alter of Satan stones.

Mikey Weinstein popped-up again last April when he objected to Franklin Graham, the son of Billy Graham, speaking at the National Day of Prayer event held annually at the Pentagon. After the Twin Towers were hit in 2001 Graham had called Islam "very evil and wicked." Later, he said, "I want them to know that they don't have to die in a car bomb, don't have to die in some kind of holy war to be accepted by God. But it's through faith in Jesus Christ and Christ alone." He also said their treatment of women was "horrid." Mikey said the invitation offended Muslim employees at the Pentagon because Graham never retracted or apologized for his description of Islam. He said it would endanger American troops by stirring up Muslims. He may get his wish for barring the event permanently since a federal judge in Wisconsin ruled that the National Day of Prayer was unconstitutional, but let the annual event continue until appeals are exhausted. As usual, the Army was mushy on anything Christian, so the Army's response to Graham's appearance was that his "presence at the event may be taken by some as inappropriate for a government agency." In other words, the founding religion of the United States is no longer welcome to merely utter a few words at the premier military installation of the United States. On April 21st the Army buckled under to the Muslims and earth-worshippers, and rescinded their invitation to Franklin Graham to speak at the National Day of Prayer event. They did this by canceling the participation of the National Day of Prayer Task Force of which Graham is the leader. This was the result of just one person, Mikey Weinstein, saying Muslims didn't want a Christian having contact with our military. My prediction is that the Wisconsin court will permanently bar the Day of Prayer since this is what Obama wants, and he controls government's side of the case. This all may seem minor, but the importance is the success of Obama's demons to remove all remnants of Christianity from every part of our public life, and then he will begin dismantling Christianity from our private lives. Important also, is that our military leaders are so weak and so under the control of a closet Muslim like Obama, that they obey without question any insane thought that might occur to their nutty Commander-In-Chief.

Getting ever further away from the designated purpose of our military, we are now going to spend more of our defense budget on non-defense items such as the abortion pill. On February 4, 2010, Obama's personal Pentagon issued an order for all American military bases worldwide to purchase and stock the morning-after pill. Surprisingly, Nancy Keenan, president of the baby-killing group, NARAL, is pleased as punch. After years of being refused by the Bush Department of Defense, Obama and his abortionist supporters, and pro-death doctors and pharmacists, were finally successful in getting this one more nail in the coffin that will be used to bury our grand old military traditions of honor and morality.

The confusing and contradictory orders under which our soldiers must adhere to in their combat and non-combat roles is absolutely insane. When one occasionally does commit suicide or beat his wife, it makes national headlines even though it happens much more often among civilians. In February 2010 the Army announced they were going to discipline at least 6 officers connected to the Fort Hood killing of 13 people. As many as 8 officers may receive reprimands when Army General Carter Ham delivers his accountability review of Major Nidal Hasan's murders. The reprimands will all be centered on the idea that the soldiers failed to alert authorities of Hasan's increasing Islamist radicalization. Like all soldiers serving in today's military, they are damned if they do, and damned if they don't. If any of these officers had gone to his commanding officer and said that there was a crazy Muslim in their outfit they would have faced a court martial for religious persecution. As it is, a reprimand is the same as a pink slip to civilians; their career is over, caput, finished. When these men are booted out of the service, regardless of their otherwise exemplary performance, don't you think that they have large numbers of associates who will see the same thing destroying their careers, and just go ahead and get the hell out of this rat-race while the getting is good? Many more will read of this in Army Times and either leave the service or lie low and do no more than absolutely required. This damages morale and performance and we lose good men.

In March of 2009 Army Lieutenant Colonel Doctor Terry Lakin, refused to be deployed to his next overseas assignment until his Commander-in-Chief, Obama, proves that he is constitutionally qualified to occupy the top of the Army chain of command. In other words, Lakin wants to see proof that Obama was born in the United States. If Lakin was a female black PFC with three out-of-wedlock dependents, and refused to be deployed because she couldn't find a babysitter, it would be a non-story. But, Lakin is a highly decorated soldier with 18 years in service who has served in Honduras, Bosnia, Korea, and Afghanistan, and is now the Chief of Primary Care and Flight Surgeon caring for Army Chief of Staff General Casey's pilots and air crew. He has been nominated for promotion to full colonel. Lakin filed an Article 138 with his commanding officer, which is a legal military avenue for redress of subordinate's complaints against superior officers. Congressman Zack Wamp of Tennessee forwarded Lakin's request to the Department of Defense, but received a reply stating only that Obama was not a commanding officer for purposes of Article 138. Then, House members Bill Posey and Marsha Blackburn sponsored legislation to provide a means for officers in the military to obtain redress for complaints similar to Lakin's. Don't hold your breath for action on this bill with a Democrat majority Congress. The only semi-official response to Larkin's action has come from an Army spokeswoman. She said an unnamed officer implied that Army generals want Lakin to have a brain scan and medical evaluation to determine his sanity. Translated, this means that the Army wants to avoid a military court martial where the defense would demand to see Obama's birth certificate. Instead, he will either be kept in limbo, or quietly discharged without controversy. All that Larkin is asking to see is a standard, full-size copy of a "live birth certificate" from Hawaii. They used to be standard until June of 2009 after which they were no longer issued by the state. Now, the state of Hawaii issues only online computer-generated birth certificates that anyone could produce without proof of any underlying documentation. Obama and his Chicago mob will go to any lengths to avoid simply producing a real birth certificate that all Americans have been issued.

How about Iraq? We are doing things a little different in Iraq, but the end result will be exactly the same as Afghanistan. In Viet Nam we were 10,000 miles from home trying to establish a Little America in a land of tyranny and communists. Despite how many men we lost or how much sophisticated equipment we employed, the North Vietnamese, Chinese, Russians, and even the Cubans would undo our work. We finally just got tired and left. In Iraq and Afghanistan we are not only fighting a half world away, but we are interlopers inserting ourselves between different groups of the same religion. The real problem is that both countries share a common border with Iran, who is the only country that intentionally churns out assembly-line, state-sponsored terrorism, and we won't bomb or invade them like we did in Cambodia or Laos. So, Iran will just keep doing what they are doing until we leave, and then they will undo what has been accomplished.

Joe Biden got a lot of laughs when he took credit for victory in Iraq, but the fact is nobody will want to claim this victory in a few years. Saddam Hussein was dictator of Iraq for 24 years (1979-2003). Everyone participating in his government's Baath party was either complicit in his atrocities, or dead. When he was dethroned in 2003 there were not any innocent bystanders to help start a new, fresh, non-Baath Iraq. The Baath party was composed mostly of Sunni Muslims. Our choices of who was to run the country after the fighting was over, was between the Sunni Baaths or the Shias who were not Baaths, but associated with Iran's extremist Shias ruled by Mahmoud Ahmedinejad and Supreme Leader Ali Khamenei. So, we put together a conglomeration of Iraqi's to rebuild the destroyed country and have some semblance of stability. Unfortunately, the majority of the Muslims in Iraq are Shia, just like Iran, though this did not keep them from warring with each other from 1979 to 1988. Not only are they from the same off-shoot of Islam, but many of the people charged with creating a new Iraq are taking their marching orders from Iran. When Iraq had their much touted elections back on March 7, about 500 members of the Baath party were excluded from running for office. That sounds good considering the history of that party under Saddam, but the problem is that the 500 selected to be excluded were chosen by a terrorist named Ali al-Lami who answers to Ahmedinejab, the nuke-nut from Iran. The story gets much more complicated than I have room to explain here. But, I would stake my life on my prediction that neither Iraq nor Afghanistan will be under stable, semi-democratic governments for more than a few months after we leave. I could not care less if they all kill each other because the only things Muslims seem to do well is kill each other, regardless of the fact that they are both born of Islam. The sad part of this Bush-Obama legacy is the lives of our brave soldiers sacrificed for nothing, and their loved ones living without them till the end of their own lives.

DEPENDENCY TO BONDAGE

As stated earlier, the United States entered the "fear" sequence on 9/11 with the collapse of the Twin Towers. Obama rather quickly thrust us into the dependency stage by exploding the unemployment rolls, converting workers into welfare dependents, and labeling political kickbacks as jobs-creation efforts. Much of this disaster, and even the election of such a miscreant as Obama, would have never been possible without the aiding and abetting of the black elite, Hispanics, and those suffering from white guilt. Unlike whites, blacks have always been racist in their voting patterns, but, the climate spawned by the pandering, paternalizing, and pronouncement of victim status on a whole race of people has exacerbated the problem into an epidemic. The more so-called equality that is heaped upon the black race, the more they blame inequality for their pitiful condition, which leads to more heaping of undeserved benefits. Rather than disproving white racism, the election of a black minority President has merely whet their appetite for increased victim status, and given their black elite the status of power brokers in furthering the demise of the conservatives and Christians who knit this country together, and whose progeny are the only remaining threads binding it together. Blacks have had over 145 years to establish themselves as a viable race that can participate in a Constitutional Republic and select their representatives based on character, morality, and honesty without thought of the superficial consideration of skin color. Given that 99% of blacks voted for a person with no experience, no work ethic, few morals, and no character, but just happens to be black, confirms that racism among blacks is raging while white racism is provably rare. Obama's election was more a result of whites crossing over and voting for him since they are still the majority. In the hope that maybe a few blacks will practice positive introspection, and see their destructive racism and the resulting damage to our country, and that whites may comprehend their share of the damage they cause by treating blacks as inferior by their ceaseless pandering, I offer this section entitled "The Black Imbroglio."

THE BLACK IMBROGLIO

No one believes in God more than I. Without a doubt, He created all men. But, I do not know <u>why</u> He created black, brown, yellow, red, and white men. Why not just one color? What I do know is we are all stuck on this one planet and have no choice but to try and live together in harmony. So far, it hasn't worked out too well. We all have to find our place in society and occupy that space without harming others. We cannot pretend to be something we are not, and each race must shoulder their own responsibilities. If we cannot do these things, then the result will be eternal conflict.

My concern here is limited to the relations between blacks and whites in the United States. Why? Because racism elected the most dangerous man ever to occupy the White House and racism is increasing, not decreasing, thanks to Obama. But, Obama didn't start racism. He is just a light-skinned dark guy claiming to be black who arrived on the scene after the stage had already been set by 60 years of farce; yes, six decades of white guilt resulting from an artificially constructed equality between the races. Each race must find its own way and establish its own identity, or natural forces will evolve in time to correct the equilibrium.

An honest discussion of race after 60 years of history revision, and ensconced black leadership in a devils pact with white liberals, is probably unattainable. The word "racist" has replaced the "IRS" as the most feared word in our vocabulary, and it is the most used response of blacks when they are confronted about any of their questionable activities. Even though the majority of blacks still occupy the lowest rungs of society economically, educationally, and culturally, this oligarchic cabal commands their unquestioned loyalty by invoking racism, painting whites as boogie men, and themselves as gate-keepers guarding their flock of perpetual victims. Less than 1% of blacks are numbered among the elitist class, but they rule like demagogues over the minds and bodies of the other 99%. This scenario has been around for years, and would not be so urgent except that it is accelerating under their victim-in-chief, Barack Hussein Obama, at the most critical time in our short history. A discussion of how we became actors in this racial charade is in order.

If and until white Americans wake up and admit that the Black Imbroglio exists, that blacks are a large part of the problem, and that they are the enemy of the continued survival of the America that was created by our patriotic founders, then there is no hope that we will survive. If Americans stay locked into white guilt, and refuse to even see blacks as their equals, not the pampered cattle herd that must be satisfied at all cost lest they rebel and call us names, then it is truly "Over." To continue giving special dispensation to the black race and now, the brown race, is to say either they are inherently inferior, or that we are inherently superior, and that it is the job of whites to care for them as invalids from cradle to grave. This kind of racism practiced by whites suffering from white guilt won't work anymore because the blacks, and now the browns, are not happy merely getting welfare and paying no taxes. They have joined forces with the Darkside, and want and will take over the whole United States. When they do, the whites will not be taken care of like cattle. They will be held in contempt for not sharing in the bounty of America earlier, or not continuing to drain their wallets. They will be hated and punished. The hatred of whites by blacks and browns cannot be extinguished by simply giving them what we have. They are not seeking a piecemeal redistribution of white wealth. They want it all.

WHITE SLAVERY

If prostitution is the oldest trade, then slavery is probably the second oldest. Long before we were even sure the earth wasn't flat, there was already slavery among the tribes of Africa, the Mayans, the Aztecs of South America, our American Indians, the nomadic hordes of Asia, and every place else. But, and listen-up **Jeremiah Wright**, the most widespread, violent and long-running practice of slavery ever was committed by black Africans enslaving white Europeans! Contrary to our revisionist history books today, slavery was not the invention of whites, but rather an uninterrupted black African, Muslim, bread-and-butter career for over 700 years before King Cotton replaced the pine barrens in our southern states. Unlike our plantations in the South, who used black slaves to till the crops, the white slaves captured by the Africans **were** the crops. Now, we can have that long awaited two-sided talk about reparations with the Rev's, Jackson, Sharpton and Wright, and tell Oprah to bring her checkbook.

In 846 AD black Muslim pirates from Africa sacked Rome, the Vatican, and 21 Italian villages, and established pirate havens along the southern coasts of France and Italy. As the Eastern Roman Empire and the Byzantine Empire declined, Africans occupied Cyprus, Crete, and Sicily from which they could terrorize the whole Mediterranean area. Over 1.5 million white European residents of seaside villages in Italy, Spain, Portugal, France, Britain, The Netherlands, Ireland, and even as far away as Iceland and North America, were captured and carried off as slaves. After Spain conquered Granada and expelled the African Muslims in the late 15th and early 16th centuries, the Africans began limiting their activities to the Mediterranean Sea. These Africans, combined with Islamic Mamelukes of Egypt, the Ottoman Turks, Arabs, and Berber tribes mounted pirate expeditions called "razzias" against Christian European nations. The pirates operated out of Tripoli, Tunisia, and Algeria and were ruled by a" beylerbey" who set up his seat of power at Algiers. The beylerbeys were dedicated slave-hunters and their cruelty to white slaves far surpassed what blacks endured in the New World. The Africans were not only driven by lucre, but also out of the Muslim belief that all whites were infidels, so Allah approved treating them as chattel property. Like present day Muslim terrorists, enslaving, raping, burning, selling, murdering, and torturing white infidels held no threat of religious repercussions in their after-life, according to the Quran.

The pirates were not the unorganized, swashbuckling mavericks depicted in today's movies. Their ships were state-of-the-art Corsairs with a sail arrangement to make use of headwinds, and a galley of oarsmen below for rapid turning, speed and capture. The *beylerbeys* were really admirals of the sultan and commanded great fleets for slave-hunting, war, and political purposes. Under the beylerbeys were *reises,* or captains, who controlled squadrons of ships organized into corporations with shareholders. The corporations fitted out the corsairs and cruisers and shared in the booty. At least the ships that later would bring Africans to the Americas had multiple purposes. They would pick-up slaves in Africa, drop them off in the West Indies, pick-up rum, sugar, and molasses, and drop that off in the colonies. Then they would pick-up tobacco and deliver that to England where they would load English products, then cruise back to Africa and trade it for more slaves. The black African pirates, on the other hand, built their ships and operated them solely for the single purpose of capturing white slaves and making a profit on them.

Piracy was such a lucrative business that it's easy to see why the skinny little blacks of Somalia are trying it again nowadays and apparently succeeding. The African Muslim pirates perfected the technique of surrounding an entire village on the European coast and capturing all the inhabitants at once. If the village fought back the Africans killed just enough to stop the resistance. Then they killed the older residents who were too aged to work or rape. The rest, from 3000 to 20,000 at a time, would either be taken back to Africa, or sometimes they would take them aboard ship, and send word to their relatives in neighboring towns that they could be ransomed for a set price at a future date. Sometimes financial factors (lenders) would be in collusion with the Africans, and arrange to loan the villagers money on their homes, land or animal stock to ransom their friends or relatives out of slavery. One raid was on a village in Iceland where 400 were captured, 31 were ransomed, and 242 taken back to Africa to be sold. Of the remaining 127 villagers, 14 had been killed outright during the first hours of the attack, and 113 of the older citizens had been herded into a church with the doors barred and set on fire. Another raid on the harbor village of Baltimore, County Cork, Ireland, captured the entire village and surrounding population of 7000. After killing 1500 of the whites they took the rest back to North Africa and sold them as galley slaves, servants, laborers, and harem concubines at the sultan's palace. I doubt that black history revisionists today can point to even one instance where their ancestors were rounded-up on the Ivory Coast by whites, and wantonly butchered or burned alive because they were too old to be useful.

In 1786 Thomas Jefferson and John Adams met in London with Tripoli ambassador, Sidi Haji Abdul Rahman Adja, and asked why his ships attacked Americans and made slaves of our white citizens. When Jefferson reported back to the Continental Congress he said that Adja had told them "it was written in their Koran, that all nations which had not acknowledged the Prophet were sinners, whom it was the right and duty of the faithful to plunder and enslave." Piracy was no small matter to America. The tribute payments amounted to 20% of the entire American government's budget in 1800. The pirates offered to stop capturing and enslaving American ships for a tribute payment of $1 million annually, but the Congress offered to appropriate only $80,000, and the African pirates kept right on enslaving whites.

Americans are familiar with the cruelty aboard slave ships heading to the United States, but the African slavers with white Europeans were equally nightmarish. Many died of disease or lack of food and water during the long voyage back to North Africa. The "lucky" ones that survived were made a spectacle as they walked through the town to the auction. The white slaves then had to stand upright from 8AM till 2PM while prospective buyers examined them from head to foot. Then the bidding took place, and later, the Dey (governor of Algiers), was allowed to purchase any slave at the price bid by the other buyers. During the auction, the whites would have to run, jump, lift up their dresses, open their undergarments, open their mouth, or bend over, for inspection by the prospective buyers. After the auction, the slaves were assigned to domestic work (mostly women), hard labor, or harem "duty." However, the worst form of white slavery was the "galley slave."

You have probably seen depicted in movies, or heard during Black History Month, of the horrible conditions of black slaves during their voyage from Africa to America. They were usually chained by eye bolts to the bulkheads in the stifling heat or cold below deck to avoid escape or mutiny. But, what if a slave never left that hell hole and endured those conditions, not for the normal 3 or 4 week Atlantic crossing, but for 10 or 20 years? The white galley slaves of the Ottoman Sultan in Istanbul were permanently confined to their galleys, and often served extremely long terms, averaging around nineteen years. Most of the white galley slaves simply never left the galley. They were shackled and chained to their seat where they also slept (very little), ate meals, defecated, urinated, and eventually died.

The African enslavement of whites did not end until 1830 when the French conquered and colonized Algiers. Now, Obama will <u>really</u> hate colonialists when he finds out they not only colonized his homeland of Kenya, but also helped end white slavery. The end of attacks by the African pirates on American ships, and the corresponding tribute payments came earlier for us in the First Barbary War from 1801-1805, and the Second Barbary War in 1815. The United States Marine Corps' (Obama's pronunciation is "corpse") actions in these wars led to the line in the Marine Hymn, "to the shores of Tripoli." Also, the uniform worn by the Marines to fight the pirates had a high leather collar to protect them from the slashes of the pirate's cutlass, and is the genesis of their nickname "Leatherneck."

BLACK SLAVERY

Only a fool or a racist (black or white) would defend or justify black or white slavery. I would never do that. But, I will say that liberal whites and blacks have exaggerated and revised history beyond reason or recognition. When one side of a debate invents "facts" out of thin air, and uses hyperbole and subterfuge, then no reasonable discussion can take place and no valid conclusions can be reached. Black History Month is not history at all, but propaganda so often repeated that everything portrayed is now believed. I have already given you a perfunctory view of slavery in the preceding "Fatal Sequence" section of this book. Rather than an exhaustive discussion of slavery, I will here offer a short glimpse of history that mysteriously has vanished from our politically correct textbooks of today.

Black Africans first appeared in Colonial America when the British pirate ship, "White Lion," with 20 Angolan slaves aboard, landed at Old Point Comfort (present day Ft. Monroe), on the coast of the colony of Virginia in 1619. They had captured the Africans in a battle with a slave ship bound for Mexico. The male population of the colony had been reduced by typhus and other diseases, so they agreed to trade food and material to the pirates in exchange for the Africans. Since over half of the colonists had arrived as indentured servants themselves, and slavery was as yet unknown, the Virginians decided to treat the Africans as indentured servants. After a period of time, the 20 Africans were all freed and given use of land and supplies by their former bondholders. One of the African freedmen was named Anthony Johnson who became a prosperous landowner on the eastern shore. He also became the first owner of the first legally recognized slave in the colonies when the Northampton County court ruled against another black, named John Casor, in 1654 for his debt owed to Johnson. So, the first black slave in the colonies was owned by a black former slave that the whites had freed. To put it more succinctly, blacks introduced black slavery into the United States, not whites.

The American colonies entered the slave business a century behind South America and the West Indies. Of the 12 million black slaves shipped to the New World, most went to Brazil and the West Indies to work in sugar cane, coffee, and other labor intensive agriculture. The total number shipped to the American colonies from 1654 to 1808 was 645,000. Even after Casor's enslavement by Johnson, blacks still represented a mixture of freed, slave and indentured servants. In 1676 Nathaniel Bacon organized free slaves and poor whites in confronting the British governor to demand that something be done about the Indian depredations on frontier settlements. This became known as Bacons Rebellion. Afterwards, the British hardened their attitude toward blacks because they had joined Nathaniel Bacon in his attack on Governor Berkeley and burned his house down. Later, 22 of Bacon's followers were hanged, both blacks and whites.

Improved economic conditions in England meant fewer people were coming to the colonies as indentured servants. This shortage of labor in the colonies, and the intensive labor required of the new cash crop, tobacco, caused the slow transition from indentured servitude to slavery. Both slaves and slave-enabling laws expanded in all 13 colonies except one, Georgia. In Georgia, slave ownership was prohibited from 1735 until 1750 when the pro-slave faction took control of the colony away from the religious faction. The three reasons behind the Georgia law banning slavery had been religious, the desire to encourage only small, owner-worked, non-slave farms, and the fear of the Spanish in adjacent Florida, fomenting a slave uprising in Georgia.

The black slaves in the northern colonies worked as house servants, craftsmen, and laborers while the southern colonies employed them mostly in rice and tobacco cultivation, and as domestic servants. Sensing future, unsolvable problems between the races, all the colonies had passed laws by 1798 banning the importation of new slaves, and the last slave ship left our shores in 1808. An "Africa Squadron" was even formed by American and British naval forces to stop slave ships from docking on our shores.

Slaves themselves had termed their ocean voyage from Africa as the "middle passage," meaning it was sandwiched between the trek from their African home village to the African coast, and the trek from the point of arrival in America to their final destination. When tobacco in the northern and mid-Atlantic colonies lost its luster and was replaced by rice and cotton, the planters started acquiring large tracts of land in the southern and western territories. The Louisiana Purchase, Texas independence, and Eli Whitney's 1793 cotton gin all hastened this relocation. This led to the mass movement of slaves to the new territories and was aptly named by slaves the "second middle passage."

To be a white slave captured by the African's on the European coasts, or a black slave taken from Africa and brought to the American colonies was a horror no American today would want to relive. Both were examples of man's inhumanity to their fellow man. What it should augur is that evil exists in the hearts of all men, regardless of color. There are thousands of books on slavery, but only a very few are historically objective. You can read Frederick Douglass's "My Bondage and My Freedom" or Eugene D. Genovese's "Fruits of Merchant Capital:Slavery and Bourgeois Property in the Rise and Expansion of Capitalism." Or, for a more rational, realistic and less agenda-driven view of slavery, you can read Robert W. Fogel's Nobel Prize winner, "Without Consent or Contract," or read "Children of Pride" by Robert M. Myers. The first two are highly opinionated, slanted, and with obvious political content as are most history books written on slavery. Fogel is definitely not pro-slave, but gives a reasonable account of the treatment of slaves. I think Myers' book, which won more awards than the others combined (from liberals no less), offers more truth because it is not based on ulterior motives. It is simply 1353 pages of letters between members of Dr. Charles Colcock Jones' extended family describing social life, and the relations of whites and slaves from 1854 to 1868. The letters were never meant to be read by outsiders so we get an unbiased insight into the goings-on of the lives of slave-owners. It even contains two instances of inappropriate sexual contact between planter and slave, and the condemnation that ensued.

Today's reparation-fanatics (Congressman John Conyers) and pity-trip extortionists (Jackson, Sharpton, Obama) pretend that blacks are incompetent, docile victims of domineering whites. And, they insinuate, had the roles been reversed, blacks would have taken the high road and acted differently than whites. Really? If blacks had arrived at a paradise of 3.5 million square miles of arable land and lush forests with no black labor force, and had the opportunity to buy some whites to work the fields and prosper, are they telling us they would have opted to stay on their plantation and till only an acre or so with their little hoe and rake? Of course, this common sense question falls on deaf, racist ears because racism has provided a lucrative career for John Conyers, Jeremiah Wright, the Congressional Black Caucus, and especially Obama and his elitists. What would these people do for a living if their whole deck of race cards was taken away? What would be their answer to the above question if their gonads were connected to a high-voltage truth-0-meter?

Slavery was a front-and-center issue from the arrival of the first slave in 1654 to the last slave birthed in 1865. They were present in every colony and state, and very visible. Slavery was referred to as the "peculiar institution" for good reason, it was very peculiar. It was true that slaves were chattel property and counted only 3/5 of a vote in elections, but they were not without redress in law. Two examples among many are Charles Quin and David White who were both hanged on November 23, 1739, for the murder of a slave, and William Pitman who was hanged on April 21, 1775, for the murder of his black slave. All three hanged were white and it was whites that hanged them. One slave, Denmark Vessey, won a lottery and bought his own freedom. In 1830 there were 3,775 black slaveholders who owned over 21,000 black slaves with 80% of them located in Louisiana, South Carolina, Virginia, and Maryland. By 1860 some 12,000 free blacks owned over 100,000 black slaves as did thousands of Native Americans and Latin Americans. The Metoyer clan of black slave-owners in Louisiana owned over 400 slaves worth over $20 million in today's currency, making them one of the wealthiest families in American history, black or white. Harry Smith, one of the most successful slave traders in Memphis was himself a former black slave. I guess when it comes to money people will not only sell their soul but include their brother in the bargain, too. Wealthy southern planters were even instrumental in giving blacks a college education when they sent the offspring of their carnal relations with their female slaves to Wilberforce University in Ohio. The school lost most of its 200 students when the Civil War broke out because the mixed-race students had to head back to their southern plantations.

The slavery abolitionist movement began long before we won our independence. A majority of the 56 signers of the Declaration of Independence abhorred the "peculiar institution," but knew that to press the issue would mean they would never achieve a consensus on drafting a constitution. They rightly calculated that the first order of business was to get their new republic on its feet and tackle the issue of slavery later. Of course, "later" never came because the issue never cooled down, and labor-intensive "King Cotton" came along. There were ongoing efforts to resolve the slavery issue right up to the Civil War. The slave, Quock Walker, sued in court for his own freedom and thereby ended slavery in Massachusetts. The American Colonization Society (ACS) solicited funds to repatriate thousands of slaves back to Africa and helped to establish the country of Liberia. The founder of ACS was Henry Clay (a slave- owning southerner) who felt repatriation was necessary because the slaves could never "amalgamate with the free whites of this country." If the United States does not find a better solution to our racial problems than the current foolishness of diversity, reparations, victimization, and disguised racism of today, then maybe Henry Clay had the right idea. The Dred Scott decision was handed down in 1857, but did not alter the abolitionist momentum. John Brown took over the Harpers Ferry Arsenal on October 16th, 1859, in an attempt to arm blacks and incite an insurrection. But this succeeded only in killing a free black employee of the arsenal and getting John Brown hanged.

While abolitionist activity continued in the North, some slaves took actions of their own. There were at least 16 slave rebellions, uprisings, revolts, conspiracies, raids, and wars from the 1712 New York Slave Revolt to the John Brown Raid of 1859. The best known slave uprising was the Nat Turner

Rebellion of Virginia in 1831. Nat Turner was a slave in Southhampton County in Virginia and was originally owned by his namesake, Samuel Turner. He had been sold twice, and in 1831 was owned by Joseph Travis. Nat Turner was known as the "preacher," enjoyed all of the privileges of a freedman, and considered his owner "a kind master." From childhood he had claimed to have had visions and strange dreams foretelling the future. For years he had been looking for signs that would signal him to start his task of "slaying my enemies with their own weapons." When a solar eclipse occurred on February 12, 1831, Nat was convinced it was God's signal telling him the time had arrived. Turner "communicated the great work laid out (for me) to do, to four in whom I had the greatest confidence," meaning his fellow slaves Henry, Hark, Nelson, and Sam.

On August thirteenth the sun appeared bluish-green and Turner took this to be the final sign. One week later, on August 21, 1831, he started out with his four allies armed with axes, knives, mauls, pitchforks, and scythes. They felt guns would sound the alarm and spoil their stealthy approach. They visited every home of white families in the surrounding area repeating the cycle of killing every white encountered, drinking all the liquor found, and then heading for the next white home. Turner knew most of the whites. The adults would greet him and the children would run up to him and embrace him before he, or one of his followers, would plunge an axe into their head or back. Before long, Turner had a following of over 70 slaves and freedmen. All were intoxicated. Many of the slaves, especially the house servants, refused to follow him. No white encountered was spared for any reason. Since many of the men were away or in the fields, Turner's group came upon mostly women, children, toddlers, and infants. The women would be held and axes would be used to split their heads in two halves, while the children would be herded together and all beat to death with blunt tools or pitch-forked. Each bedroom was sacked, and when babies were found in cribs they would be grasped by the leg and bashed against the fireplace stone. When the killing ended there was over 60 white women, children, babies, and a few men dead. There were no wounded. Only one white child had escaped by hiding in the fireplace.

The alert was sounded and the various militias rounded up their members and went after Turner's drunken mob. Forty-eight of Turner's group were caught within two days and charged with conspiracy, insurrection, and treason. In the end, the state executed 55 people, banished many more, and acquitted a few. Turner eluded capture until he was found hiding in a hole covered with fence rails by Benjamin Phipps on October 30. He was tried, convicted, and sentenced to death on November 5, and hanged on November 11, 1831, in Jerusalem, Virginia. I mention John Brown and Nat Turner because these are two of the people that Obama eulogizes in his two books as idols worthy of black emulation.

John C. Calhoun and Daniel Webster tried to hold the Union together by compromise. But the abolitionists in the North wanted slavery to end immediately, and the "fire-eaters" of the South were tired of being treated as inferiors and in no mood for compromise. Lincoln's election tipped the scale and the firing on Fort Sumter on April 12, 1861, was the final straw. In the South, with the men away fighting, and only the women left at the farms, some of the slaves slowly deserted their quarters and headed north. The majority remained in the South until the end of the war out of loyalty to their owners, or out of fear of being caught. Many were employed as labor to build the southern infrastructure such as railroads, macadamized roadways, redoubts, salt production facilities, ships, dams, and bridges. Many kept on doing what they had always done, picking King Cotton to pay for necessities and the war effort.

Most of the southern Confederate officers took their personal slave with them to act as a valet and cook. Almost all of these slaves were loyal to their master, and would even take up arms when needed to defend their owner against the Yankees. The North became so crowded with runaway slaves that they were formed into army regiments and served to the end of the war. The most famous was the 54th Massachusetts. Early in the war, General Patrick Cleburne of Arkansas suggested enlisting slaves in the Confederacy in return for freedom, but the idea was rejected on the basis that it would negate one of the very reasons for which the South went to war. The idea was actually adopted in March of 1865, but by then it was already too late.

Lincoln's Emancipation Proclamation took effect on January 1, 1863, and immediately ended slavery in all the Confederate states. Oddly, it did not end slavery in the border states, northern states, certain counties of Virginia (now West Virginia), Kentucky or Tennessee. These would be covered by the thirteenth amendment in December 1865. In effect, Lincoln freed the slaves in the states he had no control over, and kept slavery in the states where he had control. This makes about as much sense as some of Obama's ideas.

RECONSTRUCTION

From all verbal and written evidence, Lincoln envisioned a quick reconciliation with the South after the Civil War because he knew the monumental difficulties ahead in deciding what to do with 4 million uneducated, illiterate, black Africans who he felt would never assimilate with the 31 million white, educated, predominately European, urbane population. Unfortunately, John Wilkes Booth ended that hope on April 14, 1865, when he blew Lincoln's brains out at the Ford Theatre in Washington D.C. Lincoln's successor, Andrew Johnson, proposed a reasonable plan of reconciliation that was soundly rejected by the radical abolitionists in the Republican Congress and almost resulted in Johnson's impeachment. Remember, in 1865, none of the southern states were represented in Congress so the Republicans had dictatorial, absolute control. So, rather than reconciliation, we got retaliation euphemistically labeled "reconstruction."

Reconstruction officially began at the moment the Civil War ended on April 9, 1865. It ended 12 years later in 1877 when sanity and southern representation returned to the Congress. The radical Republicans lost their death-grip on the country. And even they finally realized their forced installment of blacks into the seats of power, controlling a structured, highly educated, society of whites, would not work. It took Washington about 12 years to fathom the idea that amalgamation was unachievable. The vast majority of blacks still lived in the South and the North wanted to keep it that way. It was easy for the North to abandon the effort. The northern carpet-baggers, scalawags, speculators, and opportunists had bled the South dry, so they had nothing left to steal and packed-up and left. Many of the Yankee abolitionists had lost their passion when blacks were actually free and moved north into areas near them. Even the northeast liberals realized that continuing the troop occupation of the South, and repressing their economy, would lead to migration of the blacks to the North and that was unacceptable. They were champions of the downtrodden black man, but living next door to them was another matter altogether. Let's look at a few of the more interesting aspects of reconstruction.

Lincoln, before his assassination, and President Johnson afterward, both verbally and in their written words and actions, wanted an orderly reconciliation between the North and South. They both knew the task ahead in rebuilding the country, and figuring out what to do with 4 million freed slaves, would require a united country working together.

Every village, railroad depot, county seat, and state capitol was quickly occupied by Union troops as the Confederates laid down their arms and abided by the terms of surrender to Grant, Sherman, and all the other Union Army commanders operating in the south, central, and western states. The governors of the southern states called together the legislatures and civilian authorities to restore order to the chaos and turmoil swirling throughout the South. Their attempts to help restore order were countermanded by Union military authorities who ordered all the civilian leaders to resign and disband. They imprisoned Jefferson Davis and would have tried Robert E. Lee if Grant had not stepped in to defend him. They hanged Henry Wirz, commandant at Andersonville Prison in Georgia, even though more than 6000 prisoners had died of starvation and disease at Camp Douglas in the middle of Chicago where food was plentiful. Today, people talk only of Andersonville, but many more Confederates died of starvation and cold in the northern states from purposeful deprivation. Thanks to Generals Sherman, Sheridan, Hunter, Shields, and others, the edible crops of the South had been destroyed and there was little food left for the southerners, let alone the Union prisoners. So, both starved. But, there was no reason to starve the thousands of Confederates in northern prisons or the denial of warmth except out of hatred. The Yankees intentionally placed former slaves to guard the Confederates. Empowered by this, the slaves exacted cruelty much worse than they had ever received working for the planters.

Those few southerners that could flee the country did so when fear of imprisonment or hanging spread among the former Confederates. General Jubal Early went to Cuba. Former Vice-President of the U.S. under President Buchanan, John C. Breckinridge, and Robert Toombs of Georgia went to Europe. Former Tennessee Governor Isham G. Harris and Generals Magruder, Hindman, and Price headed to Mexico. Generals Loring and Graves fled to Egypt and served under the khedive there. Enough Confederates moved to Brazil to found five ex-Confederate communities, the descendants of whom still celebrate their Confederate ancestors to this day.

However, for the vast majority of southerners, leaving was not an option. So they stayed, regardless of the depravity that lay ahead. Robert E. Lee could have left, but he had declined the job of Union General-in-Chief out of loyalty to Virginia, and was not now going to abandon her when she needed him most. The federal government issued proclamations listing the requirements for each of the seceded states to be admitted back into the Union. All of these stipulated that every southerner had to sign a loyalty oath, and then petition to be allowed to rejoin the Union. Voters of each of the southern states were to be composed of all white and freed blacks except confederate military officers above the rank of colonel, naval officers above the rank of lieutenant, governors, judges of courts, West Point officers, all civil officers of the Confederate governments, and all citizens worth over $20,000. These exclusions amounted to about 150,000. In other words, almost the entire leadership class of the South was denied participation in rebuilding their state or community. Many of them had not taken part in the war, but had just chosen the wrong side of the Mason-Dixon Line to reside.

All of the southerners joined in knitting the fabric of the nation back together. Even those denied the vote supported the ones granted the right by the military provost marshals to hold office. The state legislatures repealed their ordinances of secession, and by the end of 1865, eight of the seceded former Confederate states had joined 19 of the northern states to ratify the 13th Amendment to the Constitution- abolishing slavery.

On April 2, 1866, President Johnson announced that all the former Confederate states were fully restored and that "no organized armed resistance" existed anywhere. He went on to note that laws "can be sustained and enforced therein by proper civil authority, state and federal; that the people of said states are well and loyally disposed, and have conformed or will conform in their legislation to the condition of affairs growing out of the amendment to the Constitution prohibiting slavery within the borders and jurisdictions of the United States." This proclamation covered the states of Alabama, Arkansas, Florida, Louisiana, Georgia, North Carolina, South Carolina, Mississippi, Tennessee, and Virginia. Johnson had excluded only Texas, who had yet to meet the criteria to be re-admitted.

Unfortunately, Congress had been recessed since before Lincoln's death. They stayed out for eight months and returned in December 1865. Abolitionist Republicans ruled Congress and knew if the Democrat-dominated southern states were re-admitted, the Republican majority would be diluted or dissolved. So, they denied seating any of the newly elected southern Congressmen until they could investigate and rule on the propriety of seating them. They proceeded to appoint a 15 man committee to travel to each of the former Confederate states and report back their findings. The committee was called the "Reconstruction Committee" and was composed of 12 Republicans and 3 Democrats. Johnson had issued orders to start recalling the troops stationed in the South, but this was rescinded by the Republicans.

By excluding the largely Democrat southern Congressmen, the Republicans had a super-majority and could and did override any veto by Johnson. Besides vetoing Johnson's re-admittance of the seceded states, the Republicans also overrode Johnson's veto of a bill establishing a "Freedmen's Bureau," and a civil rights bill. In July of 1866, the Republicans passed another bill to give the "Freedmen's Bureau" police power, and appropriated $6,887,700 to hire agents to enforce the punitive laws against southern whites. All positions of authority were given to these agents and northern "carpetbaggers," both of whom were given free-rein to bring "hell on earth" to the whites with full military protection for their actions. The net effect was that while the President said the war was over, the Republicans said the new war of reconstruction was just beginning.

In the fall of 1865, President Johnson had toured the southern states with General Grant. Both agreed that southerners were making the best of their ruined lives. The people were cooperating with the Freedmen's Bureau and the military, and obeying the laws required to be admitted back into the United States. All efforts proved naught after the draconian laws passed by the Republicans. The agents of the Freedmen's Bureau were all Yankees, and made it common practice to promise every black that they would shortly receive 40 acres and a mule. Until they received these gifts, they would be fed, clothed, and housed by the Freedmen's Bureau. This they did, and asked of the blacks only that they use their new suffrage rights to vote for the agents should they run for elective office. Almost to a man, every carpetbagger agent ran for public office and won since blacks were in the majority, while many whites were still denied the vote. Not only were these agents able to promise 40 acres with a mule and provide food, housing and clothing to the blacks, but were empowered to have whites arrested, whipped, and jailed on the mere word of a black. As a result of this new found power over their former white owners, the blacks frequently fabricated disputes to take whatever assets, such as homes, land, horses, mules, and wagons owned by the whites.

The Freedmen's Bureau agents exercised total control over the blacks, who in turn looked to the agents for their every need. Every agent was from the North, and all but a few were white. The agents formed exclusive clubs for blacks and carpetbaggers called "Union Clubs," which they used to create and sustain black hatred for all non-union whites, and as their own springboard for political office. Nearly every federal, state, county, and city office was held by these agents by the middle of 1866. Since the blacks expected to receive free land taken from the southerners, they refused to work, preferring to loiter around, get drunk, and harass whites, knowing that anything short of murder was acceptable to the agents. Every court docket was full in every county and state courtroom, with over 95% of cases hearing trumped-up charges by blacks against whites. The Yankee judges invariably handed down guilty verdicts against the whites and, more often than not, gave kick-backs to the blacks, which further encouraged the practice.

From the end of the Civil War in April 1865, until almost 1870, most of the agriculture in the South was done by the sweat of the small white farmer. The blacks literally thought they would never have to work again, and took it for granted that the U.S. owed them reparations. Sounds like today doesn't it? All the cities began filling up with itinerant blacks. They had quit the fields in large numbers and equated freedom with never having to work again. They were not solely to blame, since the agents promised them a lifetime of government provided food, clothing, and care, to go with free land and stock. The Republicans purposely started the rumor that every black would receive 40 acres and a mule, and many waited 10 years for this lie to materialize.

The fact that the South had reorganized their state governments in accordance with the government's mandate, repealed their ordinances of secession, and ratified the 13th Amendment, only served to whet the appetite of the bitter Republican super-majority in Congress. It was not for love of blacks, but rather for lust of their new-found power, and their intent to never relinquish it, that made them want to make the South "howl" just as Sherman had done in his march to the sea. With the help of the abolitionist press, the Republicans added even more of their members to the Congress in the elections of 1866. Then, they by-passed the President again by opening the 40th Congress in March of 1867 rather than wait until the usual December seating of the new Congress. On March 2nd, they overrode the President's veto again, declared the reconstruction efforts already in place null and void, and also declared themselves now in charge of all reconstruction projects. They divided the 10 former Confederate states into five military districts, and placed abolitionist Union officers in charge with instructions to use severe methods in exacting justice for the blacks. They also enabled only chosen state legislatures to proceed to ratify the 14th Amendment, and threatened that the states would remain as provisional until the amendment became part of the Constitution.

Extraordinary as it may sound, ten of the former Confederate states were denied statehood until they voted to ratify the 14th Amendment, even though previously, they had been considered as legal states to ratify the 13th Amendment! So, is the 13th Amendment valid? Was Obama born in Hawaii or Kenya? Who knows, who asks, and who cares? The effect of the 14th Amendment was to deny the South the right to vote until such time as the Republicans said they could vote. Also, it specifically prohibited Indians and omitted women from voting. Besides the 13th and 14th Amendments, the Republicans passed a slew of bills, each more oppressive than the preceding one. The military was given extra-Constitutional power, such as the right to invade and quarter soldiers in the Southerner's homes. Georgia Governor Jenkins and Mississippi's Governor Walker were both Union men, but still felt the laws were so onerous that they filed suits to have them overturned. They won their cases in the lower courts and proceeded to the appellate courts. Getting wind of this, both houses of the Republican Congress rushed through bills on March 27, 1868, to deprive the appellate court of jurisdiction, and then overrode Johnson's veto of these same bills. Due to the disenfranchisement of white southerners, the blacks either held outright majorities of state legislatures, or the blacks backed the white northerners who actually held the office.

One of the aforementioned bills was the Sherman Bill. When Governors Jenkins, Throckmorton of Texas, and the Governor of Alabama told their constituents not to obey the bill's harsh measures, they were peremptorily removed from office along with the state comptroller and treasurer by order of General Pope, military commander of the district. Fort Pulaski, along with other existing and new facilities, was used to imprison the thousands of whites incarcerated for nothing more than being white. White voters in Alabama and Arkansas tried to defeat their state constitutions, which had been forced on them by the blacks and Yankees, by refusing to go to the polls and vote. Congress simply combined these two states with the others and forced them to accept the unwanted state constitutions regardless.

Let me give you just one example of the Yankee takeover of the southern states. Republican officeholders chosen from the Freedmen's Bureau for Alabama in February 1868 were: Lieutenant-Governor Applegate of Ohio; Secretary of State, Miller of Maine; Auditor, Reynolds of Maine and Commissioner of Internal Revenue, Keifer, of Ohio. From legislators to probate judges to county solicitors, northern Republicans held all offices. Many of the offices were also held by blacks who hardly knew the English language and could not write their own name. Most of the state militias were composed of blacks who roamed around consuming whiskey, and taking liberties with both white men and females of both races. Republicans welcomed the occasional problems caused by the KKK, because turmoil meant job security to both the Republican officeholders and black militia.

The scheme used today by Obama to pass emergency legislation like the TARP and stimulus bill, and to dole out these trillions to ACORN, SEIU, and Democrat politicians, was copied from what the Republican carpetbaggers did in the South. They would saddle the bleeding South with oppressive taxes, and then legislate public bonds to build railroads at grossly overpriced construction costs on overpriced land purchased from their partners. Six of these bogus railroads were started in Alabama, five were abandoned, and only one was completed. The bond brokers, railroad schemers, and land speculators, made millions off the overtaxed citizens of the southern cities, towns, counties, and states before the well went dry. As a result, the carpetbaggers packed-up and went back north, leaving both the whites broke and the blacks without their new masters.

On March 5, 1871, after the 12 former Confederate states had been readmitted, their Congressmen consisted of 22 Republican Senators, 2 Democrat Senators, 48 Republican House members and 13 Democrat House members. Most were still Yankees. These states had been so gutted by the carpetbaggers that the state and county treasuries were in deficit. In South Carolina it was noted that over two hundred black trial judges were holding office that could neither read nor write.

The Union League of the South was organized by the northern Republican Party to take ironfisted control of the southern people and keep it. The League was designed to be a clandestine black party to act as the right arm of the Republicans, and keep the blacks separated from the southern whites to avoid losing control. Strangely, this black-only Union League consisted of two segregated divisions: one all white and the other all black, except a few whites to instruct and control them in Republican ways. The members of the League were sworn to secrecy and surrounded by mystery. They had arcane handshakes, mysterious salutations, strange initiation ceremonies, and had to swear an oath of allegiance that contained veiled threats if they violated the League by-laws. A typical meeting of the League would be held in an open field with the black inductees surrounding a large bonfire. Then, the white controllers would in-turn stand up and harangue the blacks into a hysterical mob. They were reminded of slavery, and how hatred and revenge were the only courses for the black man. These meetings gave the blacks a sense of brotherhood, kept them from realizing that their station in life was not really improving, and that even the whites of the South were slowly pulling themselves out of poverty. The Republicans knew they had to keep the blacks in turmoil until they could finish draining all the value out of the South, and only then could they depart.

For every action there is a reaction, and the reaction to the criminal actions of the Union League was the Ku Klux Klan. The object of the KKK was the preservation of order and the protection of society by preventing crime, plunder, assassination, and rape by the Republican-led black Union League. Today's history-ignorant population knows only that they've heard all their lives that the KKK hanged blacks from every tree if they looked cross-eyed at a white girl. I'm sure that actually happened just as I'm sure blacks raped some of the hundred-thousand or so widows of Confederate soldiers, or committed numerous acts of depredation when urged to do so by the Union League's handlers. Usually though, the more common incident was similar to what happened in Noxubee County, Mississippi. The population of this county was about 10 blacks to one white. Recent meetings of the Union League had stirred the blacks to lawlessness, abusive language, incendiary remarks to white women, and roaming gangs of blacks punching, kicking, assaulting, and sometimes killing whites without cause. This had been going on for months and was leading to more serious results as the emboldened blacks became more belligerent with each attack.

One night about two hundred white men clothed in white sheets rode through the thickly-settled black section of the county on horseback, slowly and without uttering a word. They appeared without warning at dusk, and vanished at dawn. They did not dismount their horses, carried no weapons, and said no words. This did not make the League disband, but the black violence ceased almost entirely. Never fail to remember that the victors write the history books, and in the last 100 years the radical left has written them all, so the real story of the KKK has been skewed beyond recognition.

Today, most Americans are history-deficit and do not question the flawed, warped words of the racist revisionists of America. Isn't it enough for rational people on both sides to look at the facts of white slavery and black slavery, and say we are all imperfect, just as we continue to be today, instead of the lies and distortions?

To continue with reconstruction, let me give you a description of a carpetbagger from the 1899 "Confederate Military History":

"THE CARPET-BAGGER

His is like the world has never seen from the days of Cain or of the forty thieves in the fabled time of Ali Baba. Like the wind, he blows and we hear the sound thereof, but no man knoweth whence it cometh or whither it goeth. National historians will be in doubt how to class him. Ornithologists will claim him, because in many respects he is a bird of prey. He lives only on corruption, and takes his flight as soon as the carcass is picked. He is no product of the war. He is a "canker of a calm world "and peace, which is despotism enforced by bayonets. His valor is discretion; his industry perpetual strife; and his eloquence ' The parcel of a reckoning' of chances as he smells. Out a path which may lead from the White House to a custom house, a post office, the internal revenue bureau or perchance, to either wing of the Federal capitol. His shibboleth is 'The Republican Party.' From that party he sprung as naturally as a maggot from putrefaction. Wherever two or three or four negroes are gathered together, he, like a leprous spot, is seen, and his cry, like the daughter of the horse leech, is always, Give, give me office. Without office he is nothing; with office he is a pest and public nuisance. Out of office he is a beggar; in office he grows rich till his eyes stick out with fatness. Out of office he is, hat in hand, the outside ornament of every negro's cabin, a plantation loafer and the nation's laze-rone; in office he is an adept in' addition, division and silence.' Out of office he is the orphan ward of the administration and the general sign-post of penury; in office he is the complaining suppliant for social equality with Southern gentlemen. (Norwood) This is a splendid picture in general of the carpet-bagger during the days of reconstruction."

My reason for giving you a southern description of carpet-baggers is to show you that the enmity that developed between blacks and whites after the Civil War is more complicated than a simple resentment felt by the Southerners because they lost their slave labor. The carpet-baggers were 95% white and 5% black northerners who sowed racism for a purpose, and that purpose was greed. Then, these "Saviors of the Slaves" got back on the trains and headed north with their carpet bags full of the very cash needed by the whites and blacks of the South to start over again. The South was poor after the war, but not so dirt-deep poverty-stricken and depressed that it could not recover and learn to live with their former slaves in a more amicable society. But, what transpired under the crushing weight of the Republicans, Freedmen's Bureau, Union League, and carpet-baggers left every state bankrupt, every white broke, beaten, and hopeless and every black still waiting for a handout with no one to feed him or protect him. Being a retired CPA I have come to hate numbers, but let me give you a glance at the ruinous condition of the South after a few years of the tenure of the carpet-baggers.

Alabama's state debt (mostly from the war) was $8,336,083 in 1866 before the Republicans took over. When Republicans left the state the debt was $25,503,593. This did not include the debts of the counties and cities. North Carolina was in worse shape. Republicans had issued $25,000,000 in bonds and $16,000,000 in other securities plus stolen all funds collected for the education for all blacks and whites, so that not a single child of either race was educated for a period of two years. At the end of reconstruction the tax debt imposed was $38,000,000 while the taxable wealth was returned at $120,000,000. Additionally, municipal bonds for $14,000,000 had been issued for a railroad and not a mile of track was ever laid. In 1860, assessed property value was $292,000,000 and dropped to $130,000,000 by 1870. That's over a 50% drop. Taxes on that same property went from $543,000 in 1860 to $1,160,000, over a 100% increase. South Carolina in 1860 had taxable property valued at $490,000,000 and paid taxes of $400,000. Taxable property in 1870 was assessed at only

$184,000,000, but taxes paid amounted to $2,000,000. In Georgia all property was valued at $672,322,777 in 1860 and fell to $226,329,767 by 1870. In Florida, property values fell 45% in eight years of Republican rule from 1867 to 1875. In Mississippi 6,400,000 acres of land was forfeited to the Republican carpet-baggers via killer property taxes. Much of this land was later sold back to the citizens at exorbitant mark-ups. In New Orleans the property value decreased by $58,104,864 in the city from 1860 to1870 and in the county from $99,266,839 to $47,141,690 for the same period. It is estimated that carpet-baggers disappeared with over $140 million from just the city. Louisiana state debt increased more than $40,000,000, and city and county property decreased by 40% and 50% respectively.

When reconstruction finally ended in 1877 all 10 former Confederate states were readmitted to the Union again. But they were broke, destitute, and stuck with 4,000,000 ignorant blacks that were suddenly abandoned by their fair-weather Republican friends who had milked the South dry and fled, leaving behind the blacks to fend for themselves. The Freedmen's Bureau, Union League, carpet-baggers, scalawags, agents, and military provost marshals all went back to their comfortable homes in the North. Most had made a fortune and they took it with them. The northern black carpet-baggers had been freedmen living in the North when recruited by the Republicans, and sent south to help control the blacks and to administer the Freedmen's Bureau's enormous distributions of food, clothing, and housing. They and the white carpet-baggers had also shipped wagon trains of whiskey to the South beginning immediately after the Appomattox surrender and right on through to the end of reconstruction. Almost all was consumed by the blacks and troops stationed in the South. A common ploy was to barter a case of whiskey to the blacks in return for a staged incident, after which the black would win a settlement in the rigged court from the whites, and turn over most of the settlement to the carpet-bagger. Whiskey was so plentiful that thousands of blacks died of alcohol poisoning and alcohol-related malnutrition. They were discouraged from working so that large tracts of plantation land would lay fallow and bankrupt the white owners, so that carpet-baggers could purchase it for unpaid taxes.

The Republican northerners practically left the South overnight. When the state and municipal bond markets dried-up and state debt had reached its ceiling, they saw the handwriting on the wall and literally left by the wagon and trainload. The blacks woke-up one morning and they were alone; without food, clothing, or work and nowhere to get it but from the southern whites whom they had been taught to hate. So, they slowly went to work either as share-croppers or hired-hands on the larger farms. This period was hard on both races. The Republicans had gone home, but they still ruled from Washington and still passed bills to interfere with the South's progress. Much of what the farms and citizens produced during this period went for taxes to pay the huge debt left them by the Yankees. Investment capital of the North was spent in the new northwestern areas of the United States where there were no troublesome blacks or insurmountable public debt.

When the war ended, the cumulative war debt of all the Confederate states was $87,000,000. After reconstruction the debt of the states had grown to $300,000,000. Investment capital was rare in the South and borrowed at a rate of 75% interest when available. Most capital was flowing to the west and northwest where over a half-million immigrants had come to build railroads and cities. All steered clear of the South where only debt and ruin existed. There were blacks at all levels of government in the southern states starting in 1866. As white carpet-baggers started easing out of the South around 1872 blacks replaced them, and often were the majority office-holders since they had the vote while many whites were still denied their suffrage. In South Carolina blacks controlled both houses of Congress. Whites could just sit and watch as inexperienced, uneducated blacks, who had known only labor in cotton fields, took the reins of government in tumultuous confusion.

Federal troops were still stationed in Florida, South Carolina, and Louisiana as the presidential elections approached in 1876. The "Compromise of 1877" was a deal between Rutherford B. Hayes and southern Democrats to elect Hayes in return for removing the troops and appointment of a southerner, David M. Key of Tennessee, as Postmaster. Once the troops were gone, the majority of the Republican office-holders in the South switched to the

Democrat Party (they were called "Redeemer Democrats"), and stayed in dominance for 89 years until 1966.

As already stated, by 1877 all the troops were gone and the blacks returned mostly to share-cropping or field labor. In 1896 the Supreme Court ruled 7 to 1 in Plessy vs. Ferguson, upholding the constitutionality of segregation under the doctrine of "separate but equal" in public accommodations. Homer Plessy had agreed to be arrested to test Louisiana's segregation law. This remained standard doctrine until Brown vs. Board of Education in 1954 when Plessy was repudiated by the court.

Segregation of blacks and whites did not require a court order. The races were so divergent that they self-segregated into separate communities, or separate areas, even when they lived in the same community. Sharecropping was not a black-only activity. Sharecropping was the mainstay of 80% of the blacks and 40% of the whites for 70 years after the Civil War. Although viewed by liberal historians as an extension of slavery, it allowed the poor whites in the South, often working side-by-side with black sharecroppers, to survive in the South after the Republicans had left their devastation. Sharecropping is a system whereby a landowner allows a tenant to use his land to raise crops, and a share of those crops is paid to the landowner for the use of the land. Unlike a fixed rent, the fortunes of both landowner and tenant depend on the crop yield. Both take the same risk. If the tenant has a bad year then the owner of the land has a bad year, and vice-versa. Sharecropping kept millions of blacks and whites alive during a time when they were both literally starving.

Finding an unbiased history of racial relations in the South is like finding flattering descriptions of white folks in Obama's books. They don't exist because they are all written by flaming white or black racists who have an agenda. And, that agenda is the same as Sharpton, Jackson, and most of the black liberals of today: portray the blacks as poor, helpless, stupid, dependent, whipped incompetents that have been victimized by evil whites, and need lifetime welfare and reparations to make it all nice. Luckily, my personal library has about 2500 books, many of which cover the period under discussion. Plus, I grew up in Illinois and moved to the South in 1958 so I witnessed first-hand segregation and relations between the races in both north and south.

I have done very extensive research on race relations, both on-line and from hard-copy. Virtually all of the material contained anywhere on the post-Civil War period is dominated with lynching's, mobs, the KKK, hangings, murder, stabbings, and various other white crimes against blacks. If all of these be true then blacks would today be an endangered species. There was some white crime against blacks then just as there is black crime today against both whites and blacks, except the blacks today commit 8 times more violent crimes than whites. Try for a moment to trade places with the whites during the period from 1865 to 1877. Over 250,000 of your sons, brothers, and fathers were dead, and another 500,000 were limping and maimed from their wounds. Soldiers stationed in every village treat you worse than slaves were ever treated. You don't have the vote. Maybe you are a widow with three small children. You live in a shack and till a small garden for bare sustenance and see blacks with plenty to eat, a horse to ride, and a nicer place to live, all compliments of the Freedmen's Bureau. They never seem to do a lick of work. Wherever you go drunken blacks harass you, and sometimes even more than just words are used to abuse you. If you say anything out of line a black will summon a soldier and you are arrested and jailed. You can't pay the fine. You have nothing but some silverware you buried in the ground when the Yankees first came through. You dig it up and pay your fine. Your property taxes are trebled and come due. You sell half your land at one-tenth its value to pay exorbitant taxes. You see whites and blacks of the "Union League" meeting secretly, but if more than two southern whites get together they accuse you of conspiracy and you are subject to arrest. Almost daily your neighbors are evicted from their land for non-payment of taxes.

Then one night men dressed in white sheets appear slowly riding down the street. You flee to the house in fear. There are a few hundred of them. They do nothing but ride back and forth, stopping only to stare menacingly at known members of the "League," who cower in fear and walk away. You find out later that these are not Union men at all, but ex-Confederate soldiers who surrendered with Lee, Joe Johnson, or Kirby Smith and came home to a burned out home, a wife and three kids to work the fields and just try and survive. They wore sheets for a damn good reason. If recognized they would be visited and arrested by the military provost troops. Finally seeing some "regulators" on your side after years of subjugation by drunken ex-slaves and their handlers was a welcome sight. These ex-soldiers on average were more educated than people in the North. They were lawyers, printers, store owners, entrepreneurs, gentleman farmers, and owners of manufactories. Not only could they not vote or return to their own businesses, but blacks, carpet-baggers and Yankees of all sorts treated them like vermin. They could not even visit relatives in the next town without fear of being accosted by blacks and Yankees, and if not polite, they could take your horse, beat you, or arrest you on trumped-up charges.

Put yourself in the place of a white resident of the South or a returning Confederate soldier. Would you not be happy to finally see someone stand-up against years of abuse? Would you, as a proud returning soldier, lucky to have survived the bloody war, welcome being treated as a criminal because you tried to protect your country from the ravages of the racist North who sold the slaves to the South, and then wanted the "peculiar institution" ended immediately? When some of the later KKK members retaliated beyond just leveling the playing field - then so what? Let a white person walk down Moreland Avenue in Atlanta at night and see how long they survive. Liberal whites should visit gang-controlled black areas of L.A. or Detroit and time their survival rate with a stop-watch. White southerners only did what blacks, browns, or yellows would have done had the situations been reversed.

Never, ever forget that everything you have ever read about race, blacks, segregation, or lynchings in the South from the pre-antebellum period to the 1970's is either fabricated, enhanced, or an outright lie. Practically every book, article, or newspaper story was written by a liberal with a bad case of white guilt or a black bigot. For example, Obama's number one favorite chronicler of the southern black experience was W.E. Burghardt Du Bois. I enjoy reading his writings also, because I simply love our American history, even when most of it is fantasy. Regarding slaves, he wrote, "He emerged from slavery: not the worst slavery in the world, not a slavery that made all life unbearable, rather, a slavery that had here and there much of kindliness, fidelity, and happiness." Du Bois was not known for his solicitude toward whites. Regarding the harsh treatment of whites after the Civil War by blacks and Republicans, Du Bois said the "Bureau courts tended to become centres simply for punishing whites, while the regular civil courts tended to become solely institutions which could have maintained a perfectly judicial attitude, this arrangement would have been ideal, and must in time have gained confidence; but the nature of its other activities and the character of its personnel prejudiced the Bureau in favor of the black litigants, and led without doubt to much injustice and annoyance." Any reasonable American today that knows the true horrors perpetrated on the defeated southerners by the northern carpet-baggers, the criminal Republicans, and their robotic army of blacks, and doesn't understand why they welcomed an organization like the KKK is at the very least ignorant, and most likely an unrepentant racist.

While there were many financial crises, droughts, crop failures, and other man-made and natural disasters, the South and the two races existed up through the early 1900's much as they had in the late 1870's. Although they were segregated, both races advanced. Both white and black institutions of higher learning were founded, and both races moved from an agrarian subsistence to other fields of endeavor. Many blacks moved with their families north to work in the new automobile industry and manufacturing. The southern whites moved also, since both races were tired of fighting for a bare subsistence from the soil. They competed with the influx of immigrants pouring into the North, mostly from Europe. The blacks often found that the people of the North practiced racism more vehemently than in the South. The blacks and whites in the South had reached a sort of symbiotic cooperation. While "separate but equal" may not have been totally equal, it was far from the evil portrayed in later years by the "arms length" liberals who were critical of the system, but did not want the blacks moving in their neighborhood.

Even with segregation, blacks progressed in all endeavors just like whites. They had their heroes to emulate, too. Booker T. Washington was born in Franklin County, Virginia, in 1856 on the Burroughs farm where his mother was a cook and his father worked at another farm. He worked his way through college and founded Tuskegee Institute in 1881. Speaking on segregation at Atlanta in 1895 he said, "In all things purely social we can be as separate as the fingers, yet one as the hand in all things essential to mutual progress." He could see from his own efforts the steady progress of blacks throughout the nation and, most importantly, they were doing it on their own and not piggy-backing on white benevolence as they would later on. For his beliefs he was called an "Uncle Tom."

George Washington Carver was the most famous of black notables in this period. He was born in 1864 in Missouri and kidnapped along with his mother and sister when just a week old, and taken by raiders to Arkansas. His owner, Moses Carver, swapped a racehorse to get George back. When the Civil War ended a few months later, Moses Carver and his wife Susan adopted George as their own son. The Carvers home-schooled George and that began his interest in a life of learning that never ceased. Conquering many obstacles, George earned his college degree and eventually accepted a position from Booker T. Washington at Tuskegee Institute. Until his death in 1943, Carver developed 300 products out of peanuts, 118 from sweet potatoes, and many for cowpeas, soybeans, and pecans. He was recognized by Presidents, received laurels and awards, and, more importantly, proved to the world that the black man was capable of scientific intelligence in a league with other races. Unlike today's blacks, Carver quietly earned his place in history by intelligence and hard work, not covert reparations, victimization, or affirmative action as do today's black elites of the Darkside.

The NAACP was founded on February 12, 1909, and incorporated in 1911. The founders were composed of seven whites and one black, W. E. B. Du Bois. The first president was Moorfield Storey, a white Jewish American. The only black member of the executive board was Du Bois himself. It would be 1975 before the NAACP would elect its first black president. The organizational charter sought to advance the interest of colored citizens and secure "employment according to their ability." Of course, when Jesse Jackson, Al Sharpton, and other "victims" came along later, they wanted blacks treated the same as handicapped and disabled citizens and receive special dispensation. The NAACP was totally financed in 1911 by white and Jewish individuals and groups as it largely is today. In 1920 Eugene K. Jones formed the National Urban League to pursue better employment opportunities for blacks. In 1942 the Congress of Racial Equality was founded by James L. Farmer, Jr., George Houser, James R. Robinson, and Bernice Fisher with a goal of passive resistance to segregation. In 1955 blacks organized the Montgomery Bus Boycott to fight segregation of the city's bus lines. Later, a group of the protestors from the boycott were organized, and in 1957 the Southern Christian Leadership Conference was founded with Martin Luther King elected as the first president. The Student Nonviolent Coordinating Committee was also founded in 1957 as an activist group for more direct action, as opposed to passivism. All of these groups worked both together and separately toward the common goal of ending segregation.

The anti-segregation activities of the black organizations were swept up into, and sometimes became part of, the upheaval exploding in the United States with the Vietnam War, pot and LSD, the feminist movement, financial crises, free love, the "Great Society," and the whole counter-culture thing. Some blacks became affiliated with groups like the Students for a Democratic Society, Weathermen, and Weather Underground. They also formed their own radical groups like the Black Panthers, and even the Symbionese Liberation Army, which was a group that used robbery to finance their anti-segregation efforts. Of course, the most famous character to emerge from the black civil rights movement was Martin Luther King.

Ralph Abernathy was with King, both when he started the SCLC, and when King was shot in Memphis on April 3, 1968. He was King's closest confidant and always with him in the marches and demonstrations. Years later, in 1989 he wrote a hard-cover book titled "And the Walls Came Tumbling Down" because he could not live with his conscience concerning the perceived sainthood of King. In his book he describes King's partying and having sex with three white women while crying "I'm f---king for God" and "I'm not a Negro tonight!" One of the women was brutally beaten by King. The audio of this incident, and many others, were recorded by FBI wiretaps. Abernathy also describes King's use of church funds to hire white prostitutes during their travels in the U.S. There are many blacks that have served their race and country faithfully and honorably and should be a model to blacks, but King isn't one of them. Whites and blacks both revere John, Bobby, and Ted Kennedy, and they were all the most despicable philanderers in our history. But, at least whites didn't honor these losers with their own whore-a-day holiday like the blacks honored King.

Speaking of holidays, let's take a look at Martin Luther King, Jr. Day celebrated on January 20th every year. Within four days of King's assassination on April 3, 1968, Rep. John Conyers of Michigan introduced a bill to honor King with a holiday. If you recall, Conyers was the same idiot that made the statement during the Obama, Obamacare hearing that he, of course, "hadn't read the legislation because it would take two lawyers two days to read that stuff." Another black, Shirley Chisholm, resubmitted the MLK holiday bill every year thereafter until successful. Ronald Reagan signed it into law in 1983. Arizona Governor Mecham objected to the holiday, so the NFL moved the Super Bowl that year from Arizona to Pasadena, California, plus the NAACP browbeat companies into boycotting the state. Finally, like most whites, when faced with black threats, Arizona backed down. Most states didn't mind blacks honoring whomever they pleased, but forcing hundreds of millions of citizens to share in a holiday for somebody that did little more than get himself killed by a nutcase was overkill. As usual, the whites retreated when faced with looting and riots, which usually occurred when blacks were denied even minor demands. Of course, the blacks and others make the argument that black folks need one of their own people honored by a holiday because of their torture at the hands of whites. Fine, and keep the MLK Day, too, if you admire gutter behavior. But, if equality is the goal then whites should get at least 6 white-only holidays and Hispanics need at least one of their own, too. I nominate George Washington, Ben Franklin, Robert E. Lee, Stonewall Jackson, Thomas Jefferson, Davy Crockett, and Daniel Boone for our white holidays. I've checked these guys out and they all make MLK look like a lightweight. I can hear the screams of "racist" as I write this. Whites are supposed to avoid defending themselves or other whites, and always defer to blacks lest they be forever labeled a racist.

National holidays cost billions of dollars because millions of workers get paid-days off and work does not get done. Another aspect that the white cowards did not consider is the streets that disappeared forever to make room for the MLK street signs. There are now streets, avenues, boulevards, ways, courts, and lanes named for King in every state, county, city, and village in the United States. Before the white fear and white guilt backed down from the King hordes, these streets were named Washington, Jefferson, Adams, Pulaski, Houston, Lee, and perhaps some for local heroes or events of significance. In effect, whites have sacrificed their heritage for a philandering soapbox preacher who no more believed in God than Judas. Does exalting an icon of blacks require the destruction of real white heroes or notable men? We are a 234 year old superpower republic founded and persevering because of the efforts of mostly white citizens, yet we have only one holiday devoted to a single individual, and it is to honor a black who added nothing to this nation. That's stupid. And, for those thinking that giving blacks their own holiday will even partially satiate their hatred of whites for slavery, then think again. They look upon MLK Day as a down-payment only on reparations. The payments are just beginning under the reparations-in-chief Barack Hussein Obama.

Even though Brown vs. Board of Education struck down segregation in 1954, actual integration was not immediate. My family moved south from Illinois to Florida in 1958 and I was sent alone on a Greyhound Bus down to Florida. The whites sat in the front and the blacks in back. During the long trip we stopped in Alabama and a black boy of about 8 years old boarded the bus with his mother, or maybe it was his grandmother. He ran ahead of her and sat down next to me. Being from the North, I just kept reading whatever I was reading. The lady came along after him and said something like, "Get up from there and get on to the back where you belong." I was 14 years old at the time, much more interested in the two girls that were sitting a few seats away, and didn't care where anybody sat. When we made stops, there were "colored" and white bathrooms and drinking fountains. I entered Pompano Beach High School which was a white senior high school while Blanche Eley High School was the black high school. There were never any racial problems at either school. Today all schools are integrated and most of the races, black, white, and brown self-segregate without the law ordering them to, and there are fights and problems on a daily basis. Education now costs 10 times more and graduates are illiterate. What have we accomplished?

Integration was virtually complete in the early 60's. Elementary schools, high schools, colleges, the military, trains, planes, and public facilities were all open to all races.

Whites in the North and South accepted integration of public facilities, but objected to integration of their neighborhoods, and simply moved out if blacks moved in. Most acted out of economic necessity, not racism, since home values plummeted when blacks moved in. Neither did they mingle with blacks socially. That was all supposed to change when President Lyndon Johnson signed the Civil Rights Act of 1964. Although the term "Affirmative Action" had only appeared in John Kennedy's executive order number 10925 in 1961, and applied also to other human parameters besides race, it became increasingly part of every liberal civil rights legislation in Washington. It also began the decline in American exceptionalism which continues to this day.

If you have not heard George Santayana's quote, "Those who do not remember the past are condemned to repeat it," then Obama probably has a job for you because you are too ignorant to see what is happening today. The demise of our nation started in the 60's and it came fast and furious. Drugs, homosexuals, feminists, Vietnam War, so-called war on poverty, Medicare, food stamps, environmentalism, sexual promiscuity, stagflation, radical leftist groups, and the portrayal of blacks as victims all hit us at once. Nazi, fascist, socialist, communist, liberal and progressive criminal gangs like SDS, Black Panthers, Weathermen, and SLA sabotaged businesses, bombed offices, and committed murders. Fortunately, America at this time still had enough reserves of hard-working, educated, mostly white citizens who stood like a stone wall between these destructive forces and our constitutional infrastructure. Unfortunately, none of these anti-American forces withered or died after the turbulent 60's. Instead, they expanded and multiplied until today they threaten to unravel our republic. Exacerbating our very real 11th hour emergency in 2010 is a leader that embraces all these radical, anti-American philosophies, and he is advancing his agenda every day. Heretofore, a radical minority fought the government. Now, this minority has grown into a cohesive coalition of hate groups aligned with the Obama radicals against the shrinking conservatives of America. Although this section deals primarily with the black imbroglio, it cannot be separated from the other radical groups because blacks form a large part of the forces trying to tear apart our republic, and the radicals used the blacks and the civil rights movement to get their camel's nose in our collective tent.

Earlier, I gave you a brief glimpse of post Civil War Reconstruction in the South. Roughly, it lasted from the end of the war in 1865 to 1877 when President Hayes pulled the troops out of all but two of the former Confederate states. That same year most of the carpet-baggers, both blacks and whites, skedaddled back up north and left the black Republicans and former slaves to fend for themselves against whites who had been beaten into submission and destitution for 12 years. Contrary to what history revisionists and Obama and his acolytes hold forth as the truth, a few of the blacks escaped being lynched, and many migrated to the other states and did quite well when you consider that most were former slaves or descendants of slaves. Then, beginning in the 60's a coalition of liberal whites and black opportunists entered into a symbiotic pact that ushered in what I will call the "Second Reconstruction." Until the 1960's, blacks had been a negligible force in elections because they simply didn't go to the polls in any of the states, regardless of whether a poll tax existed or not. White liberal Democrats saw an opportunity for trading government largesse for votes. The devil's pact was made, liberal whites got their votes, black opportunists got their guaranteed voting block, and the vast majorities of blacks were enslaved again by masters of both races, and entered a cycle of economic and mental depravity where they are to this day.

THE SECOND RECONSTRUCTION

(RISE OF THE BLACK ELITE)

I have already briefly touched on white slavery and black slavery. The 1.5 million whites enslaved by Africans either died as slaves or were ransomed and returned to Europe. Either way, their European brethren multiplied and migrated to North America and other lands, and pioneered most of the scientific, cultural, and industrial advancements of the world. The blacks that were enslaved in Europe and the American continent were eventually freed, and most of their offspring achieved a level of prosperity only after the playing field was artificially leveled by the sacrifice and benevolence of whites. This prosperity is still denied to their ancestral homeland. Most blacks in Africa today are still in the stone-age. Not a single black African nation can be considered a stabile, highly developed, industrialized power. Tribal wars abound, AIDS is rampant, and infrastructure is basic. The African continent was richly endowed with minerals and natural resources, but these were all discovered and developed by non-Africans. When an earthquake or tsunami hits anywhere in the world it is never African nations that come to the rescue. The only African nation to approach near the status of an industrial power was South Africa which was founded by a Dutch-English consortium, and turned into a wasteland simply because it's phenomenal success had forced importation of black labor, which led to a one-man, one-vote, one-time scenario. Prior to the surrender of South Africa to the blacks there were more black millionaires in that single nation than all the other nations of Africa combined! Universal suffrage may sound egalitarian, but it simply rewards rapid procreation at the expense of civilization. Look at South Africa today and you see the United States of America tomorrow.

The Bible and our earliest physical evidence of written history show us that mankind has been on earth about 6000 years. Assuming that all races on our planet today also existed in the beginning, then we should deduce that all would have reached their level of achievement or hierarchy by now as a result of natural selection or survival of the fittest. To be sure, there was much position-changing between the races during these 6000 years. But, the general habits, characteristics, mores, intellect, socialization, cultural development, and all other classifications of human behavior should be a settled issue after six millennia. In other words, all of the four races should have arrived at their respective niches by 2010.

So, if all the races had reached their equilibrium, then why is equality and racism even an issue in the United States? And, how can equality be artificially created and expected to last without reverting to its normal state of previous equilibrium? The blacks had been sold to white slavers by other black tribes on the Ivory Coast of Africa, and delivered to America from the mid-1600's to 1808. Once there, they consisted of free, but mostly un-free, residents until all were set free in 1865. For twelve years they were in absolute power. They served in the U.S. Senate, U.S. House and all the state legislatures. There was an absolute black majority in the South Carolina legislature, and blacks were in the majority party with their Republican counterparts in all the former Confederate states. In Mississippi, blacks outnumbered whites in total population. Why were they not still in power just 10 short years later? Were all 4,000,000 blacks lynched as the history revisionist's claim? Were they unable to keep the power they had been given without the help of their white Yankee handlers and armed soldiers? Black apologists will say that these were ex-slaves and not prepared to become administrators and legislators. Blacks had a minimum of 12 years with total military, political, and financial control over the whites in all the Confederate states. Many of the black U.S. Congressmen remained in office as late as the early 1900's. It's not like they were all kicked-out of office the day the troops left in 1877.

One reason that the out-gunned whites slowly regained control in the South is that the blacks mimicked their Republican white handlers. After both had filled-up their carpetbags with cash and negotiable securities from the bankrupt South, the blacks headed north with the white Yankees when President Hayes withdrew the troops. It wasn't just northern blacks who had come down south to rob the coffers and then flee, but the former slaves, too, that had stuffed their pockets and decided fear was the better part of valor. Instead of sticking around with their soul-mates, they scurried out of town by the trainload, leaving their former fellow-slaves to face a poor, but proud, South without benefit of armed soldiers to cower the whites. So, the blacks left behind by their fair-weather friends had no choice but to return to agrarian pursuits like their white neighbors. Like the whites, most entered into share-cropping agreements. Gradually, some started migrating north.

The southerners accepted their plight, and did what any affluent society would do when forced to live among another group so divergent that they had almost nothing in common. The two races self-segregated and interacted only when necessary. The Civil Rights Act of 1875 had tried to guarantee equal access to public accommodations, but had been declared unconstitutional by the Supreme Court in 1883 because Congress had no power to regulate the conduct of individuals. The Fourteenth Amendment prohibits discrimination by the state, not by individuals. Jim Crow laws were passed in the southern states mandating "separate but equal" facilities for blacks in all public accommodations. One effect of the Jim Crow laws, which you will never read in today's text books, is that over 130,000 whites in the South effectively lost their suffrage, too, when the poll tax, literacy and comprehension tests, residency, and record-keeping requirements were required before voting. The "separate but equal" clause was tested by Homer Plessy in Plessy vs. Ferguson, but the court ruled against him. The Isaac Woodard case of 1946 brought further attention to the unequal status of blacks after the intervention of President Truman, Woody Guthrie, and Orson Welles in defense of the returning WWII vet who had been beaten by a South Carolina sheriff. The beginning of the end of "separate but equal" came with the Supreme Court's ruling on "Brown vs. Board of Education of Topeka" in 1954. The school systems in Kansas were not only fully integrated, but by all standards, equal also. But, the NAACP (like the ACLU today) needed a reason to meddle and decided that it was unfair to force children to attend schools out of their neighborhood. So, they canvassed the area and found 13 families willing to join a test case. The lawyers finally settled upon the argument that separating the races at school can never be equal because it has a deleterious effect on the psyche of the black students. Strangely, this had little to do with the original complaint. But, when the NAACP and ACLU appear before activist judges, who pay attention to the stupid Constitution or laws? The Brown ruling had little effect on Kansas, but it was a boost to the pending plans of the NAACP to obtain "de facto" integration.

While writing the opinion for the Missouri vs. Jenkins case in 1995, Justice Clarence Thomas referred back to the Brown case and stated, "Given that desegregation has not produced the predicted leaps forward in black educational achievement, there is no reason to think that black students cannot learn as well when surrounded by members of their own race as when they are in an integrated environment. Because of their distinctive histories and traditions, black schools can function as the center and symbol of black communities, and provide examples of independent black leadership, success and achievement." Of course, Justice Thomas was right, but the NAACP was not interested in educating blacks in 1954 or 1995 or 2010. They saw that the grass was greener in white people's yards, and blindly forged ahead with the idea that the illusive idea of "equality" would make their grass just as green. They thought that whites and blacks were interchangeable, like automobile parts. They thought, like they still think today, that equality is simply a matter of passing laws and putting words on a piece of paper. Rather than face reality, they accepted Brown as the opening salvo and the impetus to move up to the next level. Just think of the millions of black students today who have been cheated out of a quality education because liberal whites and black elites have been hell-bent on pushing the two races together, regardless if it helps the blacks to reach higher levels of achievement or not.

In 1955 the Supreme Court heard Griffin vs. County School Board of Prince Edward County, Virginia, concerning ending segregation in the public schools in Virginia. This case became known as "Brown II." The resulting ruling was to order the district courts to carry out the desegregation orders "with all deliberate speed." When, by 1959, the schools still had not ended segregation, the district court told them to do so immediately. The local school board simply stopped appropriating funds for the schools, and gave financial assistance to white students to go to private schools. The NAACP knew that Brown II simply would not do, and sought further relief.

"Brown III" came along in 1978 when the ACLU joined forces with the NAACP and reopened the 25 year-old Brown case in Kansas. Although the Topeka schools had always been integrated for over 100 years, the 10th Circuit ruled that they still had vestiges of segregation with respect to student and staff assignments. A municipal bond issue was passed to pay for the suggested changes, but the installed racial balance standards were not approved by the courts until 1999.

The assassination of John Kennedy on November 22, 1963, was the turning point in the civil rights and "equality" movement. The death of Kennedy had changed the mood of the country, and Lyndon Johnson capitalized on this in pushing through the Civil Rights Act of 1964 on August 6, 1964. In a short time, black voter registration increased dramatically. The "Voting Rights Act of 1965" put teeth and specifics into the '64 Act and covered discrimination of language as well as race. It was renewed and amended in

1970, 1975, 1982 and 2006. It was specific to the point of requiring southern states to secure "preclearance" before they could even change the address of a voting location within a precinct.

The black elites ruling the majority of blacks today actually had their roots started long ago with the passage of the 13th, 14tH, and 15th Amendments, and the civil and voting rights acts passed since 1875. This legislation permitted the rise of the black elitist class to rule over their ignorant black brethren. The axiom that "absolute power corrupts absolutely" describes perfectly the chains of bondage attached to blacks by their own black opinion leaders. The dramatic increase in black suffrage and the resultant potential power achievable by harnessing millions of black votes attracted a new brand of scoundrel. These bloodsuckers came as black messiahs, champions of the black people, but were really just more carpet-baggers from their own neighborhood. Only this time around the carpet-baggers would not align themselves with Republicans, and they would not clear out of town with their 30 pieces of silver after their bags were full. The new generation of black carpet-baggers taking advantage of the "second reconstruction" were all attracted by money and power, and they were not all politicians. Let's look at a few of these unrepentant reprobates who unabashedly took advantage of the nations white guilt, and cared not a whit about the millions of disenfranchised blacks. Ladies first.

Maya Angelou (Marguerite Johnson) read her poem, "On the Pulse of Morning" at Bill Clinton's 1993 inauguration. This woman has an IQ of minus-three and had she been white she would have been thrown in a dumpster along with her nonsensical poems. Wake Forest University paid her a salary of $100,000 for doing nothing. A reporter went to interview her at the university and found her office was a broom closet. Carol Moseley-Braun was the first black female U.S. Senator and was elected from Illinois in 1992. Supposedly, she was defeated in 1998 for selling favors and stealing campaign money, but I think even the Soviet Republic of Illinois voters could look into her eyes and see that nobody was home. Clinton punished poor New Zealand by making her our ambassador there after she lost her Senate seat. If you remember Joycelyn Elders, you will understand why liberals today revere pariahs like Algore,

Michael Moore, Harry Reid, and Obama. As Surgeon General she undertook such monumental tasks as sex education, condoms, abortion, legal use of marijuana, and masturbation. She was too much for even Clinton to stomach so he fired her and she returned to Arkansas to teach. Pray for her students. Now, for the guys.

You probably remember Henry Louis Gates from the "beer-gate" affair where Obama called Police Officer, Sgt. Joseph Crowley, and the Cambridge Police Department "stupid" for the serious offense of asking Gates what his name was, and if he lived in the house he was trying to break into. Anyone that has read Gates' biography will understand his indignation at being questioned by a white guy. Gates, like his messiah Obama, is an unrepentant racist in addition to being perhaps the dumbest PhD in America. He is a product of affirmative action and like most black liberal professors, knows and teaches just one subject, "Black History." This is an easy subject for Gates and the others because they just make it up as they go. Gates can't spell or define "meritocracy," but he sure has "t-e-n-u-r-e" down pat. Gates' guiding principle throughout his life has been Afrocentrism.

Afrocentrism loosely translates into the idea that all civilization emanated from the African culture. It seems to have all started with the "Afrocentric" theory developed by one of Obama's heroes, W.E.B. Du Bois, who first employed it in the early 60's. Du Bois' theory was plagiarized by Molefi Kete Asante who used and expanded the idea profusely in his speeches and writings. I tend to agree with Robert Todd Carroll's position that Afrocentrism is "Pseudohistorical" with its prime goal of encouraging black nationalism and ethnic pride, but I disagree that it was the result of racism. Carroll uses the race card for the same reasons that members of the Black Caucus and other black elites use it; they can't explain their blunders any other way. Black professor, Clarence E. Walker, who teaches at University of California at Davis described Afrocentrism as "a mythology that is racist, reactionary, essentially therapeutic and is eurocentrism in black face." Another black, Gerald Early, has been especially critical, dismissing Afrocentrism as just another North American experiment in "group therapy"; "intellectual fast food for his less sophisticated brethren." Although I have read extensively on Afrocentrism for this book, I will not here refute all the many arguments by Cheikh Anta Diop, Cain Hope Felder, or George James. I will simply say that, were I a black man, I may have been desirous of finding truth in Afrocentric theory also, because it is human vainglory to want pride in yourself and your ancestors. But, if and when I discovered that the theory was supported on a foundation of clay and riddled with historical inaccuracies, I would have then abandoned it, and sought pride in myself and the provable accomplishments of my predecessors. The disproven theory is preached by most black college professors because it gives them something to add to their other hogwash in African-American studies. The manufactured tenants of Afrocentrism are like the manufactured tenures of the black college professors; meaningless and existing only to satiate vocal blacks. Whites always surrender to blacks, like Neville Chamberlain surrendered to Hitler, always thinking that this retreat will be the final one. It never is. All colleges and universities in the United States have blacks on their faculties teaching useless studies like black history, Afro-American Studies, and African this and African that. Please understand, if blacks want to believe what they teach and teach it to young blacks, then that's okay. But, why should schools pay these high salaries and make these subjects part of the core curriculum for all students when they are based on fabrications and have no useful application in our society?

To me, a black defending his belief in Afrocentric theory is like a white person saying they descend from a royal bloodline. Part of being an American and not living in Europe is not giving a damn whether your distant relatives lived in a castle or dug potatoes outside the castle. I make it a point to buy every one of Thomas Sowell's books because he is one of the wise men of our era, not because he is black or all culture emanated from his relatives. The same is true of Walter E. Williams, regardless if I read his column on the Townhall website or listen to him when he subs for Rush Limbaugh. Nobody could pay me enough to debate Alan Keyes. I've yet to find a subject on which he is not expert. If intelligence, wit, dark complexion, real slave blood in his veins, and morality were electable credentials he would have beat Obama in the 2004 Illinois Senate race, and maybe we would not be facing Obamageddon today. If you read "My Grandfather's Son" by Supreme Court Justice Clarence

Thomas you would better understand how blacks could rise to any level in any society and be a credit to the human race, not just the black race. I could go on and on about blacks like Herman Caine, James Golden (Bo Snerdley), Charles Payne, and a hundred other blacks who make me look like a rookie. But why? Ninety-nine percent of all blacks ignore these great Americans, and prefer the victimhood and government dole offered by the whoremongers and false prophets like Jesse Jackson, Jeremiah Wright, Al Sharpton, Lewis Farrahkhan, and Obama.

There are thousands of other blacks who leaped on the civil rights money-wagon, but space is short, so I will just mention the most flagrant ones. We have already covered the "reverends" in an earlier section who are blasphemous in their use of God to get into the pockets of both white corporations and the drooling black legions of these false prophets. I can't begin to write about all of the black "educators" who can't spell, or the corrupt black mayors and councilmen, or the inept national politicians who feed and nurture the perpetual "victimization" beast to keep their power and money flowing. But, let's mention a few.

Alcee Hastings is at the top of my list, but off the radar for most people, because scum like him would not even occupy a seat in the U.S. House if blacks voted for anybody besides other blacks. Hastings was appointed a federal judge for the Southern District of Florida by none other than "Jimma" Carter in 1979. In 1983 he was charged with soliciting bribes from defendants already convicted and awaiting sentencing, repeatedly lying throughout his trial, and actually passing along sensitive information obtained through a federal wiretap. His crimes were so onerous that the House of Representatives voted 413 to 3 (the nays were all from the black caucus) for the 17 articles of impeachment. The Senate followed suit and Hastings was kicked-off the bench. Not surprisingly, Alcee used the race card and yelled "racism" and the usual card players, Farrakhan, Jackson, Innis, and fat Al Sharpton, raced to the rescue of their fallen black victim. Then, Hastings added the charge of double jeopardy to the racism charge to see if either would stick. Being black and bold, he even sued the U.S. Senate and some of its staff. So obvious and blatant were his crimes that, lo and behold, even the NAACP abandoned him after all but three of his black brothers in the caucus turned their backs on him.

So, Alcee was an impeached federal judge destined to live a life of poverty, begging on the back alleys of Miami, right? Wrong! Luckily for Hastings there were only two requirements necessary to become a U.S. Congressman from Florida House District 23: (1) be a black brother and (2) have a (D) next to your name. Fortunately, there were no restrictions on being a crook, lying, disclosing secret wire taps, impeachment, or well, anything. So, easily meeting the two prerequisites, Alcee simply walked through his 1992 campaign, and didn't have to actually run a hard race for the office like most white candidates would have to do. Being a black guy in a black district he, of course, was elected in 1992 and was re-elected seven times since. He has proven once again that the only way a black Congressman can fail to be elected in a predominately black House district is to assume room temperature.

Charlie Rangel. How do you top this guy? He was elected to the 92nd Congress in 1971 and has been stealing and dealing ever since. Like Hastings, he represents a congressional district (15th New York) with a minority of whites. He had beat out Adam Clayton Powell in the 1970 election. Powell was another black House member who got caught with his hand in the cookie jar. But, since his constituent area is one of those "once black, never go back" gerrymandered congressional districts, Rangel easily won his first time out, and the next 18 times, too. Actually, Rangel is a likeable guy even though he is a whiner, thief, and racist. If he would just keep stealing, lay low, and shut-up about it like Hastings, it would be no big deal. But the guy is Chairman of the powerful Ways and Means Committee which materially impacts our nation and our lives.

Rangel has been a high-flyer and a free-spender for the last 40 years, but the Darkside media was too busy tailing Republicans around to notice that Rangel had been a very naughty boy. It took the privately-run National Legal and Policy Center (NLPC) to compare Charlie's House financial disclosure forms with the obvious and provable facts of the real world. After a lot of snooping and gumshoe sleuthing, the NLPC accumulated enough evidence to catch the attention of the House Ethics Committee, which is controlled by the majority Democrat Party and reluctant to investigate or indict their own crooks. After a lot of hand-wringing, the Ethics Committee finally is "looking" into six separate charges. Briefly, Rangel owns rental property at the Punta Cana Yacht Club in the Dominican Republic that rents for up to $1100 per night and is usually booked 100%, yet he has claimed income from a high of $5000 per year to $0 in most years. Like most good husbands, he first blamed it on his wife, and then blamed it on his non-fluency in the Spanish language. They are also investigating exemptions claimed on his Washington home, illegal fund-raising for the Charles B. Rangel Center for Public Service at City College of New York, and four rent-subsidized apartments in Harlem. Don't hold your breath if you expect to see Mr. Rangel behind bars. He has two cards he is fond of playing: the race card and the Korean War Vet card. Democrat crooks never go to jail. Like old soldiers, they "just fade away."

All 42 members of the House Black Caucus are dyed-in-the-wool racists, but most have enough smarts to fool their black constituents, and stay out of the limelight while stuffing their pockets, and giving a semblance of civility. Not so Maxine Waters. Her ignorance is on display for all to see. The beauty of being stupid is that when you are acting stupid, you are too stupid to realize you are acting stupid. This woman is not only stupid, but is a double-dip minority (female and black) and therefore exempt from being openly called stupid by her non-Democrat, non-black colleagues. She gets a free pass when accusing the CIA of creating AIDS to kill blacks in L.A., or claiming George Bush was seen planting dynamite in the levees around New Orleans, and then seeding clouds to create Katrina. More importantly, she and Barney (the Sodomite) got away with forcing the Treasury to bailout her black-owned OneUnited Bank for $12 million of TARP funds, so that she and hubby can pocket the capital gains profits. When the black officers of the bank were caught cruising around in Porsches, and buying Santa Monica beachfront homes with bank funds, they used the old standby and screamed, RACISM! Reprobates like Maxine Waters definitely benefited from their black victim status created by the civil rights propaganda and the feminazi hoopla from the 60's.

Of course, Waters' 35th Congressional District is blacker than black. She has managed to stumble through 10 terms and, assuming she does not assume room temperature, her blackness and (D) will keep her around to perpetuity. To really savor the unadulterated dumbness of this person, and add some humor to a deadly serious defect in our Congress, you must go to crewsmostcorrupt.org and see the dialogue between Waters and Federal Reserve Chairman Ben Bernanke on February 25, 2010. Forget about her basic understanding of the difference between the fed funds rate and the discount rate. This black dummy must have a hard time even dressing herself. What a pity that we have turned over the greatest nation on earth to subhuman primates like Maxine Waters.

Jesse Jackson Jr. is a good example that the fruit never falls far from the tree. His father's fame began with a lie that he held MLK in his arms while King was in the throes of death. Jesse Sr. then went on to bigger and better things, like extortion of funds from corporations and government, and knocking up a woman on his staff and paying her off with the extorted funds. His namesake son is an eight-term House member from the, you guessed it, all-black 2nd District of the Capone-controlled duchy of Chicago in the Soviet state of Illinois. When Chicago "Don" Obama became POTUS it left a vacant Senate seat to be filled by Governor "Hair" Blagojevich. Junior wanted to make Daddy proud and eliminate that bothersome procedure of a Senate campaign all in one fell swoop. So, he, his brother Johnny, and Raghuveer Nayak, got together with Hair and struck a deal to pay the latter $1.5 million. Too bad for both because the FBI had been listening to Hair's boring conversations until "Senate Candidate No. 5" came on the recorder and perked them up. Junior used the Clinton defense which was to deny and play dumb which, being his father's son, came natural for him.

The House Office of Congressional Ethics launched a "preliminary review" which in "congress-speak" means *"you got caught red-handed but since you are black we'll let this thing blow over and after most people have forgotten it we'll slap your wrist."* If you think that the FBI agents will include poor junior Jackson in their "political corruption crime spree" case against "Hair" Blagojevich, then you think wrong. Guess who the boss is over the FBI. If you guessed Eric "The Red" Holder, you would be correct. If you guessed he was black, you got it right again. Since Holder has made it a rule never to prosecute Black Panthers threatening whites with batons and nightsticks at a voting precinct, or pursue ACORN prostitution centers, or inconvenience poor innocent terrorists with an awful military trial, then do you think he will go after black junior Jackson who is the son of a famous black philanderer and extortionist? NOT!

When asked if he read the 2000 page House healthcare legislation before he voted on it, who said, "Of course not. It would take two lawyers two days to read that stuff"? If you guessed John Conyers, you would be correct. Conyers was one of the founders of the Congressional Black Caucus (CBC) way back in 1969. The CBC raised some $55 million from 2004 to 2008 extorting corporations and unions, and spent it on conventions, a new headquarters building, playing golf, and gambling. They gave less in scholarships to blacks than they spent on any single one of their conventions. The Black Caucus is a segregated group that opposes segregation. They worship diversity, but do not allow diversity of races in their group even though many white liberals have begged for admittance into the CBC. They pray at the altar of affirmative action, but deny all but members of the black race to participate in their closed society. Makes sense to them I guess. Conyers also authored and submitted the MLK holiday bill starting in 1968 and every year thereafter until it passed in 1983. So, now we dedicate a day each year to a philandering, traveling, false prophet who helped give us the incompetent Black Caucus, incompetent employees through affirmative action, and ultimately the worst joke ever played on Americans, Obama. Conyers has also authored and submitted H.R. 40 in 1989, and every year since, asking for white people to give reparations to blacks for slavery. Every black in the Black Caucus is a millionaire many times over. Are their relatives in Africa millionaires? How about thousandaires? Hundredaires, maybe? Or, do their African ancestors left behind make closer to the annual income of Obama's Kenyan half-brother, George, who makes $20 per year in the best of times and resides in his 6 ft. by 9 ft. "Hut, sweet hut?" How much should white people pay to billionaire Oprah Winfrey? How much do Conyers and the 40 million blacks owe us for their relatives enslaving 1.5 million of our white European relatives for 700 years? How much are we owed for the 619,000 whites who died in the Civil War or the 1.7 million that were wounded? I look forward to that reparation discussion, since their black bro Obama has ruined our economy and we whites sure could use some of Oprah's and the caucus's big bucks.

But, before we bother brother Conyers let's give him a little time to get accustomed to visiting his wife Monica in prison. It seems that pay-offs, bribes and kick-backs run in the Conyers and other black political families around Detroit. She was sentenced to 37 months in prison on March 12, 2010. This did not set well with her, so she screamed at the judge and begged to recant her confession. The Darkside, and even their spouses and lovers, are not accustomed to actually owning up for their crimes. Hubby John used his prestige to help her get elected to the Detroit City Council, and she took John's prestige and used it to squeeze contractors for favors. John got entangled in Monica's mess, too, when he reversed his opinion on a plan to inject sewage into the earth's subsurface after a contractor paid Monica $10,000. It's amazing how a man's mind changes when somebody gives his wife ten grand, huh? Monica was involved with Detroit Mayor Kwame Kilpatrick (who is now in the slammer) and tons of other black gangsters, but I get dizzy just trying to connect the dots. So, we won't go there right now. Kwame Kilpatrick, by the way, is the son of Carolyn Cheeks-Kilpatrick, another of the infamous Congressional Black Caucus members. The entire Black Caucus is a den of inequity and mimics the city of Detroit which is a crime-ridden, disgusting, and filthy place that should be razed to the ground and replaced with a productive asset like a landfill. Like all cities populated and run by blacks, it has no direction, no hope, and no future.

A simple way to calculate the likelihood and degree of corruption within any particular city in the United States is to compare the percentage of blacks. In other words, if the population is 50% black then there is a 50/50 chance of serious corruption. Detroit and Washington are virtually 100% controlled by blacks, so the corruption is 100%. Atlanta is about 60% so there is always black crime and corruption, but not enough to shut-down the whole city. We all know and love Washington's Mayor Marion Barry, the coke-smoking, whore-hopping, kick-back taking, and all around fun-loving guy. Finally, even D.C. had enough of old Barry and gave him some hard time to get his head screwed on right. After his vacation, the astute voters of D.C. checked his credentials and, sure enough, he was still black and still a Democrat, so they elected him again to the city council. Then, last year Barry did it again. At 73 he was caught smoking crack. Who wants to put a court jester like this in the slammer? He is not going to stop his bad habits, so why not put him out to pasture and give him a prescription for medical marijuana?

Barry's successor in Washington D.C. is 38 year old Adrian Fenty. Not to be outdone by his hyphenated African-American contemporaries, Fenty decided to call himself an Afro-Panamanian. Actually, he is an African-American-Italian-American-Afro-Panamanian American. Being young, black, carrying three Blackberries, and wearing a black fedora means Fenty will be around a long time. So far, the state-run media has chastised Fenty on his secret trips to the Middle East, using motorcades to shadow his jogs around D.C., not clearing-up the snow during February's snowstorms, stealing skybox seats at the Washington National's games, and awarding a mere $80 million in city contracts to his friends. No big deal in a black city of black folks that love all black people, especially crooked ones. If he can keep his girlfriends and dope-smoking behind closed-doors he will not have to suffer the distress of poor Marion.

Only in comic books or New York would you see a blind, black, philandering lieutenant governor replace a bald, ugly, bad-breathed (a guess on my part), white governor who charged visits to his prostitute on his credit card. That's exactly what happened when David Paterson took over the reins when Eliot Spitzer and his pay-for-play girlfriend got caught in the sack. Can you wrap your brain around the thought that the best our second largest state can do is pick two guys who cheat on their wives and smoke dope while the state goes bankrupt?

Above and in other parts of this book I have named some of the black beneficiaries of the civil rights movement. As so often happens in social change, the original goals of an honorable crusade get ambushed and bastardized by seedy, greedy usurpers. There were a number of sincere blacks in the civil rights movement starting in the latter 1800's right up to the 1960's. After that, things changed, and now all blacks in the civil rights, affirmative action, diversity, reparations, victimization movement speak with one tongue (forked), and act in unison like an automaton. Their brains are now all wired together. Whether one is a preacher, legislator, mayor, educator or SEIU thug, there are metes and bounds, rules and regulations, written and unwritten, standards by which all must comply or suffer chastisement by fellow blacks. They all feed at the common trough and must toe the line lest their house of cards will fall. I'm sure that among the thousands of multi-disciplined blacks included in this self-serving cabal there are a few with morals that find abortion or sodomy detestable. I know this to be true since I saw a video recently of John Conyers saying he is against federal funds for abortion. But, when crunch time came to vote on Obama's healthcare bill which included the federal funding for abortion, Conyers fell in line and voted for it. Conyers would have gotten the evil eye, and worse, from Obama had he done otherwise.

Prior to the "Second Reconstruction," people like Justice Thomas or Alan Keyes would have received the accolades they justly deserve. But, the devil's pact between the Darkside Democrats and the liberal black whores ended their recognition before it began. Imagine the strength and courage of these men who chose the right path, not the easy path. They and a handful of others like them would rather be called "Uncle Tom" than swim in the sewer of filth occupied by the likes of Jesse Jackson and Al Sharpton. Unlike Colin Powell, they had the courage of their convictions even when it came to not supporting the first semi-black President. Powell had been promoted way beyond his "Peter Principle" level all during his career just because he was black. But when his hand was called, he played the "race card" and voted for skin color, rather than what was good for the country that had been so good to him.

Great American minds like Justice Thomas, Walter E. Williams, Thomas Sowell, and Alan Keyes would be exactly where they are today had affirmative action, diversity, or racial equality never entered our vocabulary. But, virtually all of the black puppeteers of the Darkside would not be threatening America's very existence today were it not for these artificial props that branded all blacks with the stigma of inferiority. These black opportunists helped create the white guilt, and then used it, plus victimization, to entice a mass black following. There were many blacks from the 1870's to the 1960's that just wanted to ride in the front of a bus, drink out of a fountain not marked with "colored," and vote without paying a poll tax. These and many other requests or demands were reasonable. But, as the Darkside delivered the goods with affirmative action, welfare, and government largess, the majority of blacks increasingly gave blind obedience to them just as the German people did when Hitler first put bread on the tables of famished Germans. With virtually 100% of the world media in lockstep with the Darkside, and bolstered by our Victim-in-Chief, I think that blacks will continue marching right over the cliff with their pied pipers leading the way. It took 234 years for the greatest minds, combined with the lives of millions of whites, to create a society so fair that it allowed a 13% minority President to rule over the majority. When they succeed in tearing asunder the most extraordinary nation on earth they need not think of replacing it with one built in their own image. Once America is gone, chaos will reign till the end of time. Only then will the Darkside realize they not only stole the golden eggs, but killed the goose that laid them.

WHITE GUILT

Obama won the 2008 election with 52.6% of the popular vote. These voters were an assortment of communists, socialists, racists, abortionists, homosexuals, greennuts, Algore's global-warming freaks, unions, <u>and</u> ignorant whites that just felt terrible that somebody's white ancestors enslaved somebody's black ancestors. We'll call this group "guilters," since "birthers" and "truthers" are now a part of our lexicon. After 60 years of brainwashing by the media, liberal whites, and the black victim class, these whites hit upon the solution to erase this crushing stigma from their conscience. In one fell swoop they would make-up for their relatives' crimes by electing a black guy as President. It didn't matter which black guy; just any black guy would do. He didn't need to have real slave blood coursing through his veins, be a U.S. citizen, or even have worked a day in his life. It was okay if he hung around with terrorists like Bill Ayers and Frank Davis, and racists like Jeremiah Wright and Lewis Farrahkan. His consumption of alcohol and designer drugs just made him more like the rest of us. None of this really mattered because he had the one critical ingredient: blackness. They couldn't believe their eyes and ears when "their" boy-wonder beat out John McCain. They felt like the weight of the world had been lifted from their shoulders, and the shackles of slavery had finally been broken.

White guilt is not really a new phenomenon. Neither is it politically correct because it may offend both races. It is a disease contracted mostly by whites who have consumed, swallowed, and digested huge quantities of drivel spewed out by the progressive elitists until the virus reached their brains and filled their empty skulls. It is actually a form of racism. But this brand of racism is against their own race, because they feel other whites don't "feel their pain" about the plight of the poor black race like they do. They mollify their conscience by pandering and patronizing a whole race of people based solely on the color of their skin. It matters not if they are rapists, murderers, or thieves. They see all blacks as helpless, hopeless, and hapless; incompetent to drag themselves up from the Stone Age by themselves without the continuing extended hand of white benefactors. They didn't know enough history to realize that every individual and every race must eventually succeed on its own effort because equality artificially created is always unsustainable over time.

I would not write about white guilt were it not one of the critical elements that placed this nation in critical mass by facilitating the election of Obama. There is no empirical scientific method to arrive at the number of votes shifted to Obama by whites ashamed of their own skin color, and seeking redemption of a perceived wrong. But, from personal observation, even from my home here in the South, I think it was possibly as high as 5% to 7% of the popular vote. Since Obama won by a margin of less than 3%, white guilt was a critical factor in electing him.

Being an avid reader of everything printed for the past 60 years I admit never being aware of "black guilt" in Africa, or "brown guilt" in South America, to justify blacks or browns electing a white guy as president. Therefore, I must not only conclude that white guilt is a phenomena unique among whites, but that whites are the only race capable of self-flagellation for being a member of their own race. They see the prosperity of the white race and the white race itself as inherently evil, and will support any and all legislation to "equalize" the races. I have developed my personal theory to refute the guilters.

The underlying foundational belief of the white guilters is that the white race alone is evil and preys on the weakness of other races, mainly the black race. The real question is: would the other races have acted similar if the rolls of whites and blacks had been reversed in history? This is the gist of my "If they could've, they would've" concept. Since we can't create a parallel universe I will try and revisit some past perceived white injustices and determine if it was really a "white thing."

Imagine thousands of blacks looking over millions of square miles of beautiful arable land and not a damn lazy fellow black around to help till the fields. Along comes a ship full of young white slaves and their black captain offers to sell them to the black land owners for field labor. The blacks have a tough choice: scratch out a meager subsistence on a couple acres, or buy these white guys and cultivate thousands of acres while sipping mint juleps on the veranda. Let's see, what to do? Will they say, "We be po now and we'll just stay po cuz dees here white folks be humans jus like we'inz and just cuz daa be dumb don't mean we should deny them dere civil rights"? Do you suppose they would forego prosperity and growth and improvement of their land out of humility and self-sacrifice? Or, would they buy the whites and mostly treat them like the valuable assets they represented? The logical, common sense conclusion is the latter.

Let's apply my theory to more recent events to see if blacks are inherently superior to the evil whites in their compassion. There are now more black millionaires (and even a black billionaire) in the United States than the rest of the world combined. There are 42 members of the Congressional Black Caucus. They wield great power and are all millionaires. Black Obama is President of the only superpower. Blacks have "arrived," right? They are now equal, right? Sorry, like Obama said in his book, "Better is not enough." It will never, ever be enough. Has the new power and wealth of the black elites been spread around to their own less fortunate people? No, black unemployment is still twice the national rate. Has the new affluence and secured civil rights improved out-of-wedlock births, education, or crime rate? No, again. Over 70% of black babies are born to single black women, 60% of blacks drop out of school and 25% of young black men are in prison. Do blacks perform better in the cities run by blacks? If you mean like Washington D.C., New Orleans, Atlanta, or Detroit, the answer is no, again. They are all the murder capitals of America, and all the black mayors and city councilmen leave office early on their way to prison.

Saying that some people are guilty of white guilt is really a euphemistic way of calling them racist. In other words, they hate members of their own race based only on color of skin. They differ from other whites who vote against anyone who is conservative, pro-life, Republican, or anything pro-American. No, these "guilters" are ashamed of perceived racism and can't understand why other whites don't feel the same. They think any white person that fails to see their logic or don't become instantly enamored with their messiah is a bigot beyond help. They see every white as related to some distant plantation owner who kept blacks in chains and servitude. Any garbage man, rapper, dumpster diver, and yes, even community organizer, is preferable over any white guy as long as he is black. Poor Hillary. She sure picked the wrong year to run for prez, huh?

I live in the beautiful North Georgia Mountains about a 100 miles north of Atlanta. We have virtually no blacks and consequently little crime. We do have many blacks that come up from Atlanta to rent cabins. There was a letter to the editor in our local newspaper on February 5, 2010, from a black lady who had visited our scenic mountains. She wrote the following:

"On Friday, Jan. 29, 2010 my boyfriend and I visited Chase Mountain on Kyle Road for a weekend trip. Not heeding to the weather alerts, we ventured on our way up Chase Mountain. Upon rounding a few curves and bends, our car became stuck, as it was clear that the roads on Chase Mountain were impassable. Having very few options, we attempted to walk up the mountain to our cabin. While walking, I became extremely fatigued and experienced dizziness and lightheadedness and collapsed. My boyfriend called 911 after getting me to a nearby residence of a Mr. Curtis Young. This is where the purpose of my letter starts. The Fannin County EMT's, volunteer firefighters, paramedics arrived on the scene in spite of harsh conditions. They cared for me with the utmost of care. They attended to me and were extremely helpful and generously kind with their time, actions and deeds. What later

proved to be a menial panic attack and exhaustion, the Fannin County EMT's, volunteer firefighters, and paramedics treated me with the same care and concern as if I were in the most severe of conditions. Through snow, sleet and bitter temperatures compounded with rugged terrain, they transported me by sled down the mountain to a waiting ranger truck and then to a waiting ambulance that transported me to the Fannin County Hospital. After being released from the hospital, a sheriff's deputy transported us to a local hotel to retire for the evening. I am a young black female, and I was raised with the notion that people in mountain towns were racist and rude. Fannin County proved me so wrong today. The volunteers and emergency workers that came to my rescue were some of the nicest individuals I have ever met. I am grateful and Fannin County should be honored to have such extraordinary men on its team. While I feel completely awful for imposing on the times of individuals that could have tried to help people in much worse conditions, I am also extremely appreciative of the time, care, concern and efforts of the Fannin County EMT Department, the volunteer firefighters, volunteer rescue personnel, paramedics, rangers, and sheriff's department that came to my aid. Please find a way to thank these guys for what they do to help people. It is my prayer, that God will bless them abundantly. May God bless your county. Signed Paquita Austin Morgan."

    This young lady was from Atlanta. Her preconceived, prejudgment of southern people is not unique or surprising. Just as the northeast liberals brought on the Civil War with their skewed ideas about the South, and just as the black elites today foment racism with manufactured southern beliefs, so do racists like Jeremiah Wright and Obama stir the race pot every chance they get to keep their black cattle herd from straying. Regardless whether Ms. Morgan was visiting a mountain cabin or walking along the nearby Appalachian Trail at night, she would be infinitely safer here than we whites would be strolling along Moreland Avenue in Atlanta in either day or night. I do not blame Ms. Morgan for her apprehension. After sixty years of media propaganda and liberal hype from the black elites, you would think we southerners have lynchings of blacks for entertainment following our possum barbeques. Like I've said, white racism is rare, black racism is raging.

A few personal observations on white guilt. I think out of the box a lot and seem to notice things other people don't. For instance, have you seen the Broadview Security (formerly Brinks Security) ads on TV? They are on Fox News every day. Typically, they show a white woman alone or with her daughter, coming into their home and immediately punching in their code on their security keypad. The scene shifts outside to one or two burglars sneaking around the yard, or a guy in a track suit tying his shoe laces out front. Next, the burglar(s) burst or kick-in the door and sets off the alarm. The burglars scatter and the phone rings. It's the security company asking if all is okay. The lady says, "No," and the police are on the way. Crisis over! All would be normal with this ad except for one detail; 100% of the burglars are 100% white, no blacks, Asians, or even Hispanics, just white. FBI crime stats tell us that 73% of all violent crimes are committed by blacks. Is that equality or diversity at work? Why are blacks not angry at being under-represented in the honorable field of burglary? Can you spell P-A-N-D-E-R-I-N-G or P-A-T-R-O-N-I-Z-I-N-G?

In the same vein, have you noticed TV ads in general since Obama became President? Every ad it seems now has a black actor in it. You can hardly see an ad on anything without blacks. We have always seen blacks in TV ads since they represent 13% of the population, but if population percentage was based on blacks in TV commercials I would have to conclude they made up at least 75% of the population. Another change is the number of blacks on TV sit-coms, serial shows, and movies. I have local Atlanta stations included in my satellite programming and would expect more black exposure because Atlanta is 63% black. Black talk shows, anchors, and reporters actually outnumber whites and that's fine based on the population. My theory on the explosion of blacks on TV is that the companies producing the products in the ads, and the companies owning the products, think that Obama or the "black police" (Jackson/Sharpton) will somehow look more favorably on them if they put more blacks in the ads. I even see blacks selling and demonstrating products which few blacks use or buy. Again, this is pandering and patronizing, but I think I am the only one who notices these things. So I guess it doesn't matter.

Another peculiarity that I have picked-up on in TV and movies that nobody but me has noticed, is the pecking order that has evolved since the civil rights tripartite of affirmative action, diversity, and equality came into being. This pecking order has also been more pronounced since Obama took office. The pecking order from highest to lowest is black women first, then black men, then other minorities, then white women, and finally, white men. By "pecking order" I mean that, for example, black women are shown in a better light, or perhaps more intelligent that those lower on the totem pole. If the ad is about a particular product it will be the one higher up the pole explaining the advantage of the product to one lower on the pole. A black male is never shown to be inferior or stupid unless it is a black woman doing the dirty deed. White guys are always slow, fat, bald and stupid. Since white guys represent most of the world's physicists, scientist, inventors, and researchers, is this depicting reality or again pandering to blacks? Is this a "feel good" practice or does it give minorities a false sense of superiority that they will not see in the real world? If whites really see blacks as equal then why can't blacks sometimes be portrayed as a dunce even once in a while?

When either blacks or whites commit heinous crimes I want to see the perpetrators caught and hanged, electrocuted, shot, guillotined, or euthanized. But, do the majority of blacks feel this way when blacks are the perps? I think not. Let's look at a few crimes on both sides of the race scale.

Three civil rights workers, one black and two Jewish males, were murdered on June 21, 1964. President Johnson, the FBI, and even the Colombo crime family of the Mafia was asked to assist. Six men were tried, convicted, and sentenced to prison. Two were released, including Edgar Ray Killen, because the jury refused to convict them. Three movies, "Attack on Terror: The FBI Vs. The Ku Klux Klan," "Mississippi Burning," and "Murder in Mississippi" dramatized the case. A white reporter for the Jackson Clarion-Ledger produced a documentary for the National History Day contest, and worked tirelessly on his own investigation. Mississippi Governor Haley Barbour (evil white Republican) joined 1500 residents of Philadelphia, Mississippi, in calling for a new trial for Edgar Ray Killen. Finally, on June 21, 2005, 41 years after the crime, Killen, then 80 years old, was sentenced to 3 terms of 20 years each, i.e.: death.

Medgar Evers was killed on June 12, 1963. Byron De La Beckwith was tried twice for the murder in 1964, but acquitted. Beckwith was a Marine combat vet having fought at Guadalcanal and wounded at the Battle of Tarawa, and awarded the Presidential Unit Citation (twice), Asiatic-Pacific Campaign Medal with three bronze service stars, Good Conduct Medal, World War II Victory Medal, and Purple Heart. This all would make no difference in the pursuit of justice. Beckwith was 74 years old in 1994 when a jury of 8 blacks and 4 whites found him guilty of the 31 year-old crime, and sentenced him to life in prison where he died in 2001.

On January 24, 2007, James Ford Seale was charged with two counts of kidnapping and one count of conspiracy in the murders of two black men, Charles Eddie Moore and Henry Hezekiah Dee on May 2, 1964. On August 24, 2007, 43 years after the crimes, Seale was sentenced to three life terms.

The above three cases involved crimes against blacks by whites. The prosecutors, FBI agents, investigators, judges, and a majority of the juries were all white. Even though it took sometimes over 40 years, the crimes were solved and the criminals brought to justice. Can white victims of black crime expect the same courageous, colorblind pursuit of justice from blacks? Let's look at a few black on white crimes and see.

Between 10:15PM and 10:40PM on June 12, 1994, Nicole Brown Simpson was found outside her Brentwood condo stabbed through the throat to the point of near decapitation with her vertebrae almost severed completely. Nearby was the body of 26 year old Ronald Goldman also with multiple stab wounds. Nicole's two children were asleep inside the condo. A bloody glove and other evidence pointed to Nicole's ex-husband, O.J. Simpson. Simpson's lawyer, Robert Kardashian, convinced Los Angeles Police to allow Simpson to turn himself in voluntarily, even though he was facing a double murder charge which carries a possible death sentence. Immediately after the murders, Simpson had flown to Chicago. He promised to return to Los Angeles right away. When Simpson failed to turn himself in by 2PM the next day police issued an all points bulletin.

Kardashian read a note from Simpson to reporters that said, "First, everyone understand I had nothing to do with Nicole's murder...Don't feel sorry for me. I've had a great life." Taking this as a suicide note, the police traced Simpson's cell phone and found him driving north on I-405 in a white Bronco with his friend Al Cowlings. Cowlings yelled to police that Simpson had a gun to his own head so they dropped back from following him too close. Driving only 35 MPH Simpson and Cowlings drove to Simpson's home where he surrendered. Being a millionaire and famous, Simpson hired a "dream team" of lawyers that included F. Lee Bailey, Robert Shapiro, Alan Dershowitz, Robert Kardashian, Carl E. Douglas, and Johnnie Cochran. Even DNA lawyers Barry Scheck and Peter Neufeld were employed.

A grand jury was seated to hear the evidence. Brentwood resident, Jill Shively, testified that she saw Simpson speeding away from Nicole's house so fast on the night of the murders that his Bronco almost collided with a Nissan at the intersection of Bundy and San Vicente Boulevard. Jose Camacho, a knife salesman at Ross Cutlery, said he sold Simpson a 15-inch German-made knife like the one used in the murders just three weeks before the crime. Neither of these witnesses was allowed to testify at the trial because they sold their stories to "Hard Copy" and "National Enquirer." On July 29 the judge ruled that there was sufficient evidence to try Simpson for murder, and when asked how he pled Simpson said, "Absolutely, one hundred percent not guilty." The trial began on January 25, 1995.

The prosecution called dozens of expert witnesses that proved that Simpson drove to Nicole's with intent to kill her. She answered the door; Simpson grabbed her before she could scream and started stabbing her. Ronald Goldman showed-up while he was stabbing Nicole so Simpson held Goldman in a choke-hold with one hand while stabbing him repeatedly in the neck and chest. Then, he returned to Nicole, pulled her head back by the hair, put his foot on her back, and slit her throat severing her carotid artery. He had left a trail of blood from the condo to the alley behind it, and all the way to his home on Rockingham Drive. One dark glove was found at the murder scene with its match found at Simpson's home. One had Goldman's blood on it. Many witnesses said Simpson had previously beaten Nicole and thrown her across the room while threatening to kill her many times. No witness refuted the prosecutions charge that timing and evidence left only the conclusion that Simpson killed both the victims. Former NFL player and pastor, Rosey Grier, and Los Angeles County Jail guard, Jeff Stuart, both testified that during Grier's visit Simpson had yelled that he didn't mean to do it. Rosey said he urged Simpson to come clean. The evidence was ruled hearsay and not allowed.

I don't have the space in this book to detail over 134 days of testimony. Suffice it to say that the evidence was overwhelming. So, Johnnie Cochran decided to use a tried and proven tactic, racism and white guilt. When Cochran played the race card, prosecutor Darden disputed the charge of racism saying that police had gone to Simpson's house 8 times on domestic violence calls without arresting him before finally citing him on the ninth call. Also, they had waited 5 days before arresting him on a double murder charge. Then Cochrane hit the jackpot. He had discovered that detective Mark Fuhrman had lied when asked if he ever uttered the term "nigger." When Fuhrman said no, Cochrane produced a 19 year old tape from a female former friend where he had said the word. During Cochran's jury summation he compared Fuhrman to Adolf Hitler and called him a racist, a perjurer, America's worst nightmare, and the personification of evil.

The verdict was predictable. First, the trial was not held in the Brentwood jurisdiction where the murders occurred. This was standard practice. Instead, it was held in a largely black-dominated jurisdiction nearby. Next, assistant Darden was an inept black who was duped into allowing Simpson to try on the glove by Cochran who knew it had shrank from exposure to blood and freezing temperatures. This was the source of Cochran's "If it doesn't fit, then acquit" chant which was picked-up by the crowds of blacks outside the courtroom. But, the real death knell was the selection of the jury. The racist "dream team" got even more than they could have hoped for: 9 blacks, 1 Hispanic, and 2 whites. None read newspapers, 8 watched tabloid TV shows, 5 thought it was sometimes okay to use force on a family member, all were Democrats, 5 reported they had a negative experience with the police, and 9 thought Simpson was less likely to be a murderer because he was a professional athlete. The white guilt of the judge, public, media, and even the prosecutors worked again to give Simpson every benefit of every doubt, and it was sufficient to remove whatever doubts the racist jury may have harbored.

I could easily write a lengthy book on how white guilt aids and abets black crime because of the fear of whites to confront the "race card." But, I won't. Well, maybe a few comments on Rodney King.

Rodney King was tooling down Interstate 210 on March 2, 1991; doing about 100 MPH. Cops got on his tail, so Rodney exited the freeway and zoomed through residential streets at 80 MPH with squad cars and helicopters after him. After about 10 minutes the cops cornered his car and asked him and his two passengers to exit the vehicle. King had been drinking and toking all day, and feared a DUI charge would look bad on his parole conviction for burglary. So, he started dancing around, grabbing his butt, and generally acting silly and refusing to cooperate. Officer Stacey Koon told the other three officers to execute a "swarm," which is a technique involving multiple officers that grab a suspect all at the same time with empty hands to subdue him. King went crazy, and being a huge man he tossed the officers around like toys. Koon ordered them back and tasered King twice. When King attacked the officers again they whacked him with batons, wrestled him to the ground and cuffed him.

As usual, a guy named George Holliday was videotaping all this from his apartment balcony. Mr. Holliday called the police and told them he had the video, but they brushed it off. Big mistake. The media didn't brush it off and the rest is history. King had suffered a fractured facial bone and a broken right ankle along with bruises and lacerations. Although the officers had followed SOP for subduing doped-up drunks, the bleeding-heart public is used to kinder-gentler treatment of criminals and, unlike the police, they don't put their lives on the line every day. They would have preferred the officers sit down, have a beer with Mr. King, and ask him to please slip the handcuffs over his wrists. The public outcry demanded a trial and they got one. The four officers, Koon, Powell, Briseno, and Wind went on trial and were all acquitted on April 29, 1992, except Powell, who was charged with using excessive force, but no punishment was decided upon. It's an established American custom that when a white police officer gets away with hitting or shooting a black criminal that the blacks receive free TV's, liquor, furniture, and whatever else they can haul out of stores after breaking the windows. It is also the signal for opening day of hunting season on whites, and there is no daily bag limit on this species of big game. So any white seen roaming around is fair game. Being aware of this practice, the Los Angeles riots of 1992 officially got under way.

The verdict came at 3:15PM on Wednesday, April 29, 1992, and the blacks started without delay looting, attacking vehicles, and any white person they could find. Who can forget watching truck driver Reginald Denny get his brains bashed out with a concrete block on live TV. Besides his physical damage, his speech, and ability to even walk were permanently damaged. Fidel Lopez was ripped out of his truck, smashed repeatedly in the head with a car stereo, had his ear cut-off and had black spray paint covering his chest, torso, and genitals. The next day started off more calm because the blacks were hung-over from Wednesday's festivities and were deciding where to put all their new shiny appliances and other loot. Later, after resting up, they decided to go back for a second helping of free stuff. They brought their Zippos along this time.

While the blacks were enjoying a fun day of looting and toasting marshmallows over the burning buildings, some of them made the mistake of looting businesses in Koreatown. They had grown accustomed to robbing and killing whities because they were full of white guilt, and didn't put up much of a fuss. These damn Koreans hadn't lived in the states long enough to realize that blacks were the incompetent victims of society and permitted to loot, rob, rape and burn at will. The Koreans still believed in that foolish thing called "work." So, the Koreans surrounded their stores and stood on rooftops with shotguns and rifles. Soon, the blacks left Koreatown for easier "pickins." Bill Cosby, President G.H.W. Bush, Mayor Bradley (black), and even the idiot Rodney King went on TV and uttered those immortal words, "Can't we all just get along?" Too late, the word was out about free TV's and liquor and all of the blacks wanted their fair share of the booty.

To avoid being a distraction from the black festivities, the Los Angeles Lakers, Portland Trail Blazers, Los Angeles Clippers, Utah Jazz, Dodgers, Expos, horse racing, Van Halen and Michael Bolton concerts, and even wrestling events were cancelled.

By the 6th day of the L.A. riots, blacks had forgotten what had happened to cause all these free things to fall into their laps, or the unexpected, unscheduled hunting season for shooting whites on sight. Also, they were running out of places to loot and burn. Most distressing of all was that whites were getting scarce on the streets, and Koreans were shooting back so that it was not fun anymore. Then, two things happened to make them call it a day and go home and count up the loot. First, thousands of Army and Marine troops came pouring in. Their guns weren't loaded, but blacks didn't know that. Second, the white guilt had surged in the hearts of our valiant leaders and the Justice Department in Washington said they would bring justice to the blacks if nobody else would. So, they began a federal investigation into poor Rodney King's beating.

Of course, Maxine Waters, Jesse Jackson, and the first black Presidential candidate, Bill Clinton, came to heap their pity on the poor black folks. Until the federal Gestapo could punish the cops, the local justice system threw the blacks a bone by sentencing Korean shop-owner, Soon Ja Du, to 5 years probation for shooting a black who was looting his store. President Bush said the riots were "purely criminal" and Vice-President Dan Quayle said they were caused by a "poverty of values." This didn't sit well with the black community because they do not like to hear the truth uttered in plain English. They much preferred the mushy words of Clinton, Jackson, and Waters telling them they were blameless, that TV's and liquor were a down-payment on reparations, and that all will be well if they keep voting Democrat.

Blacks kept voting Democrat and sure enough all turned out well. Officers Briseno and Wind were reprimanded and lost their careers. Officer Powell and Koon were sent to prison for 30 months. Hero Rodney King was awarded $3.8 million bucks, part of which he used to open his own hip-hop music label "Straight Alta-Pazz Recording Company." In '93 he was placed on probation for crashing his car into a block wall. In '95 he spent 90 days in the slammer for trying to run-down his wife with the family car. In '03 drunken Rodney slammed his SUV into a house, breaking his pelvis. In 2007 he said he was shot in the face and body by another black trying to steal his bicycle. Yes, if it hadn't been for those racist white police officers Rodney King would have continued to be a credit to his race.

The Los Angeles Riots lasted six days. Although many blacks didn't even know who Rodney King was during, or after, the riots, they still managed to get 53 people killed, injure another 2000, set 3600 buildings on fire, destroy another 1100 buildings, and cause $1 billion in damages. What should have been a source of shame for the blacks was transformed into political advantage for the likes of Bill Clinton, Jesse Jackson, and Maxine Waters. Is it any wonder that we see only hopelessness and despair with arsonists like these throwing gasoline on the fires that are consuming our republic.

I've shown you briefly how whites relentlessly pursued other whites who had committed crimes against blacks, and how blacks all over the country were flushed with joy that one of their own could legally slaughter two innocent whites and laugh about it. Then, their joy turned to euphoria as their brothers and sisters were rewarded for killing people and burning down Los Angeles, and finally to ecstasy upon seeing four white cops lose their careers and two of them go to prison. Yes, white guilt was alive and well.

White guilt is the gift that keeps on giving. Obama said it better when he said in his first book "better isn't good enough." He meant that while blacks have raked in a lot of bucks and accumulated enormous power by playing the role of victims, they must now adopt Ethan Allen's brave last words, "we have just begun to fight." Like Jackson, Sharpton, and thousands of others feeding at the public trough, Obama has indeed struck it rich in the victim business. But, unlike the "Justice Brothers," Obama has used his blackness to catapult him to the top spot, while the reverends remain in the trenches groveling over the miniscule millions extorted from the nervous white corporations. Obama knows he has the whites on the run and now is not the time to relax the reins. Like Hitler, Marx, and Stalin before him, he knows the shock value of rapid fire initiatives and changes to keep the enemy (white conservatives) confused and dazzled. He allows John Conyers to submit his reparations bill, but knows his white opponents will feel a victory when it never even advances to committee, and doesn't get his Obama's support. Why pursue a lump sum, one-time, complicated payment like reparations when blacks can be assured of a lifetime annuity unto death from the white money machine. Why work, be competent, or actually produce anything when white guilt supplies all needs and upward mobility, too. If the white guilt was sufficient to elect to the Presidency a pot-smoking, cocaine-sniffing, racist who never broke sweat, and can't say two words without a teleprompter, then the best advice is to keep doing the same thing. Don't rock the boat. The whites are like the "shmoos" in Lil Abner; they just keep on supplying all that blacks need and require nothing in return. When whites get out of line, blacks need only remind them that their ancestors were once enslaved and no amount of money or effort can ever repay them for the horrors endured. It matters not that their messiah is President, or Oprah is a billionaire, or that thousands of blacks have become millionaires living in this racist country while their more fortunate African brethren remained behind in the luxury of the motherland in their cute little mud "Hut, sweet huts."

DIVERSITY, AFFIRMATIVE ACTION AND EQUALITY

Supposedly, the civil rights movement was intended to end segregation, and achieve equality between the black and white races. When I grew-up in Illinois' integrated schools blacks were referred to mostly as negroes and rarely as "niggers" when parents weren't around. Back then we meant no ill feelings toward blacks by the term. Even though we lived only 10 miles from East Saint Louis, which was 100% black, our area had no blacks, so we had no reason to like or dislike them because they were not a big part of our lives. It was about the same when we moved to Pompano Beach, Florida, in 1958 even though segregation was in effect in Florida then. The blacks had a new high school and neither school had much contact with each other. I only remember that the black high school seemed like a quiet, well-run school where the students were clean, well-dressed, and went there to learn, not what they go to school for today. The school system was integrated after I left, but I know that all schools in the U.S. have gone downhill since integration. We never had stabbings, fights, or riots in the late 50's.

So, did the civil rights successes from 1865 to 2010 end segregation of the races and make everybody equal? No, on both questions. The minute segregation officially ended blacks promptly renamed it "diversity" and went right on complaining about everything. When they reached equality they didn't even slow down, but kept on zooming ahead to inequality. Only this time the blacks wanted to be "more" equal than the whites, like Obama's "better isn't enough" statement. Understandably, they didn't want to be called "niggers," so that word was virtually banned and replaced by "negro." Not happy with negro, we were told to call them "colored" which covered mixed-bloods, also. Then, they decided to exclude mixed-bloods and limit membership in their race by labeling it "black." Later, the black "powers that be" decided to make membership even more restrictive in their race club by calling themselves "Afro-American." Last, but not least, since Afro seemed chic and less proper, and more like a hairdo, they settled on "African-American." Now, they were among the exalted hyphenated class while whites kept their same old boring moniker with no hyphen.

Affirmative action entered our vocabulary when John Kennedy mentioned it in his 1961 inaugural speech. Lyndon Johnson put it into action after Kennedy was gone. It slowly leeched into every part of our government, education, and private sector economy. It became standard operating procedure at all federal, state, and local governmental offices to give blacks special treatment when hiring or promoting. Civil rights activists next scrutinized every university, college, junior college, and grade school, making sure blacks were receiving handicapped, "victim" recognition ahead of whites, both in faculty and student considerations. Simultaneously, they made the rounds at private employers making sure blacks got preferential treatment.

The first serious obstacle to the expanding use of racial quotas throughout the nation came in the 1978 Supreme Court's decision in the Alan Bakke affirmative action case. Bakke was white. He had applied to attend the medical school at the University of California at Davis and was denied because the limited openings had been given to blacks with inferior scores. The court ruled that racial quotas were unconstitutional. As usual, liberals in the federal and state governments and the courts continue to this day to find ways to bypass and circumvent this silly notion that we should actually pay attention to our Constitution.

When discussing affirmative action there are two competing theories in the Civil Rights Act of 1964 according to the Supreme Court: "disparate impact" which supports the use of affirmative action programs to increase minority representation in the work force, and "disparate treatment" which precludes the use of race in an employer's decision-making process and thus supports claims of reverse discrimination. Even with the Supreme Court ruling in favor of the disparate treatment theory most government, educational institutions, and private businesses willingly or unwillingly adopted disparate impact as their SOP. Later, in the 1971 case, Griggs vs. Duke Power Company, the Supreme Court further defined disparate impact theory to disallow consideration of a high school diploma or aptitude tests in hiring practices, saying it violated the Civil Rights Act. California and Michigan both amended their constitutions to prohibit racial quotas, but even that does not stop liberals from circumventing the law. Ward Connerly (black), former University of California Regent, wrote an article entitled "Study, Study, Study-A bad Career Move" in the June 2, 2009, edition of "Minding the Campus (www.mindingthecampus.com)." Mr. Connerly tells of a conversation with a high-ranking UC administrator in which the administrator wanted to increase diversity. When asked why he wanted to increase diversity his response was that the school would be overrun with Asians if something wasn't done. When Connerly asked what was wrong with that, the administrator said that Asians are "too dull...they study, study, study." Then he warned Connerly that he would deny having the conversation if he mentioned it to anyone.

The reason the administrator was trying to increase diversity, and cull the number of Asians is that California had passed Proposition 209 back in 1996 outlawing racial discrimination in college enrollment. Asian enrollment at all nine UC campuses shot up to over 40% with Riverside at 43%, UCLA at 38%, UC Berkeley at 42% and UC Irvine at 55%. Asians make up just a 13% minority in California. The UC Regents have drawn-up a new set of rules to reward the dedication of the Asian students by barring them from admission to the University starting in 2010. Among the new rules will be one eliminating automatic admission for students in the top 12.5 percentile, and eliminating the need for some students to even take the SAT tests. Connerly concludes by saying, "There is one truth that is universally applicable in the era of diversity, especially in American universities: an absolute unwillingness to accept the verdict of colorblind policies." Commenting on this article, Thomas

Sowell (black) said "Hypocrisy is part and parcel of the liberal academic elite. But the American people, who fund universities either as parents, donors or taxpayers, should not accept this evilness and there's a good way to stop it - cut off the funding to racially discriminating colleges and universities."

I have yet to disagree with Thomas Sowell on anything. To me he's an icon. However, cutting off funds for educational institutions that discriminate is going to be tough. On March 4, 2010, students, teachers, unions, and radicals held protests all over the United States. They called it the "National Day of Action to Defend Education." It was held to protest the cut-backs by states and the federal government necessitated by a sick economy. It was really about thousands of spoiled kids getting grants and tax money cut off, and teachers not getting their usual increases to their exorbitant tenured salaries. What's scary are the groups organizing the protests. Reading the lists of groups makes memories of the sixties come streaming back. Most of them represented socialists, anti-imperialism, communists, revolutionists, anti-war groups, progressives, and radicals wanting to take back the southwest states or kill all capitalists. Some of the hundreds of groups in 127 metro areas screaming and carrying signs were Young Democratic Socialist, Students for a Democratic Society, Movimiento Estudiantil Chican de Aztlan, Million Worker March Movement, and Solidarity & Defense Fighters of America.

Returning to Connerly's article about UC Asians, I would like to add a few comments of my own. The last time I looked in the mirror I was still a white guy. I graduated from the University of South Florida in 1969. Unlike Obama, no group paid for my tuition. I had the GI Bill, unloading semi-trucks, and working as a student assistant to thank for paying my way through college. Even back then we had a lot of Asian students and my recollection is that most of them were pretty sharp students. It seemed to me they were very disciplined and from families that encouraged them to excel. I think that is still true today. If the Asians are smarter than the blacks or whites then let them occupy any and all admission slots that they earn on a merit basis. The people that want to artificially "level" the field are either blacks, or PC administrators and professors that fear blacks. In the real world intelligence cannot be faked for long. Blacks are fine to teach black history or Afrocentrism, but these are useless subjects, heavy on pride, but light on substance, and would be best removed from the education curricula. Of course, that would put all the so-called black professors like Henry Gates out of a job. But, if Asians are denied admission then who would enter the fields of chemistry, physics, and medicine? Who would do the scientific research and make advances in medicine? Just as the same-sex dinosaurs in "Jurassic Park" found a way to reproduce, so will Asians find a way to get into the education system and excel. So, why hold them back? Equality cannot be forced even if affirmative action is perpetual because it cannot create something that does not exist. As stated in earlier arguments, the races have had 6000 years to be judged, and laws today are not going to change the innate intelligence generally existing in each race right now.

Like Asian superiority in the abstract sciences, blacks are obviously better in physical endeavors. They represent over 70% of the college basketball players and 95% of the NBA basketball players. They are also 61% of the NFL football athletes and 43% of the professional baseball players. That's okay with me. Being a minority, if affirmative action, diversity, and equality had been enforced when I was in college, I should have played basketball and football to balance the black dominated teams. I would not have lasted a New York minute on the court, and even less on the gridiron before being stomped by the black players, because I would have been where I was out-classed and didn't belong. Why will blacks and liberals not realize that they are placing blacks where they are also out-classed and do not belong?

We have been told to "Celebrate Diversity" for the past 30 years. If this means to be proud of your heritage, then that's fine. If it means you are content being inside your particular skin color and its associated ethnicity, that's okay, too. But, we Americans tend to overdo everything; to go to extremes and push the envelope. And that's exactly what's happened. Diversity, as defined in the United States, was intended to give blacks pride in their heritage while they integrated into a society in which they felt no part of, prior to civil rights laws. Diversity, practiced meaningfully, would help bridge the gap between segregation and integration until the blacks truly equaled the whites in all areas. Unfortunately, it was subverted from diversity to divisiveness, and has accelerated under Obama. Obama gave many, if not most blacks a sense of superiority they did not have before he became President. Obama's election elicited euphoria from many blacks similar to blacks that were freed after the Civil War. Back then, blacks were made so many promises that they thought the government would never make them work again for the rest of their lives. Many took free food, board, and clothing from the Freedmen's Bureau for 12 years, and stayed drunk on alcohol supplied by the carpet-baggers in return for their vote. When the Freedmen's Bureau folded in 1877 the blacks had to work or starve. Some blacks today are benefiting under Obama (mostly the elites), but for the rank and file their condition has not changed much since Bush left office.

The divisiveness produced by the rush to diversity has almost created a nation within a nation. Blacks increasingly see themselves as existing above and apart from their white countrymen. The quest for differentiation and the implementation of those differences to anything non-white has been strictly a black exercise. Before "negro" became "African-American," blacks were already advocating the wearing of the jellabiya, djellaba, dashiki, kaftan, bogolanfini, and kanzu. Black men started wearing the African kufi hats to set them apart from the crowd. All of a sudden blacks no longer were named James, or William, or Jane, or Wilma. They were now Afram to Zareb, and A'sharia to Zahra. Christmas was replaced with Kwanzaa. "Juneteenth" is celebrated as Black Emancipation Day. Their choice of music was originally associated with jazz, and it was a good and profitable association for them. But, when the white guys started not only enjoying it, but playing, singing, and recording jazz music the blacks moved on to hip-hop, funk, hip house, new jack swing, and rap. Black male hairstyles went from the short kinky to the afro to the fade, dreadlocks, braids, cornrows, and shaved heads of today. They replaced the "Star-Spangled Banner" with "Lift Ev'ry Voice and Sing" which was adopted by the NAACP as the Negro National Anthem. About half of all blacks switched their religion from the Baptist of the South to either African Methodist Episcopal, Black Liberation Theology, or the Muslim religion. About 17% of U.S. Muslims are black.

Back in the 50's, the blacks and their liberal hand-wringers were crying for integration with white society. Since then I can't tell you how many times white-dominated golfing clubs, men's clubs, fraternal organizations, and social groups have been rooted out, exposed, and ridiculed for excluding blacks. This is still happening today and will continue until the last holdout is eradicated. Apparently, this form of discrimination applies only to white organizations. You already know about the Congressional Black Caucus, Miss Black USA, the United Negro College Fund, and the Black Mayors Association, but have you heard of Black Women in Sisterhood for Action, Jack and Jill of America, Black Wall Street Merchants Association, Black Culinarians Alliance, African- American Speaker Bureau, 100 Black Men of America, and hundreds of others? They all have one hard and fast common denominator: no whites allowed! Every year bleeding-heart, white- guilt-saturated liberals beg and plead to be allowed to join the Black Caucus. The answer is always the same, a resounding no!

Affirmative action, diversity, white guilt, and demands of equality have placed millions of blacks in jobs both high and low that they were not qualified to perform. This has cost our nation trillions in tax dollars and lost opportunity costs. We have surrendered to black demands for the only national holiday named for a single individual. We have retreated on every front and awarded every demand made by blacks. Now, we are broke and the housing market crash was the spark that spread to an inferno, and was largely due to blacks running Freddie Mac and Fannie Mae and blacks receiving the undeserved loans. This victimization of blacks and their official designation as an inferior underclass has, and will, accelerate geometrically under Obama. Rather than heal the chasm between the races, Obama is working to widen the divide and the result may be armed conflict. The fact that Obama received 99% of the black vote should tell astute observers that all the untold trillions, work, and lives expended in the reconciliation attempts between the races over the last 155 years have all come to naught. No white candidate for President has, or will ever have, the luxury of receiving 99% of the white vote for the sole reason of being white. Black racism is alive and well and still raging, while white racism is still rare.

INCONVENIENT TRUTHS

Reconstruction after the Civil War was supposed to give blacks a jump-start. It didn't for the reasons given in that section. The second reconstruction isn't working either because history is repeating itself. The black elitists are simply the 21st century version of the 19th century carpet-baggers. How would blacks have conducted themselves if the liberal white do-gooders and the black "victimizers" had just left them alone to stumble and fall and get back up again? Of course, wannabe totalitarians have never just let people alone. They must round-up the masses like cattle and indoctrinate them repetitively with the idea that their salvation depends on the benevolence of their select few leaders. In 1940 BTD (Before The Darkside) the illegitimacy rate among blacks was about 19%. Now, after the modern day black carpet-baggers made unrepentant beggars of their herd, about 74% of blacks are born out of wedlock. In 1950 approximately 82% of black households had a married man and wife in the home raising children, and they had the same last name. Now, only 25% of households are headed by a married man and wife. The disintegration of the black family has destroyed the lives of millions of the black offspring who now have no father at home. The hundreds of welfare programs legislated by the Darkside since the 1950's have rendered the black father's presence in the home unnecessary. Black men happily accepted their new role since sex without responsibility is every man's dream. The black women looked at their illegitimate kids as a badge of honor; proof that they were an adult and had the side benefit of a heftier welfare check. The kids went on to achieve a 55% high school drop-out rate, and commit 8 times more crimes than evil white people. Those that did manage to graduate high school found that new forms of welfare called affirmative action, and cash dispensations for just being black, would take-over where welfare left-off. When they entered the real world, white guilt and the victimization mentality of the Darkside assured them a position they could never have achieved independently.

I am not a phrenologist, anthropologist, sociologist, bigot, or racist, but I do know that blacks are way behind in the learning curve. American blacks will counter that slavery held them back. Then, I will counter that, and say that I think 145 years is enough time to catch up, isn't it? They will say that after slavery the white man kept his foot on their head, and didn't let them progress until the civil rights laws started kicking-in around the late 60's. Okay then, let's switch continents; Americans didn't enslave the one billion blacks in Africa. Why are they not going to the moon and creating wealthy, industrial, stabile societies? I'm sure my phantom debater would then say that the other colonial powers raped their countries of the natural resources and enslaved the Africans, thereby retarding their progress. My comeback would be, if Africa is the seat of civilization, then why did the Africans allow themselves to be ruled by the colonial powers? Why didn't they have guns and gunpowder and kill the hell out of the Europeans when they first set foot on their shores? I am sincerely looking for answers and solutions to our race dilemma. My taxes have been supporting our state and federal welfare programs for years, and blacks consume more than the 13% represented by population percentage. Everybody says we are all equal, so why is there such a thing as affirmative action? Why did we end segregation only to have blacks unilaterally re-segregate? I believe in real equality. If Asians, Hispanics, East Indians, Chinese, or Blacks can outperform me in anything, then they win, and I lose whether its academics or sports. But don't give any race an artificial advantage. Not all, but a large percentage of our dismal education system in the U.S. is the lowering of standards for all students rather than programs to elevate just the lagging black students. Many young blacks are chastised by other blacks and called Uncle Toms when they try to better themselves because they are perceived to be adopting the white man's ways. Much of the gang-related and drop-out problems are because of the 75% unwed pregnancy rate and single-mother households. This is not a wholly black problem, but rather a joint crime by the black elites and liberal Democrats. But, it still exists and the black race is still regressing, and there is no indication it will improve. Obama's "Road to Serfdom" is colorblind in this regard since he wants the mass of the population to be on the lowest rung, black and white, because he needs a proletariat to form his fascist regime.

I'm not really expecting any definitive answers to the above questions because nobody will dare answer in today's racially-charged atmosphere. As a Christian, if a truly objective study would find that blacks were slow in learning, and required supplemental financial help to get past the more difficult curriculums or else take jobs that perhaps did not require advanced studies, then that would be fine with me. But, to have people like Henry Gates being a high paid, tenured professor at Harvard is crazy. I have come across many black professors at what I formerly called prestigious universities teaching non-subjects like "African Studies" and "Afrocentrism" that are not only useless subjects, but instill a false pride of achievement in black skulls that is based on a lie and will contribute nothing to the student. Why do these schools employ these people? Do they suffer from white guilt, and this is their way to make amends for slavery? Sending these fakes a check and barring them from filling young brains with silliness would benefit society more. Don't think I'm just picking on blacks. There are more white dummies out there than blacks. I was at my ophthalmologist's office the other day and picked-up a copy of Newsweek. On the front cover was the words "The Thinking Man's Thinking Man" and it had a picture of Algore. This guy is one of the dumbest human beings on earth. Well, I'm not sure about the human being part. Returning to our black imbroglio, I have served on important missions with blacks, Asians, American Indians, and Hispanics, and race was a non-sequitur. I don't care if all sports are 100% black as long as they achieved their status fairly. I just do not believe in artificial equality because it cannot last, and will eventually cause more problems than it solves. A few years ago Walter E. Williams wrote an article about how blacks were on their way to carving out their rightful place in American society in the 1950's. Black families mostly had a mother and father and a good work ethic. Then came the devil's pact between the white liberals and black elite, and now look at black statistics; Drugs, prison, crazy clothing, unintelligible language, low morals, violent crime, and no chance of improvement. The election of Obama has exacerbated the problems giving them false hope that they will now be given everything without working for it. This may indeed come true if his fascist state is successful, but that luxury will be short lived.

    To me, the lack of incentive and ambition among blacks is similar to what state lotteries have done to many blacks and whites. I voted against the state lotteries both in Florida and

Georgia because I knew what it would do to the working poor. My business sells lottery tickets, so I see first-hand the people that buy the tickets like addicts every day. All of them think that the next ticket will be the one that frees them from ever working again. They do not try to better their life through working harder. They do not save for the future, and many waste money on lottery that should be spent on necessities. Blacks have become so dependent on the handouts of the Darkside that they have become like the freed slaves during reconstruction, waiting for the 40 acres and a mule that never materializes. Blacks think that the election of Obama is the culmination of all their dreams. The messiah will finally redistribute the wealth of the whites and spread it to the blacks, who will now sit on the veranda drinking mint juleps and watch the whites picking cotton. For the black elites this vision came true already starting about 1970, but for most blacks it will never come true. The way Obama is bleeding America it is but a short time before the entire gravy train derails for all of us. When that happens, we will all be on our own again just as we were when this nation started carving a civilization out of the wilderness. Obama and his Darkside know well how to bring down a capitalist society since they've perfected their strategies since the 1960's. But, will they know how to create their utopian dream? I think not since Fascist experiments always fail. If indeed anyone survives Obama's intentional war on the whites it will be the fittest and most cunning among us. Contrary to the beliefs of some, Obama just ain't that smart, and the black caucus and other black elites belong in a zoo. But, the snowball is too far down the slope to stop now, so we'll just have to see who is still standing after the dust clears.

It's difficult to accept the fact that the progeny of our founders, and the offspring of the trail-blazers and pioneers that built America, have handed it all over to a hollow-headed non-performer like Obama. Make no mistake, whites elected him, not blacks. Do you think the 13% made him President? No, Obama knew he could count on the racist vote from 99% of the blacks, but he still needed 30% of the white vote to combine with 70% of the Hispanic vote to put him over the top. So, there were more white votes than the votes of blacks and Hispanics combined. None of these whites had guns put to their heads, so we must conclude that they indeed voluntarily turned over their country to a person that considers their forbearers vile and disgusting. Blacks cannot be held responsible for their actions because, unlike most whites, they have not matured beyond the base attributes of hatred, discrimination, and victimhood. They have been led around by the nose, and propagandized so thoroughly that original thought is foreign to them. Their mentors have been black elitists who have founded, established, and prospered in careers whose sole purpose is perpetuation of a black victim class. Black victimhood is a virtual industry run by black elites in both private, so-called non-profit, and government entities, and produce only a single product - pity for a whole race of people who blame their shortcomings on everything but themselves.

WHITE RACISM IS RARE, BLACK RACISM IS RAGING

The above title makes two statements. First, is that real dislike or hatred of blacks by whites is a highly unusual occurrence in the United States in 2010. I know this to be true because I live in the Deep South where any liberal worth his salt would expect any residual pockets of racism to reside. I am an avid daily consumer of local, state, national and world news, so I am immediately informed of any racial news wherever it may occur. The overwhelming majority of whites have never been racists. They have always been more concerned with school, fishing, hunting, sports, family, God, raising children, chasing women, playing golf, and a thousand other activities that have nothing to do with race. Only a microscopic minority of whites in the last 50 years ever spent much time or effort on affairs of race. Of course, liberals and their media twins thirst for the rare racial incident and pump it up into an earth shaking event. I think there are more full-time, well-paid race baiters staffing the Southern Poverty Law Center in Montgomery, Alabama, than there are of the so-called domestic terrorist groups or race crimes they claim to track. If you believe in God or home-schooling watch out, the SPLC will probably have you on their extremist list. The SPLC represents the ultimate extremes of white guilt. Of course, like government agencies that create crises to justify their expanding budgets, the SPLC must constantly manufacture race chaos and race-baiting or liberals would stop donating big bucks to them.

The second part of the above title means that blacks espouse and practice overt, and covert, racism often and increasingly. Don't take my word for it. Watch your TV, go on the internet, or read your newspaper. Black elites are incapable of subtlety. Their hatred and anger pours forth like a burst damn. Witness the unbridled anger, hate, lies, and poison spewed-out by Maxine Waters and all other black elitists after hurricane Katrina. For the first time I saw racism weaponized by Darkside blacks and even some of their white mouthpieces. Their vitriol was not aimed at black Mayor Ray Nagin of New Orleans who was right there in the bathtub city sitting on his hands scratching his head. Neither was their anger directed at Democrat Governor Kathleen Blanco who, like Nagin, had days of warning and did little to prepare. The largely black New Orleans City Council left the city and offered no help to anyone. The mostly black New Orleans police force just faded into the woodwork, and couldn't be found until a few of "New Orleans Finest" were arrested for looting.

On August 27, 2005, Max Mayfield of the National Hurricane Center phoned Nagin and told him the dire threat posed by Katrina. The next morning President Bush made a televised appeal saying, "We cannot stress enough the danger this hurricane poses to Gulf Coast communities." The residents of New Orleans were specifically told that the levees would probably topple and flood the city. Over one-million evacuated the metro area, but 100,000 stayed behind, mostly blacks. The Superdome was quickly filled with 20,000. Over 300 school buses had been parked in strategic locations, but not one of them was used to evacuate people out of the city. Immediately after the wind stopped blowing blacks poured downtown, systematically broke into every business, and carried off anything they could carry or cart away. They stole only items necessary for survival in a crisis such as flat-screened TV's, IPods, jewelry, and liquor. With dead blacks floating around in the sludge and sewerage, the other blacks were looting and raping rather than helping each other. When Washington got involved Governor Blanco finally called in the National Guard to stop the killing and looting. After it was all over 1546 mostly black residents of New Orleans were dead and 73 criminals had been shot. Hundreds of thousands of blacks were taken to other cities where they repaid their generous hosts by increasing the murder, rape, and assault statistics of every town that had taken them in. Nagin got reelected since he was black and a Democrat. U.S. taxpayers have spent $200 billion to rebuild the city (which was already a slum) and will probably spend that much more. Eleven thousand brand new mobile homes were sent to the largely black refugees for temporary shelters, but they all preferred apartments and food at government expense. The government later sold them for one-third of the purchase price. Every black elitist in the U.S. looked around for the nearest white guy to blame and they found him - George Bush.

The eye of Katrina actually missed New Orleans. It hit Waveland, Mississippi, directly and traveled right up the middle of the state spawning 11 tornadoes and bringing a 28 foot storm surge with it. Unlike Louisiana, Mississippi had a conservative, honorable governor, Haley Barbour, who not only gave warnings, but managed to evacuate over 400,000 residents of the Gulf Coast so that even though the area was damaged more than New Orleans the loss of life was 80% less. Most of these residents were white. Unlike Louisiana, Haley Barbour had already decided on the evacuation plan and activated the National Guard three full days before the hurricane struck. The devastation was much worse in Mississippi, but there was only 20% as many killed and there was little looting, no rapes, and order was established and maintained. Many said the area looked like Hiroshima after the atomic bomb was dropped. Mississippi took the disaster in stride and is still rebuilding today. They blamed it all on nature, not George Bush. Raw racism was on display by the Darkside after Katrina as they violently attacked Bush, his subordinates, Army Corps (oops, I mean "corpse"), FEMA, and any white person remotely connected with disaster relief, but steered clear of criticizing the in-charge blacks who could have saved many black lives. I may be called a racist for pointing out that blacks acted differently in this catastrophe, but unlike the black elites and white liberals, there is no substitute for truth when you are a conservative.

Have the vast majority of blacks improved the quality of their lives with the perceived success of the civil rights movement? The black elites would answer in the affirmative if asked the question about their personal lives. Since they are the problem and not the solution, my question is directed only at the 35 million or so blacks who have not shared in the spoils of the Darkside. Were the lives of those blacks that work at trades and on assembly lines, and are never seen disappearing behind the closed doors of the Black Caucus or laying bare their ignorance on TV like Maxine Waters, improved by the civil rights acts and court opinions?

Before WWII blacks had a poverty rate of about 86%, few of them voted, and therefore they had minimal political clout. After WWII and before any serious civil rights activity or laws came about the poverty rate had dropped to 47%. Why? Because blacks had decided on their own to take advantage of the industrial boom, the WWII build-up, and lack of white labor since most white men were overseas fighting the war. If the Army didn't want to integrate them into the service then at least they would help the country and themselves by working in the defense industry. They cut their poverty in half without the drivel of the self-efficacy crowd like Jackson, Sharpton, and the Black Caucus, and without anti-poverty programs or affirmative action. Of course, black poverty continued falling after the 1960's when civil rights movements declared blacks officially handicapped and wards of the state, but by less of a percentage than before. Who can say that blacks would not have done it on their own without the help of the black elite interlopers and their white handlers?

Were the social aspects of blacks improved by the black elites? Before WWII 87% of black children were born into families with a mother and father present. The illegitimacy rate among blacks stood at 13%. Today, after the black elites "rescued" their brethren over 70% of black babies are born out of wedlock. The pitiful decline of the black family is not just the result of civil rights. The civil rights movement was part and parcel of the rise of the welfare state, and affected both blacks and whites. The white illegitimacy rate quadrupled from before WWII to today. The black elite had very much to do with increasing welfare. They had all taken home the bread and tossed their black constituents a few crumbs in the form of welfare. Like the blacks 100 years earlier during reconstruction, they found it easier to forego working and punch out babies. The more babies the more welfare. Fathers were expendable.

The black family was well on its way to joining in the prosperity of America by 1960 of its own volition without the artificial "jump starting" by the white liberals and black elites. Before these derelicts got involved, black women and men intuitively understood that marriage was the norm of a stable society. In 1961 before the civil rights acts had taken effect, over 67% of black women and 75% of black men of marriageable age were married. Today, those percentages have been halved. For the same period black women with children who had never been married were only 4%, whereas today they represent 41% of the black mothers. Although liberals despise the comparison, black income is directly related to education, and education level increases with the stability of the black family unit. When the economy spirals down like today, the uneducated are hit harder and faster. Witness the black unemployment rate now of 17%, while the white rate is around 10%.

With the breakdown of the black family came the even more saddening statistics of black crime. The following statistics are from the "Color of Crime" by the New Century Foundation, and are not biased against minorities. Blacks are 7 times more likely than people of other races to commit murder and 8 times more likely to commit robbery. When blacks commit crimes of violence, they are nearly three times more likely than non-blacks to use a gun, and more than twice as likely to use a knife. The single best indicator of violent crime levels in an area is the percentage of the population that is black. Of the nearly 770,000 violent interracial crimes committed every year involving blacks and whites, blacks commit 85% and whites commit 15%. Blacks commit more violent crime against whites than whites against blacks. 45% of their victims are white, 43% are black, and 10% are Hispanic. When whites commit violent crime, only 3% of their victims are black. Blacks are an estimated 39 times more likely to commit a violent crime against a white than vice versa, and 136 times more likely to commit robbery. Blacks are 2.25 times more likely to commit officially designated hate crimes against whites than vice versa. Only 10% of gang members are white. Blacks are 15 times more likely to be members of gangs than whites. Blacks are 7 times more likely to be in prison than whites. These statistics mirror the national FBI figures and the numbers from other law enforcement agencies. It's scary to realize that a 13% minority commits over 45% of the murders.

The Centers for Disease Control in Atlanta issued its "Deaths: Leading Causes for 2004" report on November 20, 2007. Since this is 2010 the figures are probably conservative, but shocking nonetheless. The 96 page report says that the leading cause of death for both young black men and women is black men. The deaths are attributable to two causes: HIV/AIDS and homicide. Black men are 10 times more likely to be diagnosed with HIV or AIDS than white men. For those black men that say they are not homosexuals the rate increases to 15 times that of heterosexual white men. Also, black men are more likely to spread the disease to more partners because it remains undiagnosed due to a macho attitude. Unfortunately, black women suffer the brunt of this attitude by being diagnosed with HIV/AIDS at a rate of 20 times more than white women. Oddly, the source of the HIV/AIDS is prison. When released, these black men then have heterosexual relations with black females. About 75% of HIV/AIDS among black women is contracted in this way. The importance of HIV/AIDS deaths hits home when you realize that it is the number one cause of death among black women aged 25 to 34, and only the 11th leading cause of death among white women in the same age category.

The same CDC report states that homicide is the leading cause of death among black men aged 15 to 34, the 2nd leading cause of death among black women aged 15 to 24, and the 5th leading cause of death for black women aged 25 to 34. Black women in the 15 to 34 age slot are four times more likely to suffer premature death by homicide than white females of the same age. Comparing the homicide death rate among men 25 to 34 in both races shows that just 12.5 per 100,000 white males died, while 101.8 black males died of homicide. The latter statistic accounts for 48% of all black premature deaths.

Since black males are usually the perpetrators, black females represent the more unfortunate side of homicide statistics. The CDC labels black women killed by their current or former boyfriends as victims of "femicide." Being married and black helps, but still the spousal homicide for blacks is 8.4 times that of whites. Mixed marriages exacerbate the problem even more with a 7.7 times greater incidence of homicide than same-race marriages. Black females aged 15 to 19 are 3.9 times more likely to die of homicide or AIDS than white females in the same age group.

For ages 20 to 24 and 25 to 34 this jumps to 4.4 and 7.3 times respectively.

I am reprinting the following from the "American Thinker" dated March 12, 2010. It was written by E. W. Jackson whom I admire a great deal. Mr. Jackson is a radio commentator and President of STAND (Staying True to America's National Destiny). I think this one article encapsulates what I am trying to tell you about self-interest of the black elitists, and the irreparable damage they are doing to their race and this nation. It proves that, while the black elitists may hate whites more than they hate their black followers, it is the latter that suffer the greatest harm.

"On Thursday, September 24th, after an apparently productive day at Fengler High School in Chicago, Derrion Albert, a black 16 year old honor student was knocked to the ground by a blow to the head with a railroad tie. He was then punched, kicked and stomped. Those who responded to rescue him were too late. Derrion had walked into the middle of a fight between two rival black gangs. He attempted to help one of the victims in the melee and was killed for his trouble. This took place in Barack Obama's Chicago. All his work for "social justice" did a great deal for Obama, but it did nothing for Derrion Albert. Of course the President is not responsible for this tragedy, but it does expose the fatuous claim that such occurrences are the result of social injustice rather than the personal choice to engage in lawless behavior. The ghettos, drugs, gangs and violence are on display for all to see in spite of Jeremiah Wright, Louis Farrakhan, Acorn and all the community organizing.

Treating poor black people as victims to be "organized" has been an abject failure. They are human beings to be educated, inspired and required to take responsibility for their own lives. The tragedy here is that Derrion was doing just that and it was working, but the malignant pathology of the ghetto spread to him on that unfortunate day and ended his promising life.

There is another tragedy. The so called black civil rights leaders have been mute. Had this been a white gang attacking a black gang member, they would have jumped in front of every camera and microphone available to decry racism and injustice in America. If it had been a black criminal with a long rap sheet, killed in a confrontation with a white police officer, there would be protests and perhaps riots against systemic racism in the police department.

Yet in this case and others like it, there is a deafening silence from some of the biggest mouths in America. Jesse Jackson, Al Sharpton, Julian Bond, Louis Farrakhan and the Congressional Black Caucus see no evil, hear no evil and speak no evil. When Prof. Henry Louis Gates, Jr. was arrested by a white police officer, President Barack Obama -- without any facts -- found it necessary to put in his two cents. Here in Chicago, the salient facts are abundantly clear and a heinous murder has been committed in his home town, but the president is silent. Malicious, homicidal maniacs brutally killed a decent young man on the streets Obama "organized," but he has nothing to say. The self-appointed, media supported "black leaders" have not seen fit to hold a press conference or a rally supporting Derrion Albert and his family and condemning the perpetrators of this vicious crime. They have not called for witnesses to come forward.

There's a reason for their uncharacteristic silence. Derrion's murder does not fit the black liberation narrative. As one civil rights leader said to me, "If we focus on black on black crime, we let white folks off the hook." Never mind that the leading cause of death among black males ages 18 to 24 is homicide by other black males. In one interview before Obama was elected, Michelle Obama commented on threats to Barack Obama's safety saying, "As a black man, Barack can get shot going to the gas station." What she did not say is that his likely killer would be another black man. Blacks are only 13% of the population, but over 40% of the murder victims. Ninety Three percent of those black victims are killed by other black people. As a black man, I am far more wary of the real black criminal than the imagined white racist.

Absentee fathers, abortion, drug use, gangs and black on black crime have a much greater impact on people's lives than theoretical systemic racism, but these issues do not fit the liberal paradigm to which civil rights leaders are hostage. The problems of the black community must be understood solely as a social justice problem inflicted on blacks by whites. No other explanation is worthy of discussion, and woe to those dare suggest otherwise. In truth the civil rights spokesmen have another agenda which supersedes the well-being of black folks -- their personal financial and political well being.

Liberal benefactors and foundations are not interested in addressing social pathologies which can only be eliminated by change of values, stable families and the willingness of fathers to parent their children. The government's coffers are closed to moral judgments and spirituality. Faith in God, parental love and discipline to instill values of decency and responsibility are the antidotes to gangs, crime and drugs. However, allegations of racism, discrimination and social injustice are far more marketable for the Rainbow Coalition and the NAACP.

The people who killed Derrion are monsters. Monsters come in all colors, but these happen to be black. They are not victims. They are cold-blooded criminals with no regard for human life. Maybe when the so called black leaders start speaking out against gangs and criminals as parasites instead of victims of society, there will be fewer real victims like Derrion Albert."

I appreciate Mr. Jackson's optimism, but it ain't gonna happen. The so-called "black leaders" he references look at Derrion Albert as a sacrificial lamb; a single, inconsequential casualty that falls on their sword for the "greater good" derived from the contrived victimization of the black race. To specifically criticize the black gangs, or the coalition of black and white "dons" of Chicago that depend on black chaos to justify the victim status of blacks, is to weaken their reason to exist and show a chink in their solidarity with the Darkside. White guilt and fear of being called a racist have put the black elite in the catbird seat, and with the election of Obama the sky is the limit. To retreat now on even minor points, like the deaths of innocent blacks like Derrion Albert, might permit a weakening of the victim status of blacks. The established credo of the black elites differs little from the core beliefs of Hitler and Stalin; sacrifice many for the good of the few. They and their few thousand fellow blacks must keep up the illusion that their 40 million peasants are incompetent, and will revert to slavery without their parentalism.

The overt racism of the black voters in all black congressional districts is so obvious and so thoroughly entrenched in the United States that to question its existence is to prove blind stupidity. A good example is Congressman Hank Johnson of Georgia. Johnson beat out nutty Cynthia McKinney in the 4th district of Georgia. Like all black districts, if you are not black you can forget even entering the competition. While McKinney was certifiably crazy, Johnson is just flat demented. He uses his disease of Hepatitis C to cover his mental shortcomings. During a March hearing before the House Armed Services Committee, Admiral Robert Willard told the congressmen that a small contingent of Marines was being added to the troops already stationed in Guam. Hank Johnson said in a serious tone to the Admiral, "My fear is that the whole island will become so overly populated that it will tip over and capsize." He said this with a straight face. The Admiral, knowing that to laugh or smirk would bring the race card out, simply replied, "We don't anticipate that." The point I'm trying to make is that in a black district they would send an idiot to Congress before they would send a white regardless of qualifications. Johnson is just a pea in the pod called the Congressional Black Caucus.

In this section of the Black Imbroglio we have seen how slavery is a human issue, not a race issue. We have seen blacks alone advance their race gradually up the ladder for 100 years, only to be stalled, and then begin the slide back down at the hands of a black elite that prospers from their suffering. Their individual and group efforts were co-opted by and transferred to a group that cared not a whit about their fellow blacks. We have seen that all the artificial equality schemes in the world cannot make equal for long that which is not naturally equal. White racism in 2010 is a virtual myth, while black racism is rampant and on the rise. This racism dovetails with Obama's Cloward-Piven strategy of crises-nurturing and creation. Sadly, under Obama's racist policies, and with the help of groups like the Southern Poverty Law Center and the upcoming power consolidation legislation of Obama's Darkside, our future looks bleak indeed.

SUICIDAL WHITES

If white Americans want to be the first society on earth to have created the most perfect, harmonious system of government ever, only to foolishly and voluntarily turn it over to an undeserving, self-serving rabble of misfits, then they should keep doing exactly what they are doing. Turning over this nation to the Darkside is effectively saying that the million and a half lives lost in gaining and keeping our sovereignty for 234 years was in vain. It is stating unequivocally that our founder's efforts meant naught. It means that we are not worthy of the great legacy left to us by our American ancestors. And, finally it signifies that we were not capable of keeping the great gifts of life and liberty bequeathed to us by our larger-than-life unbroken chain of American heroes.

Unlike both liberal and conservative writers I am appealing to white Americans, not black. Blacks gave almost 99% of their votes to Obama. That is raw racism. Therefore, why appeal to blacks? Blacks do not vote for whites, just as they do not riot and loot when a white gets shot running from the cops. For those whites that want to continue pandering to blacks in the hopes that blacks will become conservatives and love this country like the rest of us, then good luck. They have had 145 years of freedom to join the rest of Americans, and have chosen not to do so. They chose to be called African-Americans, dress and act differently, talk their own language, have their own music, and if whites say "up," they say "down." And, don't even bring up slavery. Most of us Americans started out as indentured servants. Nobody had to hold our hands, pass civil right laws, and give us affirmative action to level the playing field.

Blacks need to get over it. A very few of our white ancestors put a few of their ancestors in servitude. Africans put twice as many of our white relatives in chains as we put theirs. Blacks worked on big farms called plantations, and most provided labor in return for cradle to grave room and board. Now, they want the room and board without providing the labor. There are more black millionaires in the United States from the progeny of the half-million blacks brought here, than there are millionaires among the one-billion blacks living in Africa. Oprah is even a billionaire. Most of the football, basketball, and baseball players making millions are black. Half of the actors in Hollywood are blacks. Blacks own their own holiday and month. What more do they want? How many more centuries do they need to get "equal" to whites?

Blacks keep bringing up silly things like Afrocentrism, postulating that all culture came from Africa. Really? Then what the hell happened to them? Why isn't there a single industrialized, stable, high-tech, peaceful, wealthy, and moral black nation that produces planes, trains, and automobiles? How many physicists, chemists, and doctors are black? Why do blacks butcher each other to death with machetes by the millions each year in Africa? Why are there more cases of AIDS in Africa than in all the other continents combined?

If you respond to my criticism above by saying that there are plenty of intelligent blacks, then you are right. The problem is blacks don't listen to any of them. They drool and froth over whores like Jesse Jackson and Sharpton, or the messiahs like Obama, all of whom keep them groveling in the dirt and never achieving their rightful place among the races of the earth. This would all change if they ever emulated men like Charles Payne, James Golden, Justice Thomas, Thomas Sowell, Herman Caine, Walter E. Williams, or Alan Keyes, but that will not happen.

Contrary to what you have seen, heard, and read during Black History Month, America was founded and given birth by white Europeans, not blacks. If blacks were removed from America for the past 400 years all of the important advancements of this nation would have still been made at the same or higher rate. Whites fought the Revolutionary War, War of 1812, Civil War, Spanish-American War, WWI and WWII almost wholly without blacks. Many whites came to the new world as indentured servants, and worked for years to get their freedom. Some of them had black slaves, or would later acquire slaves, as they prospered in the new country. They didn't buy slaves because they were racists. Slaves came in one color, black, and we needed labor because we were an agrarian society and everything was done by hand in those days. Also, all the other whites were entrepreneurs and starting their own farms so white labor was scarce. Whites were not alone in securing black labor. Indians were basically lazy and could get just so much work out of their squaws, so they also bought black slaves, too.

And, shock of shocks, blacks owned black slaves by the thousands from 1754 right up to 1865. Do you realize there are more black slaves owned right now in Africa by other blacks than there were owned by whites in the United States in 1865? What I'm trying to say is that what happened in the settling of America was just a natural progression of a society of people, not a concerted effort to punish a single race of people.

Regardless of whether you accept or reject the above criticisms, the white race in the United States is destined to fall from its state of grace into a sort of serfdom within a very short time. With the influx of brown immigrants, the rising Muslim influence, and the overbearing blacks, the white population will lose dominance in all areas. After 60 years of brainwashing, I don't blame you for automatically thinking that race is not a problem because we are all melding into one big happy family. It is not your fault, just as it was not the fault of the Jews that didn't listen to their neighbors who got out of Germany before the borders slammed shut. We have been on this planet for six centuries and never have we been more divided on all issues than we are right now. What makes you think all the world will suddenly see the light and the races will reside in harmony for evermore?

The majority of whites in the United States like to think they are members of the middle class. Most of them are. That is changing as we speak. Over 10 million Americans have lost their jobs since Obama took office, and that many more again will lose their jobs in the near future. And, please don't cite Obama's government unemployment numbers to me. If you believe anything that comes out of his mouth you are a fool. Those jobs will never return. The foundation of America's strength has always been the middle class, but they are being converted to a permanent underclass by design. The majority of the people voting for McCain/Palin in 2008 were white middle class Americans. The vast majority were Christians. Therefore, Obama is targeting specifically white middleclass Christian Americans. There will be a white middleclass and small white upper-class left after Obama completes his purge, but they will be union members, homosexuals, abortion advocates, environmental radicals, earth worshipers, education fascists, and the chosen kingpins of industry and finance who will run the quasi-governmental sector of Obama's fascist empire. The rest of the whites will be dependent on the government for either welfare handouts, or the lower-paying jobs that survived the collapse of the economy.

The supposedly savvy Republicans are perhaps not among the suicidal whites, but they are still proficient at shooting themselves in the foot. They have been chasing after the black vote for the last 60 years and captured a whole 1% for their efforts in 2008. So, to increase this percentage, they really pulled a coup and hired Michael Steele as their head of the Republican National Committee. Boy, that'll do it. If the black elite and their frothing followers despise anyone, it's an "Uncle Tom" and that's what they label any black Republican or conservative. Obama responded, "Clarence Thomas" when asked, "Who on the Supreme Court do you think is least competent?" My educated, considered, and intelligent opinion is that Obama is not worthy of shining Clarence Thomas's shoes.

If the Republicans and white guilters would act more like a herd of cats instead of cattle, they would stop the parentalizing of the black race in the false hope that blacks are going to undergo an epiphany. It ain't gonna happen, folks. You are wasting valuable time and money. Michael Steele is a nice guy, but he is not the charismatic wartime leader needed to combat the evil that is Obama. Unless and until Obama becomes a conservative, pro-life Republican, then we must treat him as we would any enemy of the people. Don't cater to him. This arms-length attitude should not be limited to Obama and politicians. Go after the idiots Jackson, Sharpton, Wright, the NAACP and Black Caucus. Meet bitterness with bitterness. When the black Congressmen obviously lied about being called racial names during the Obamacare debate, then we should call them liars. If the wannabe Harvard racist, "professor" Gates, screams racism, then we should fire racism right back at this idiot. Instead, we feature him on the History Channel to tell us how blacks created America. And, if any of these black elites want to boycott Arizona or a business, then we should show them what a real boycott is by threatening a boycott by the 50 million white conservative consumers. Rush can influence 20 million by himself. If Republicans had a charismatic national leader chosen by ability and not color, much could be done. I see no national leader appearing on the horizon anytime soon.

Before I move on to a discussion of President Barry let me say a few words about the pampered, spoon-fed, coddled, black minority that has been privileged to be born in the United States, but acts and dresses like we ripped them up from their affluent African roots and tossed them into an abyss called America. How have other nations treated their minorities? The Muslim Turks didn't particularly like the minority Armenians, Greeks, Nestorians, and other Christians living inside their country, so they systematically started killing them in all kinds of unique ways and just couldn't seem to stop until they had slaughtered 4,000,000 of them. Closer to the homeland of our "imprisoned" African-American minority is the wannabe country of Rwanda in Africa. The Hutu majority was sick and tired of the minority Tutsi's always telling them what to do, so they decided one day to do something about it. They announced over the country's radio stations that Hutu's should hit the streets and kill every Tutsi they found regardless of sex or age. Now, Hutu's are typically shorter and plumper, and Tutsi's are thinner and taller, but much comingling between the two had occurred over the years, so many times you could not tell one tribe member from the other. This didn't stop the Hutu. If a black person fit the general description then they were killed. Tutsi hospitals were a favorite target since patients can't run too fast on crutches and wheel chairs. The Hutu kept this up until the murdered totaled about one-million. Also, in the wonderful land that is Africa is the Muslim paradise of Sudan. Within Sudan is a region called Darfur which is populated with Christians, otherwise known as infidels. Sudanese President Omar al-Bashir has systematically made the minority Christians even more minor by murdering 450,000 of them. This is continuing as you read this.

Closer to home, our neighbor of Mexico has an interesting history with their minorities. There were many indigenous tribes of Indians roaming around that the Mexicans couldn't seem to blend into their society. So, they tried to enslave them and even conscripted them into the military. That didn't work out too well, so they decided to start murdering them. During the period from 1900 to 1920 the Mexicans killed about 1,400,000 of them. Minority problem solved. Finally, I'm sure that the favorite Caribbean vacation playground of Cuba is dear to the hearts of the

Congressional Black Caucus, but it holds a special place in the heart and souls of about 100,000 Cubans because their hearts, souls, and bones are buried in mass graves outside of Havana. Although the idol of the CBC, Fidel Castro, calls these Cubans "counter-revolutionaries, I simply call them Cuban "citizens."

Now, being familiar with the rhetoric of Jackson and Sharpton, I imagine that most blacks would say about now, "you whites lynched us minority blacks by the hundreds like piñatas before civil rights put a stop to it, so you're no better than the other countries." Tell ya what; let's have a murder show-and-tell, one-on-one game of wits. You show me a lynching, and I'll show you a white killed by a black <u>before</u> civil rights laws were passed. I'll start it off. Your black Nat Turner and his gang killed a documented 57 babies, women, and men. Now, you show me 57 documented blacks lynched, and then I'll show you the next mass killings of whites by blacks. After I show you proof that blacks murdered bounteously more whites than vice versa, both during slavery and before civil rights, then we will start comparing the murder rates of blacks and whites today. If you want the numbers from an outside source just go to the FBI or CDC stats, and you will see that blacks murder at a rate of about 7 times that of whites. They are even more proficient at the lesser crimes of car-jacking, auto-theft, and smash-and-grab. If you doubt this, then watch "Cops" or "Bait car" or the other police reality shows. You'll see that about 90% of the fleeing criminals are black. Of course, the white guilters producing the shows will never violate political correctness by commenting on the lopsided number of blacks or, heaven forbid, suggesting a little profiling may be in order.

VERY MERRY BARRY

Why is Barack Hussein Obama merry? Would you not be merry if you were walking around Chicago one day just hating white people, teaching black folks about how to avenge the horror wrought by whites in bringing their ancestors to such a despicable country as America from their beloved, peaceful Africa and attending but, not listening every Sunday to your mentor Jeremiah when . . . . . WALA!, you wake-up one morning and you are the most powerful man in the world with control over 309,000,000 people and

9,000 nuclear weapons at your disposal. You look around and, son-of-a-gun, the Senate and House are in the hands of the Darkside, too! Even a smart young light-skinned black guy like you didn't imagine the depth of ignorance of the whites, or the guilt that whites felt over slavery. The incessant drumbeat of liberals over the past 60 years had paid-off and convinced whites that they were the genesis of evil, and that blacks were the incarnate of docile, innocent, incompetent victims unable to defend themselves against the conniving evil of whites. So, they placed into the hands of a neophyte (who was not even descended from slaves) the power to destroy the world, and Barry was that neophyte!

In the beginning, our nation was blessed with 3 million square miles of abundant, arable land filled with minerals, fresh water, and beauty, surrounded on two sides with oceans, and on the other two sides with non-belligerent nations. Then, along came our profound, unique group of humble, intelligent, fair-minded founders who donned the accoutrements of war when angered, but just as quickly, reverted to civilian life when tyranny was no more. When confronted with the need for a more comprehensive set of rules to govern the loose confederation of colonies, they went to the Bible, the writings of John Locke, the Mayflower Compact, Magna Carta, English Bill of Rights, and documents from the ancient Athenian democracy. They wanted to know what had worked in the past and what had failed and why. Being almost all Christians, they knew only God could create a perfect Constitution. But, they wanted to come as close as mankind could in writing a document that would serve through the ages. They succeeded. There have been over 10,000 attempts to amend the Constitution, but only 27 times in 234 years has it occurred. Keep in mind that the first 10 amendments had already been promised at the original convention in 1787, and that the 18th and 21st amendments nullified each other. That leaves only 15 times we have altered the single document that has kept our republic from spinning out of orbit like all other attempts at democratic republicanism. The problems we are having today are not the fault of the Constitution, but rather those miscreants that wish to dilute, bypass, and abrogate its precious articles. The current Miscreant-in-Chief may just succeed.

Rush Limbaugh returns often to his belief that Americans are "exceptionalists." We have always strived to be the best and that's why we have excelled as a nation. We have built supersonic fighters that radar cannot see. America's charitable giving is unmatched by any nation on earth, and I'm not talking about Obama's giving of our tax revenues to Haiti or Chili, because that is our money to give, not his. Our SR71 Blackbird flew over 3000 miles per hour over 50 years ago. We went to the moon and back over 40 years ago. No nation responds better than America to the world's natural and manmade disasters. We lead the world in everything we attempt to lead the world in. We occupy less than 7% of the planet's surface, and make-up just 5% of the population, but control 25% of the world's economy. We have truly been blessed.

We could not have accomplished any of the above feats if we were not exceptionalists. We bring home the gold at the Olympics because our athletes are competitive and trained to perfection. Our soldiers are the best equipped and trained in the world. The former prime minister of Canada and thousands of others forsake their socialized healthcare in their home countries, and come to America when they need medical attention because we have the best doctors and healthcare. Remove the United States from the world today, and within weeks there would be 100 wars tearing the planet apart. So, the whole world depends on us to keep it from imploding or exploding. To do that, we must ourselves keep from disintegrating. But, that is exactly what is happening as we all witness the destruction of the greatest nation on earth at the hands of someone who should never have risen above the level of community organizer or dumpster diver.

In most of our industries and businesses we still strive for excellence. We still give drug tests, look at resumes, and check backgrounds to hire the best people. We strive for excellence in all those areas except one, our elected leaders. Right now, the Congress has an approval rating of about 11%, but don't get too giddy about cleaning house. After the dust has settled from the 2010 elections over 90% of the incumbents will still have been reelected, and they will be the very ones that should have been defeated. And, with or without a Democrat majority in Congress, Obama's Stalinist demons will intensify their incremental dismantling of what it took over 200 years and the lives of millions to create; the nearest mankind has ever come to a perfect system of government on earth.

For a country that has always strived for the best, how did we select not only the least qualified person, but one who has views that are totally antithetical to America? If a jihadist terrorist was installed in the Oval Office and told to dismantle America intelligently and slowly, so as not to arouse suspicion, a better candidate than Obama could not have been found. Most white Americans today do not consider race when they go to the polls. That cannot be said about blacks, since 99% of them voted for Obama. The rest of us are interested only in a candidate's accomplishments, positions on important issues, and the requisite of a profound appreciation and love for our unique country. Right off the bat, we couldn't even ask where Obama was born without being called "birthers." For the few of us who read his books, we knew his mom was named "Stanley", and his dad was a lazy black semi-Muslim who philandered between black and white women until he drank himself to death. We learned that "Barry" drank every kind of booze, smoked pot and crack, snorted, and most likely sold cocaine, used every curse word, chased women, spent his life hating whites, and feeling sorry for himself, and was always on a pity-trip until he got a free ride to Occidental, Columbia, and Harvard (Of course, these are all pluses if you are a Democrat candidate). When we asked to see his grades in college we were treated as if we had asked about his birth records again. We then found out that he took a non-job as a welfare-funded community organizer. Then he taught constitutional law so he could better evade and defeat its precepts. From there he advanced to another public-funded job as an Illinois State Senator, and then a tax-supported job as a U.S. Senator. He finally hit the POTUS jackpot as the beneficiary of the perfect storm of a Democrat-driven recession, a media-destroyed outgoing President, a racist black voting bloc, white guilt from 60 years of black-victim propaganda, and hordes of special-interest liberals who had laid the groundwork for the arrival of their messiah.

Most Americans, even some savvy conservatives, are sort of like the passengers aboard the first three airliners hijacked on 9/11 who thought they were taking a detour to Cuba, and would be late for dinner at the worst. They think Obama is simply president #44, just another light-skinned black guy, a little too liberal, can't decide whether he's a Christian or Muslim, and just wants either a four year ride in Air Force One, or maybe even an eight year jaunt at the most. The dizzying overnight leap from organizing on the streets of Chicago to sitting on the throne of the most powerful superpower on earth is not easily forgotten by the likes of Obama, and will never be relinquished voluntarily. Anyone who has read his books, listened to his speeches, investigated his friends, cabinet posts, czars, appointments, and non-government associates, and read all available information on him, cannot fail to see the seething anger and hatred in this man. The common thread throughout Obama's books is hatred of whites, and heaping all blame for every shortcoming of the black race on the white race. This hatred is too ingrained, too much a part of his psyche, to ever be excised. Every black he has ever admired and every black that he has appointed is of like mindset. Obama and the Darkside have not spent all their lives preparing to kill the "great Satan" only to come this close to victory and have it snatched from them. They will never be content to be put back in Pandora's Box.

If Obama embraced even a modicum of the biblical quality of humility and combined it with common sense, he would appreciate just how amazing our unique republic really is. We went from a nation who defined blacks as chattel property just 145 years ago to electing one of those chattels to the highest office in the land. He is not humble enough to simply admit that our system worked, whereas all others in every country have failed. Where else has a member of a 13% minority been elected to head a nation? And, it was whites who elected him, not blacks. Blacks voted as a bloc, not for experience or accomplishments, but for pure racist motives. But, even after the black voters robotically voted for another black (as usual), Obama still needed another 30% of the white vote to win. And, he got it. The horrible white race that had dragged Africans from the Stone Age to Oprah-land was the same white race that enabled a whining, dope-smoking, small-time Chicago mobster to rule over 309 million people.

Obama said in his book it was the sword that severed the black man's chains when dialogue failed. Yes Barry, it was the sword (as if you knew anything about weapons), but it was the white man's sword that severed whatever chains you are talking about, not the black man's sword. Just as it was the white nations of Europe who ended enslavement of whites by your ancestors, it was the 619,000 whites who died in our Civil War to give blacks their freedom. It was also whites that forcibly ensconced your people into all the seats of power over all 11 of the confederate states. Blacks had all the votes, all the seats, and all the power over all the whites in the south. The power was theirs to lose. And, within 10 years they lost it. Maybe every black needs a white paladin assigned to them from cradle to grave. Is that your definition of equality, Barry? The NAACP was formed, founded, and funded by whites. Every black school and college was funded by whites. You may think that marches and sit-ins earned your civil rights, but you would be wrong. The 88% majority never gives the 13% minority anything that the 88% majority doesn't want to give. I don't think Barry hates whites so much as he hates the fact he was born half-black and will never be white. If this sounds absurd then consider Michael Jackson, who had it all. Every material desire was fulfilled for him except one, he was not white. Rather than be content with success and money, he spent millions to chemically change his handsome features and light-brown complexion to a sculpted cartoon character with a pasty, chalk-like pigment; a grotesque disfigurement that resembled a ceramic doll that needed shielding from the sun like a vampire. He then paid white women to copulate with him so that his children would be white. I wonder if it was all worth it. This is one source of Obama's anger and, since his birth color can never change, his drive to destroy this white-created superpower of a nation will never change.

Let's look at Obama through the pages of his two books, "Dreams from My Father" and "The Audacity of Hope." By the way, if you go to the acknowledgements section of his second book you will count no less than 49 people who helped him write his own biography. How many people do you need to help you write about yourself and your own life? That's weird. My book may not sell many copies, but I will be thanking only one person other than myself and that is Dianne, my wife for proof-reading. Anyway, for those who do not know from whence the title of his "audacity" book came from, it was the name of the first sermon heard by Obama at Jeremiah Wright's church. We should count ourselves lucky it was not one of Wright's many four letter word sermons.

Speaking of audacity, Obama says in his second book that he underwent his epiphany after meeting Jeremiah, and of his own free will he walked down the aisle, gave himself to Christ, and got dunked in the baptismal tub. His claim to be a Christian should be the basis of using the word "audacity" in his book since one of his prime goals is to destroy the Christian religion. He says that neither his parents, grandparents, nor step-parents had much effect on his religiosity. His Kenyan grandfather, Onyongo, said he rejected Christianity because he could not understand giving mercy to your enemies, or how Jesus could wash away sins. He thought Christianity was only for women. Onyongo's real reason for opting for Islam was that it justified his multiple wives, casual sex, and he could look forward to 72 virgins without earthly Viagra required. Obama held his nose and associated himself with the Christian church simply because no non-Christian has ever been elected President.

On page 243 of Obama's "audacity" book he says his mom was an atheist and denied God, but said she taught him the same qualities that the other kids were learning in Sunday School, namely honesty, empathy, discipline, delayed gratification, and hard work. Really! Come on Barry, watching and reading your campaign promises, and then comparing them to your subsequent actions is like viewing two dissimilar, unrelated people. So much for the honesty. Likewise, does Barry's empathy cause him the same pain felt by the late-term babies with their caved-in skulls and vacuumed-out body parts? Then, there is the discipline of beer, booze, marijuana, coke, and sundry controlled substances. Sounds more like "if it feels good, do it." Next, the only gratification that Obama delayed, according to his books, was getting up late in the mornings after his many binges with his fellow radicals. And, last but far from least, Barry said his mom taught him hard work. He flitted from Hawaii through Indonesia, Los Angeles, Chicago, New York and Washington, never breaking a sweat or breaking a manicured nail. So much for Obama's maternal gifts.

Obama's hypocrisy is foretold on pages 38 and 39 of his first book. His step-father, Lolo, tells him to stop giving coins to beggars because if he gives everything away he will become a beggar himself. The moment he moved into the White House he immediately started giving away everything he could lay his hands on. When he ran out of our grandchildren's money he started on our great-grandchildren's money. Thanks to Barry, we are now those beggars that Lolo warned him about, but we have no one to beg from. And, China now owns the street corner on which we might have used to operate our begging business.

Were I back in college and my English Literature Prof asked me to read Mr. "O's" two books and name the common theme for both, I would have to say it is the perpetual, incessant, never-ending drumbeat of white cruelty to blacks. He throws in white cruelty to all other races here and there in the books too, but I think he did this in the hopes that Hispanics, American Indians, Asians, and Filipinos would join him in his crusade against whites. His hatred encompasses the whole spectrum of whites from the first colonist that landed on our shores, to the founders, to every generation of whites, right up to the present time. Obama is an equal opportunity hater of anything white. Since he is the offspring of black and white parents he could have been a uniter of the races and rule both with fairness. He had the opportunity to join George Washington and Thomas Jefferson as icons of America. But, this was not his destiny. He has chosen to deny his white heritage because the black side offers an easier path to the totalitarian system soon to replace the decaying republic of America.

Although our constitutional republic is in tatters and crumbling daily, there are still enough shreds remaining to prevent Obama from moving too quickly. He must dismantle us one brick at a time until enough has been removed to allow greater speed. Like a predator, he chooses the weakest prey first, and saves the stronger prey for later when perhaps other tactics can be used to advantage. If a prey doesn't fight back, then he will remember and use the same tactics again and again. Who could have imagined a few years ago that our President would fire the head of General Motors and then take over both General Motors and Chrysler? I remember years ago when banana republics in South America or oil-rich nations like Libya and Saudi Arabia, would take over companies unilaterally. Back then, we called it "nationalizing" or "expropriating" of companies without their approval. Did you hear anyone say these words when Obama did the same thing? Who is next and will anybody fight back or even say anything? Obama is turning up the heat, and boiling the frog, while our leaders are either silent or providing the fuel for the fire.

Compared to over half of the white male population of the United States, Obama lived a life of privilege and never wanted for any of the material things the rest of us were denied. His mother and grandparents provided him with a middle-class childhood, and an upper-class pre-college education at the prestigious private Punahou School in Honolulu where his grade average was a "C". He never had to work at a job or want for anything. He, his wife, and his Chicago mob are tight-lipped on his college years, but we do know some things for sure.

Obama attended Occidental College in Los Angeles from 1979 to 1981. No one has ever been able to uncover a single transcript from this college for Obama. We do know he was a heavy drug user, changed his name from Barry to Barack, befriended only Marxists, radicals, and homosexuals, and traveled to Karachi, Pakistan, for unknown reasons. The mere fact that his grades are locked-out to all comers means they were something he is ashamed of. He left Occidental without earning a degree.

Obama arrived at New York's Columbia University in August 1981. Here he met terrorist Bill Ayers, "professor of terror" Edward Said, and Zbigniew Brzezinski (Jimmy Carter's personal socialist). Wayne Allyn Root was a political science major at Columbia and graduated in 1983. He was active in student affairs and has no memory of Obama. He attended the 20th class reunion in 2003, and was chosen to be the speaker of the class. He said not even one of the attendees had any recollection of Obama. Fox News contacted 400 students who had attended Columbia the same time as Obama and not a single person remembers a student named Obama. His photograph does not appear in the school's yearbook. Obama refuses to talk about his years at Columbia, provide the names of classmates, or his school records. Obama supposedly fell in love with a white woman there, but refused to marry her for fear he would have to adapt his life to her white world. Obama states he graduated from Columbia, but his diploma has never been produced.

After spending four years organizing in Chicago, Obama, at 27 years of age, entered Harvard in 1988. Again, his grades had been so pitiful at Columbia that he had to rely on affirmative action to push aside qualified whites that had worked years for a chance to be the 1 in 14 candidates admitted to Harvard. But, Obama had more than just his victim-status going for him. A jihadist, orthodox Muslim, Khalid al-Mansour, lobbied for him with Manhattan Borough President Percy Sutton to intervene on Obama's behalf at Harvard. It worked because even with affirmative action for black incompetents like Obama, Harvard still wanted the best of the worst, yet what they got was the worst.

During the 2008 campaign and even now we hear nothing about Obama's college grades, but we do hear about Obama being president of the Harvard Law Review. Again, luck and blackness came through for him. In early 1990 radical black professor, Derrick Bell, was inciting demonstrations and near-riots to bolster his demands that Harvard appoint more blacks to the faculty. Even Harvard had enough Black History professors teaching this useless subject, but Bell was using the race card like all blacks do when they don't get their way. This racial pressure spread to the editors of the Harvard Law Review who reluctantly decided to elect their first black president. Obama was light-skinned, didn't have corn-rowed hair and wasn't frothing at the mouth like some of the black radicals. This made him a more acceptable choice. Also, Harvard had recently replaced its policy of choosing the student with the highest grades to be president, and now chose half of the editors through a writing competition. For this competition Obama wrote his first and last literary note on the subject of abortion; arguing for unlimited killing of the unborn to save them from having to grow-up in a repressive country like the United States. The note was full of grammatical errors and misspelled words. When debate day arrived there were 18 other candidates vying for the law review presidency. It turned into an all-day affair.

It seems Obama became president of the HLR the same way he became POTUS. As an article in the New York Times reported, he "cast himself as an eager listener, sometimes giving warring classmates the impression that he agreed with all of them at once." The single note written on abortion for the contest to fill one of the 43 editor slots at the HLR was the only writing Obama ever did at Harvard. There is no record, anywhere at any time, of another single word written by Obama at the HLR. Rather than advance to a clerking job for the Supreme Court, as do most HLR past-presidents,

Obama returned to Chicago for bigger and better opportunities. He had already lived in Chicago for five years and had a coterie of radicals, Muslim money men, street thugs, and just ordinary everyday mobsters awaiting his return.

So, Obama graduated from Harvard in 1991 and returned to Chicago where he got married and joined the firm of Davis, Miner, Barnhill & Gallard. He also signed with publisher, Time Books, to write an autobiography which he eventually called "Dreams from My Father." In the acknowledgements section he credits 49 people that helped him write the book. Most authors credit their wife, their editor, and perhaps 2 or 3 people who proofread or gave advice, but I have never known the author of a simple autobiography to need 49 people to help him write it. Supposedly it was his life he wrote about and usually the author is personally and uniquely alone in knowing what to write about himself. Why would anyone need 49 outsiders to tell him how to write about the simple, privileged life described in his first book? Even more extraordinary, is that it took Obama and his 49 ghost writers until the middle of 1995 to finish the simple book. But, never fear, the gushing, racist media heaped praise on Obama for this tome disclosing his "personal struggles," and so far, he has collected over $8 million dollars on his two simple little narrative books that took 49 people to help him write.

In 1996 Obama ran for and was elected to the Soviet Socialist Republic of Illinois State Senate. Being from Illinois myself, I can vouch for its corruption from the top down, and with Muslim money and black racism it's easy to understand Obama's election. Blacks compose about a third of Chicago and it matters not if you are a rapist, pedophile, murderer, queer, felon or wife-beater, as long as you are black and Democrat you have a life-long career. So, in 1998 he was re-elected.

Anxious to move up the ladder, Obama ran for Chicago's first congressional seat held by another black, Bobby Rush. It was an uphill battle since blacks adored Rush's hatred for whites, and he had earned their love by organizing the Chicago chapter of the Black Panthers and spending time in prison. He had proven 35 years ago what the Black Caucus only recently discovered: Castro was a really great guy who we just needed to get to know better. Rush and other black racists had ridden in on the coattails of Harold Washington, first black mayor of Chicago, who in turn rode into the Chicago mayoralty on the coattails of communists. Anyway, Barry lost his first try at national office and like all good Democrats, he hadn't resigned his Senate seat to run for Congress, so he just stayed put. Of course, he was re-elected in 2002. In all three terms as Illinois State Senator, Obama originated no legislation, and made no impact on anything.

In 2004 Obama decided to run for the U.S. Senate. His opponent initially was Republican Jack Ryan who quit the race due to a sex scandal. Many think Obama and his Chicago mobsters planted the personal information about Ryan with their media friends to knock Ryan out of the race. The Republicans quickly secured Alan Keyes to fill-in for Ryan on short notice. Keyes didn't have a chance. He was moral, honest, and God-fearing while Obama was immoral, corrupt, and thought he <u>was</u> God. Once again, it proved that blacks do not want quality in their representatives; they want welfare, victim status and reparations. So, On January 4, 2005, Obama was sworn in as the junior Senator from Illinois behind Dick "Turban" Durbin. He spent the next four years voting either "absent" or "present" in the Senate.

Anxious to reach the next rung, Obama announced for the Presidency on February 10, 2007. He defeated Hillary Clinton in the primary, and became the Democrat candidate on June 3, 2008. Without having any idea who or what Obama is all about, the voters gave him 53% of the vote and made him President on November 4, 2008. Why would 300 million people place a stranger in charge of the only superpower on the planet? Why would Obama spend $1 million guarding his original birth certificate from release, hundreds of thousands to make sure no media talked to his grandmother, refuse to disclose his kindergarten records, Punahou school records, Occidental College records, Columbia University records, Columbia thesis, Harvard Law School records, Harvard Law Review articles, scholarly articles from the University of Chicago, passport, medical records, files from his years as an Illinois State Senator, his Illinois State Bar Association records, or any baptism records? Just as December 7, 1941, is remembered as the "Day of Infamy," so too will November 4, 2008, be remembered as the day that America entered its death throes.

Some empires fall by violence from without and others are attacked from within. In other words, some nations die by homicide and some die by suicide. Our demise is the latter type and will happen faster than most realize. Our death will be a self-inflicted one. Many find it easy to simply lay the blame on ignorant voters, since a despotic racist- socialist like Obama could not have arisen from the depths of obscurity overnight without really dumb people voting before making themselves aware of Obama's Hitler-like intentions. Of course, ignorant, ill-informed and uninformed voters are the direct cause, but the voters themselves were the victims of 60 years of relentless attacks on their foundational beliefs by the Darkside. Drugs, homosexuals, leftist media, pornography, feminist movement, faux-enviro radicals, destruction of our education system, and black victimization disguised as civil rights, all worked to dumb-down present day voters. By the time Obama arrived on the scene, Americans were filled with global-warming hysteria, pre-occupied with drugs and sex, and felt so terrible about slavery that they would vote for anybody as long as they were black and had a "D" next to their name. The 40 million blacks in the U.S. needed no such propaganda or brainwashing since almost 99% of them are racist and vote the straight color ticket.

If Americans had not been drunk, drugged, dumbed-down, or brain-dead they would have been alarmed at what Obama openly said he was going to do in the campaign, or his lack of accomplishments, or the nuts he surrounded himself with in his 47 years of life. To me, the state-controlled media was absolutely crucial in Obama's election. For eight long years they had pounded on Bush and the Republicans. When Obama came along the press kept beating-up on Bush and McCain, but combined that with adulation and worship of Obama. This double-whammy was too much for the voting public, so even moderates were numb and indecisive when they went to the polls.

Neither this book nor ten more like it can explain to you all the intricate and complicated overt and covert activities being conducted by Obama and his apparatchik apparatus. Obama is not only the most dangerous and evil personage ever to reside in the White House, but he threatens the stability of the planet by weakening and destroying the United States. Make no mistake about his intent to bring

America to its knees. Even Obama can plainly see that America is unique and exceptional in the history of the earth, but his only concern is that blacks did not participate as full partners in this prosperity. He holds whites alone guilty of this crime of exclusion. Bringing down the only superpower on the planet with its 234 years of history and institutions is a monumental task. But it can, and probably will happen no later than 2012. If you doubt this then study every empire that fell primarily by the actions of its own citizens as opposed to a siege or attack by an enemy force. Obama has set in motion, in all strategic points of our government and private sectors, his operatives to dismantle and so alter the structures of the United States that a point will soon be reached from which it will be impossible for us to return to an America that we even recognize.

THE PERFECT STORM

As you know, the movie "The Perfect Storm" was based on a real-life event about three weather systems that came together off the northeast coast of the U.S. to create the storm of the century. It killed all 6 men aboard the "Andrea Gail" sword fishing boat, and did millions of dollars in damage on shore. It took a perfect storm of timing, personages, and circumstances to place a person in charge of the very nation for which he has only enmity and hatred. Typically, empires are brought down either by foreign powers or peripheral dissidents from within. Very rarely, if ever, has a viable nation invited and installed as their emperor someone who openly vowed his disgust for its people and institutions. What were the elements of this perfect storm, and how did they all develop and lead to Obama's rise to the Presidency?

Anyone who read Obama's two books, and looked beyond his pity-trip over being born "a poor black child," will see a hate-filled sociopath who yearns for revenge against the very nation that made him President, despite his questionable credentials and coming from the same 13% minority that used to be labeled "chattel" property. This "poor me" slobbering appeal for people to think of all blacks as victims, and needing dispensation to compensate for slavery, dove-tailed nicely with the thinking of the diversity, affirmative-action, crowd. These people snapped-up copies of Obama's book and said, "Right-on" and "Go, brother Barack." So, one of the elements of the perfect set of circumstances that paved the way for Obama's messianic arrival was the sea of disaffected blacks who had been kept in servitude by the black elite, who had in turn shifted the blame for their plight to the whites. Democrats had enjoyed getting 90% of the black vote for the past 50 years, but they were joined in 2008 by another 9% of blacks. Together, this was the unabashed racist vote. It didn't matter that Obama had done nothing in his life, that he was a fascist, or that he had no slave blood in his veins. Only color of skin mattered. Had Obama been a white guy with the same absence of credentials, most blacks would have stayed home on November 4th of '08.

Perhaps the most important element of the perfect storm was the prepping of the electorate by the media. Most Americans go to a job, come home, watch a half-hour of news on broadcast TV, and go to bed. They are not exposed to and do not seek alternative news, or question what liberal talking heads say. Having only a superficial knowledge of the plethora of events occurring constantly, they don't have the time or desire to dissect or question the news. They don't even know that there is leftist bias in everything they see, read or hear.

Bias used to be limited to the news shows. Now, leftist views are expressed in every movie, situation comedy, variety show, TV series, and even cartoons. The most common theme in the big screen movies is the big, bad, capitalist corporation picking on poor little green people. In "Law and Order" you may see them commenting derisively about Rush Limbaugh. Oprah Winfrey refused to have Sarah Palin as a guest until after her messiah was immaculated. Even on "fair and balanced" Fox you will see liberals like Shepard Smith and Geraldo Rivera attacking conservatives and coddling liberals. Lately, they are having more liberals like Bill Press on their panel discussions, as if we don't already have liberals dominating every other channel. If Fox keeps drifting south, there will be no reason to watch Fox anymore. Saturday Night Live and David Letterman pounded viciously on Sarah Palin both during and even after the 2008 election. Glenn Beck was only on radio before Obama was elected, so on TV we had only Hannity on Fox, and on radio we had Rush and just a few others to get the truth to us. But, most Americans either ignore the news or get it from liberal sources. Human beings are incapable of being exposed to propaganda day in and day out without being affected. We really have no newspapers anymore that are conservative. The Wall Street Journal is fair and balanced like its sister company Fox, but it has a relatively small readership.

George W. Bush is the best example of how destructive the media can be. The media beat up on Bush for everything from the WMD's to his dog Buddy. Nothing was off-limits whether it was his Texas Air National Guard service or his pronunciation of "nuclear." For seven days a week all that people heard was what an idiot he was, nothing ever good, never a compliment. Many people knew they hated Bush, but couldn't tell you exactly why. Mind control, propaganda, and psy-ops have been around since Adam and Eve, and there is no more refined state-of-the-art information dissemination system than the American media.

In the early days of broadcasting most of us detected a bias, but it was denied so vehemently by the press that we even doubted ourselves. We wrote it off to compassion for the downtrodden and didn't take it too serious. And, really it wasn't too serious back then because we still had two viable political parties. And, we were comfortable with them sparring back and forth since we kind of knew they both loved the same country we did. But, starting with the election of Bill Clinton the bias became more sinister and evil. The press sort of fed on themselves without the need for leftist input from the Democrats or other liberal groups. The media became their own self-serving entity; more an integral part of the left-wing than just a mere helpmate.

The internet has been a help to both the liberals and conservatives. Other than Rush and Glenn Beck, I depend on the internet for all my news. Unfortunately, I think the liberals make more and better use of the internet than do conservatives. When you use search engines, 9 out of 10 hits are liberal sites, so it takes a while to get to a site that hasn't been co-opted by the left. Obama made extensive use of the internet to solicit contributions and hide the identity of donors. Contributions came in to his coffers from Daffy Duck, Bart Simpson, dead people, and people whose identity was stolen. We hear of the growing numbers of Americans on the web, but the majority of those not on the web are the folks in rural areas who just happen to be largely conservatives. Hopefully, conservatives can make better use of the internet in the next election.

White guilt is another element of Obama's perfect storm. It took many years of constant propaganda, by both the media and government, to build the perceived guilt of white people to the highest level possible just prior to Obama's election. I think it actually declined after the fact, but it was too late to help stop the messiah's immaculation. I covered white guilt in other sections of this book, and won't dwell on it here except to say it is real and was a deciding factor in his election.

The final element, combining together with the others, and never before existing, were two generations of black, white, and brown Americans that had never known hardship or adversity of any kind. They saw America as oppressive, not sharing its wealth, and were not appreciative of its uniqueness. Whites thought education was a right and college was for parties, sex, and booze. They were also products of 50 years of propaganda by the civil rights elites and media telling them how blacks had suffered at the hands of whites. Blacks saw affirmative action and welfare due them as victims. Browns saw the Democrats as the route to everything free including amnesty. For once, the students and professors were on the same side and both were pro-Obama.

THE MADHI COMETH

Of course, I am referring to Obama, and not the Mahdi as discussed in another part of this book. Although, when you have a chance, Google "Mahdi Obama" and see what comes up. I discovered that quite a few people think he really is the 12th Imam. I'll just play ignorant on that one even though the Mahdi, Hitler, and Obama share a commonality. All three require(d) chaos to come to power and bring order to the masses. More folks think Obama is the anti-Christ. I don't think he is that either. No, Obama is just one very lucky, fascist, light-skinned black guy who came along at the right time after Clinton, Bush, the media, white guilt, black elites, and white radicals had already prepared the way.

Obama's most difficult opponent in the Democrat primary was Hillary Clinton. At the beginning of the campaign all the pundits and talking heads thought she had it all wrapped-up. She and Obama had no differences on any of the issues. When the Kennedy clan got behind Obama and the money dried-up for Clinton, the writing was on the wall. What Clinton failed to realize was that she was further down the pecking order of the new liberals. Due to racism, Obama automatically had 100% of the black vote which would have normally been spread among all the Democrat contenders. Once Republicans picked the fair-weather McCain, the race was over. With the media on Obama's side, and Obama taking in as much as $150 million a month from suspicious sources, McCain didn't have a chance. A lot of conservatives stayed at home because McCain was simply boring and not inspiring of anything. Plus, the Darkside and George Soros had been corrupting and defrauding the electoral system for years and probably skewed the total votes by 3% to 9% anyway.

Obama was the first President to be elected before anybody knew anything about him. We weren't sure if he was a U.S. citizen, and couldn't even talk to his grandmother because she was guarded day and night by Obama's henchmen. We couldn't see Obama's college transcripts or talk to anyone that attended college with him. The media protected him, but even when one of his mentors like Imam Wright or Bill "bomber" Ayers surfaced they were ignored by all but Fox. The ignorance of Americans was on full display for all to see.

The media was absolutely giddy over Obama. Many white Americans suffering from a guilt complex after being told for 60 years they were the source of the black second-class status, sent money, and voted for Obama. The media knew their role was to amplify the good and conceal the bad. McCain's side was handicapped right from the start. They had to avoid any hint of race, or Obama's watchdogs would use the race card. McCain already had a reputation of being an apologist, and crossing the aisle on the amnesty and campaign financing legislation. He even apologized for Bill Cunningham uttering Obama's middle name during a rally. Can you wrap your brain around how silly it is when you cannot even speak your opponent's full name without being called a racist? What if Cunningham had told the crowd that Obama's mother's first name was Stanley? What's the penalty for that, death?

Like most conservatives, I was ABC (Anybody But McCain), but was elated to see him pick Sarah Palin as his running mate. I donated $600 to them, but now feel it was a bad investment. They didn't have a chance against blacks, leftists, unions, white guilt, and the propaganda machine of the media. Obama's Chicago mob used the same tactics that had worked for 75 years in Chicago to whip and organize the electorate. I am from Illinois where my brother was a lawyer in Chicago, and his wife was director of the Illinois Educational Service Center for Chicago. She was caught "helping" the kids of influential politicians get preferential treatment and fired in 1995. I don't know where she is now, but if you help politicians in Chicago and get caught, you may lose your job and have to lay low for awhile, but they find a spot for you somewhere. She and my brother split-up before she made headlines.

Obama came to Chicago in 1982. As a community organizer making $13,000 a year he traveled extensively around the city and started up the chain of command. Although Chicago is the third largest city in the U.S. it manages to stay out of the headlines more than New York or Los Angeles or even smaller cities. This is because it is a controlled, stratified city-state with rigid rules and discipline. In a way, it exists as if Al Capon and his gang moved from Cicero to city hall and they are still there. Like a Mafia crime family, it has its own set of dons, captains, consigliores, and soldiers. It has a large black and Hispanic population, but run by a white mayor, Daley. It also has a large and active socialist/communist community. All these groups and many more cooperate and make deals to maintain the machine so all can get their share of the power and the treasury. Virtually every Chicagoan in any way related to politics is in on the fix. Every once in a while a few members of the outer circle get indicted by an ambitious U.S. Attorney, so they sacrifice a few judges or gang members, but never will the big fish be hooked. Governor Rod Blagojevich got nabbed and may have to cool his heels for a few months in the pen, but nothing more will come of it. Jesse Jackson Jr. is on tape trying to buy Obama's vacated Senate seat and there is hard evidence that Valerie Jarrett's supporters tried to do the same for her. But, nothing will happen to either of them now that Chicago has moved to Washington. The same is true for Burris, the "Rent-A-Senator" dummy sitting in Obama old Senate seat. In the past, many Illinois governors have always made unexpected career detours straight to prison before permanent retirement, but they now have Obama to cover for them. What will change is the pecking order. Blacks have always gotten their share of the Chicago pie, but less so since Chicago's black mayor, Harold Washington, croaked back in 1987. With Obama's ascendancy, the white political bosses in Chicago have come to the realization that blacks are in the catbird seat so they tread softly.

People have long said that California sets the trend for the whole country. Obama's election shows that Soviet Illinois now sets the trends of the future. Blacks, unions, socialists, communists, Muslims, and radicals have long controlled Illinois, and are busy installing that same mob apparatus to control the entire U.S. Illinois was the testing ground for Obama and his rise to power that surpassed his most ambitious expectations. He has now used his Chicago mob and Illinois model, and extrapolated it to the remaining 49 states. It too, is working greater than he imagined. Yes, the Mahdi has arrived. The only thing he must do to become the 12th Imam is to manufacture the crises Rahm Emmanuel said they need to create the chaos that will allow Obama to ride in on his white horse, and rescue us all from the fairy-tale, fabricated dilemma that is coming soon to your neighborhood.

OBAMA MANIFESTO

There is no official document titled the "Obama Manifesto." All we can do is examine his life, spoken word, actions, and writings to compile his Mein Kampf. Obama is a fascist. I could have labeled him a Nazi, since the two are very close in definition, but I think fascism fits him better. I also declined to use socialism or communism because both theoretically are administered by a committee, not a dictator. And, Obama does want to be a dictator. These two forms of totalitarianism own the means of production, and this has proven unworkable in the USSR and China. If Obama is good at anything, it is being able to "change" to accommodate his ambitions. No, fascism fits Barry better because it is defined as: "a governmental system led by a dictator having complete power, forcibly suppressing opposition and criticism, regimenting all industry, commerce, and private enterprise and emphasizing an aggressive nationalism and often racism." Obama is absolutely consolidating power. He is using our tax money to increase the membership of unions, vastly increase the number of federal employees, and targeting all monies directly to Democrat districts. He is nationalizing industries to pay back his donors, and destroying small companies to help the larger ones that have agreed to cooperate in his schemes. His radical racism is evident in all his actions.

To convert capitalist America to fascism requires using techniques from all of the "isms" Obama can employ. To give him time to develop and install his other control and financial plans he first needed to deflect the blame onto others to hide his own misdeeds. Both during Obama's campaign, and even after his first year, George Bush served this purpose. The Jews served the same purpose for Hitler.

When the folks started tiring of the "Bush bashing," Obama added other scapegoats like Rush Limbaugh, Fox, and the Tea Parties. The Obama lapdog media latched onto this tack and added their own embellishments to enhance the attacks. Every time the public wakes up from their apathy and sees through Obama's latest veiled fascist shenanigans, he and his demons will drag out another one of Saul Alinsky's axioms from his "Rules for Radicals." Alinsky taught his followers to "Lie, dissemble, ridicule and deride your opponent...do what you need to do to get ahead. Listen to and learn their needs and take advantage...do not care. Manipulate the morals. Lying is never wrong as long as it leads you to a position of power. Say what you need to say to get ahead. The ends justify the means." He also said the organizer's job is "first to bring folks to the realization that they are miserable, their misery is a result of greedy corporations, help bond them together and demand what they deserve from said greedy corporations." To emphasize class warfare, Alinsky said, "We have a war on our hands...a war between those with the money and those with the people...if we can convince the people they are miserable, then we can gather the people." In case you ever wondered where Obama got his "Hope and Change" slogan let me enlighten you. Alinsky wrote, "The use of the ideology of change and hope as a power technique is key to mobilizing the dispossessed to ban together and create pressure on the system."

Although Obama never met Alinsky (Hillary did) he literally worshipped him and religiously adhered to Rules for Radicals in organizing. Obama had been prepped for receiving and incorporating Alinsky's philosophy into his own ambitions years ago by his mentor Frank Marshall Davis. Obama tried to hide his relationship with Davis by referring to him in his first book as merely Frank the "poet." Actually, Obama looked to Davis as a father figure during their 8 year association in Hawaii. Davis was an active member of the Communist Party USA (CPUSA) and was investigated by the House Un-American Activities Committee. Although Obama avoids mention of Davis, another known communist, Paul Robeson, spilled the beans and said Obama and Davis were close, and Davis spent years teaching Obama the superiority of communism. Frank Chapman, a member of CPUSA, wrote in their official publication concerning Obama's election,

"Obama's victory was more than a progressive move, it was a dialectical leap ushering in a qualitatively new era of struggle. Marx once compared revolutionary struggle with the work of the mole, who sometimes burrows so far beneath the ground that he leaves no trace of his movement on the surface. This is the old revolutionary 'mole' not only avoiding showing his traces on the surface but also breaking through." Like I'm trying to tell you in this book, if you do not believe that Obama's intent is to create chaos and transform that chaos into fascism, then I can do no more for you.

After being mentored by Davis and studying Alinsky's community organizing handbook, Obama moved on to integrate himself into the real world of social activism. In Chicago, Obama met Bill Ayers and Carl Davidson, two of the original organizers of the Students for a Democratic Society. In Chicago, Davidson helped organize the rally in 2002 where Obama spoke against our coming involvement in the Iraq war. He is an admitted Maoist Communist, organized Progressives for Obama, and is active in socialist and communist circles. Ayers is a whole lot more interesting.

Obama worked with Ayers in Chicago at the Chicago Annenberg Challenge (CAC) where both sat on the board deciding how to spend foundation money on leftist causes. Recent info on Ayers is rare since Obama has told him to keep his mouth shut. But, many examples of his writings are still around. In 1970 he wrote, "Kill all the rich people. Break up their cars and apartments. Bring the revolution home. Kill your parents, that's where it's really at." He went underground when his girlfriend and two other SDS wackos were blown-up while making bombs in Greenwich Village. Another girlfriend, Bernardine Dohrn, was put on the FBI's 10 most wanted list. J. Edgar Hoover called her "the most dangerous woman in America." After the Manson murders in Beverly Hills, Dohrn told her SDS audience, "Dig it! Manson killed those pigs. Then they ate dinner in the same room with them. Then they shoved a fork into a victim's stomach."

While heading up the Chicago Annenberg Challenge Foundation, Obama helped dispense hundreds of millions of dollars directly for the funding of leftist groups like ACORN and the Developing Communities Project of the Gamaliel Foundation. Bill Ayers sat on the Annenberg Foundation, also. He makes no apologies for bombing the Pentagon or other radical acts with the SDS. Like all radical revolutionaries and communists in the U.S., he easily secured a distinguished Professorship of Education at the University of Illinois, where he is today, teaching American youth his brand of anti-American terrorism. He joins the thousands of other socialists, communists, and anti-American professors that now constitute the majority at all of our universities; your education tax dollars at work.

One definite player in the formulation of Obama's manifesto is Jeremiah "Imam" Wright. While Obama merely claims to be a Christian, Wright even had the audacity to include Christ's name in the title of his so-called "church", The Trinity United Church of Christ. For 20 long years Obama listened to this Imam's sermons, was married by him, had his kids baptized by him, and dropped money in his collection plate. He even named his second book and speech before the 2004 DNC after one of Wright's sermons. And, Obama then said he never listened to the ranting nutjob! Of course, many white Americans believed him as he knew they would. Wright is actually a racist and worships at the altar of black liberation theology which simply means black Marxist victimology. His closest friend is Louis Farrakhan who admitted he murdered Malcom X and took over the Nation of Islam, another racist group who hates whites and Jews. Few people even today have grasped the significance of Wright's influential impact on Obama and, coming soon, the entire United States.

Kyle-Anne Shiver actually visited Wright's church in 2008 to see what Obama and Wright were all about. Wright's frothing rants and telling the congregation to vote for Obama was expected, but the pamphlets and books in the church bookstore were eye-openers. Instead of the normal volumes on Christianity, the books were on Black Muslim belief systems and Marxist ideology. Most common were books by James H. Cone, the founder of the Black Liberation Theology movement. Cone is the mentor of Wright just as Wright is Obama's mentor. Shiver found that the common foundation of both Wright's "Christianity" and Farrakhan's Black Islam church is Marxism. The fact that Christ is used as a tool, rather than worshiped, is proven by Cone's simple statement that, "The appearance of black theology means that the black community is now ready to do something about the white Jesus, so that he cannot get in the way of our revolution."

In Jeremiah Wright's sermons and private talks, Obama had found a faith that melded with the atheist beliefs of his mother, Stanley, and the Marxist beliefs he had come to embrace. On page 207 of Obama's "Audacity" book, he describes his euphoria at realizing he can keep Marxism and still use Christ to reach his destiny: "In the history of these (African people's) struggles, I was to see faith as more than just a comfort to the weary or a hedge against death; rather, it was an active, palpable agent in the world...It was because of these newfound understandings (at Trinity under Wright) that religious commitment did not require me to suspend critical thinking, disengage from the battle for economic and social justice...that I was finally able to walk down the aisle of Trinity... and be baptized." Obama's chants of "We are the ones we've been waiting for" and "Yes, we can" mean that he is the first to ever have the power to finally bring to fruition and combine the dreams of black liberation theology and Marxist ideology.

So, Obama had now matured his Marxist dogma beginning with his mother and expanded by Frank Marshall Davis in Hawaii. From Bill Ayers and Carl Davidson he learned of the methodology of persuasion and brute force, if necessary, to achieve Marxism. From Saul Alinsky he gleaned the written rules to follow to hoodwink the masses into following him. He put all these lessons to work in his community organizing, but he still lacked the critical ingredient to use politics as his vehicle to deliver black theology and Marx in a palatable form. He knew no President had ever been elected without Christian credentials. Wright and Cone showed him the way to cloak his Marxism with the shroud of Christ, and shed it only after the war on whites and Christians was won. He now had his Manifesto.

OBAMA'S ROGUES

By "rogues" I refer to Obama's cabinet, his appointments, his czars, and the inside people that generally are helping him to dismantle the American republic and reassemble it into a fascist oligarchy. If you are a patriotic American and proud of your heritage, and want to preserve this exceptional nation for your children, then you would never, ever employ, let alone hire, any of the following people. In fact, if it was your intention to destroy America and you needed to assemble a hit squad, then Obama has made excellent selections. Space doesn't allow for all of them so I'll be selective. If you do not investigate in detail all of Obama's rogue gallery then you will simply never comprehend your imminent danger and will be unprepared when our point-of-no-return is beyond recall.

Bill Clinton - Clinton is the first of Obama's rogues because he and his radical leftist' wife wanted to do the same things Obama is doing, but America wasn't quite ready for Fascism in the early 90's. Between bimbo eruptions and knocking-off a few of his Arkansas mob buddies like Vince Foster, he had precious little free time to spare for the hard work of creating a Fascist state. To witness the helter-skelter path of destruction caused by Bill Clinton to the United States we should all be thankful that his brain was between his legs most of the time. Had he concentrated his full energies, like Obama is now doing, we would be much closer to Fascism. Had Russia, China, Iran, and North Korea gotten together and hired a saboteur to destroy the U.S. from within they could not have chosen a better person for the job. If you ask the typical Walmart-American their opinion of Bill Clinton they will snicker and say he couldn't keep his pants up, but he wasn't such a bad guy. This blissful ignorance prevails even more today than during Clinton's tenure and is masking the dire consequences ahead. Clinton brought his Little Rock Mob, just as Obama took along his Chicago Mob, when invading Washington. But the alley-cat morality of Clinton was a diversion for the media, and hid the very real damage that he was doing to prepare the United States for take-over from within. This is a book about Obama, so I will present just a sketch of Clinton's damage and maybe you will do some research on your own.

When Presidents take the oath of office, they promise to "protect and defend" the Constitution. This means the President promises to defend the American people and their property against all threats, foreign and domestic. This was Clinton's greatest failure, and if not intentional, then perhaps you can ascribe another term for his actions that is more PC and less conspiratorial. On February 26, 1993, after Clinton had been in office one month, al Qaeda tried for the first time to bring down the Twin Towers with a truck packed with explosives. It blew a hole 60 feet deep, killed 6 people and hurt 1000, but wasn't powerful enough to cause the collapse of the supporting columns. The FBI captured, tried, and convicted 6 Palestinians and 1 Egyptian and they were sentenced to life in prison. But the leader, Iraqi intelligence agent Ramzi Ahmed Yousef, got away. This was obviously state-sponsored terrorism. Clinton was warned that it was just the beginning, but his response was to avoid "over-reaction."

In 1993 Clinton and his willy-nilly Defense Secretary Aspin sent Rangers and other troops as part of a UN "humanitarian" mission to Mogadishu, Somalia, to stop the take-over by Adid and his al Qaeda-linked cohorts. I remember attending the funeral of my aunt in Illinois and found out from my Uncle Jim that his only son, Jimmy, my first cousin, was in Mogadishu, and had recently had the tips of four of his fingers severed in an attempt to capture Adid and his henchmen. In a phone call home he had told my Aunt Karen that they were going on missions outnumbered and unprepared, and he feared something bad was going to happen. Jimmy was a tough Ranger and didn't scare easily. The next week I got a call from my cousin, Monty, telling me Jimmy had been killed and drug through the streets of Mogadishu. I headed back to Illinois for his funeral. Another cousin of mine, Master Sergeant Sandy Wendt, was in Mogadishu also, and accompanied Jimmy's body home. I found out from her and Captain Castel who brought Jimmy home that what was later depicted in "Blackhawk Down" was largely true. No armor and no support were given to the special ops guys in case of trouble. Jimmy's buddies commandeered a Pakistani armored personnel carrier, and brought his body back to the UN soccer field after 9 hours of fighting. Two weeks later Clinton detailed some of Jimmy's fellow soldiers to guard Adid, so that he could attend negotiations to resolve the leadership void in Somalia. Clinton took no action against al Qaeda. Somalia was forgotten by all except the families of the dead and wounded. My uncle and aunt appeared on "Good Morning America" and blamed Clinton, but who cares what bereaved Americans think.

Soon after the Somalia debacle al Qaeda groups tried to blow-up the Lincoln and Holland Tunnels, but were caught before they could pull it off. At about the same time, a group of al Qaeda terrorists were caught planning to hi-jack airliners, and use them as guided-missiles to attack structures too large for car bombs or suicide bombers. The planner behind this was again Ramzi Yousef. Another plot was discovered to blow up Los Angeles Airport during the millennium celebrations there. The only thing Clinton did was to appoint Algore to look into improving airport security, but he ended up advising a need to protect the "civil liberties" of terror suspects and avoid "profiling," lest we anger our Muslim friends. Ijaz Mansoor was Clinton's liaison with Sudan President Bashir. Mansoor told Clinton that Bashir would give him Osama Bin Laden and intelligence on the Islamic Jihad, Hezbollah, and Hamas, if Clinton would lift sanctions against Sudan. Instead, Clinton pressured Bashir to expel Bin Laden, which he did, along with Ayman Awahiri who later planned the 9/11 attacks. Along with Bin Laden's entourage that left Sudan for Afghanistan were two of the terrorists who flew the planes into the Twin Towers. Clinton passed on no less than three opportunities to capture Osama Bin Laden.

One month after Bin Laden landed in Afghanistan, a 5000 pound truck bomb killed 19 Americans at the Khobar Towers military barracks in Saudi Arabia. Hezbollah was responsible, but since they were friends of Iran, and Clinton was pursuing relations with Iran, he blustered but did not act. He went even further by saying Iran had legitimate complaints against the U.S. because they have "been the subject of quite a lot of abuse from various Western nations." Like Obama, he never missed an opportunity to apologize for the United States being the cause of all the world's problems. He took a bunch of black elitists with him to Uganda in 1998 to apologize for slavery, even though no slaves ever came from Uganda or any East African state. Slavery started in that part of Africa 1000 years before slaves were brought to America and is still practiced there today. Four months after this apology trip, al Qaeda blew-up United States embassies in Kenya and Tanzania killing 245 people and injuring 5000. Again, there was no retaliation because Clinton was embroiled in his bimbo eruptions, and we were effectively "without a President from January 1998 to April 1999," according to Dick Morris. He did manage to distract attention from his eruptions when he launched cruise missiles and destroyed a pharmaceutical factory in Sudan that produced antibiotics. That action resulted in over 20,000 deaths from malaria due to the lack of the drugs to fight the disease.

On October 12, 2000, the USS Cole in a Yemeni Harbor was rammed by a small boat loaded with explosives and killed 17 American sailors and wounded 39 others. Clinton again handled it like a misdemeanor shop-lifting offense, and took no action or even called it an act of terrorism. Clinton, his National Security Advisor, Sandy Berger, Tony Lake, and others were all products of the 1960's radicals and anti-war protestors who hated the military. Together, they reduced our military from 2.1 million to 1.6 million service members. Clinton brags about reducing the federal payroll, but 286,000 of the 305,000 reduction were American soldiers who Clinton riffed out of the military. We had a 546 ship Navy when Clinton took office and 380 when he left. Squadrons in the Air Force went from 76 to just 50 by the end of his second term. He did manage to make it easier for homosexuals to enter service and remain in uniform, and spent a large part of the military budget to refurbish ships and barracks to accommodate women, since he assumed our soldiers had his same affinity for illicit sex. He also worked to change the mission of troops from "killing people and breaking things" to "consciousness raising" and "softer and gentler." Clinton thought the United States was more like a satellite of the United Nations than a sovereign nation. His two big excursions into the military arena were a "peace keeping" venture in Haiti, and a "humanitarian war" in the Balkans to rescue Muslims from the Christians, even though the former had supported the Nazis and had been killing Christians since the 1300's.

Clinton and his Department of Energy Secretary did manage to transfer millions of pages of formerly classified nuclear secrets to the Chinese, Iranians, and North Koreans to speed-up their nuclear programs. In return, Clinton got campaign money for his second term from James and Mochtar Riady, John Huang, Charlie Trie, Ted Sioeng, Maria Hsia, and Wang Jun, all operatives of foreign powers. He also gave control of both the Atlantic and Pacific ports on the Panama Canal to Hutchinson Whampoa Ltd. which is controlled by China's People's Liberation Army. I'm sure you've heard of our various intelligence agencies blaming 9/11 on their lack of communications with each other. Well, you can thank Bill for that problem, too. Jamie Gorelick (who went on to rob Fannie Mae of $27 million and help cause the housing crisis) was Clinton's Deputy Attorney General and strictly forbid cooperation between the intelligence agencies under the guise that it would bypass the Foreign Intelligence Surveillance Act (FISA). One month after Gorelick joined Clinton, he issued Presidential Decision Directive (PDD) 24 which said all intelligence collected would go through the White House. The purpose for this was to thwart the agencies' investigations into Clinton's transfer of technology to the Communist states, but the result was 9/11 because the intelligence alerting us about the 19 hijackers taking flying lessons and studying 747's from U.S. Attorney Mary Jo White, never got to the NSA, FBI, or CIA.

Even though Clinton was aware of North Korea's work on nuclear weapons, he pushed through an agreement to give them two light water nuclear reactors, and 500,000 metric tons of oil annually in return for their "word" that they wouldn't develop weapons with them. The reason for this was twofold: cover-up his transfers of our secrets and to help General Electric and other industries who would profit by exporting technology to the Communists.

Clinton didn't wait till the end of his term to start pardoning criminals and terrorists. On August 11, 1999, he pardoned 16 terrorists of the Armed Forces of National Liberation (FALN), a Marxist-Leninist group who detonated 130 bombs in Chicago, New York, and Washington D.C. killing 6 people and wounding 80 more in their quest to make Puerto Rico independent. Clinton also pardoned Susan Rosenberg and Linda Evans of the Marxist-Leninist Weather Underground who had participated in the Brinks armored car robbery in Nyack, New York, where two security guards and two police officers were shot, three of whom died. This shortened Rosenberg's sentence by 42 years and Evans' by 24 years. Rosenberg promptly went to work for Congregation B'nei Jeshurun, which leftist radical lawyer Alan Dershowitz called a "congregational victory." These two pardons were payback to New York Congressman Nadler for his help in Clinton's impeachment. Clinton's most famous pardon was for Marc Rich, who had made over $100 million on illegal sales of Iranian oil. His wife slipped contributions to Clinton of over $1.5 million, plus joined the string of bimbos in his harem.

The complete list of Clinton's crimes would fill thousands of pages, omitting his philandering and violent assaults on women. The United States survived his attack; wounded, but still alive. It may not survive Obama. The United States can barely defend itself against foreign enemies today, but it definitely cannot survive a war planned and executed against us by the same person that is our constitutionally mandated protector.

Tim Geithner - Geitner is Obama's Treasury Secretary. Tax evasion and hiring illegal aliens made the headlines, but that was merely a canard used to distract citizens away from Geithner's real threat to your future. He is doling out our $700 billion TARP funds and $787 billion misnamed "stimulus" dollars to AIG, Goldman Sachs, and Citibank who will be Obama's personal cash cows, and UAW, SEIU, ACORN, and special interest groups who will be Obama's indebted, loyal voters. Geithner is the prime facilitator of Obama's financial arm of his fascist regime.

Paul Volcker – Volcker is Obama's economic czar. To gauge either his level of incompetence or his level of complicity in Obama's planned scheme of wealth redistribution, you need only listen when he said: "It is only Barack Obama, in his person, in his ideas, in his ability to understand and to articulate both our needs and our hopes that provide the potential for strong and fresh leadership. That leadership must begin here in America but it can also restore needed confidence in our vision, our strength, and our purposes right around the world." Now that's sick. Volcker was one of the founding members of the Trilateral Commission, served as the President of the New York Federal Reserve Bank, and later was Chairman of the Federal Reserve System. Before joining Obama's regime his most visible job was his appointment by UN Secretary Kofi Annan to head the investigation into the Oil for Food program. This was the program put in place after the first Gulf War to make sure Saddam Hussein sold his oil for necessities and not weapons. Even though hundreds of millions in oil money had been spent on everything but food, Volcker concluded in his report that all was fine. Two of the lead investigators promptly resigned saying the report was a sham. It turns out that Kojo Annan, Kofi Annan's son, worked for one of the Oil for Food contractors and tens of millions could not be accounted for. The missing information just happened to be available in thousands of documents that Annan's Chief of Staff, Iqbal Riza, spent hours shredding. Paul Volcker assured all that his close friend Kofi knew nothing of his son's involvement in the crime. Of course, Volcker's four years as a director of the UN Association and Business Council could not possibly have influenced him. In April, Czar Volcker proposed a Value Added Tax (VAT) to help the U.S. crawl out of the recession he and his messiah created.

Janet Napolitano – Janet was picked as Obama's Homeland Security Secretary because she's against any security at all for our homeland. She thinks our only enemies are "right-wing extremists" like Christians, people who own guns, and heterosexuals. She is most likely a lesbian. As Governor of Arizona she vetoed 7 pro-life bills and refused to spend one cent on Arizona's long border with Mexico. Over 20% of the judges she appointed were homosexuals. She will help Obama allow illegal immigrants to receive amnesty, and give Obama the votes he may lose because of his socialized "Obamacare" legislation. She uses the term "man-caused disasters" instead of terrorism. She has repeatedly emphasized that "right-wing extremists" are much more dangerous to the U.S. than are foreign terrorists. She seriously classifies right-wing extremists as Christian, pro-life gun owners. When the government comes to get your guns she will be leading the charge.

Eric "The Red" Holder – Holder is Obama's Attorney General and one of his few true insiders charged with the enforcement arm of Obama's fascist take-over. He controls the FBI and all United States Attorneys representing the government. He oversees the disposition of terrorist prisoners which means they have a friend in Washington. He has over 80,000 armed, jack-booted thugs at his disposal. Holder was instrumental in pardoning Marc Rich and the 16 terrorists of the FALN described above under Bill Clinton.

David Axelrod – Axelrod is Obama's Senior Advisor. He was born of leftist parents and followed in their footsteps. He is a fascist like his boss, but worked for sex-addicted leftists like John Edwards and Eliot Spitzer, and your every day lefties like Hillary, Rahm Emanuel, Deval Patrick, Tom Vilsack, and crooked leftists like Chris Dodd. He hit the jackpot when Obama hired him.

Valerie Jarrett – Valerie is described as the other side of Obama's brain, confidant, conscience, and female twin. If possible, she is more radical than him. Her father-in-law was Vernon Jarrett, a fellow communist with Paul Robeson, DuBois, Frank Marshall Davis, Studs Terkel, Ishmael Flory, and many others. She alone hired Van Jones, the greens communist. She is whiter than most whites but, like Obama, she weighed the advantages of the two races, and chose to call herself black given the advantages of white guilt and increased leftist leanings of the country.

Rahm Emanuel –Rahm Emanuel is Obama's Chief of Staff. His loyalty to Obama and fascism supersedes his religion, Judaism. He is crude, rude, violent, and can't hide his anxiety for speeding-up the morphing of America into fascism. He is a Cloward-Pivens fan.

Ezekiel Emanuel – Ezekiel is an oncologist and bioethicist advising Obama on how to structure the new universal, socialist, so-called healthcare boondoggle. In assessing Ezekiel, or anyone in Obama's mob, you must listen to what they admit to. And, if it scares you, then what they will actually do will terrify you. Trust me; this Emanuel will codify euthanasia and death panels in the final healthcare program. If you doubt it, investigate yourself.

Hillary Clinton – Hillary is Obama's Secretary of State and was chosen because of the "keep your enemies closer" concept. I lived in Arkansas when her and Bill started their climb to the top. Their politics are left, but Obama makes them look like Reaganites. He will keep Hillary out of the country and out of the loop.

Robert Gates - Gates, like Hillary, is really just a useful idiot. Obama kept this leftover from Bush because he had carryover experience as Bush's Secretary of Defense, and is a "yes" man who will do as he is told. Plus, Gates, like Obama, never served his country, and has no problem with our soldiers being harassed by homosexuals trying to creep in bed with them while they are facing death every day.

Mark Lloyd – Mark is the diversity czar of the FCC. His assigned task is to get rid of Rush Limbaugh, and take over the internet and all other communications between Americans. He is against private ownership of any media. Until all media is nationalized, he wants to take money from them now and give it to public-owned media or those not doing too well. He is a disciple of Alinsky and worked for George Soros. He is an unabashed racist.

Hilda Solis – Hilda is the Secretary of Labor. She has been a member and officer of the Socialist Progressive Caucus, and sends her representatives to Socialist International, Democratic Socialists of America, and the Communist Party USA meetings.

Carol Browner – Carol is Obama's climate czar. She was formerly Clinton's EPA administrator and didn't finish destroying our economy with her greens hysteria, so she is back to finish the job. She is an admitted socialist and a charter member of the Commission for a Sustainable World Society. If you like Algore, you'll love Browner.

Chai Feldblum – Feldblum was appointed to the Equal Opportunity Employment Commission as one of the 15 recess appointments in late March. Republicans were holding up her confirmation because of her perversion, but the pervert-in-chief won when Congress went on a two-week Easter vacation. She's a lesbian, hates marriage, hates America, hates Christians, likes group sex, and thinks sex with animals is a good thing, supports having multiple husbands or multiple wives; you name it, and this pervert is for it. She will be deciding what is okay in our workplaces. WOW!

Cass Sunstein – Sunstein is Obama's regulation czar. He wrote a book with a long title saying all rights come not from God, but rather the government. Like his boss, he would like to tear-up the Constitution and dissolve the Supreme Court, or at least kill the conservatives on the bench. He believes that your dog should be appointed a lawyer and sue you if you do not treat him as a human. Typical Obama-ite, huh?

John Holdren – Holdren is Obama's science czar. He supports compulsory sterilization and abortion to control population and size of families. He advocates withholding food from certain population groups to starve them. He believes in world control of natural resources and redistribution of wealth according to Obama's directives.

Saul Alinsky – Saul (1909-1972) was the most noted community organizer in America. He worked primarily organizing blacks in large cities. He wrote "Rules for Radicals" in 1971 aimed at helping the 60's generation achieve power. He stated that Machiavelli wrote "The Prince" for the "Haves" and he wrote Rules for Radicals for the "Have-nots." Alinsky was not a communist, or a Nazi, or religious, but concentrated on making community organizing a pure science. Most of the people we recognize today as leftists, like Obama, Hillary, Ceasar Chavez, and Jesse Jackson have followed Alinsky's philosophy.

Nancy Polosi – Polosi is a pro-death Catholic Speaker of the House. Nancy's favorite mode of transportation is a broomstick although she has been known to fly a C-32, 45 passenger Boeing 757 since becoming Speaker. The previous speaker, Dennis Hastert, traveled on an Air Force C-20B Gulfstream III with a measly 12 seat capacity. Nancy needed more room to hold all her free-spending homosexual contributors from San Francisco who sometimes need extra room to stretch out on the long, slow, relaxing flights from Washington. At 70 years old, Nancy is no longer able to join them in their gaiety. She's had so many face-lifts that just walking too fast may rearrange the taunt skin stretched tight over her little round skull. If she ever cleaned-up the "swamp of Washington" as threatened, she would probably uncover a proverbial sea of Democrat corpses.

Harry Reid – Harry is Senate majority leader and a Mormon who supports killing babies. He may be a bi-sexual because he is consumed in passing laws to bring them and homosexuals into your bedroom. He even tacked-on a sodomy protection addendum to the defense authorization bill. He is now pushing preferential laws for homosexuals, transsexuals, and cross-dressers. All of this pro-homosexual activity is in addition to his dedicating much of his time in the Senate to facilitate Obama's fascist goals. He has made millions and millions on inside land deals in Nevada. Rush calls him "Dingy" Harry.

David Plouffe – Plouffe was Obama's campaign manager in 2008, and was brought in again as an "outside advisor" in late 2009 after Scott Brown's election in Massachusetts scared them. He was connected to David Kernell who hacked into Sarah Palin's emails during the 2008 campaign. His wife is Olivia Morgan with the Dewey Square Group; left-wing lobbyists who aid left-wing organizations. Plouffe's early successes as a campaign manager included socialist Senator Tom Harkin of Iowa and leftist John Oliver of Massachusetts. Plouffe was working to get Robert Torricelli reelected to the Senate in 2002, when it was disclosed that one of Torricelli's supporters and contributors was a spy for North Korea, David Chang. Torricelli lied about his connections to Chang and many other charges, but lying in public is permissible in New Jersey if you are a registered Democrat. Torricelli opted out of the Senate race. His Republican opponent, Doug Forrester, should have been declared the victor in the Senate race because the time for registering in the election had passed according to state law. Again, laws mean naught when you have a (D) next to your name, so the New Jersey Supreme Court tossed out the law and replaced Torricelli with the old, tired communist, former Senator Frank Lautenberg. Since Obamacare passed, the Republicans think people will flock to kick-out Democrats in 2010. I suggest they postpone any celebrations and recall that Plouffe learned his trade from reading Hitler's minister of propaganda, Joseph Goebbels', tactics and will do whatever necessary to make Obama look like the Phoenix bird when November rolls around.

Donald Berwick – Berwick is Obama's new Medicare and Medicaid czar. He wants a "radical transfer of power" in the health industry and likes to ask people, "What determines whether a patient will live or die in this country?" After listening to answers like smoking cigarettes or being overweight, he provides the answer, "Just look at the color of their skin." So, we have a white racist who hates whites. That's not so unusual nowadays. An extensive profile of Berwick in the Boston Globe labeled him a "revolutionary" who wants to "blow up" the healthcare system. Berwick is a pediatrician and professor at Harvard. I must assume there has to be a lot of racism in Berwick's neighborhood in Massachusetts to make a statement indicating that blacks get inferior healthcare. I live in the Deep South in Georgia and blacks, as usual, get free medical care at Grady Memorial in Atlanta much faster than paying white folks. In fact, I would say that blacks make up about 80% of the patient population there. I live in the rural mountains and any black that comes up here will get treated just like any white patient would. Mr. Berwick, like all radical racists, likes to use the race card to impress his racist boss. My advice to all the 50 million baby boomers that are white is to follow Rush Limbaugh's example and arrange for your medical care in New Zealand or the Czech Republic. Soon, you will all be depending on Medicare and Medicaid to take care of you in your old age, and Berwick may have shifted all the care to blacks since they are dying like flies, according to him. If he was spewing out this nonsense before he took the czar job from buddy Obama, what will he do when he gets revved-up?

Ben Rhodes – Rhodes is Obama's Deputy National Security Adviser charged with the monumental task of telling us which nations and groups in the world want to kill us, and prioritizing each according to their level of threat. Rhodes wrote the Iraq Study Group Report for the 9/11 Commission, Obama's Cairo speech (where he praised Islam and criticized Israel), and, most importantly, outlines our overall national security strategy. The words, terms, and speeches outlining the perceived threats to the United States delivered by Obama and Hillary Clinton to Americans are written by Rhodes. One of his prime responsibilities is evasive and contradictory word-smithing, sounding like the strong, sovereign, America we all know and love, but meaning something totally different. For example, he writes that "the gravest danger" faced by America is weapons of mass destruction, but never mentions Iran, North Korea, or al Qaeda because it would offend them. He writes that we cannot afford to fight two wars in Afghanistan and Iraq, yet we cannot leave until they are both stabile, which will never happen. He avoids the term "terrorist" because it may be offensive to terrorists, and considers the real threats to America to be cyberthreats, climate change, our dependence on foreign oil, and non-Islamic, gun-owning, church-going, pro-life Americans. He believes that there are no really bad people trying to harm America, just misguided Muslims who can be "engaged" diplomatically and peacefully. So far, this "engagement" policy has China and Russia laughing at sanctions for Iran, North Korea sinking a South Korean Corvette, and Iran delivering advanced missiles to Hezbollah in Lebanon to kill Israelis. Much more could be written about this loser, but let's look at his credentials for this national security position.

Rhodes had just received his master's degree in "fiction writing" from New York University in 2002, when Lee Hamilton hired him to help draft and write policy recommendations for the 9/11 Commission. Hamilton is the leftist former Congressman from Indiana and was co-chair of the 9/11 Commission with James Baker, and is often called on by Democrats because he speaks moderate and thinks leftist. If you recall, Hamilton's recommendations in his report were that we need to "reach out" to Iran and Syria, put pressure on Israel, and appease the terrorists. Rhodes is all of 32 years old, has no military experience, and really no experience in anything except deceiving the public. When you hear Obama telling a teleprompter-driven, heart-rending story of our military it probably originated from the pen of Rhodes. Obama borrowed Rhodes from Hamilton to write his speeches during the campaign, and Rhodes was so proficient in the art of facilitating Obama to speak out of both sides of his mouth that he promoted Rhodes to Deputy National Security Adviser.

John Brennan - is Obama's laughable "counterterrorism adviser." Brennan, Hillary Clinton and Jim Jones, Obama's National Security Adviser, all fanned out across the U.S. to sell Obama's new national security strategy to Americans last May. The 60 page "strategy" report should be labeled the "Muslim Terrorist Protection" report since it prohibits the use of such terms as terrorists or jihad. It says that security begins at home and calls for economic recovery, a commitment to education (more money to the NEA), clean energy (high oil prices), advancements in science and technology, reduced federal budget (yeh, right), and the report mentions climate change 24 times as the greatest threat to our security. These people are crazy! Brennan called jihad a "legitimate tenet of Islam," and said "jihadists should not be used to describe America's enemies." During a speech at the Center for Strategic and International Studies, John Brennan described violent extremists as "victims" of "political, economic and social forces," but said that those plotting attacks on the United States should not be described in "religious terms." Obama has instructed Brennan, Napolitano and other rogues to downplay the threat to us from Obama's Muslim terrorist's friends and emphasize the danger of "homegrown" terrorists to hasten the day that they can make use of a Rahm Emmanuel "crisis" to abrogate our 2nd Amendment rights.

OBAMA'S DEMONS

Just as the biblical demons were an extension of Satan and scurried around doing his dirty work, so does Obama have legions of people and groups who act as surrogates, and physically execute his orders either by direct command or autonomously as if by telepathy.

ACORN – ACORN was formed in 1970 as the Arkansas (later changed to "Association") Community Organization for Reform Now by communists Gary Delgado, George Wiley, and Wade Rathke. All three were left-over, but unrequited, radicals from the Students for a Democratic Society. Their "Peoples Platform" manifesto proclaimed, "We are the majority, forged from all minorities. We will wait no longer for the crumbs at America's door. We will not be meek, but mighty." They started in Arkansas because then Republican Governor Winthrop Rockefeller paid them $5000 cash to register voters. Delgado later said, "Of course, they thought we were going to register Republicans. We did not register a single Republican voter in that election. However, we did use those resources early on to build the organization." They use the Cloward-Pivens strategy of creating chaos by violence, assaults, spitting, striking, throwing, screaming, chanting, clubbing, biting, scratching, cursing, lying, and any other illegal actions to reach their radical objectives. They have 400,000 dues-paying members and 1200 chapters. They are actually Obama's personal army of radicals. If he needs demonstrations at Congress, mobs to block voting places, or marches to block traffic he need make only a phone call. So far, they have been used to browbeat citizens at malls and urban areas to register to vote, advise prostitutes, demand welfare, and crowd into banks demanding loans for welfare blacks. Soon, they will be demanding bans on guns, and voting rights for felons since many of them are felons. Almost all of them are black. Like Jackson and Sharpton they extort money through threats, but with their messiah now in the White House they can look forward to your tax money financing their violence. Don't be fooled by the closing of ACORN offices due to the undercover videos exposing them for advising clients on underage prostitution and tax evasion. They are merely changing names, keeping the same employees, and doing the same dirty work for Obama. Some of the many new names are Alliance of Californians for Community Empowerment, New York Communities for Change, New England United for Justice in Massachusetts, and Arkansas Community Organizations.

Obama has tried to distance himself from ACORN both during his campaign and after his election. Try as he might, he can't erase history. Starting in 1992 Obama was a lawyer for Project Vote, an ACORN project to infiltrate, overload, and crash our voting system. He helped Project Vote register 125,000 blacks in Illinois to get Democrat Carol Moseley Braun elected to the Senate seat he eventually won in 2004. Obama so impressed Madeline Talbott of ACORN that she sought this "radical young lawyer" to craft a lawsuit to impose Bill Clinton's 1993 "Motor Voter Act" to finish crashing the voter registration rolls that Project Vote had started. The lawsuit prevailed and eliminated what little credibility Illinois' voter registration system had left after years of corruption. Talbott also hired Obama to help train the ACORN/Project Vote troops. Obama posed with his "trainees" in a newspaper photo headlined, "This is a mass organization directed at political power where might makes right." Obama sat with Weather Underground bomber Bill Ayers on the Woods Fund Foundation, and together they gave many grants to ACORN to finance their radical, illegal, and confrontational politics. During the 2008 Democrat Primary, Obama's campaign paid an ACORN subsidiary, "Citizens Services, Inc.," $832,598 to make sure he won the Ohio primary. ACORN and it's over 100 newly named surrogates is flush with cash donations from George Soros, leftist foundations, and your tax revenue. They and other groups like SEIU and the Black Panthers will be Obama's front line thugs in the coming confrontations with Americans who see their country being irrevocably taken-over by fascists.

Don't underestimate ACORN, regardless of their new nice sounding names. They represent hordes of blacks that hate whites, and will do anything for their black messiah. Sol Stern of the Manhattan Institute wrote, "Instead of trying to overturn the system, to blow it up, as Wiley wanted to do, ACORN burrows deep within the system, taking over its power and using its institutions for its own purposes, like a political 'Invasion of the Body Snatchers'."

SEIU – SEIU stands for the Service Employees International Union. Think of ACORN as a high school street gang throwing rocks, and SEIU as Mafia enforcers using AK47's and grenades. They are the thugs Obama calls on when Tea Partiers need pushed off the sidewalk or their fingers bitten off. SEIU provided Obama with 100,000 campaign volunteers and 3000 full-time workers. They, all by themselves, gave Obama $61 million and a promise to beat-up Republicans on demand. He in turn gave them cabinet appointments, executive orders, key personnel slots, unlimited visits to the White House, and all sorts of legislative goodies. The chief thug of SEIU is Andy Stern who said, "We prefer to use the power of persuasion, but if that doesn't work we use the persuasion of power." Stern copied Jimmy Hoffa's Mafia style threats and intimidation, and it works. Let's see if he becomes part of a sidewalk like Hoffa.

SEIU has over 2.5 million dues-paying members with 317 affiliates, and 25 state councils in the United States, Canada, and Puerto Rico. Presently their members work in the hospital system, long-term care, public service and property services, but will expand to other areas under Obama's tutelage. SEIU president, Andy Stern, was trained at the Midwest Academy which was founded by former Students for a Democratic Society leftists Paul and Heather Booth to teach socialist's community organizers how to infiltrate and take-over the labor movement. Stern will use absolutely any weapons at his disposal to unionize companies whether private or public. He calls his tactics "death of a thousand cuts." When he is going after a target company, his SEIU attackers harass and disrupt company activities, send vicious emails and letters to stockholders, intimidate customers, follow employees to their homes, file pseudo-lawsuits, plant false stories in newspapers via their media friends, and threaten suppliers and trade associates of companies to isolate their targets. In 2005 Stern formed the "Change to Win" (CTW) federation by combining SEIU with the International Brotherhood of Teamsters, Laborers' International Union of North America, United Farm Workers of America, and the United Food and Commercial Workers International Union. The combined membership of the CTW is over 6 million. Two of their mission goals are increasing the minimum wage, and amnesty for illegals. They quickly achieved the first goal under Obama. The second goal may require some physical force and the CTW is ready and willing to provide Obama with the muscle needed.

Stern is also a leading member of the "Shadow Party", a nationwide network of over 60 unions, homosexuals, abortionists, left-wing think tanks, tree-huggers, earth-worshippers, anti-Christian groups, and anti-capitalists. The purpose of the Shadow Party is to act as the shadow of the Democrat Party and work behind the scenes to elect leftists, and exclude moderates from entering the party. Stern and other Shadow Party members like Harold Ickes, Steve Rosenthal, Ellen Malcolm, and Jim Jordan formed "America Votes" to aid Project Vote in over-loading and collapsing our elections system. In 2007 Stern formed the "Working for Us" (WFU) political action committee to help elect hard(er) left Democrats, and defeat moderates and conservatives.

In February, Obama appointed Stern as one of four board members to serve on the "National Commission on Fiscal Responsibility and Reform" chaired by Erskine Bowles and Alan Simpson. The purpose of this commission is to make recommendations to improve our economy. You've got to give Obama credit for deception of the masses. He is openly and deliberately dismantling capitalism and he appoints a commission of socialists to save it.

In May, Andy Stern stepped down as head of SEIU feeling he could do more damage to the United States in other capacities under the tutelage of Obama. His replacement is Mary Kay Henry, who will really be a female Andy Stern, and who will change nothing regarding the theft of member's dues to buy National Socialism. She has already said the SEIU would be spending at least $44 million on political races just in 2010. Specifically, she will be targeting the governor's races in Arizona, California, Connecticut, Florida, Illinois, New York, and Ohio. I thought socialist and communist groups like SEIU believed in redistributing wealth to the masses, not distributing the wealth to wealthy politicians.

CBC – CBC is the Congressional Black Caucus; presently composed of 41 black House members and one black Senator. Every member is not only a pure, white-hating racist, but also a Castro-loving communist. They hate even the white leftists Democrats with whom they vote 100%. But, even with their miniscule mentality they know the symbiotic union between them and the white Darkside must be maintained until Obama's black power is irrevocably established. It is only when they feel secure in their black grip on America that they will turn on their white handlers, and the rolls of subservience will be reversed.

The CBC is the best example I can think of that shows the fallacy of universal suffrage. Hundreds of millions, if not billions, could be saved by replacing all 42 members of the CBC and choosing just one of them to represent all the districts of the others. The effect on how Congress votes would be identical since they all vote like automatons anyway. Every black on the CBC has an IQ no larger than the temperature on a cool spring morning.

The CBC functions as a left-wing arm of the Democrat Party. They had their own staff, offices, and lavish budget for years under their masters, the Democrat Party, but lost them in 1994 when the Republicans took power. Under Obama they have had them returned. Congressman J.C. Watts refused to join the CBC labeling them "race –hustling poverty pimps." All of the members act in unity on all subjects. All are adherents of Louis Farrakhan and his Nation of Islam, which doesn't really mean they are Muslim, but rather indicates they follow anything with a black face. Usually the members of the Black Caucus stay out of sight of the normal public, and display their ignorance only at conferences and C-SPAN hearings. But, occasionally we get a glimpse of why they are so very lucky to represent all-black districts so that normal, intelligent voters can't get a crack at them. Last year seven of these fools went to visit Castro, our favorite communist, who has imprisoned and murdered over 200,000 of his own countrymen. CBC Chairwoman Barbara Lee (no relation to Robert E., I hope) said, "The fifty-year embargo just hasn't worked. The bottom-line is that we believe it is time to open dialogue with Cuba." Another mentally-challenged black, Bobby Rush, said, "It was almost like listening to an old friend...in my household I told Castro he is known as the ultimate survivor." Another of the "brains" of the CBC bunch, Laura Richardson, said of her hero Castro, "He listened. He said the exact same thing as President Obama said. He looked right into my eyes and he said 'How can we help, how can we help President Obama?" Oh, the sincerity of it all!

The Congressional Black Caucus exists for a single purpose, self-perpetuation. Their survival depends on keeping their constituents ignorant, poor, and hating whites. Just as Hitler, Stalin, and Obama divert attention away from their evil activities, so must the CBC invent boogie-mans to keep their herds of victims content in their collective ignorance. The best and simplest way to rid ourselves of this gallery of fools is to require an intelligence test to become a member of Congress with a corresponding minimum passing IQ of 70. With the loot they've stolen from taxpayers, they could return to the ghettos and be kings of the hoods they helped create.

BLACK PANTHER PARTY (BPP) - In 1966 Huey Newton turned his Oakland, California street gang into the Black Panther Party for Self-Defense. They were at war with white Americans and considered themselves the "American Viet Cong." Black Panther Eldridge Cleaver said, "If people had listened to Huey Newton and me in the 1960's, there would have been a holocaust in this country." Like Obama, the BPP organizers based their party on Marx, Lenin, and Mao Tse-tung's revolutionary socialism through mass organizing and community-based programs. They condemned colonialism's legacy, and advocated a peasant-led revolution of absolute violence to liberate blacks. Newton wrote a ten-page program that demanded everything from free housing and jobs for blacks, to emptying out all the prisons of black inmates. They reserved especial hatred for the police. By the late 1960's the Panthers were full-blown criminals engaged in drug dealing, pimping, extortion, assault, and murder. They committed over 300 felonies in 1969. They killed at least 15 law-enforcement officers and injured many more. Any Panther not conforming to their creed suffered in-house punishment. One of Newton's many female sex partners later revealed that his favorite punishment against another Panther was "stomping": "The floor was rumbling, as though a platoon of pneumatic drills were breaking through its foundation. Blood was everywhere. The victim's face disappeared." Once, when the Panthers were escorting the widow of Malcolm X, the police tried to restore order with their night sticks. The Panthers brought out their 12 gauge shotguns and the police backed-off. When the California State Assembly met to discuss a gun-control law on May 2,

1967, thirty Panthers stormed into the room with shotguns and rifles to stop the bill from passing. In September 1968 FBI Director J. Edgar Hoover declared the Black Panthers the "greatest threat to the internal security of the country." In October 1967 Huey Newton shot and killed Oakland Police Officer John Frey. After three trials, two hung juries, and white fear and intimidation, Newton was released for the cold-blooded murder after less than a year in prison.

In 1971 Hillary Rodham (later Clinton) was introduced by her Yale Professor, Thomas Emerson (Tommie the Commie), to Panther defense attorney, Charles Garry. Hillary got personally involved with the Panthers and helped defend several, including those that tortured, murdered, and mutilated Alex Rackley, a Panther himself. Rackley had his eyes gouged-out, boiling oil poured on his genitals, limbs sawed-off, and tortured for three days before dying. In August 1974 Newton and Panther co-founder Bobby Seale had a falling-out. Newton whipped Seale mercilessly, and then sodomized him with such force that Seale had to have his anus surgically repaired. A witness later explained, "You have to understand, it had nothing to do with sex. It was all about power." On August 6, 1974, Newton shot and killed a 17 year-old Bay Area prostitute, Kathleen Smith. Later he pistol-whipped his tailor, Preston Callins, cracking his skull in four locations. Rather than face murder charges Newton fled to Cuba, and left his girlfriend, Elaine Brown, in charge of collecting "protection" payments from local businesses. She hired a 42 year-old white woman named Betty Van Patter to keep the books. When Van Patter discovered "discrepancies" in the books she reported them to Brown. On January 3, 1975, Betty Van Patter's corpse, with caved-in head, was found floating in San Francisco Bay.

The New Black Panther Party (NBPP) is the successor to the BPP. It is an avowed black supremacist organization populated mostly by breakaway members of the Nation of Islam, and headed by Malik Zulu Shabazz. The NBPP hates Jews almost as much as they despise whites. During former Georgia Congresswoman Cynthia McKinney's campaign for re-election against another black, Hank Johnson (another idiot), the NBPP attacked reporters, accused them of all being Jews, and called Johnson a "Tom." They also said that 9/11 was a Jewish conspiracy because 4000 Jews called in sick before the Twin Towers were hit. When the black whore at

Duke University accused the lacrosse players of rape, Malik Zulu Shabazz raced down to hound District Attorney Nifong to make sure the lacrosse players were punished. When the whore's accusations were thrown out of court, Shabazz appeared on the Bill O'Reilly Show on Fox TV. He refused to apologize for the Black Panthers' aggressive actions at Duke. He stated that the rich, white students and their parents had put political pressure on the legal authorities and gotten the charges dropped. When Michelle Malkin questioned him he called her a "political prostitute" and a "mouthpiece for that racist Bill O'Reilly." Michelle stated that "the only whore present is you." The NBPP organized the "Million Youth March" to protest police brutality, and called for the killing of all whites.

On November 4, 2008, Samir Shabazz and Jerry Jackson of the New Black Panther Party for Self-Defense stood at the entrance in front the voting poll at 1221 Fairmount Street in the City of Philadelphia. They wore black berets, combat boots, bloused battle dress pants, rank insignia, New Black Panther Party for Self-Defense insignia, and black jackets. They both held nightsticks or batons with contoured grip and wrist lanyards. They taunted and threatened every white voter that approached the voting precinct. Attorney General Eric "The Red" Holder refused to even look into the details of the case. Although the NBPP does not claim over a few thousand members, they all are enamored with weapons from clubs to knives and guns. And, they are sure to seek involvement in any upcoming election campaign to make sure their messiah stays in power.

GEORGE SOROS - George was born George Schwartz on August 12, 1930, in Budapest, Hungary. He is Jewish by birth, but hates Jews and Israel. I will skip details of his life until 1979 when he started his "Open Society Institute" (OSI). This is his flagship foundation which he uses to fund all of the many socialist causes. OSI donated over $5 billion to left-wing causes from 1979 to 2007. Soros launched the Soros Documentary Fund in 1996, and turned it over to Robert Redford's Sundance Institute in 2001 with the instructions to continue producing documentaries on social justice, human rights, civil liberties, and freedom of expression. To keep this section brief, I will just tell you that Soros hates all things American, but has a special hatred for

George Bush. He is an atheist, virulent gun-control fanatic, and for legalizing marijuana. He was one of the first founders of the "Shadow Party" and made use of the 527 "soft money contributions" to help leftist candidates. The term "527" refers to the part of the IRS code that allows supporters to spend money on a candidate's behalf without direct donations. In 2004 he gave $5 million to MoveOn.org, $10 million to America Coming Together (a get-out-the-vote group for Democrats), and $3 million to former Clinton chief-of-staffer, John Podesta. I will not bore you with the details of how Soros makes his money except to tell you that he made a cool $1 billion in one day by shorting the British Pound-Sterling when it was devalued, but now works with Obama indirectly and profits hugely.

Soros hosted a fund-raiser for Obama in the latter's 2004 Senate race. As early as December 2006, Soros met with Obama and together they decided Obama should run for the Presidency in 2008. The next month, January 2007, Obama created an exploratory committee. Soros immediately switched from supporting Hillary Clinton to Obama. In 2008 Obama announced he would form a "Social Investment Fund Network" to provide federal money for social entrepreneurs and leading non-profit organizations that are assisting schools, lifting families out of poverty, filling health care gaps, and inspiring others to lead changes in their own communities. Michelle Malkin said this was all pay-back to Soros to use our Treasury to pay for Soros' pet projects. You will also find Soros' footprints on the TARP bill, the so-called Obama stimulus bill, healthcare, cap and trade, and amnesty legislation. Any leftist is dangerous, but one with a net worth of $25 billion is downright threatening.

PS: Beware of "Media Matters" on the internet and elsewhere. This is Soros' vehicle for weaseling his radical leftist views into normal news and information outlets.

OTHER DEMONS - Space won't allow me to list and describe all the groups and individuals who perform the Nazi "Brownshirt" functions for Obama's Darkside. For a partial listing of just 878 of these groups go to www.discoverthenetworks.org where they start with the A.J. Muste Memorial Institute, and end with the Zayed Center for Coordination and Follow-Up. They represent the full spectrum of causes from Abortion to the Young Communist

League, but they have one thing in common: support for Obama's radical takeover of America.

USEFUL IDIOTS

Useful idiots are both government and non-government operatives who aid and abet Obama's headlong rush to fascism. Some do not even realize they are helping to move the paradigm rapidly to the left by their actions. Lenin first coined this term for the masses that helped him overthrow the Russian monarchy, and thought it was being replaced by a democracy until they woke-up and found Lenin and his Bolsheviks were in control.

FBI - Many Americans think of the FBI as it was portrayed by Efrem Zimbalist, Jr. on the TV series "The F.B.I." that ran from 1965 till 1974. Like Superman, it promoted "Truth, Justice and the American Way" sort of feelings. I suppose that many Americans who have not read past the headlines still have that perception of the FBI. Anyone that has followed the details of the Waco Massacre, the FBI sniper assassination of Sammy and Vicky Weaver at Ruby Ridge, or scores of the other FBI atrocities over the last 20 years, sees them in a different light. J. Edgar Hoover was certainly not a perfect human, but he was looking out for America and chasing down the bad guys most of the time. Hoover's career spanned from 1924 to 1971 during which time he killed or locked-up the gangsters in the '30's, and the Mafia starting in the '40's. When the Supreme Court veered left in the 1950's and allowed communists to openly subvert American citizens, Hoover covertly initiated the COINTELPRO program to go after the communist party, Black Panthers, Martin King, the Ku Klux Klan, and American Nazi's. After Hoover's death in 1972 the secret files of COINTELPRO were exposed by the Church Committee, and the FBI was changed forever into the servant of the left where it remains today.

Under the expert guidance of Bill "blue dress" Clinton and his trusty side-kick Janet "lesbo" Reno, the FBI laid siege to the Branch Davidian "Compound" (plywood barn) on February, 28, 1993. For 51 days the FBI used light and sound psy-ops to drive the Davidians crazy. Finally, the FBI sent in two tanks, set fire to the buildings, and burned 76 people, mostly women and children, to death. If you go to

Wikipedia or see the Waco story on "Cops" you will get the whitewashed version complete with the doctored tapes of Davidian conversations and their so-called "arsenal." I'm not a crusader, so if you want to accept their version of the truth then I really don't care.

On August 21, 1992, six U.S. Marshalls dressed in camouflage were on Randy Weaver's property near Ruby Ridge, Idaho, carrying MP-5 machine guns. They were hiding behind bushes when Randy's dog, Striker, started barking. His 14 year old son, Sammy, went to investigate because he thought Striker had come in contact with a deer. The agents shot the dog and when Sammy started to run they machine-gunned him to death in the back. Later, Randy found Sammy's body and laid his dead son on a table in a small shack near their plywood cabin. That evening Randy went out to the shack to prepare Sammy's body for burial. He was shot in the back by FBI sniper, Lon Horiuchi. As he ran into the cabin, his wife, Vicki, held the door open while she was holding their 10 month old daughter, Elisheba. As Randy was running past her, half of her head exploded in a shower of flesh, brains, and blood. FBI sniper Lon Horiuchi had struck again. Vicki was killed instantly, but her mother's instinct caused her to shield the baby from the fall long enough for her other daughter to stop the baby's fall. That same round wounded Kevin Harris, a friend staying with the Weavers. For 11 days the Weavers crawled around on the floors of the rickety plywood cabin while the FBI Hostage Rescue Team played loud music and taunted them with things like, "Hey Vicki, we're having pancakes for breakfast. What are you having?" They knew they had killed her and didn't care if her three young daughters inside the cabin heard them. The FBI even crept under the floorboards of the cabin, and shined blinding lights up through the cracks. The Weavers ate their canned elk meat, and covered their bloated mother and wife with blankets. Outside, over 400 agents surrounded the cabin with machine guns, night vision, and sniper rifles. At one time a helicopter hovered overhead with bladders of gasoline to drop on the cabin and burn the Weaver family alive, but decided to abort when crowds of Randy's neighbors appeared. Late in the 11 day siege, the FBI sent a robot up to the cabin and told Randy to pick-up the telephone attached to it so they could communicate. He refused. Later, he found that it was rigged with a 12 gauge shotgun. For the sake of his three daughters, dead wife and son, and his wounded friend, Kevin Harris, Randy surrendered.

To cover-up their heroic acts of bravery the FBI immediately ordered Vicki and Sammy cremated. Randy and Kevin were incarcerated. Their trial was held in Boise a few months later. Gerry Spence, a famous, very liberal Hollywood lawyer, read about Ruby Ridge and was so disgusted that he went to the trial and represented Randy at no cost. Day after day the U.S. Justice Department, FBI, ATF, and U.S. Marshalls Service paraded witness after witness before the jury. When it came time for the defense, Gerry Spence stood up and said, "The defense rests." He did not call even a single witness. After a short time the jury returned, and cleared Randy of all charges except failure to appear in court. Even that was wrong because they had purposely misdated the date on the summons.

In September 1995 the U.S. Senate Judiciary Committee held hearings on the Ruby Ridge incident. I remember seeing Randy and his daughters testifying. They brought in the cabin door to the hearing room to better understand how Vicki died. The very worst thing even the liberal Senators called Randy during the hearings was a "white separatist." The government awarded Randy $100,000, and $1 million each to his daughters, Rachel, Sara, and Elisheba. And, finally in 2000 Kevin Harris was awarded a $380,000 settlement. The FBI sniper, Lon Horiuchi, was indicted for manslaughter in 1997 by the Boundary County, Idaho prosecutor just prior to the statute of limitations. As usual, the trial was quickly moved to federal court, and the murderer of Vicki Weaver was dismissed on grounds of "sovereign immunity." During the original trial in Idaho, FBI Deputy Assistant Director, Danny Coulson produced a memo he had written on the 4th day of the siege. It had four notes written on it: "(1) Charge against Weaver is Bull Shit. (2)No one saw Weaver do any shooting. (3)Vicki has no charges against her. (4) Weaver's defense. He ran down the hill to see what dog was barking at. Some guys in camys shot his dog. Started shooting at him. Killed his son. Harris did the shooting (of Degan). He (Weaver) is in pretty strong legal position." FBI Director Louis Freeh stated before the Senate Judiciary Committee that he proposed to discipline 12 of the FBI agents involved at Ruby Ridge. He described it as "synonymous with the exaggerated application of federal law enforcement" and stated "law enforcement overreacted at Ruby Ridge." To the FBI, it was an "overreaction." To Randy Weaver, it was the loss of Vicki and Sammy forever. By the way, the 12 agents proposed for discipline...all got promoted and are doing just fine.

Randy Weaver happens to be my best friend. His only crime was to raise his family in a rural area away from the crime and silliness of a sick, racist society.

ATF – The ATF is now called the Alcohol, Tobacco, Firearms and Explosives Agency. "Explosives" was added after terrorism became a part of our lives. After the economy, terrorism is the second greatest concern of the American people. But, don't expect any help from the ATF. Even though there are 35 known Jihadist training camps within the U.S. and many cells of Muslim extremist that may start blowing us up soon, the ATF concentrates on homegrown bubbas lurking in the woods with firecrackers.

I suspect that most of the present ATF agents have no military combat experience. I have. And most guys that I know having been shot at and returning fire, are not so anxious to dress in black and play GI Joe. Waco is the perfect example and it is the only one I will mention, although there are hundreds of such atrocities committed by the ATF.

A UPS delivery truck was making a run to the Branch Davidian complex near Waco, Texas. The driver noticed that the packages contained inert grenades. The Davidian leader, David Koresh, attached the fake grenades to blocks of wood and put a sign on them saying "Please take one" as a desk paper-weight to sell as novelties at gun shows. UPS notified law enforcement, who contacted the ATF. The ATF put an informer inside the Davidians, and could not prove they had illegal weapons. Koresh offered to cooperate many times. He jogged along the rural roads almost every day. They could have taken him in for questioning at any time. But, that would not solve the problem they were having at that particular time. Their new budget hearing was coming up soon, and they needed a high visibility event to prove their worth.

On February 28, 1993, ATF agents came to the Davidian's front door and Koresh came outside to talk. Then, a cattle trailer full of swat-clad agents came up in a swirl of dust and opened-up on Koresh with MP-5 machineguns, wounding him and his father-in-law. Other agents were hanging out of helicopters, shooting down. Then four agents climbed on the roof and started shooting into the windows. The Davidians returned fire and killed four of the agents. The ATF had expected a one-way battle with them being easily victorious, so that their budget would be increased after they arrested this religious wacko. Instead, four of their wannabe jackboots had been killed and they looked like fools. So, they backed-off and called in the FBI, although they stayed around to make sure they could sabotage the negotiations.

The FBI established communications with the Davidians and talked to them every day. The main bone of contention was that the Davidians wanted to make sure that the ATF did not destroy the roof area, so they could show how many rounds the ATF had fired into the walls and windows when they climbed the roof and assaulted the second floor of the plywood building. The ATF and the FBI started a harassment program of turning off the power to the complex, faking tank attacks, playing loud music, and turning on 100 million candlepower carbon lights at all times of the night to interrupt their sleep cycle. Finally, they achieved their goal when the Davidians stopped coming out to talk. Then they started other tactics like saying Koresh claimed he was Jesus Christ, and that he was molesting children. They also politicked Attorney General Janet Reno and convinced her that CS gas was safe to use against the women and children. CS gas is actually highly flammable. The ATF was desperate. If the Davidians proved the ATF had jumped the gun, then not only would their budget suffer, but they would look like fools. The only solution was to try and kill all the Davidians, and leave no witnesses.

On April 19, 1993, the FBI tank assault began. The FBI said they attacked because the Davidians broke the phone line to cut-off negotiations, but the Davidians said the tanks crushed the lines. The Davidians held-up signs (seen on TV) saying "REHOOK PHONE," but the tanks kept coming. The FBI loudspeaker blared, "This is not an assault." The Davidians would run out to the tanks and give gestures of surrendering, but the automatic rifle fire would either kill them or drive them back inside. The tanks were systematically demolishing every building and structure on the property. Most of the women and children escaped to a school bus that had been buried in the earth for protection from tornadoes. The men in the main structure were running from one part of the building to another as each was caved-in and access blocked by the tanks crushing wall after wall.

After six hours of sheer terror a fire appeared in the corner of the structure. Americans saw it live from long-range TV cameras. The wind was already blowing at about 20 miles an hour and the swirling flames seemed to increase the wind velocity. A few of the Davidians managed to dodge the bullets and tanks, and some reached relative safety by being seen on live TV where the FBI feared shooting them in front of an audience. The tanks had run over and crushed the entrance and exit to the buried school bus and trapped the women and children. When the fire fell on the bus and spread to its flammable parts, thirty-four women and twenty-three children were all burned alive in that bus. Their charred remains were unrecognizable as human in later photos. Nineteen of the men were either burned to death or were shot in the building.

Only 11 of the Davidians survived to stand trial. What crime, you ask? How about carrying a weapon in the commission of a crime! What if government agents came to your home, shot some members of your family, and the survivors went to prison for grabbing guns and defending themselves? Nine of the Davidians received 243 years in sentences. In 1995 Congress held hearings and after two weeks said they had arrived at what had happened at Waco, and would make sure it never happened again. That's what they had said two years before about Ruby Ridge. In 1999 after some Americans wouldn't let the travesty die, the headlines read, "Reno and Freeh Agree on New Independent Probe of Waco." This was a lie to buy time and the massacre at Waco of innocent Americans just faded from memory until the next time the jack-booted thugs lusted for fresh blood. Carol Moore writes in "The Davidian Massacre" that the truth of what happened at Waco is too terrible for the American people to hear. Federal agents had cold-bloodedly, and with aforethought, murdered 82 innocent civilians, mostly women and children, and many of them were black. The guilt was equal among the executive, legislative, and judicial branches in their protection of the Gestapo-like agents. One part of the government was covering for another. Expect to see this become commonplace under Obama.

NPR - National Public Radio was created in 1970 as a result of the passage of the Public Broadcasting Act of 1967, and signed into law by President Lyndon Johnson. NPR has syndicated programming on 797 radio stations, and reaches an estimated audience of 32.7 million listeners. As any non-socialist will affirm, NPR leans left in all of its programming. It is prohibited from discussing any specific religion, but not prevented from advocating viewpoints antithetical to Christians such as evolution, homosexuals, lesbians, cross-dressers, and transsexuals. Of course, the Darkside is never happy with just receiving balanced programming or even slightly-leftist programming. They want NPR to swing all the way left so they, like all good socialists, constantly criticize them for being too far right, just too damn conservative, in the hopes that NPR will respond by moving even farther left. You can expect this to happen anyway with Obama now taking over in Washington. With Obama's planned economic collapse you can also expect to see Obama pump more money into NPR, and exercise correspondingly more control over programming.

In 1994 NPR planned to air a program of prison-life commentaries by convicted cop-killer, Abu-Jamal. Senator Bob Dole complained and they canceled the show. Besides leftist propaganda, NPR also is anti-Israel. According to the weblog "Little Green Footballs," NPR is the biggest provider of anti-Israel propaganda outside the Arab world. Marty Peretz of the New Republic calls NPR "National Palestine Radio." They refuse to call suicide bombers "terrorist" because it would be "prejudicial." NPR's show "Day to Day" features reports and interviews by reporters and editors of the Microsoft online magazine "Slate.com." A survey of this group in 2004 found that 40 planned to vote for John Kerry, while only 2 were voting for George Bush. A broadcaster with PBS (parent of NPR), Bill Moyers, was a former trustee of the Open Society Institute which is Gorge Soros' main conduit for contributions to fascist and communist movements.

U.S. MARSHALLS SERVICE – The U.S. Marshalls Service was created by the first Congress in 1789, and is the enforcement arm of the federal court system under the Department of Justice. In other words, their boss is none other than Eric "The Red" Holder, Obama's personal lawyer who represents terrorists against the United States. The U.S. Marshall Service presently has about 3000 armed agents. Like most entities, the Service has been dumbed-down by the black victimization craziness, since white guilt clouded the thinking of America starting in the 1960's. A black named Matthew Fogg sued the U.S. Marshall Service in 1998 and was awarded $4 million in a race discrimination and retaliation judgment. He had risen to the level of Chief Deputy, but found a racist court that bowed to his complaint. He borrowed the race card from O.J. Simpson and played it well. He retired with his $4 million windfall and used it to become president of "Bigots with Badges," director of "Congress Against Racism and Corrupt Law Enforcement" (CARCLE) and helped organize Law Enforcement Against Prohibition (LEAP), a pro-drug legalization organization of law enforcement officers. I think getting rid of this racist loser was worth $4 million of our tax money. The only loss suffered by the departure of Mr. Fogg will be felt by his boss, Eric "The Red" Holder. They both owe their fortunes to racism.

I.R.S. - The IRS probably doesn't require much description for most Americans. Before the black elitist convinced white Americans that they were the scourge of the planet, the IRS was the most feared word in the English language. Now, it is the word "racist". The IRS may make a comeback though with the passing of Obamacare. When fully implemented, Obamacare will add at least another 17,000 new gendarmes to Obama's IRS Army. Added to the current force, that will mean about 23,000 people doing the work of half as many competent workers. I speak from experience. When I graduated with a degree in accounting, the students with a 3.5 GPA went to work for the "Big 8" firms, while others went with private companies. The bottom-feeders accepted jobs at the IRS. But, intelligence level is not related to the level of the trouble that IRS agents can cause the productive members of our society. Not having any idea of what it means to actually work for a living, make a payroll, or produce something useful, the IRS people instinctively think that your gross income is equal to your net income, and that you should be happy to pay it all to them. Under Obama you can count on the IRS to take on a new aura of power and intimidation. He verbally assaults Americans making over $250,000 a year, but you shouldn't think that lower-paid workers will be treated any better. Like the KGB in the USSR, the IRS will be employed to instill fear in all citizens regardless of income. It is a tactic that works in all totalitarian regimes from Haiti, under "Papa Doc", to China. You can also expect more of the IRS agents to be armed. Ignoring Obama's manufactured unemployment numbers, you can be sure the number of people not working will increase. When that becomes true, there will be many more that resist paying the exorbitant taxes to finance Obama's new fascism. When people are struggling to make ends meet they will not appreciate IRS stooges wanting to take their meager savings.

BODY COUNT THUS FAR

One of Obama's first moves to rape Americans, and rescue his banking partners simultaneously, was the $700 billion Troubled Asset Relief Program (TARP), which was a gift from Bush. What very few people realize is that this $700 billion is a "rolling fund" which means that the same money keeps being loaned out over and over wherever needed. Timothy Geithner, who had bailed out global banks as head of the Fed in New York, was made Treasury Secretary so he could continue bailing out AIG, give Bear Stearns to Chase, and continue destroying our economy by transferring our wealth to the big banks. Paul Volcker, who had purposely caused the debt crisis of the early 1980's, and Larry Summers, who had decimated banking regulations under Clinton to permit wild speculation and hedge funds, were brought in by Geithner. Obama now had the bucks to facilitate the financial tentacle of his fascist oligarchy.

The next of Obama's many tentacles was created to buy and keep Democrats in line by earmarking pork directly to their districts and states. This took the form of his so-called jobs stimulus bill which stimulated nothing, and was never meant to. Following FDR's partisan blueprint, Obama pleaded for and got $787 billion with no Republican votes in the House, and only 3 in the Senate voting for it. FDR used his stimulus bills to keep the Democrats in power for 50 years. Obama is shooting for Democrat control in perpetuity. Obama's rhetoric to elicit support said the money was for jobs and freeing-up credit. He said the money was for extended unemployment checks, upgrading schools, $300 to senior citizens, energy efficiency, green jobs, and a high speed rail service among many thousands of others. As of March 2010, less than $300 billion had been spent and that was specifically targeted to help out Democrat districts, most of them predominately black. The remaining $500 billion will be used similarly. Virtually no jobs have been created.

More proof that Obama's IQ is commensurate with his age is his silly $5 billion "Weatherizing Program" to caulk homes and save energy costs. He spends trillions like it was monopoly money, and then makes a big deal out of caulk. Since he's never broke a sweat in 47 years he wouldn't know caulk from toothpaste. In one of his daily TV appearances he proclaimed that his army of caulkers would produce thousands of jobs and save millions in energy cost. The only shovel-ready part of this foolishness is the BS coming from Obama and his ever-present teleprompter. He had already so destroyed the economy that states didn't have enough employees left to add their bureaucratic overseeing role to watch over the army of expected caulkers. He is finding out in his attempts to make sure only blacks arm themselves with caulk guns, that they are less adept at shooting caulk than they are at shooting liquor store clerks. Indiana was inundated with blacks wanting to caulk and be paid large paychecks, but it turned out the art of caulking was beyond their pay grade or mental ability. In California, with a population of 37 million, only 12 homes have been caulked with a gross increase of 84 jobs statewide. Don't ask me why it took seven people to caulk each house.

The "Fairness Doctrine" is an old tired idea resurrected by an old tired Congressman named Henry Waxman of California. Waxman is the only Congressman on C-SPAN that when he looks directly into the camera you can look right up his nostrils, at which time you should look away before throwing-up. Rush Limbaugh calls him "Commisar Nostrilitis." Waxman has been around Congress for 36 years and is Chairman of the House Energy and Commerce Committee. Calling him a leftist is an understatement.

Waxman facilitated delivery of $600,000 in cash and medical supplies in 2004 to the terrorists in Fallujah, Iraq, who were concurrently killing American soldiers every day. He and verifiably insane Dennis Kucinich drew-up impeachment documents for Bush and Cheney. He obstructed the work of the special prosecutor looking into Bill Clinton's scandals. He hates the 2nd Amendment, loves socialized health care, and has authored a Cap and Trade Bill. The 1200 page Cap and Trade bill phases out all coal-fired power plants and will actually reduce our Gross National Product by $3 trillion, while adding $9 trillion to our energy costs. It passed the house in June 2009. It was found out later that Waxman paid other members $16,000 in cash to vote for it. Who needs lobbyists with creeps like Waxman? It will be the largest tax increase in the history of the world. Even though Senators Boxer and Kerry have introduced the companion bill in the Senate it has yet to pass. There's much more, but let's get back to the "Fairness Doctrine."

The so-called "Fairness Doctrine" is a regulation that requires all broadcasters to provide equal air time for contrasting views on controversial subjects. It was in effect until 1987 when it was repealed by the Federal Communications Commission. Now that Rush Limbaugh and other conservative radio hosts dominate talk radio, Waxman and other lefties want to bring it back. So far, Waxman hasn't been too good at getting either partisan or bi-partisan support for the bill. Obama has said not to push it, but don't you just know he hates Rush and would relish giving one of his fascist friends equal time with Rush? Waxman is not just looking at getting leftists on the radio. He also wants to somehow fabricate a fairness doctrine for the internet. If he is successful in getting either the radio or internet legislation passed it will be another of our freedoms lost.

Another of Obama's covert attempts aimed at revenge against the whites for succeeding where blacks have failed is the federal student loan bill, which he and the Darkside piggy-backed through Congress on the Obamacare bill. The rates of repayment on student loans have been decidedly lopsided whereby whites repay their loans faster and have had 50% fewer defaults than blacks. Predominately black colleges also have historically lagged behind white colleges in GPR and achievement. Obama decided to kill both of these birds with one stone by putting the student loan program under the brainless bureaucrats of the government who have never run anything efficiently in 234 years. Now, instead of the loans being administered by private for-profit financial companies with real employees who support real families and pay real taxes, it will take twice as many dunces to perform the same work and they will all be Democrats, and vote for the messiah. Black students will now go from 50% defaults to near 75%. The bill limits yearly repayment to 10% of gross income, but in reality, if the debtor makes a low salary or chooses to enlist in Obama's civilian volunteer force for a few years, he will pay only about 10% of the original loan, anyway, before it sunsets after 10 years and is all written off the government's books. The pouring of more money into the black hole of black colleges is just a bone thrown to the blacks by Obama to bolster their continued support for their lost cause. They have miserably failed at increasing the standards of blacks and this will not change.

Most Americans now realize that the changes already wrought by Obama were not what they visualized, whether they voted for him or not. What many still don't comprehend is the depth and breadth of the sea changes coming. Everything that he is doing has been done before in Russia, Europe, and Canada. Only this time it is being done to us. When he fired General Motors CEO Rick Wagoner in March 2009 we asked each other, "Can he do that?" When Wagoner immediately left his office and never came back our question was answered. He had joined GM 30 years before and had been CEO for 8 of those years. From March through May, Obama's surrogates and the state-controlled media eviscerated Wagoner and GM management for all Americans to hear. After he fired the GM president and nobody complained or tried to stop him, he took a step back and let the shock soak into the brains of the business community. We all saw that Chevys were still being made, and the dealerships were still changing our oil and rotating our tires, so the furor died away. In June he came back and effectively nationalized General Motors by taking 60% for himself, 12.5% for Canada, 17.5% for the UAW and 10% for the bondholders. The root cause of GM's problems, the United Auto Workers, left the bankruptcy table with the new ownership stock plus no reductions in hourly pay, pensions, or health care benefits. The $13.1 million in union funds, plus the $4.9 million in independent donations, and the $2 million in other money given to only Democrat candidates in 2008 paid off handsomely for the UAW. Paying UAW members an average $73 per hour compared to the $35 per hour earned by the non-union American plants of other foreign car-makers would make any company bankrupt.

The United Auto Workers Union and Obama really made a killing when they killed Chrysler in May 2009. They ended up owning 55% of Chrysler's stock while Fiat got 20%, Obama 23%, and Canada 2%. Obama retains defacto control of the board of directors also, since his Treasury Department and UAW (over which he has virtual control) combined, hold 5 of the 9 seats. Hundreds of thousands of retired police officers, teachers, firemen, and investors lost billions. Parts suppliers and creditors lost hundreds of millions while the UAW lost zero, and walked away owning the company. The saga of the UAW's role in the General Motors and Chrysler bankruptcies proves the prophetic words of the prediction that democracies exist only until the voters learn they can profit by voting themselves the riches from the Treasury. In return for giving all their contributions to Obama, he in return gave them two of the big three automobile companies in the United States. In the Democrat party the UAW had identified and paid the compliant whore, and she had delivered the goods.

Even more important to the unions than owning GM and Chrysler is "Card Check." As usual, the Democrats named the legislation for this union scam for monopoly control over labor, the fairy tale title of "Employee Free Choice Act." Rather than holding a secret ballot election of employees to see if the majority want to unionize, card check would allow a union to contact union members one at a time and coerce them into signing an authorization card until they had a majority. Anyone knows that when a group of union thugs visits an employee at his home on a dark night, and asks him to sign a card or bad things may happen to his family, he is going to sign anything stuck in front of him. Since taking office, Obama had been trying to appoint Craig Becker to one of the five slots on the National Labor Relations Board. Becker has been perhaps the most outspoken union lawyer advocating for Card Check, and his appointment had been held up by the Republicans because of his radicalism. Well, a day after Congress left for their Easter vacation in late March, Obama made 15 recess appointments and one of them was Becker. The real danger posed by Becker is that he will not wait for congressional action to introduce Card Check into unionizing companies. With the power of the NLRB Becker can exert his influence over non-union workers and achieve Card Check unilaterally. This may add tens of thousands of new union members, most of whom will vote for Obama and other liberals in 2010 and 2012.

On July 2, 2008 Obama made a campaign speech in Colorado Springs where he stated, "We cannot continue to rely only on our military in order to achieve the national security objectives that we've set. We've got to have a civilian national security force that's just as powerful, just as strong, just as well-funded as our military." Of course, many of us that were sickened at the thought of Obama becoming President immediately thought that this socialist, or whatever he was, was already going to form his own army. It is now almost two years later and, while I don't think it was an armed militia he was describing, I do think it will have almost the same effect. Like all successful dictators, Obama is initiating a blinding array of multi-pronged attacks on every brick of our American foundation until it crumbles. He is simultaneously rebuilding another structure right in front of our very eyes, but we do not see. Most Americans will see it for the first time after it is completed, operational, and irreversible.

The "civilian national security force" described in Obama's speech is now called the "Corporation for National and Community Service" on Obama's website at www.barackobama.com/pdf/. It would serve some purposes during times of peace and emergencies, but the primary purpose of the effort is akin to the "Hitlerjugend" (Hitler Youth) which was for propaganda and political service. Obama had already set the precedent for using our tax revenues to finance his personal 24/7/365 perpetual campaigning when he used the $700 billion TARP funds to buy control of the banking industry, and the $787 billion "porkulus" to repay the unions and politicians for their help in electing him. He is already well on his way to expanding this private "Army of Obama" and paying for it all with your tax revenues, again. I will briefly describe this vast army that is in every state, county, and city right now, and growing every day.

Totaling about 75,000 members and forming a part of the Corporation for National and Community Service is AmeriCorps. Subsidiaries are AmeriCorps National, AmeriCorps State, AmeriCorps VISTA, and AmeriCorps NCCC. Each of these in turn have subsidiaries, chapters and sub-organizations too many to mention. The work descriptions for all of these organizations include "intensive service to meet critical needs in poor communities," whatever that means. The only specifics mentioned on their website are flood relief in Iowa, rebuilding Gulf Coast communities, and Katrina relief. Meaningless phrases like "support a broad range of local service programs that engage thousands of Americans in intensive service to meet critical community needs," and "provides full-time members to community organizations and public agencies to create and expand programs that build capacity and ultimately bring low-income individuals and communities out of poverty" are common in their literature. It sounds like a lot of people wasting their time and our money on people that are too lazy to help themselves, and probably never will. It is the usurpation by the government of what used to be performed by the churches, charities, and neighborhoods helping each other and the sweat of good people.

Speaking of AmeriCorps, Obama said they will do things like "provide health care and education, saving our planet and restoring our standing in the world." What the hell does that mean? Most of them are not doctors or teachers, and how do they save the planet or increase the standing of the only superpower on earth? Is Obama ashamed of the United States? He said he will increase their membership to 250,000. The added 175,000 new members will form 5 new corps. The "Classroom Corps" will help teachers. The "Health Corps" will provide public health information. The "Clean Energy Corps" will promote energy independence. The "Veterans Corps" will help veterans. The "Homeland Security Corps" will work with FEMA and help in national emergencies. The entire AmeriCorps apparatus is a retread of FDR's Worker's Progress Administration (WPA), which my dad worked on during the depression and called "We Piddle Around," and the Civilian Conservation Corps (CCC). They were FDR's failed welfare programs that cost billions from our bankrupt country, accomplished nothing useful, and created no permanent jobs. Of course, creating jobs is the last thing on Obama's mind until he finishes-off the capitalist beast called America.

Similar to AmeriCorps is the "Senior Corps" of the new Obama Army. Senior Corps is composed of three divisions: The "Foster Grandparent Program," "The Senior Companion Program," and "RSVP." Approximately 500,000 people age 55 and over are involved in Senior Corps. Another similar program that is part of the Obama Army is called "Learn and Serve America." It grants a college student a $4000 "American Tax Credit" in exchange for 100 hours of community service. Approximately 1.3 million students participate in this program. The Peace Corps is a part of Obama's Army, also. Right now it numbers about 8000 volunteers, but Obama wants to increase it to 16,000 by 2011. Yet another is called "America's Voice Initiative" which is located within the State Department. They will train Americans who are fluent in languages of the Muslim nations, and who will travel to the Middle East and work in mass media outlets. Other programs in Obama's Army are "Global Energy Corps," "Green Job Corps," "Youthbuild Corps," "Green Vet Initiative" and others.

The exact number of Obama's "corps" and the total costs are impossible to calculate because they are shape-shifting constantly. I am a CPA and still get lost in the numbers or simply can't reconcile the figures. All I can say is that this army will cost between $150 billion and $300 billion. Spending this kind of money with our present economy is foolish enough, but spending it so that Obama and the Democrats receive lopsided laurels to further their devious takeover of our country is criminal.

The total number of The Corporation for National and Community Service members by the end of 2010 should be between 2.1 and 2.7 million members. All of them are paid out of Treasury; your tax revenues at work. Virtually all of the work and functions performed by the members of the CNCS were formerly done by private enterprise, charity, or simply good people with good hearts. Obama has already increased our federal work force by 51,000 to a record 2.2 million employees. That's over 2.5% of the workforce. And Obama is not only hiring in record numbers, he is forcing them into the unions as fast as they arrive. Over 40% of the federal workers will be unionized by the end of the year. Besides hiring at a record rate, those employees making over

$100,000 represented 14% of the total when Obama took office, and now they make up 20% of the number. A recent survey found that Obama's government is paying an average 83% more than comparable jobs in the private sector. Guess who all these holders of cushy jobs will vote for should there ever be another Presidential election in this country? This is happening at a time when 8 million Americans in the private sector lost their jobs. What do you call a society where everybody works for the government? Pick one: (A) socialism, (B) communism, (C) Nazism, (D) fascism or (E) all of the above. We are heading in that direction and the rate of increase in federal workers is itself increasing. Each well-paid, cushy job with benefits and perks is another vote in Obama's corner.

You can bet that most of Obama's rogues, demons, and useful idiots voted for him in 2008 and will do so anytime he runs for President or Dog-Catcher. But, some of the newbie's in AmeriCorps, Senior Corps, and even in the new IRS hires for the Obamacare fiasco, and others crowding on the already sinking federal payroll ship, are actually Americans just wanting a job and career. They will get their job, but with it will come covert and subliminal propaganda right out of George Orwell's "1984." We have all become accustomed to signs at highway construction sites, bridges, and signs posted at the borders when you enter another state that tells you your governor welcomes you or is building a particular improvement because he loves you. The same is true at city, county, state, and federal buildings. The mayor, commissioner, governor, and president use every government-owned facility to influence the citizens to think of them positively. This is especially true in the military. On November 22, 1963, I was standing naked with about 100 other guys getting physicals for induction into the Army. Looking at me from a picture on the wall was John Kennedy. We were still naked when a sergeant rushed in to say Kennedy had been assassinated in Texas. It didn't take two weeks before Lyndon Johnson's picture had replaced Kennedy's at all Army bases.

But, I think this time around the new, young recruits in the AmeriCorps, the old recruits in Senior Corps, and the millions already on the government dole will be treated to something closer to Goebbels' propaganda which was spoon-fed to the German people to make them think Hitler was their God. Our military has been getting away from the tried and true philosophy of "killing people and breaking things" to a "kinder and gentler" approach to defend America against our enemies. First, there was the "time out" card which a soldier holds up when he needs to take a break from running or physical training. Then came "sensitivity training" where soldiers were taught to be politically correct. Now, Obama wants homosexuals sleeping with them, so it will be against SOP to sleep on their backs because it will convey distrust for their fellow soldier's tender sexual feelings.

The propaganda under Obama's regime is guaranteed to be rained on the heads, eyes, and ears of all new and old government employees in monsoon-like torrents. If you go to Obama's description of his plans for the Corporation for National and Community Service at the website barackobama.com/pdf/nationalserviceplanfactsheet.pdf you will find Obama's and Biden's names mentioned no less than 53 times. You can be sure that every one of the millions of employees connected in any way to the federal largesse will be bombarded by Obama propaganda. Every job application, every factsheet, report, piece of literature, brochure, booklet, manual, procedure, and video will be full of Obamafacts to let you know who you are working for, and who you owe for your paycheck. You will receive newsletters and updates on what your hardworking President has done this week to improve your life and your country. And, you will also gain the knowledge of the enemy: those damn Republicans, conservatives, and Teabag people who are trying to meddle in your exalted President's struggle to make your life better. This used to be called brainwashing, but now it's called "Obama-cleansing." The media already prepared the masses for this cleansing by eviscerating George Bush for eight years, and the McCain/Palin ticket after that. When election time came, it was like voting in Cuba; there was only one suitable candidate left on the ballot who would rescue us from these corrupt, racist, white tyrants and that was the new messiah promising "hope and change."

THE FASCIST MEDIA

It is impossible to make wise decisions in your personal or business life without knowledge of the cause and effects those decisions will impact. Whether it is figuring out what to plant in your home garden or what stock shares to invest in, you must first see the pros and cons of each before deciding. In most areas and issues affecting us we can obtain objective, non-controversial information to help us make decisions. In one area, politics, we have no direct objective source of intelligence. For those few of us that still care about America and pay attention to what's happening, we have no choice but to gather information from the media and try and make sense of it. If the media has an agenda which it pushes into your head day after day, then you become like Pavlov's dog and salivate for the wrong reasons. Huxley's "Brave New World" and Orwell's "1984" were fictional books about the persuasive powers of propaganda that have become non-fictional under Obama. Obama's success in transforming the United States into a Fascist Empire will depend on whether enough people care enough to seek the truth by circumventing the state-controlled media. Looking around at average Americans today I don't see that happening.

I label the media "Fascist" because it is not owned directly by Obama, but it acts in lockstep with the Democrats. There is no longer a free media in the United States with one exception, Fox News. A good example was given by Dan Gainor of Foxnews.com in writing about the media's shrill and repetitious support for Obama during his maniacal rush to pass the nationalized health care bill. I will give a few excerpts:

> "It didn't matter whether it was NBC using the Winter Olympics to tell a positive story about Canada's socialized health system or Time senior political analyst Mark Halperin saying it's "immoral" that America is "the only industrialized democracy that doesn't cover every citizen." Journalists in the United States told one side of the story: Obama's."

> "From the President's attack on insurers to the bogus prediction the bill was going to pass any day to claims that

opponents were "Astroturf" or phony grassroots, the media mirrored the President's position almost constantly. The Washington Post went so far as to cede much of its coverage of the issue to liberal blogger Ezra Klein, who naturally supported even the lamest attempt at national health care."

"Nearly a year ago, during what ABC's Diane Sawyer called "D-Day for health care" reform, the broadcast networks devoted 10 stories to Obama's May 11 speech. Only one of those segments included a critic. And Sawyer was using the talking point for the administration's plan, claiming it would benefit patients. "What's the first thing they'll do for you and your family?" It was inconceivable to journalists that the result of so-called health care reform might do something **to** most Americans, not **for** them."

"Those pesky, ordinary voters who dared oppose something so "great and necessary" were labeled "radical" or "dangerous" and abused in the media. Even this week, MSNBC's looniest guy without a show, David Shuster, claimed tea party protesters were "far right" and said they were "going nuts" because of maneuvering on the Hill."

"His nuttier colleagues had worse things to say about the voters who opposed health care reform. "Hardball" host Chris Matthews blamed it on racism: "I think some of the people are upset because we have a black President." Fellow host Keith Olbermann preferred to blame tea partiers for another ism … "terrorism." "When Hamas does it or Hezbollah does it, it is called terrorism. Why should Republican lawmakers and the Astroturf groups organizing on behalf of the health care industry be viewed any differently?" he ranted."

"The few folks who watch Ed Schultz saw him saying Republicans were the party of death for opposing health care reform. "The Republicans lie! They want to see you dead! They'd rather make money off your dead corpse!'"

"The so-called professional journalists on the broadcast networks weren't much better. While sleazy Democrats were contemplating passing health care reform without *ever even voting on it, the evening news shows were largely silent. The bogus claim that the government can seize one-sixth of the economy through "deem and pass" received little coverage, let alone scrutiny. Imagine if the GOP had tried to ram through a similar controversial law. The media would have filled the airwaves with concerned citizens, experts and advocates. Since Democrats are embracing the corruption, it's just a blip in the coverage."*

"And journalists repeatedly got the scope of the problem wrong. Before Obama changed his claim about the number of uninsured Americans, networks parroted the bogus figure 80 percent of the time. ABC's Robin Roberts was typical when she told "Good Morning America" viewers that "50 million Americans" were uninsured. Her claim was wrong by at least 14 million people. But when Obama downgraded his number during a September speech, most of the media fell into line."

We have historically looked to our media to report political scandals, corruption, kick-backs, padded contracts, and scams uncovered by investigative reporters interested in truth and honesty in government. The media started leaning left in the 60's but Clinton ushered in a new era of increased bias. It grew worse during the Bush 43 years and became virtually government-owned when Obama announced for the Presidency. He added a new dimension because of the sheer complexity of the existing Chicago crime syndicates combining with the labyrinth of alphabet agencies, secret alliances, slush funds, and covert relationships that defied understanding even by an independent media. Thousand of strange-looking operatives came pouring into Washington, occupying all levels of government, and shuttling and shifting trillions of dollars like it was small change. If ever there was a time that we needed a watchdog media it is now. What a bonanza of secret deals and concealed schemes could be discovered and uncovered by the media if we only still had one. There would be Pulitzer prizes galore. Clinton set new highs in corruption, immorality, and criminal activities, but Obama would make him look like a piker if only we had a media to ferret it out. The media has actually become a part of Obama's administration and increased its destruction of

America since the lack of oversight allows Obama to operate freely and openly with no fear.

I think most reporters suffer from an extreme case of white guilt. The one that comes to mind first is Chris Matthews. Remember when he said that he felt a tingling down his leg when Obama spoke? He is really serious. He has a terminal case of white guilt. People like him cannot comprehend that a white person can criticize a black person and not be a racist. He is so ashamed that some white people 150 years ago owned black people as slaves. He will never get over it no matter how much time goes by, or even if a former "chattel" of a 13% minority becomes President. Nothing, but nothing, will ever atone for the horror that whites have done to blacks. His feeling toward anyone that has an ounce less white guilt than him is a borderline racist. He harbors a rabid hatred so intense that it comes bursting out without warning. For anyone that doubts the existence of white guilt they need only watch Chris Matthews in action. Thank God I already know all about white guilt, and do not need to suffer through a half-hour of watching the rants and raves of a maniac like Matthews.

I am 66 years old and have done more, seen more, and been to more places than most Americans. Many years ago I saw a free press and a free media thriving in the United States, and I've seen countries where the press lives in fear of printing anything controversial or detrimental to the government. Currently, our media thinks it is free because, like Pravda and Izvestia, they mimic the party (Obama) line. They should think back to last year when Obama, Gibbs, and their demons piled on Fox for awhile. That is absolutely nothing compared to what will happen to them if, and when, they wake-up someday and find themselves in a totalitarian state where their copy is written for them, and if they try to express their objectivity they disappear.

NATIONALIZED INTERNET

A democracy cannot exist without a free press; a free media. We have been losing our free press for 60 years and it finally died in 2008 with the coming of Obama. What little remains of our late, great free media consists only of Fox on TV and Rush, Glenn, Mark, Hannity, and a few others on radio. Fox is increasingly creeping leftward, and Congress and Obama's FCC is designing schemes to limit or eliminate conservative talk radio. The internet then will be our only means of a free and unencumbered exchange of ideas, right? Wrong.

We have the most leftist Congress in 234 years, yet even they would not bow to Obama's wishes to pass legislation allowing him to tax and control the internet. As far back as the Carter administration, the White House had tried to control the Computer industry, but had been rebuffed by an honest FCC. Even Clinton's FCC had not allowed tampering with the internet. But, like the unisex dinosaurs in Jurassic Park who found a way to multiply, Obama has found a way to bypass Congress. Since Congress would not give him the authority, he simply told his FCC to start regulating the internet web providers "as if" Congress had given the go-ahead. When they tried to do this Comcast sued the FCC in the D.C. Circuit Court of Appeals and won. Comcast is one of the largest internet providers in the U.S. Obama, always the recalcitrant optimist, told his old leftist Harvard comrade from Chicago, Julius Genachowski, who he appointed to head up the FCC, that he needed for him to find a way to circumvent the court ruling. Being a part of the Chicago mob, where criminality is instinctual, Julius announced his intention to reclassify broadband internet to resemble an old-fashioned telephone system as a pretext for pervasive regulatory control. If Genachowski is successful it will reverse 30 years of precedent for the FCC which has always operated independent of the politics of Washington.

The most amazing attribute of the internet is that it is an interactive means of communication. We can only listen to or watch radio and television, but we can respond to each other, have chat rooms, watch videos, and perform a multitude of other functions on the internet. It has flourished into a remarkable engine of economic growth, innovation, competition, and free expression. Obama's interest is manyfold. He can monitor the exchange of information like most fascist do. He can place limitations on it to control interaction of the masses. And, he can tax it. Robert McChesney, founder of the radical leftist "Free Press" (who you'll read more about in "Pravda Rebirth") said, "What we want to have in the U.S. and in every society is an internet that is not private property, but a public utility." He went on to say, "At the moment, the battle over network neutrality is not to completely eliminate the telephone and cable companies. We are not at that point yet. But the ultimate goal is to get rid of the media capitalists in the phone and cable companies and to divest them from control." Not surprisingly, the so-called Free Press and McChesney get their funding to finish killing our independent media directly from none other than George Soros.

The goal of Obama's fascists is "Net Neutrality" which, in Obamaspeak, is socialism of the internet. As in all nationalist takeovers of private industry, they say it will level the playing field and make the internet more available to the masses. It will level the field like Obamacare and financial reform, but Team Obama will be the only players on the field. Besides Julius "Julius Caesar" Genachowski the other socialists taking-over the internet are Obama senior technology advisor Susan Crawford, and senior FCC advisor Colin Crowell. FCC Commissioner Robert McDowell wrote a letter to House member Henry "nostrils" Waxman (D-Calif.) explaining the FCC's planned take-over, and said it may need his help in fending-off attempts by non-socialists to prevent "Obamanet." Waxman promised to provide the cover and will be introducing legislation if the FCC needs help.

All of America watched as Obamacare unfolded day after day on CSPAN, and pundits discussing it 24 hours a day. We were all stunned how Nancy Pelosi and "Dingy" Harry used every dirty trick to pass legislation that 80% of Americans were against. Finally, it took the 535 members of Congress to vote up or down on Obamacare. It was a big deal because healthcare represented one-sixth of our economy. Why haven't we heard similar screams of socialism about the FCC taking over the internet and communications industries? The industry represents the same one-sixth of our GDP. The main difference between the two industries is that the takeover of the communications industry requires only 3 votes of the FCC, and Obama owns all 3 votes.

PRAVDA REBIRTH

For those of you too young to remember the cold war, the state-owned propaganda organ of the U.S.S.R. was Pravda, where the official position of the communists was promulgated. Just as a free, unencumbered press is the lifeblood of a free society, so is a controlled press, a propaganda mouthpiece, necessary for converting a free society to totalitarianism slowly by progressivism, or quickly through revolution. Had we been blessed with a fair and non-aligned media over the last 25 years Obama would never have become President. They brought him to power and will keep him there. Just as he rewarded the UAW, tort lawyers, Planned Parenthood, and homosexuals, so too must he keep alive his propaganda arm of his revolution. The miniscule conservative wing of the media is alive and well and needs no government support. This is not true of the left. Gore and his "Radio America" finally died after limping along for years. Rush, Hannity, Mark Levine, and all other conservative talk radio hosts are more popular than ever. Fox is stomping CNN, MSNBC, and the rest of the cable news programs. Even though the conservatives have no newspapers to call their own, the liberal press, which has no competition, is in the red for over $75 billion total. If Obama leaves it up to the conservatives only to get his words out to the public, the message may be fair and balanced, but that's the last thing he wants. Without Chris Matthews saying that Obama makes his legs tingle, or reporters throwing softballs at him, his movement will lose momentum. So, Obama will approach this problem from a couple different fronts.

You will soon see Obama extolling the virtues of the unlimited free press. He will say that "without the multitude of media outlets, dissenting views will be suppressed. The more conflicting views the better. Therefore, we must prevent this vital industry, this icon of our American heritage from ever disappearing from this great land that our forefathers fought for. Being the oldest source of our news in the country, the newspaper industry must be one of the first forms of media rescued." Or, in Obama's own words, newspapers are "critical to the health of our democracy." He went on to say, "I am concerned that if the direction of the news is all blogosphere, all opinions, with no serious fact-checking, no serious attempts to put stories in context, then what you will end up getting is people shouting at each other across the void but not a lot of mutual understanding." In other words, he likes newspapers because 100% of them lean left, or more left, or far left. He also said he is "happy to look at" any bill that gives struggling news organizations tax breaks if they were to restructure as nonprofit businesses.

Following Obama's advice, Senator Ben Cardin of Maryland introduced S.673 titled the "Newspaper Revitalization Act" to give government funds to newspapers in trouble if they become not-for-profit 501(C)(3) corporations. Even as non-profits they would still be allowed to report on all issues including political campaigns, which means every article would favor Democrats. Every newspaper in the U.S. has experienced reduced revenues, but many like the Chicago Tribune, Los Angeles Times, and the Baltimore Sun have declared bankruptcy while the San Francisco Chronicle, Seattle Post-Intelligencer, Rocky Mountain News, and Baltimore Examiner have either stopped daily publication or soon will. Anyone familiar with "Washington-Speak" should interpret Cardin's bill to result in government controlled nationalized newspapers just like GM and Chrysler. Being non-profit means nothing. Salaries could still be whatever is required to attract the highest paid liberal writers who would beat-up on any Republican or conservative. Unlike government financed and controlled NPR broadcasting, where we know and expect leftist propaganda, which is off-set by conservative radio talk shows, the "National Public Newspapers" will have no competition and they will fill every page with "Obamaganda."

Steve Forbes wrote a piece about the lobbying efforts of anti-capitalist socialist groups that want to go further than Senator Cardin. They are part of the "media reform" movement in the U.S. and headed by a professor named Robert McChesney. McChesney is the founder of the so-called "Free Press." We have all become aware of how Democrats title their bills to sound nice even though they usually do bad things to people. McChesney's "Free Press" is like this and sounds like a freedom-loving newspaper, until you realize that he would like us to pattern our press like that of Hugo Chavez of Venezuela who has been documented as ordering the murder of journalists in his country. Like Obama, you need only listen to McChesney's words to easily catch his intent. He said, "Any serious effort to reform the media system would have to necessarily be part of a revolutionary program to overthrow the capitalist system itself."

McChesney thinks media reform is the first step in the struggle to force Americans to discard capitalism and embrace socialism. Besides Chavez, he is an admirer of Marx, Hitler, Lenin, and Obama. He takes his message often to Washington and is welcomed on his regular visits to the House and Senate to lobby for his radical changes, and even visits the Federal Communications Commission (FCC) and the Federal Trade Commission (FTC). He must be having an effect or he would not be welcomed back so often. The Democrats are listening and making notes of McChesney's ideas. They and the agencies will try and put something together before the 2010 elections while they are still sure of a majority in both houses of Congress. But, don't think Obama will wait on Congress to assure that the newspapers don't miss a beat in helping him push his fascist agenda.

While you would think the FCC would be the logical agency to deal with newspapers since communications is part of their name, Obama uses the Chicago mob approach and has multiple means to reach his pragmatic goal of controlling the media. The FTC has historically limited its influence to matters of commerce, and left all forms of communications to the FCC. That has changed since the immaculation of the Propagandist-in-Chief. The FTC came out with their 47 page "Potential Policy Recommendations to Support the Reinvention of Journalism" that outlines a major government push to rescue the country's failing newspapers. The recommendations are many, but let's take a look at just a few. The report suggests that we create a journalism division within AmeriCorps, Obama's private army of 75,000 government paid volunteers. Also suggested in the report are tax credits for every journalist hired by news organizations, public funding for public radio and television, postal subsidies for print media, grants to universities to have their own investigative reporters (no bias there, I'm sure), a tax on consumer electronics to provide at least $4 billion for public funding of journalists, and lastly, establishing "citizenship news vouchers" which "would allow every American taxpayer to allocate some amount of government funds to the non-profit media organization" of their choice.

Of course, Obama and his Demons console conservative critics by saying the report is just a draft of ideas so they shouldn't get alarmed. This is an old ploy and the tried and true methodology of the left to jump-start radical changes when no change is necessary and no discussion is even needed. In other words, their scheme creates an issue from thin air, starts the ball rolling and puts the conservatives on the defensive. The authors of the report said "we seek to prompt discussion of whether to recommend policy changes to support the ongoing reinvention of journalism, and, if so, which specific proposals appear most useful, feasible, platform-neutral, resistant to bias, and unlikely to cause unintended consequences in addressing emerging gaps in news coverage." The only "bias" is on the left and the only "gaps in news coverage" is the left failing to do their job since the "Holy One" took office. Cliff Kincaid, editor of Accuracy in Media, said that the FTC's job is to protect consumers, not mess with newspapers. He added the point that consumers have always made it clear to the newspapers that they are sick and tired of the slanted news and have switched to other modes of communications such as the internet, talk radio and Fox News. Dan Gainor, VP of business and culture for the Media Research Center, was more direct and said, "The mere fact that they're holding these hearings is the beginning of the problem. They should have no hand in the future of journalism."

Professor Jeff Jarvis of the City University of New York's Graduate School of Journalism said, "I find it dangerous for government to have a role in speech because the government gives and the government taketh away." He went on to say, "The problem with this is that the FTC is trying to set an agenda here, that some sort of government intervention is necessary. It's a power grab by the FTC and it's also an example of one old power structure circling its wagons around another." Jarvis said he found it odd and disturbing that the report would use the perspectives of newspapers since they are a dying form of journalism and not use the internet and the more modern forms that people are turning to today. He pointed out that the term "blog" was used only once in the report and that the proposals seek to "support the old power structure of the dying model of newspapers." Jarvis concluded by saying that "Everything you see in that document is an attempt to stifle new competition by sustaining the incumbents" and "I don't even understand why they're doing this. This document is an anti-competitive and even unconstitutional world view." As in healthcare, Obama, if he is anything, is tenacious. He will not let go of his goal of total control of all propaganda reaching the ears and eyes of Americans. He will have his Pravda, come hell or high water.

CLOWARD-PIVENS MEETS THE DARKSIDE

Even if you have watched Glenn Beck and have an idea of what the Cloward-Piven Strategy is, let me give you a quick primer. Richard Cloward and his wife Frances Piven were sociologists at Columbia University. They are members of the largest openly socialist organization in the U.S. They wrote a paper called the "Cloward-Piven Strategy" in 1966 which described how the poor could destroy capitalism by overloading the government bureaucracy with a flood of impossible demands, thus pushing society into crisis and economic collapse. Society would then accede to the demands of the poor to escape the chaos. The original idea had been inspired by the August 1965 riots in the Watts district of Los Angeles that erupted after a drunken black man was arrested. Cloward and Pivens argued that, rather than be content with the welfare handouts of society, blacks should overload the system, cause it to crash, and then force society to redistribute all the wealth instead of parceling it out to them. Like Obama would do later, they used Saul Alinsky's "Rules for Radicals" as the basis for replacing capitalism with socialism.

Specifically, the Cloward-Piven Strategy calculated that about 8 million people in 1966 were on the welfare rolls in the United States, but that at least 16 million would qualify for welfare. They proposed that a "cadre of aggressive organizers" use militant demonstrations to demand welfare entitlements for those currently not on the rolls. Making use of friendly, left-wing journalists coupled with black violence, the politicians would force the government to redistribute income. This would spread from city to city, and finally to Washington where redistribution of wealth would be accomplished on a national basis. This was all based on the Trojan Horse concept where radical change was disguised as an attempt to help the poor. The chaos, fear, turmoil, and violence would throw the government into such crisis that the central powers would be at the mercy of the revolutionaries.

Cloward and Piven actually did a trial run of their theory. They recruited a black militant named George Wiley in 1967 to form the National Welfare Rights Organization (NWRO). By 1969 his NWRO thugs numbered 22,500 families with 523 chapters across the country. Their typical tactic was to storm violently into welfare offices, and demand all that was due them as poor people living in a wealthy society. The economy in the late 60's and early 70's was thriving, but many of the blacks found pro-active welfare activity more lucrative than working. From the welfare offices they expanded to sit-ins in legislative chambers, lay-ins at United States Senate committee hearings, mass marches of thousands of blacks, school boycotts, and picket lines. Later, their actions turned to rock-throwing, glass-smashing, turning over desks, ripping out phone lines, and scattering trash in offices. Mounted police, police cordons, tear gas, and arrests did not slow them down. The number of households filing welfare claims soared from 4.3 million to 10.8 million in a short time. When New York City reached a point where two blacks were on welfare for every one person working, the city declared bankruptcy in 1975. The whole state of New York nearly crashed with it. Cloward-Piven was not just a theory anymore, it worked. It hadn't worked nationally, but it had brought a city and almost a state to its knees. It worked like a Trojan Horse in that nobody really knew what was happening until chaos hit. Before the entire nation suffered a similar fate the Republican Congress passed the 1996 Personal Responsibility and Work Opportunity Reconciliation Act which imposed time limits on federal welfare, along with strict eligibility and work requirements. Since Bill Clinton was a willing player in the Cloward-Piven game he did what he could to water-down the bill, but finally was forced to sign it into law. Both Richard Cloward and his wife Frances Piven were invited to the signing as the personal guests of Bill Clinton. Clinton and his guests were all smiling at the ceremony; they knew this was just round one.

Cloward and Piven remained largely unknown, but not by people that saw New York almost go down the tube. Rudolph Giuliani saw through their scheme and said in a 1998 speech that what they had done was the "result of policies and programs designed to have the maximum number of people get on welfare." Cloward and Piven were convinced that they had not succeeded in bringing down the whole capitalist American system for one reason: secrecy. Their Trojan Horse plan had been too visible and too concentrated, largely in the northeast, to work simultaneously throughout the country. They decided that the next attack on the country would be stealthily approached and undetected until it was too late for the capitalist system to survive the onslaught. The next target chosen for the Cloward-Piven Strategy would be to overwhelm, paralyze, and discredit the voting system of the United States through fraud, protests, propaganda, and vexatious litigation. Keep in mind as you read the following that it is the culmination of reams of material surrounded by layers of intertwining groups and individuals purposely obfuscating the real nature or goal of their efforts. In other words, the Trojan Horse was coming again but this time he was cloaked in invisibility.

In 1970 the aforementioned George Wiley (NWRO) and his lead organizer, Gary Delgado, and another of his protégés, Wade Rathke (SDS), formed the Arkansas Community Organizations for Reform Now (ACORN) with a mandate to organize all poor and working-class people into a viable political force. The "A" in ACORN was later changed from "Arkansas" to "Association" but the acronym remained unchanged. In 1983 Cloward and Piven founded the Human Service Employee Registration, Voting and Education campaign Fund (Human SERVE Fund) to increase the voter turnout of the poor. ACORN co-founder and former NWRO and SDS militant, Zach Polett, formed a not-for-profit 501(C)(3) front group called "Project Vote," and shared the responsibilities of voter registration of the poor with the Human SERVE Fund. Project Vote went door-to-door, in food stamp lines, welfare lines, unemployment lines, soup kitchen lines, and anywhere else the poor congregated, to register voters. Human SERVE lobbied government officials directly to enact laws and regulations directing public employees to offer to register citizens applying for services at government agencies like Medicaid and food stamp lines, recertification centers, libraries, and driver's license bureaus. From "discoverthenetworks.org" the following was written by Cloward and Piven:

"[B]etween March and September of this year [1985], Human Serve helped obtain six gubernatorial executive orders permitting registration assistance in state offices. The Governors of Texas, Ohio, New York and Montana directed that such services be provided by all agencies; in New Mexico and West Virginia they limited the services to public welfare offices. Governor Rudy Perpich of Minnesota publicly endorsed the plan but did not mandate it. Orders were also issued in two dozen counties and cities, including such metropolitan centers as Austin, Texas; Newark; Dayton, Columbus and Cleveland, Ohio; Portland, Oregon; Miami and Tallahassee, Florida. There were even some legislative victories. Washington, Florida and Maryland passed bills directing state employees to offer to register citizens."

It took 10 years, but Cloward and Piven reached their second milestone on May 20, 1993, when they again stood behind Bill Clinton as he signed the National Voter Registration Act of 1993, better known as the "Motor Voter Act." The gist of the act was to order every state to provide resources enabling people to register to vote at state agencies at the same time they applied for drivers' licenses, welfare, Medicaid, and disability benefits.

A few years later Cloward and Piven closed down the Human SERVE Fund figuring their part in collapsing our capitalist republic was successful, and the rest was up to ACORN and Project Vote to overload the voting system until it collapsed. John Fund of the Wall Street Journal wrote in his book "Stealing Elections: How Voter Fraud Threatens Our Democracy":

"Perhaps no piece of legislation in the last generation better captures the 'incentivizing' of fraud... than the 1993 National Voter Registration Act... Examiners were under orders not to ask anyone for identification or proof of citizenship. States also had to permit mail-in voter registrations, which allowed anyone to register without any personal contact with a registrar or election official. Finally, states were limited in pruning 'dead wood' – people who had died, moved or been convicted of crimes – from their rolls. ... Since its implementation, Motor Voter

has worked in one sense: it has fueled an explosion of phantom voters."

In an editorial titled "Too Easy to Steal" in the WSJ on December 11, 2001, it was stated that the Motor Voter Act had resulted in over 8 million new voters registered, but only 5% of them bothered to vote, meaning that the remaining 95% were available for fraudulent use by people other than the registrant. This is especially likely since most states do not require a photo ID at polling booths. In San Francisco, California Secretary of State Bill Jones said that 3600 votes could not be found even though they were certified by his predecessor. Jones also found a discrepancy of 9% between the counts of the precincts in the city and the total reported by the city. After the 2000 election, workers found 240 ballots jammed in the voting machines, and the Coast Guard found the tops of 8 ballot boxes floating in San Francisco Bay. The problems are nationwide and growing yearly. Just in St. Louis the U.S. Postal Service can't locate 28% of all registered voters.

John Samples, PhD of the Cato Institute, appeared before the Committee on Rules and Administration on March 14, 2001, to address the disastrous consequences if the Motor Voter Act was not rescinded immediately. He said the two stated goals of the Motor Voter Act, namely, to protect the integrity of the electoral process, and to produce accurate and clean voter rolls, had produced the opposite results. The basic problem was that the Act made it extremely easy to register without verifying identity, and once on the rolls it was almost impossible to remove the voter even though they are dead or do not exist at all. Once on the rolls, the election office would have to call, mail, or visit each and every voter to verify existence. In Indiana alone a single, one-time mailing for verification would cost more than the entire Election Division's budget for the entire year. The Indianapolis Star did their own examination and found that "tens of thousands of voters are registered more than once, that 300 dead people were registered, three convicted killers and two child molesters were on the rolls." A study in Georgia found 15,000 dead people on the rolls. In Alaska the Federal Elections Commission did their own study and found that there were 502,968 registered voters, but only 437,000 people of voting age in the whole state according to the census.

Doctor Samples selected St. Louis, Missouri, as especially fraudulent in its voter registration. An ACORN affiliate, Operation Big Vote, had been organizing black voters aggressively in St. Louis, and delivered 3800 registrations on the deadline date of February 7, 2001, for the March mayoral election. A quick check of the registration cards turned up a few questionable cards so the elections staff spent a full day examining each one. They found that every one of the 3800 cards were fraudulent and included dead people, convicted felons, prominent citizens using their childhood addresses, and dogs. When some of the people on the cards were contacted they said some guy calling himself "Big Mike" came to their house, said he was from the Election Board and wanted to register them. They had no intention of voting. Another 29,500 cards came in a few hours before the deadline for the November 7, 2000, Missouri governor's election. Democrat Bob Holden won the race by just 21,000 votes statewide, so you can see how corrupt groups like ACORN and Project Vote can and has criminalized our suffrage rights and succeeded in getting the loser declared the winner.

Samples makes a good point when he asks, "Why would anyone go to the trouble of committing registration fraud if they did not intend to follow through and commit vote fraud? Otherwise, committing registration fraud becomes a senseless act. Are we to believe that individuals commit registration fraud for thrills or simply as a practical joke? The existence of fraudulent registrations suggests the greater threat of a corrupt election, a danger that we dismiss at our peril. Given the state of the registration rolls, a major vote fraud disaster remains a distinct possibility." Samples went on to mention that thousands of votes were fraudulent in the Florida 2000 elections, including 452 felons and non-existent people. He said that Missouri Republicans now believe Democrats are guilty of voter fraud. Of course, the Democrats have learned how effective using the race card has been for the blacks, so they merely brushed off the Republicans by saying Republicans just wanted to disenfranchise their constituents. In other words, anytime blacks are involved in voter fraud (which they always are) pull out the race card and let the fear of being labeled a racist do the rest. Samples concludes by saying that the Motor Voter Act should be judged a failure.

In 1996 Project Vote was involved in "Teamstergate", a criminal conspiracy to embezzle funds from the Teamster treasury, launder it through outside organizations, and then funnel it back to Teamster President Ron Carey. According to trial testimony, the operation was approved by high-level White House and Democrat officials. In another case, a Project Vote contractor, a single mother of three, forged 400 voter registration cards in 1998. "Some of the addresses listed on these applications were traced to vacant lots, boarded-up buildings, abandoned buildings, and nonexistent house numbers," reports the Employment Policies Institute. The former field director for ACORN's 2004 voter mobilization in Miami-Dade County, Mac Stuart, testified that fraud was standard procedure and encouraged by supervisors. He said it has been operated illegally since it was started.

Voter fraud may not mean much to most Americans, but when you remember that if just 4% of the votes were fraudulent in 2008, John McCain and Sarah Palin would now occupy the White House, and the United States would not be facing disaster. After studying multiple sources and data bases on the many scams and schemes of the Democrats to destroy our sacred right to vote, I conclude that there is at least a 5% to 9% discrepancy rate in our vote counts in all elections in the United States. In most races for President, Senate, House of Representatives, Governor, State Senate, State House, and on down the line the spread is often less than 10%. Consequently, every Democrat that won by a margin of 9% or less is occupying an office that should be held by his losing opponent. When you realize the sheer numbers of ACORN, Project Vote, SEIU, and other special interests coupled with the hundreds of millions of dollars pumped into both legal and illegal operations, it is a wonder there are any offices held by Republicans at all.

The Democrat voting drives have seen their Cloward-Piven Strategy succeed beyond all expectations. They now smell more blood and will go for the final kill starting in the 2010 elections. They will use their mass voter registration drives to again overload the election boards throughout the country with fraudulent voter cards and understaffed offices. They will use systematic intimidation of election officials, frivolous lawsuits, the usual unfounded charges of racism and disenfranchisement, and direct action in the form of violence. These criminal malcontents have introduced a level of fear, tension, and foreboding among the Republicans and knowledgeable Americans never before experienced outside third world countries. The final death knell for American suffrage rights is on its way, and it is called "Universal Voter Registration." This basically allows the federal government to take over all voter registration.

In January, John Fund of the Wall Street Journal reported that House member John Conyers and Senator Charles Schumer were submitting companion bills to allow universal voter registration. The bill could just as well be titled "The End of Democracy in America." Everybody whose name appears on any list, anywhere, for any reason in the United States and its territories will automatically be placed on the voter registration rolls. This includes drivers licenses, food stamps, tax returns, Social Security, Medicare, Medicaid, SSI, unemployment compensation rolls, etc. Schumer and Conyers could just save a lot of effort and stipulate that the 2010 Census become the new federalized voter registration list with a few additions. Those additions may be the 5 million felons and the 11 million illegal aliens. All of the liberal blogs, newspapers, and left-wing magazines are pumping out stories about how the United States will finally be like Canada, France, Venezuela, and Russia where voter registration runs as high as 90%. Articles in "The Nation," Los Angeles Times, AlterNet, and reports by the Brennan Center for Justice and many more, are heralding the day when universal voter registration arrives.

Hans A. von Spakovsky, a legal scholar in the Center for Legal and Judicial Studies at the Heritage Foundation and former commissioner on the Federal Election Commission, wrote that the universal registration idea is "gathering momentum." He said the left is pushing for this by saying large numbers of voters had trouble registering for the 2008 election. He countered that by saying, "The contrary evidence is much more powerful: The Census Bureau just reported that there was an increase of 4 million registered voters in 2008 from the 2004 election and voter turnout increased by 5 million." In other words, 20% or 1 million more people registered than existed thanks to ACORN, Project Vote, and the criminal Democrats.

The infamous, leftist 9th U.S. Circuit Court of Appeals overturned a Washington state law prohibiting convicted felons from voting until they are released and off parole. The basis of the ruling was that the law penalized minorities because they had a higher incarceration rate. The ruling means that felons will now be allowed to vote while still in prison, not only in Washington state, but also possibly in Oregon, Hawaii, Alaska, Montana, Nevada, Idaho, Arizona, and California. Massachusetts currently allows convicted felons to vote after they are released from incarceration. That is not good enough for them and they have taken their case to the U.S. Supreme Court. Their argument is that the law is unconstitutional and violates the 1965 Voting Rights Act because there are more blacks in prison than whites, so it is therefore racial discrimination. The convicts claim the state law "resulted in disproportionate disqualification of minorities from voting" and is therefore impermissible. The Supreme Court announced on May 3, 2010, that it wants to know the views of the Obama Administration before deciding whether to hear arguments in their case. Does the possibility exist that there are more blacks in prison because more blacks commit crimes? Naw, it must be racism pure and simple. And, let's all guess on how Obama will decide on whether the case should be heard by the Supreme Court. Of course, when Obama's universal voter registration becomes law this will all be moot since anyone occupying space can vote.

The Darkside Democrats have been whittling away at our suffrage rights for years and have already made deep inroads. Arizona, Washington, Kansas, and Indiana already allow registration online. Michigan Democrats have sponsored a bill to allow online registration by submitting a driver's license number, electronic signature, and a valid email address by 4PM the day of the election. Oregon and Nebraska are soon to have their own brand of online registration. New Hampshire, Maine, Minnesota, Wisconsin, Idaho, Wyoming, Montana, Iowa, North Carolina, and Washington D.C. all allow same-day registration. John Fund says, "They don't care and you can't stop it." I agree, since the Democrats have majorities in both houses and they are on a roll.

Obama and the Darkside are by no means finished with removing your suffrage rights totally, and making your vote an exercise in futility. After Obama puts his fascist spin on the 2010 decennial census results, the manipulated numbers will benefit the Democrats in gerrymandering the congressional districts, increase the number of registered Democrats for federal and state welfare programs, and make it much easier to stuff the ballot boxes in future elections. Congressman Patrick McHenry of North Carolina said, "President Obama has made clear that he intends to employ the political manipulation of census data for partisan gain." To achieve this manipulation Obama selected Robert Groves to head the Department of Commerce which oversees the constitutionally mandated census. Groves has stated that he is "researching ways to improve survey response rates." That is "Obamaspeak" for including and inflating the numbers of blacks, Muslims, Hispanics, Haitians, illegal aliens and any other minority group where Democrats gain votes.

In a 1999 ruling the Supreme Court ruled that the statistic sampling done by the census should never be used for apportioning House seats, but that the numbers could be adjusted when redrawing congressional districts. Democrats in the past have taken full advantage of the second part of the ruling by gerrymandering districts into strange-looking mixtures of lines and curves that would drive a surveyor crazy. The Congressional Black Caucus owes its very existence to gerrymandering. The zigzag borders of their districts can be used to determine where the majority of blacks reside, and who, in turn, can be depended on to keep them in office until another black replaces them due to old age or prison. Of course, gerrymandering in the northeast is now more of a racial issue than a partisan problem since liberal politicians and their state-owned media partners have decimated the Republicans to the point where they have become an endangered species in that geographical area. When Obama's subalterns redraw the districts after the scammed 2010 census, it will pit leftist black against leftist white or leftist Hispanic to see who gets another leftist congressional seat. If it were a horse race my money would be on the black horse since the owner of the stable is also black.

Under Obama's specific orders to look under every minority rock and ignore budgets to root out more Democrats, the Census Bureau has pulled-out all the stops. They hired Raul Cisneros to head the Census Publicity

Office, and Cisneros in-turn brought onboard subordinates from every nationality, color-shade, creed, and ethnicity he could find. Radio, TV, magazine, and newspaper ads are in 28 languages from Spanish to Farsi. Although minority groups comprise only 26% of the population, over half of the $140 million budget for ads will be targeted at them. Not only are the ads language-specific, but even the culture displayed in the background of the ads is designed for the different minorities. And, the messages for each of the minority groups are written to appeal to whatever that particular group is thought to feel are most important to them. For example, an ad aimed at Mexicans will have a plump, brown Mexican senorita speaking the Mexican dialect of Spanish, with typical Mexican furnishings in the background, telling you that your census data will be confidential, and will mean you will receive money from the federal government under your new leader Obama. An ad targeted at blacks from sub-Saharan Africa will have a former Congolese basketball player named Dikembe Mutombo, surrounded by black kids in an African motif, talking about the free money from their homeboy, Obama, by just filling out a single census form. Only one group is receiving no special attention, and if some of this group is missed then it is poetic justice. That group would be the evil Christian white Americans whom Obama has targeted for punishment rather than for his census ad campaign.

So, when Obama and his Census Bureau number-manipulators have completed his tabulations of the population, don't be surprised if the racial make-up of the nation has miraculously flip-flopped since the 2000 census, and whites now compose only about 15% of the population. When he finishes draining the Treasury, eliminating capitalism, and installing his fascist elite who cares what part of this wasteland belongs to any particular race of people?

Although the Cloward-Piven Strategy was used to bring down our welfare system and suffrage rights, it was also applied to our capitalist, free-enterprise system, even though this dynamic duo of destruction make no claims nor participated directly in our economic collapse. To understand how the Democrat Darkside collapsed our economy you must go back to 1977 to one of my fellow Georgians, and also the most useless President ever elected, "Jimma" Carter. Jimma signed into law that year the Community Reinvestment Act (CRA) designed to encourage banks and savings associations to loan money in accordance with good business practices to borrowers in their immediate community, including low-income neighborhoods. Chief promoters of the legislation were Barney Frank, ACORN, and the Greenlining Institute. The Greenlining Institute was formed by radical racists who followed Saul Alinsky's playbook "Rules for Radicals" in forcing banks to change their lending practices in California. They took their name from a play on the term "redlining," which was used by lending institutions to denote borrowers that did not meet the criteria for loan requirements. The Greenliners would select individuals from racial minorities who had been rejected on home loans by banks, and either file lawsuits or, more often, would storm into bank offices and scream "racist," disrupting the offices and personnel of banks. Banks rarely, if ever, refused to make a loan back in 1977 or 1907 because of skin color. At the center of the capitalist system is capital or, in plain English, money. If you got the income you get the loan, it's that simple. I know. I'm a CPA who's dealt with banks all my life. But, when you are a racist who hates the capitalist system you have a more sinister motive than race for fomenting chaos in the banking system. Race was merely the vehicle to get the proverbial foot in the door.

One of the main reasons that entrepreneurs charter new banks or lending institutions is in the hope that they will grow, and either establish branches or merge with other banks and thereby increase the value of their stock ownership. Therefore, the Community Reinvestment Act stipulated that before a bank could have their application for a branch or merger approved, they must first show that they had complied in accordance with fair lending practices in making loans to minorities. So, to avoid their applications being denied, the banks employed representatives of ACORN and Greenliners to advise them on whom to loan money to. Consequently, these two racist groups would direct many of the loans to their friends and similar leftist organizations. The volume of loans made in this manner never satisfied the two groups because the banks still had to meet their stringent regulations, and also market the loans to mortgage holders like Freddie Mac and Fannie Mae. Although the Financial Institutions Reform and Enforcement Act of 1989 and other laws were passed to both tighten-up lending practices while still making it easier for minorities to get loans, it was not enough to satisfy the Alinskyites of the left. In response to the never fulfilled left, the Federal Housing Enterprises Financial Safety and Soundness Act of 1992 was signed. This act mandated that HUD set specific goals for government-sponsored Fannie Mae and Freddie Mac, regarding setting aside a percentage of the mortgages they buy specifically for low-income minorities.

In their never-ending struggle to redistribute the wealth of those that earned it to the slackers who merely want it, the leftist groups lobbied their willing leader, Bill Clinton, to lessen restrictions further for minority borrowers. The Riegle-Neal Interstate Banking and Branching Efficiency Act of 1994 repealed the restrictions on interstate banking, but tied it to the CRA rules which gave even more power to the leftist groups like ACORN and the Greenliners. In 1999 Clinton signed into law the Gramm-Leach-Bliley Act (GLB) which repealed most of the Glass-Steagall Act of 1933 that had prohibited banks from making risky loans. Glass-Steagall had been enacted to prevent the bank failures of the depression in the 1930's from recurring. The GLB Act also made any bank wanting to be re-designated a holding company, or expand into non-banking businesses, subject to the CRA rules regarding minorities. While signing the GLB Act, Bill Clinton said that it "establishes the principles that, as we expand the powers of banks, we will expand the reach of the Community Reinvestment Act."

So, we now had a booming economy with banks that wanted to grow and expand which required lending ever larger amounts to unqualified borrowers. This in turn pleased ACORN and the other leftist groups who must give their approvals to the banks before they could grow. In the 90's the banks started making subprime loans and Adjustable Rate Mortgages for people and businesses who couldn't afford fixed-rate loans. Round and round this spiral went upward with the help of Fannie Mae and Freddie Mac, who would buy the mortgages from the banks so they could turn around and reinvest the funds again, and pass it through to Fannie and Freddie again. The politicians were muted in this period of prosperity by Freddie and Fannie stuffing $4.8 million in their pockets. Chris Dodd got $165,400, Obama $126,349, Kerry $111,000, Reid $77,000,

Hillary $76,050, and so on. The Democrats got the lions' share of the shut-up money, but the Republican's hands are dirty, too. The insiders at Freddie Mac and Fannie Mae are the real crooks who doctored earnings over six years, and exaggerated income by $10.6 billion to collect hundreds of millions in bonuses. Obama's black buddy, Franklin Raines, stole $90 million, James Johnson took $21 million in just his last year at Freddie Mac, and Jamie Gorlick lifted $26 million. Of course, both Raines and Johnson went to work for Obama to advise him on crashing the whole economy since they had valuable experience at crashing things. I'm no friend of John McCain, but I will say he and George Bush were two of the very few voices screaming in the wilderness in an effort to stop the out-of-control lending practices.

Barney Frank, the sodomite House member from the 4th district of Massachusetts, stonewalled all attempts at controlling Freddie Mac's and Fannie Mae's runaway lending practices. He received cash of $42,350 from the two mortgage giants and, as a member of the Progressive Caucus, joined with the far-left in crashing the economy. A third motive for defending their subprime and lax lending practices was that his boyfriend, Herb Moses, was an executive with Fannie Mae, and his bonuses depended on the volume of mortgages accepted. Frank had been censored by the House Ethics Committee back in 1987 when it was discovered that his live-in "lover," Steve Gobie, had been operating a house of prostitution from Frank's Capitol Hill apartment for 18 months. This didn't really concern him since he is routinely reelected from his district by a margin of 20%. As the ranking member of the House Committee on Financial Services, Frank had immense influence while overseeing the housing and banking industries, and was front and center every time the Republicans tried to reign-in the runaway mortgage subprime market. In 2001 he said he had "no concern about housing." In 2003 he said, "Fannie Mae and Freddie Mac are not facing any kind of financial crisis....the more people exaggerate these problems, the more pressure there is on these companies, the less we will see in terms of affordable housing." When Bush expressed concern over the risky lending practices, Frank joined Pelosi, Maxine Waters, and Charlie Rangel in sending Bush a letter warning that "an exclusive focus on safety and soundness is likely to come, in practice, at the expense of affordable housing."

Frank's response to a 2004 211-page letter from the Office of Federal Housing Enterprise Oversight (OFHEO) condemning irregularities in Fannie Mae's accounting was, "It is clear that a leadership change at OFHEO is overdue." In 2007 Frank became the chairman of the House Financial Services Committee. Later, when the subprime crisis hit he said, "The subprime crisis demonstrates the serious economic and social consequences that result from too little regulation." This is why debating with the Democrat Darkside is like talking to a tree. They all lie, deceive, and get angry because they are simply incapable of honesty.

While Barney, Nancy, and angry Maxine were pushing for loans to people who would never pay them back, and their friends and spouses were pocketing pay-offs and kick-backs, private millionaires were scamming us from the other end. Hedgefund billionaire John Paulson and two other creative subprime kingpins, Herb and Marion Sandler, gave a $15 million "gift" to the Center for Responsible Lending (CRL). CRL is a Durham, North Carolina based non-profit that works with such reputable groups as ACORN, helps the government draft legislation to protect consumers, and is a registered lobbyist. They and similar groups lobbied for Congress to ease restrictions on subprime loans while simultaneously pressuring banks to make bad loans to unqualified borrowers. Paulson meanwhile paid another $15 million to Goldman Sachs to create a portfolio of collateralized debt obligations consisting mostly of the bad loans that CRL had forced upon the unsuspecting banks. . He, in effect, shorted the bad loans just as investors short stocks when they think the price will fall. He made $1 billion in profit (3333% return) while the economy crashed, and hundreds of thousands of working Americans lost their jobs and homes. These were Obama's friends who engineered the housing collapse and the unemployment. Now, he will convince you that he is the messiah here to rescue you from people like Goldman Sachs, and the bankers who will in turn stuff his pockets like they have stuffed theirs. We the American people are the only losers.

Freddie Mac and Fannie Mae were placed under the conservatorship of the Federal Housing Finance Agency on September 7, 2008. Believe it or not, Eddie Bernice Johnson (female), representing the intellectual arm of the renowned Congressional Black Caucus, had the guts to introduce a bill titled "The Community Reinvestment Modernization Act of 2009" on March 2, 2009, to take up the destruction where the original Community Reinvestment Act had left off. The debacle of Freddie Mac and Fannie Mae will eventually cost American taxpayers over $150 billion dollars, but what the hell, members of the Black Caucus like Charlie Rangel take money and don't pay taxes on it anyway. They look at taxes as white man's reparations. The Cloward-Piven Strategy had achieved a milestone toward replacing capitalism with fascism, but there was still a way to travel. On October 6, 2008, the DOW fell 700 points and was below 10,000 for the first time in 4 years.

In reaction to the subprime crisis, Congress passed the Emergency Economic Stabilization Act of 2008 on October 3, 2008, which included $700 billion for the Troubled Asset Relief Program (TARP). The stated purpose of this money was to purchase distressed assets, especially mortgage-backed securities, and make capital injections into banks. The beneficiaries of the $700 billion that had been earned by working American taxpayers were companies that had earned trillions, and paid their owners and officers hundreds of billions. Rather than let them fail, as those of us do when we make bad business decisions, your government took money that we can never pay back and used it to prop them up. Once Obama took office in January 2009 he took control of the $700 billion as his own slush fund for the triple purposes of nationalizing banks and the auto industry, repaying friends and supporters like the United Auto Workers, and most important, the building of the financial arm of his ultimate fascist regime. Recall that in a fascist or Nazi government the means of production remains in private or semi-private ownership while answering to the head of government. To date, Obama has effective control over General Motors, Chrysler, Federal Reserve Banks, AIG, and many more will follow.

Obama's stimulus bill or, officially, the "American Recovery and Reinvestment Act of 2009" (ARRA) was signed into law on February 17, 2009. It contained 1071 pages; nobody read it and it passed the House with all the Democrats except 11 voting for it, and all 176 Republicans voting against it. In the Senate all the Democrats voted for it, and all but 3 Republicans voted against it. When asked by a reporter if he had read the bill Rep. John Conyers (D, of course) said, "Of course not, it would take two lawyers two days to read that stuff." For those of you that remember the hectic months preceding the signing, and the ominous predictions if Congress failed to act, should also remember that it sat on Obama's desk three days while he played golf on vacation. My favorite economist, Thomas Sowell, said that Obama was in a rush to get the bill passed "before the economy begins to recover on its own." The stated cost of the bill was $787 billion, and the stated purposes were to create jobs and promote investment and consumer spending to help recover from the deepest recession since the 1930's. I am a CPA and do my own research, but will use some figures from the work of Robert E. Rector and Katherine Bradley of the Heritage Foundation in examining the real purpose of this financial stake through the heart of America. Rector helped write the 1996 welfare reform law. I will refer to this bill by its acronym, ARRA, and avoid calling it a "stimulus" bill as much as possible since it is actually the most massive, permanent increase in welfare spending in U.S. history. It makes the attack on our welfare system to achieve income redistribution by Richard Cloward and his wife, starting in the late 60's, seem like a warm-up to what Obama has already wreaked by this Trojan horse.

Remember the 1996 welfare reform bill the Republicans forced on Bill Clinton and the Darkside? Well, Obama killed it dead with the ARRA. The '96 bill made people get off welfare and work, or helped them get training for a new job. That's why they called it a "work-fare" bill. Obama's ARRA brazenly tells states that the more welfare they hand-out, the more federal money they will get. Not only will states get bonuses for increasing the case loads, but the payments will be higher than before. For example, prior to the ARRA the federal government would pay a state 67 cents back for every dollar they paid to Medicaid patients. Now, they will pay the states 80 cents on the dollar. Some say that at least Aid to Families with Dependent Children (AFDC) remains under state control. But, I personally see so many violations of this program even in rural Georgia that it probably couldn't be run any worse if it were in federal hands. Federal funds for education will double, which means Obama's pornographic, anti-American, pro-abortion, homosexual indoctrination of our children will double also; especially under the limp-wristed Secretary of Education, Arne Duncan.

For the first time, Americans will get a refundable tax credit every year whether they are single or married or merely need it; just pure manna from Obama so we will remember who to vote for in the next election. The recognizable welfare in Obama's so-called jobs bill is $264 billion, but it will trigger another $523 billion in hidden budgetary gimmicks to total $787 billion. Our federal expenditures on welfare in fiscal year 2008 were $491 billion. But, just the first year's effect of Obama's ARRA added over $100 billion in FY 2009, the largest increase in our history. The combined federal, state, and city welfare cost for FY2008 was $679 billion, and with normal anticipated growth would have been close to $8.97 trillion over the next 10 years. The ARRA will increase this by at least $1 trillion meaning every working household in the U.S. paying taxes will have a $127,000 share of the burden. Obama and the Democrat Congress indicated that most payments in the ARRA were Keynesian in nature, and would be phased-out after two years. Keynesian simply means injecting money to stimulate the economy. This is another one of Obama's Trojan Horses. He knows that you will have forgotten about this little matter in two years, and politicians never take things back from voters anyway if they want to get reelected.

So, what Obama and his Democrats told us was a jobs-creating stimulus bill, turned out to be a Trojan Horse filled with wealth redistributing welfare. And, it is permanent because once a privilege is granted it becomes a right, and no politician that wants to be reelected will change that. Obama and his mob have given us many different numbers of the jobs created by his $800 billion "spendulus" ranging from two to four million. Believe not a word of it. It has probably killed at least one million jobs by sending welfare checks to people instead of encouraging them to get out and find a job. Punish the workers and reward the lazy is what redistribution of wealth has always been about.

Thus far, the well-organized radicals from the 60's have won many battles in their siege against capitalism. They have exploded the number of welfare recipients, and so infected our voter registration rolls that they are still on life support. But, bringing down the only superpower on earth is no easy task even if the besiegers own the media. Obama swept into office and took the baton from the Cloward-Piven's gang and is now sprinting for the goal line. His strategy is blitzkrieg:

multiple targets attacked simultaneously to confuse the enemy. Obama is everywhere; TV, newspapers, internet, and I hear his teleprompter-inspired voice even during Rush Limbaugh's news breaks. Speeches, signing nuke treaties, making recess appointments, interviews, and so on; the guy is non-stop. If he misses a day then Baghdad Bob Gibbs starts blathering. They are on a roll. They added their do-or-die spendulus package to Bushes' gift of TARP, threw some crumbs and bones to special interests for a few months to keep their troops in line, and all the while preparing behind closed doors to unveil the cornerstone of their fascist redistribution of our earned wealth and the Waterloo of our republic: Nationalized Health Care.

NATIONALIZED HEALTH CARE

The "Healthcare Reform Bill" passed the Senate (S1796) in December 2009, and passed the House on March 21, 2010, and was signed into law on March 23, 2010. It is thousands of pages of detail which no members of Congress read and you don't need to read it either. The Darkside wants you to get lost in the minutia while the juggernaut grinds ever forward. First, lose the names "healthcare," "universal health care," "healthcare reform" and even "Obamacare" from your vocabulary. "Nationalized Health Care" lends to this crime the aspect of a bully taking by force that which belongs to others. Nationalized Health Care (NHC) has more far-reaching manifestations than even most conservatives realize. First, it means virtual or actual ownership of hospitals, doctors, nurses, health workers, clinics, the pharmaceutical industry, vitamin companies, and distributors; every person, business, or manufacturer involved in any way with the health of over 310 million people. That represents almost $3 trillion of our total $15 trillion gross national production of labor and products in the United States. Secondly, it is the largest transfer and redistribution of wealth from the lazy to the not lazy by taxing one half of working Americans to pay for the other non-working half. The bill contained the word "tax" 124 times, "taxable" 158 times, and "excise tax" 12 times, according to the Americans for Tax Reform. Another term for this transfer of wealth is welfare. This also surpasses the recent spendulus bill as the largest increase in welfare ever.

This welfare-dependent "permanent underclass" of half of all Americans will give their allegiance and votes to the Darkside because they view NHC as a windfall.

Many of you know the politicians who were hell-bent on passing NHC, but most don't know the identities of the puppeteers pulling the strings. Space doesn't allow for an in-depth discussion, but I will show you the tip of the iceberg. John Conyers submitted H.R. 676 "U.S. National Health Insurance Act of 2005" on the first day of the 109th Congress back on February 8, 2005. This universal health care and single-payer bill morphed into what eventually became H.R. 4872 "Reconciliation Act of 2010" in the House and S1796 in the Senate; which was actually an amendment to H.R. 3590 that had passed earlier in the House. The authors of the House and Senate legislation were senior staffers brought in especially to write a bill so voluminous and confusing that only they could decipher it. On page 158 is the following:

(D) MEMBERS OF CONGRESS IN THE EXCHANGE-
(i) REQUIREMENT- Notwithstanding any other provision of law, after the effective date of this subtitle, the only health plans that the Federal Government may make available to Members of Congress and congressional staff with respect to their service as a Member of Congress or congressional staff shall be health plans that are–
(I) created under this Act (or an amendment made by this Act); or
(II) offered through an Exchange established under this Act (or an amendment made by this Act).

In "Congresspeak", this means that the senior staffers that wrote this passionate and loving health care package for the downtrodden people of America want no part of it, and are therefore exempting themselves from the law's provisions. These senior staffers were the front-office bean-counters that pieced the puzzle together. The interlocking pieces of the puzzle were provided by many groups and individuals. I only have room to discuss a few of them.

One of the prime early advocates of NHC was Quentin Young of the Physicians for a National Health Program (PNHP), a very close and personal friend of Obama's since his days as a community organizer in Chicago. Young was a member of the Young Communist League in Chicago in the

1930's. In the 1970's he was a member of the Communist Party of the USA (CPUSA) and the Bethune Club which was a group of communists limited to doctors only. In 1972 Young went to North Vietnam with Jane Fonda's group to encourage the communists to stay the course until enough Americans were killed to sour the public on continuing the war. In the late 1970's Young was active in the pro-Marx/Gramsci New American Movement. In 1982 he was a co-founder of the Marxist "Democratic Socialists of America" along with both Richard Cloward and Frances Piven. In 1995 Quentin Young and terrorist Weather Underground bomber Bill Ayers and his foul-mouthed wife, Bernardine Dohrn ,welcomed to their group a young light-skinned, up and coming leftist, Barack Obama, who was chosen to replace fellow-communist Alice Palmer as State Senator.

Young's co-founder of PNHP was Peter Orris, the son of a staunch member of the Chicago Communist Party and brother of Maxine Orris, another communist who got her medical training in Cuba. Peter Orris was a member of Students for a Democratic Society before joining the Chicago branch of the CPUSA. Besides PNHP, Orris is a member of "Doctors Council of SEIU."

Another key member of PNHP and prominent in the Democratic Socialists of America is Joanne Landy. In 2008 Landy and PNHP President Oliver Fein wrote, "We Can Do It! The Case for Single Payer National Health Insurance." Mark Almberg is the communications director of PNHP, and also a prominent member of the Illinois Communist Party since the 1970's.

In 1981 Quentin Young founded the Chicago-based single-payer advocacy group "Health and Medicine Policy Research Group (HMPRG)." Co-founder was John McKnight, a radical community organizer who worked for three years with Barack Obama in the late 1980's. He wrote a letter of recommendation for Obama to the Harvard Admissions Office in an attempt to override Obama's low GPA at Columbia and Occidental Colleges. On March 7, 2008, HMPRG held a dinner to celebrate the 85th birthday of Quentin Young themed "A Rebel without a pause" for his single-handed efforts at single-payer health care. The guest list was like an old homecoming gala for single-payer, anti-capitalist radicals. All were members of either the Communist Party of the USA and/or Democratic Socialists of

America, and all were close friends of Barack Obama. Some of the guests were: Timuel Black, Danny K. Davis, Leon Despres, Jeremiah Stamler, Jan Schakowsky, Jane Ramsey, Peter Orris, David Orr, Calvin Morris, William McNary, Roberta Lynch, Jacky Grimshaw, and Miguelle del Valle. Illinois Senator Dick (Turban) Durbin and Governor Pat Quinn were also in attendance. The guest speaker who drove all the way from Detroit to Chicago was none other than the Honorable John Conyers, long-time communist sympathizer and single-payer fanatic. He stated, "We were pushing for single-payer long before Barack Obama came out in favor of the idea as an Illinois State Senator." Barack Obama had attended Young's 80th birthday back in 2003, but could not make the 85th party in 2008.

By 2004 the leftist movements in the U.S. in all sectors could see the fruits of the efforts of ACORN, SEIU, and the Cloward-Piven Strategy working. PNHP joined other socialist, labor, religious, and community organizing groups to form a coalition for the final drive to get nationalized health care called "Healthcare-NOW!" Besides PNHP, the Board of Directors of Healthcare NOW! was composed of Muslim Women's Institute for Research and Development, League of Young Voters, National Black Women's Health Project, Health Care for the Homeless Council, National Interfaith Committee for Worker Justice, Labor Party, Ruckus Society, Progressive Christians Uniting, United Mineworkers of America, Industrial Unions Council, International Brotherhood of Electrical Workers, Women's Economic Agenda Project, and Latinos for National Health Insurance. There are many more, but no room to list them all. Individual members of Healthcare Now! include Medea Benjamin of Code Pink and Michael Lighty, Director of Public Policy for the California Nurses Association. Lighty is a long-time member and former national director of the Democratic Socialists of America. Medea Benjamin helped found the "Committees of Correspondence" which has representatives from all groups pushing for single-payer health care, and meets often to coordinate their efforts. The name was taken from the committees selected from each of our original 13 colonies to coordinate activities against the British.

Other members of Healthcare Now! are Flavio Casoy and "Reverend" Lucius Walker. Casoy is a long-time CPUSA member and revolutionary activist with the leftist Medical

Students Association. Walker is a Sharpton-type reverend (God who?) with the Interreligious Foundation for Community Organization, a radical member of CPUSA, and organizes "Peace Caravans" to Cuba for Americans to go there for medical training.

The Obamacare legislation passed in March 2010 is not even universal healthcare or nationalized health care, and does not contain the single-payer requirement that all the above individuals and groups want. But, just as Cloward-Piven accepted retreat on welfare in 1996 only to come back later and kill the 1996 bill in 2009, so will the radicals take what they got in March 2010 and turn it into single-payer. They are in a rush but will take their time. When they succeed in nationalizing healthcare it will become the single largest employer in the world. Right now the largest employer on the planet is the British National Health Service, followed by the Indian Railway System and the China Military Industries. The U.S. Healthcare behemoth will supplant all three. Of course, all of the millions working for the healthcare monster will be propagandized by Obama and the Darkside. Healthcare is the largest single event in the Darkside's success in criminalizing our economic and electoral systems to maintain a grip on voters and their pocket-books, until the near future when voting will be a robotic, meaningless exercise like Cuba, Iran, and North Korea.

While the Republicans are figuring out how to put the healthcare bull back in the pen the Darkside has moved on to cap-and-trade, more control of our financial sector, immigration, and more assaults on capitalism. I'll just write a little about Cap and Trade first.

CAP AND TRADE

The Cap-and-Trade bill, H.R. 2454 passed the House on June 26, 2009. Conservatives call it "Cap and Tax." The vote was 219 for, and 211 against with 3 not voting. Since it's primarily a tax increase, Democrats voted for it and Republicans against. Cap-and-Trade is a Trojan Horse just like welfare, voting rights, and healthcare. The Darkside uses these seemingly humane arguments to appear egalitarian while they are really seeking power through control and wealth redistribution. In the case of Cap-and-Trade, they are using the ultimate fairy-tale of the destruction of the planet caused by imaginary global warming to force the reduction of greenhouse gases like carbon dioxide. Of course, without carbon dioxide all plants on earth will die, and unless you are on a rock diet and inhale nitrogen, you will die, too. The "green" Democrats say the bill will reduce greenhouse gases by 17% by 2020 and create some green jobs. Each industry will be issued pollution credits for various pollutants like acid rain, smoke particles, and carbon dioxide. The fossil fuel burners will have tremendous initial costs because they must install high cost equipment to monitor pollution, whereas wind turbines and solar collectors do not have this complicated equipment to monitor their relatively simple operations. Coal-fired power plants will produce more pollutants than solar plants and, therefore, must buy carbon credits from the solar plants. Since fossil fuels like coal, oil, and gas produce most of our electricity our power bills will increase substantially. Since global warming exists only in the brain of idiots like Algore, the Cap-and-Trade foolishness is just another Democrat tax to take from working Americans and redistribute it to Obama's lazy herds. Algore has invested millions in the green industry, and lobbies for Cap-and-Trade often. He, Goldman-Sachs, General Electric and other Darkside companies and operatives stand to rake in billions in selling, swapping, and trading carbon credits. So far, the Senate has not shown much interest in passing a companion bill. The farm and coal producing states fear their economies will suffer if the bill is passed. But, don't relax because any number of things can change quickly to get the bill re-started. Nothing the Democrats do makes sense until you read between the lines. Then you find out that they are lining their pockets with taxpayer money.

Of course, waiting for Cap and Trade to pass is not the Chicago mob's way of doing business. Like spoiled children, they are accustomed to instant gratification. Obama's socialist head of the Environmental Protection Agency (EPA), Carol Browner, is moving forward on a staggering regulatory power grab that includes about 18,000 pages of appendices and will eventually regulate every aspect of the United States economy. Whether Cap and Trade passes or not, Browner and her EPA will regulate cars, trucks, buses, motorcycles, planes, trains, ships, boats, tractors, mining equipment, recreational vehicles, lawn mowers, fork lifts, and even wheel chairs. Obama previously stated that his primary objectives in legislation were nationalizing the health care industry and global warming. With health care out of the way he and Browner will move ahead to nationalize every means of transportation and power production in the U.S. He and his fascists will never be satisfied until they have brought down the great Satan, us.

ILLEGAL ALIENS
(OR UNREGISTERED DEMOCRATS)

As soon as the ink was dry on Obama's Nationalized Health Care bill, he said that he would be able to give the "broken immigration system" the attention that it deserves. A few days after signing the health care bill, the Congressional wing of his regime blocked the funds to build the electric fence along the border that was supposed to stop illegal immigrants from crossing the borders. The passing of Nationalized Health Care angered many Americans and dropped Obama in most polls. Even worse for Obama was the election of Scott Brown in Massachusetts to take Ted Kennedy's seat in the Senate, and McDonald of Virginia and Cristy of New Jersey, both upsetting their Democrat opponents after Obama supported them. The messiah may feel he is losing some of his magic and 2010 has him worried. He and Cloward-Piven succeeded in the following: ballooning the welfare rolls, expanding the number of federal employees at high salaries, funneling billions to his supporters with his personal slush funds (TARP and spendulus), registering the dead and non-existent, and hopefully tampering with the census enough to add a few million more Democrats. The question is, "Can he count on all these tactics to be enough to squeak by the 2010 elections?" Once past 2010, with the Congress still in Darkside control, the United States will be his own playground forever. If legislation falls short, then executive orders and the bully pulpit will do the rest. But, how to make 2010 a sure thing is the priority. Only immigration will cement the Democrats in perpetual power.

Democrat Congressman Luis Gutierrez of Illinois submitted his immigration bill in April 2009 called "C.I.R. ASAP" which stands for Comprehensive Immigration Reform A.S.A.P. Although it is close to what Obama wants, it has gone nowhere because it is actually an amnesty bill that will add 12 million new legal citizens at a time, when we have at least 10% unemployment. On March 21, 2010, just as Obama was rushing around twisting arms, threatening, promising executive orders, and giving special deals to get Obamacare passed, there were thousands of brown people outside the Capitol National Mall chanting and carrying signs. Not one to ever miss an opportunity to be seen or heard, Obama videotaped a message and presented it on a giant screen to show and tell the demonstrators that he is committed to do everything in his power to forge a bipartisan consensus on immigration reform in 2010. He warned them that the cost of inaction would mean more families would be torn apart, employers would keep gaming the system, and police officers would be struggling to keep the communities safe. What he was really saying is that he needs their votes counted by November, or one of the houses of Congress might shift to the enemy.

Congressman Gutierrez took his campaign for cramming illegal's into our country to Capitol Hill on April 20th when he got with other Hispanic radicals to push for action on the amnesty bill. The headlines read, "Democrat Pressures Obama on Immigration Bill." The article went on to say that Gutierrez was threatening Obama with telling his brown people to stay home on Election Day if Obama didn't get moving on the bill. Gutierrez, like the other Hispanics, is a member of the "Hispanic Caucus," a racist, exclusive club of elites that ignores the needs of America and caters only to the racist demands of Hispanics. Frank Sharry, with the radical immigration group, America's Voice, accompanied Gutierrez and backed-up his hollow threat to Obama. Obama gave lip service to Gutierrez the same way he did to the homosexuals that screamed at him at a rally for Barbara Boxer, demanding an end to barring them from military service. He knows homosexuals and Hispanics have nowhere else to go, so empty threats are meaningless.

Obama does not lose any sleep worrying about Hispanic families being torn apart. Obama is aware of the same statistics that I am aware of. Hispanics are the largest minority and now total over 46 million, or a little over 15%, of the U.S. population, while his own black minority is a little over 13%. In 2008 Obama got 67% of the Hispanic vote. Without the lopsided Hispanic vote Obama would not be

President, so he needs to keep them voting for him. If he can, by hook or crook, get his amnesty passed as he did Obamacare, he will not only increase his percentage of legal Hispanics over the 2008 figure, but add the majority of illegals to his vote count.

Most of you think you know enough about the illegal immigration problem because it is in the news all the time. You see the shorter than average Mexican men with their wife and 3 or 4 toddlers at the supermarket or construction site going about their daily lives. They just seem like hard-working people that escaped from the perpetual poverty of Mexico and want to start a new life here. They seem this way because it is a true depiction for most of them. Back in 1964 I served in the U.S. Army Medical Corp with a handful of Mexicans who would later receive their American citizenship for their service. I was on the first aircraft to land at Benito Juarez Aeroputo (Mexico City) after the earthquakes in 1985. I filmed truckloads of dead Mexicans being hauled to open pits for burial. I've hired Mexicans to work on my ranch in Florida and my home in Georgia. Recently, I went to Canton, Georgia, to pay a traffic ticket and half of the court room was set-aside for Mexicans with their own Spanish language interpreter. Until about 1987, Mexican immigrants were just like any other immigrant, mostly good, some not so good, some criminal. That has all changed in the last 17 years so that we now have probably 15 million Mexicans, and about half of them are radicalized. How did this happen to these seemingly docile, hard-working, family-oriented, and humble people?

I know the answer to this mystery. And no, Obama is not personally guilty this time of subverting millions of Mexicans to his perversions. But, like many of the other ruinous pogroms of the Obama regime, he has latched on to an already-existing Cloward-Piven going-concern hatched by other America-haters. If you remember, the ultimate goal of Cloward-Piven was to kill capitalism by creating such an overwhelming permanent underclass population that the sheer numbers would dilute individual wealth through income redistribution. This is pure Marx. In "Importing Revolution" William Hawkins says that the radical left must first destroy the working class through lower wages and living standards before they can save them. That is half the battle. The other half was spelled-out by Marxist Mike Davis in "Prisoners of the American Dream" when he wrote, "The real weak link in American imperialism is a black and Hispanic working class, fifty million strong. This is a nation within a nation, a society within a society, that alone possesses the numerical and positional strength to undermine the American empire from within."

Presently, we have about 15 million illegal Mexicans already here, and more pouring across porous borders every day. About 17% of Americans that could work are not working. Wages and living standards are down and going lower daily. Admittedly this is not all due to immigration, but the fact that Obama's collapse of the economy by design is achieving the same result does not detract from the fact that the left is well on its way to accomplishing the first half of their objective. How are they doing on the second half? The black and Hispanic populations together represent 87 million people. Add illegals and you get 102 million. Obama proved in 2008 that blacks are racist since he got 99% of their vote. I know many writers say 96%, but I simply disagree. Most poll results are based on exit polls, and I think many blacks do not want to appear racist, so some of them claim they did not vote for Obama when they actually did. He also got an average of 67% of the Hispanic vote. If he can get Senate aisle-crossers like Lindsay Graham and a few more limp-wristed Republicans onboard, and make a few back-alley deals with fence-sitting Republican House members he will get amnesty for the 15 million illegals. That will give him a lock on the black-Hispanic vote, which he can add to the whites that are liberal or suffering from white-guilt, and continue the destruction of America without undue stress over reelection.

It has long been an axiom of the left that the easiest groups to recruit are newly arrived immigrants, because once they have joined in the upward mobility of American society they are less likely to be attracted to socialism or communism. This was proven to be the case with the communist party in the early 20th century, and it is true with the Mexican immigration today. Unfortunately, I have personally counted over 123 separate and distinct organizations today that are recruiting Mexicans to be radical activists in demanding not only citizenship immediately, but free medical care, college tuition, healthcare, and other rights not even granted to American citizens of long-standing. Of the 123 organizations, I will discuss only a few to give you an idea of what we are facing.

The League of United Latin American Citizens (LULAC) founded on February 17, 1929, is the oldest and largest Mexican immigrant organization in the U.S. Its purpose originally was actually pro-American assimilation where Mexican immigrants were encouraged to speak English, serve honorably in the Armed forces, and be loyal Americans. Then, in 1954, they got involved in litigating an American of Mexican descent who had been convicted of murder in Jackson County, Texas. They contended that the 14th Amendment guaranteed that the jury would be representative of the population, and there were no Hispanics on the jury that found the defendant guilty. The infamous Earl Warren court ruled that people of Mexican descent were neither black nor white, but represented a distinct class and therefore overturned the lower court and released the convicted murderer. This not only whet LULAC's appetite for litigating for Hispanics, but encouraged them to pursue a race classification unique from whites and blacks. As a direct result of the Supreme Court ruling, the Office of Management and Budget issued Directive Number 15 recognizing "Mexicans" and "Hispanics" as separate and distinct from "European-Americans," and therefore eligible for affirmative action privileges just like blacks. Once they realized the advantages of victimhood and the free entitlements available to non-whites, they never again considered themselves part of the integrated American population. Just as the blacks had fought for integration and, once achieved, self-segregated to the extreme to reap the benefits of minority victimhood, so the Hispanics pursued their share of the liberal pie cooked-up by Lyndon Johnson, and multiplied by every succeeding President thereafter.

LULAC quickly transformed into a separatist organization and aligned itself with radical leftist groups like the ACLU, Rainbow PUSH, NAACP, NOW, Mexican American Legal Defense Fund, and The National Lawyers Guild. They opened their membership and leadership positions to illegal aliens, and fought for open borders with no legal requirements for citizenship. In the 1998 LULAC Legislative Platform the organization appears to condone, if not actually promote, the violation of our election laws. Jose Velez, head of LULAC from 1990 to 1994 and a convicted criminal, used his special status with the Immigration and Naturalization Service to pocket millions of dollars by submitting documentation for 6000 illegal aliens seeking amnesty. Although when founded, LULAC encouraged all Hispanics to learn English, they now actually discourage them from speaking anything but Spanish. LULAC claims a membership of over 120,000 members with 700 offices nationwide. They have full-time lobbyists roaming the halls of Washington to make sure Hispanics get their share of any federal monies, and constantly monitor Hispanic representation in all federal agencies to make sure affirmative action guidelines are followed. LULAC is a strong advocate of racial preferences. LULAC opposes any deployment of the military to defend U.S. borders, not even to interdict drug smugglers. After 9/11 when the Patriot Act was proposed to fight terrorism, LULAC opposed it, when it required additional Border Patrol agents be placed along the Mexican border. Funding for LULAC comes from the Ford Foundation, AT & T Foundation, Open Society Institute, Verizon, and many other foundations. Like Jesse Jackson, LULAC extorts "donations" under threat of boycott from companies like Bristol-Meyers Squibb, General Motors, Chevron, Chrysler, Lockheed, Rockwell, Southwestern Bell, Quaker Oats, J P Morgan Chase Bank, Ford Motor Company, and General Electric.

One reason that LULAC changed from being an American-oriented organization to a racist, leftist, anti-capitalism group is the success of a rival Hispanic group, the "Mexican American Legal Defense and Educational Fund" (MALDEF), who discovered the benefits of victimhood early on in their founding. The MALDEF is actually a creation of the Ford Foundation with an initial seed grant of $2.2 million in 1968, and a total of over $25 million donated to date. It is the most influential Hispanic advocacy group in the United States, and fights for totally open borders, free college tuition for illegal immigrants, lower admission standards for all Hispanics, and voting rights for Hispanics convicted of felonies. At any one time MALDEF may have over 50 ongoing lawsuits against the federal, state, county, and city governments for education, affirmative action, immigration, and civil rights claims. They will often sue any jurisdiction that does not provide bi-lingual ballots for Hispanics, claiming they are similar to the literacy tests administered to blacks in the South prior to civil rights legislation. MALDEF condemned our "Operation Gatekeeper" in 1994 along the California-Mexico border saying the program "callously diverted" illegal border crossers from California to the harsh and dangerous Arizona desert. MALDEF charged that Americans opposing unrestricted immigration were motivated largely by "racism and xenophobia." After the 9/11 terrorist attacks, MALDEF lead a protest campaign against Operation Tarmac, a federal crackdown on airport workers with immigration violations. According to MALDEF, such law-enforcement efforts amounted to "actions that harm the civil rights of Latinos rather than protect them." In MALDEF's view, biases against minority immigrants pervade virtually every aspect of American life. Of course, they in-turn were biased against Alberto Gonzales' appointment as Attorney General, who was of Mexican ancestry, because they feared he might actually enforce immigration laws.

MALDEF joined with the Hispanic National Bar Association, National Association of Latino Elected and Appointed Officials, and League of United Latin-American Citizens, and demanded that Michael Chertoff, U.S. Secretary of Homeland Security, place a moratorium on worksite raids designed to find illegal aliens. Their General Council, John Trasvina, said, "Federal officials have the obligation to enforce the immigration laws consistent with civil rights laws and good judgment. Putting over 1200 immigrants, only 5% of whom have criminal charges, in jails across the country and separating them from family members raises concerns." Although many of their suits involve charges of race discrimination, MALDEF founder, Mario Obledo, in 1998 said, "California is going to be a Hispanic state and anyone who doesn't like it should leave. They should go back to Europe." MALDEF is composed of only a board of directors who comb the nation seeking legal redress for Hispanics and work for their on-staff platoons of lawyers. Most of their huge funding comes from the Ford Foundation, Rockefeller Foundation, Carnegie Corporation, Ahmanson Foundation, AT & T Foundation, Joyce Foundation, John D. & Catherine T. MacArthur Foundation, Open Society Institute, David and Lucile Packard Foundation, and the Verizon Foundation. Only 2% of MALDEF's budget comes from grass-roots donations.

The prime mover and the source of most funding for illegal immigration comes from the Ford Foundation. I want to emphasize the fact that the Ford Foundation is not a simple provider of funds, but has actually sought-out, pushed, and instructed Hispanic groups on the finer points of the mass-illegal immigration agenda. The organizations below are from Robert Locke's "The Open-Borders Conspiracy" and shows a partial list of the pro-immigration groups financed by the Ford Foundation:

"Arizona Farmworkers Union, African-American Institute, American Bar Association Fund for Justice and Education, American Civil Liberties Foundation, American Council for Nationalities Service, American Friends Service Committee, American Immigration Law Foundation, American Public Welfare Association, Asian-Pacific American Legal Center of Southern California, Bilateral Commission on U.S.-Mexican Relations, California Rural Legal Assistance Foundation, Casa de Proyecto Libertad, Center for Constitutional Rights, Center for Economic and Social Studies of the Third World, Center for Migration Studies of New York, Center for Southeast Asian Refugee Resettlement, Center for Teaching and Research in Economics, Central America Resource Center, Centro Presente, Chinatown Resources Development Center, Christian Community Service Agency, Clinica Monsignor Oscar A. Romero, Coalition for Immigrant and Refugee Rights and Services, Farmworker Justice Fund, Haitian Centers Council, Haitian Refugee Center, Haitian Task Force, Immigrant Legal Resource Center, Indochina Resource Action Center, Institute for Regional Education, International Refugee Center of Oregon, Inter-University Program on Latino Research, Intertect Institute, Lawyers Committee for Civil Rights Under Law, Lawyers Committee for International Human Rights, Legal Aid Foundation of Los Angeles, Lutheran Council in the USA, Lutheran Immigration and Refugee Service, Mexican-American Legal Defense and Educational Fund, Migrant Legal Action Program, Multicultural Education Training and Advocacy Center, National Association for the Southern Poor, National Bureau of Economic Research, National Chicano Council on Higher Education, National Coalition of Advocates for Students, National Coalition of Haitian Refugees, National Council of La Raza, National Immigration Project of the National Lawyers Guild, National Immigration, Refugee and

Citizenship Forum, New York Association on New Americans, Policy Sciences Center, Population Council, Population Reference Center, Potomac Institute, Refugee Policy Group, Salvadoran Humanitarian Aid, Research and Education Foundation, Social Science Research Council, Southeast Asian Mutual Assistance Associations Coalition, Texas Legal Services, Travelers and Immigrants Aid Society of Metropolitan Chicago."

Most foundations in the United States are left-wing and many are Marxist. The Ford Foundation is especially onerous because it bribes and coerces the above organizations if they are not aggressive enough in their pushing the agenda of the left. Even the grandson of Henry Ford could stand no longer the communist tilt of his family's foundation and resigned.

The government of Mexico openly proclaims to its own people that it is their intention to re-take the parts of the Southwestern United States that were conquered from them in 1845. It also secretly financed the notorious 1982 Supreme Court case, Phyler vs. Doe, in Texas which established a "right" for the children of illegal immigrants to attend school in the United States with the same rights as American children. Mexico also has a deliberate policy called "acercamiento" (reconciliation or bonding) to gradually envelope the southwestern states. Mexico is attempting to use Americans of Mexican descent as a voting bloc to advance its political interests, and also to increase legal and illegal immigration until Hispanics outnumber whites. As part of this goal they want to expand trade across the border, and solicit funds from the United States to finance their foreign debt.

It should not come as any surprise that the country of Mexico is complicit in all legal and illegal immigration across our southern borders. The U.S. and Mexico currently have counter-complementary objectives in the employment numbers of both countries. In other words, Obama's objective of ruining our economy, exploding welfare, increasing unemployment, redistributing wealth, giving the vote to illegal immigrants, and diluting the white population of the United States, is all simultaneously accomplished in one fell swoop by having his open borders policy, and encouraging every illegal possible to cross the border and not get caught or return to Mexico. Mexico, on the other hand, reaps huge benefits. First, they get rid of 12 to 20 million excess, unskilled laborers which saves hundreds of billions of pesos in subsidies. More important is that the money orders and wire transfers sent from illegal Mexicans in the United States back to their families and relatives in Mexico are the second largest source of revenue behind petroleum production. Obama supporters that are not in the Obama-loop may argue that the illegals were here before he took office, so their presence cannot be blamed on him. They are correct. But, the organizations and forces encouraging mass illegal immigration before the arrival of Obama's regime were working for the same goals as Obama; crashing capitalism and redistribution of wealth. Now, they have a leader, a friend in the White House, who can quietly assist them in finishing what they started, and give them what they have been pursuing since 1950: a government-run socialism that will take care of them from cradle to grave and a life far superior to the one they had in Mexico.

On May 5 of this year El Presidente Barack Hussein Obama and First Senorita Michelle held a party at our former White House to celebrate Cinco de Mayo. The purpose was to show unity with the 20,000,000 illegal alien wetbacks and secure their vote once he gets the amnesty bill passed. Meanwhile, out at Live Oak High School in Morgan Hill, California, hundreds of Hispanic students were not only wearing colors of the Mexican flag, but many had painted their faces and arms with the colors of Mexico: red, white and green. Five clean, well-groomed American students, Daniel Galli, Austin Carvalho, Matt Dariano, Dominic Maciel, and Clayton Howard wanted to show their colors also, and wore American Flag T-shirts and bandannas. While sitting at an outside table they were approached by Assistant Principal Miguel Rodriquez and asked to remove their American Flag bandannas. The boys did as they were told, but were told by Rodriquez to follow him to the principal's office. Once they arrived, Principal Nick Boden told them all to turn their T-shirts inside-out or they would have to go home. The boys replied that turning the shirts inside-out was disrespectful so they were taken home by their parents. School officials at the Morgan Hill Unified School District said that the boys "could wear it on any other day, but today is sensitive to Mexican-Americans because it's supposed to be their holiday so you are not allowed to wear them." Few realize that Cinco de

Mayo is celebrated only in the Mexican state of Puebla and the United States to commemorate the battle of Puebla on May 5, 1862, where the Mexicans whipped the French. Big deal, the French came right back, beat the Mexicans, installed Emperor Maximilian, and ruled Mexico for five more years. This is America, not Mexico. If the stupid people involved in our pseudo-education system like Mexico so much, they should just head south and participate in the drug gangs and murder pastimes of our southern neighbor.

The Darkside's nonsensical response to Muslims killing 3000 Americans on 9/11was to elect two of them to the U.S. Congress, give building permits for two mosques next to Ground Zero, and give Muslims the red-carpet treatment in all their demands, while simultaneously attacking Christians. This weird logic is applied to illegal aliens, too. Washington State is infested with Darkside Democrats, and if something makes no sense to normal people you can expect to find it codified into law in the silly state of Washington.

One illegal alien, Gregorio Luna Luna, somehow accidently got sent back to Mexico by some ICE agents who had not been briefed by Washington's Darkside that illegals were a protected species in this northwestern land of silliness. Luna Luna was deported because he just couldn't seem to stop using his live-in girlfriend, illegal alien Griselda Ocampo Meza, as a punching bag. Less than three weeks after being shipped back to Old Mexico Luna Luna was back in Washington. Figuring time was of the essence, and he may not get another opportunity, Luna Luna decided to go ahead and murder Ms. Meza rather than continuing to make the bothersome round trip back and forth between the two countries. Franklin County prosecutors reluctantly put Luna Luna in jail and now have to figure out how to let him go. After all, Luna Luna had a rough childhood, and our cruel American authorities put him through the hell of paying his own transportation north, and did not include enough ethnic Mexican food in their food stamp programs.

In the city of Edmonds, Snohomish County, Washington, a passerby noticed Jose Lopez Madrigal forcibly raping a woman next to a dumpster behind a Safeway Supermarket. Being of the Darkside mentality, the passerby felt that surely the alien-friendly state of Washington could provide better accommodations for our alien friends from the south to do their raping regimen, so he hailed the nearest cop to see if they could find a more suitable raping location. Upon checking around, the police found that poor Jose had been deported at least 4 times back to the "old country," and was probably worn out just from traveling back and forth. He is currently resting in the Snohomish County jail until he is well enough to be deported again, and has to walk back across the border again, and head north again, before his next welfare check arrives at the dumpster behind Safeway.

Another "round-robin" illegal alien in Whatcom County, Washington, heard about Jose's trips back and forth from Mexico to the U.S. and became jealous. So, he made the round-trip at least five times and probably raped a different woman on each trip. He got caught on two of the rapes, but since his protected status as a poor Mexican alien allowed rape as one of the benefits of his newfound homeland, the kinder and gentler authorities refused to press charges, and just sent the playfully horny guy back home to Old Mexico after each rape. Unfortunately, the third time he was caught raping a homeless woman created a dilemma for the kind folks in Washington. You see, homeless people are a protected species in this silly state, also. Plus, this rape was the third time they caught him and some idiot, years ago, had passed a "Three strikes and you are out law" and it was still on the books. So, our poor misguided Mexican is cooling his heels in the can, but at least the Washington jails serve tacos and enchiladas to their southern guests.

The alien-loving, silly state of Washington is home-sweet-home to about 150,000 misunderstood, fun-loving Mexicans who came north to enjoy the never-ending drizzle of rain in Washington State, and liked it so much they stayed and stayed and stayed. Being only 2% of the population, they found it hard to make themselves noticed. So, they hit upon the idea of becoming criminals and being famous for at least something. They exceeded all expectations. In Franklin County alone they extrapolated that puny 2% into a whopping 14% of the jail population. Statewide they are up to 4.5%, but working hard to increase that disappointing figure. They are doing even better in other areas of their drive to succeed in the field of criminality. In the Washington State Patrol's Most Wanted List, the Mexican aliens have outstripped all competition and now represent over 50% of suspects. Fully 18 of the 26 on the list are Hispanic, but have no place of birth noted. We know where they were born though, don't we? Most of the aliens on the list are wanted for killing people with their automobiles, and have been on the list for years without much hope of finding them. If you've ever driven in Mexico City you can understand how difficult it is for these guys to learn how to drive without killing people. Maybe the silly state of Washington should give them a three-strikes law on vehicular homicide, and thus allow them to kill at least two Americans with no legal penalty, and perhaps a misdemeanor charge only for killing the third American. This will serve the dual purpose of increasing the number of Mexicans and decreasing the number of Americans, thereby speeding-up the imbalance between the races so that Mexicans can quit fretting over their minority status.

When asked the immigration status of the illegal aliens on the Most Wanted List, the Washington State Patrol replied that they didn't know, didn't care, and that immigration status is not important in locating the poor aliens. Even mentioning the immigration status comes too close to the "P" word (profiling) and makes the Washington Patrol very nervous.

Of even more importance in the Mexican Criminal Marathon to excel in the Criminal Olympics, is the Washington State Felony Warrant competition. Unlike the pitiful small number on the Most Wanted List, there are about 50,000 felony warrants in the whole silly state of Washington, and the heroic 2% Mexican minority have somehow magically exceeded all hopes by representing almost 40%, or 20,000, of the 50,000 named honorees on the list. The goal of both the Mexican aliens and their adopted Washington State homeland is to help the former achieve majority control of the Felony Warrant Marathon. To facilitate this honorable effort, silly Washington's largest silly city, Seattle, not only declared themselves a "sanctuary" city, but has boycotted Arizona because of Arizona's refusal to participate in the various Mexican Alien Criminal Olympic Games. Not to be outdone, the silly city of Tacoma joined Seattle against mean old Arizona, and invited additional Mexican aliens to leave that bad old state, and bring their crime up north to Tacoma rather than face the likes of Sheriff Joe and his pink brigades in Maricopa County. Stay tuned to the latest Mexican alien news.

NATIONALIZING OUR ECONOMY

In December 2009 Nancy Pelosi said, "We are sending a clear message to Wall Street: The party is over." The Democrats had just passed the Financial Regulatory Reform Bill with a vote of 223 to 202 without a single Republican vote. The Senate passed it on May 20th with four Republicans joining the Democrats. Obama said the 1,297 page monster was going to create a new federal agency to regulate the size, scope, and activities of Wall Street firms, give shareholders a say in executive compensation, control credit-rating agencies, and set-aside billions of dollars to aid unemployed homeowners. Barney Frank, who, along with his boyfriends, caused the housing market to crash and helped bring Wall Street down, was the one who pushed through the new legislation. This bill will effectively give Obama the power to unilaterally take-over any financial institution he chooses, for any reason he chooses, at any time he chooses. He can wipe out stockholders equity and even break-up the company and sell its parts separately. It does not allow for any judicial review, or require any objective evidence of wrong-doing to trigger a take-over by Obama. It will give Obama the power to fire one or all of the board of directors, the CEO's, and management teams. Like Rush Limbaugh said it "is really more of an exercise of eminent domain than it is an extension of traditional federal regulatory power." It is the government nationalizing companies at will. Of course, Obama did the same thing to General Motors even before he was given this power by Congress.

The Senate version of the Financial Regulatory Reform Bill was authored by Chris Dodd, the long-term dishonest Senator from Connecticut who philandered around with Ted Kennedy before Teddy assumed room temperature. Dodd is retiring this year, but he wanted to push through this last piece of destruction before he goes. The legislation will authorize a new agency called the Consumer Financial Protection Agency with powers so great, and a budget so large, that it can virtually exercise control over the entire economy. It is actually a much larger and more significant takeover of our economy than General Motors and Chrysler combined. To show you just how corrupt the circle of power, greed, and control is manifested in our corrupt government,

Eric Stein used to work for the Center for Responsive Lending, which I discussed in the Cloward-Pivens section, and helped Dodd write the so-called reform bill. He now works for the Treasury Department. But, if the bill passes, he will take over the Consumer Financial Protection Agency and "regulate" all of his friends in the business. If all this comes to pass you can expect Mr. Stein to help his friends prosper, while their competition unexpectedly declares bankruptcy.

The Consumer Financial Protection Agency is only part of the sweeping legislation impact on our economy. Like Obamacare, it will give government so much control over both consumer industries and Wall Street that Obama will have virtual dictatorial control over who lives and who dies in the financial sector. The transference of power from the private sector to Obama's government is far-reaching. The very nature of the stock market is risk taking. Investment companies will be more likely to stay in low-risk markets like treasury notes, and stay out of higher-risk items like mortgages and commercial loans. This will stifle start-up businesses and kill job creation. Even more onerous is the political pressure that will be brought against businesses to contribute money to the Democrats. Obama will have access to books, records, and correspondence of every Wall Street firm. Any who donate to Republican politicians may suffer any range of punishments including nationalization, or government confiscation like General Motors where they divided-up the stock of the company with friends of Obama. Dick Morris cited the fact that Goldman Sachs gave Obama $954,795 in 2008, and wasn't that probably the reason Obama's buddy, Hank Paulson, allowed Lehman Brothers to fail since Goldman profited enormously from the failure? Obama and his Chicago mob will pick and chose who survives and who fails. Since Dick Morris calls this bill "totalitarian," and Rush says it is "Fascism," I will simply say it is par for the course for the Darkside.

Obama's head mobster, Eric "The Red" Holder, has filed charges against Goldman Sachs for their part in causing the financial collapse in 2008. Don't believe a word of it. Goldman gave Obama about a million bucks for his campaign, and even if the kangaroo trial makes Goldman pay a fine of $100 million they will just pay it out of petty cash. They are in bed with Obama and will be a large part of the financial arm of his fascist regime. Most of the former

Sachs people already work for Obama anyway. Just watch, learn, and laugh how this all unfolds, but never, ever believe it is anything other than a show trial to make Obama and Goldman look like adversaries, which they are not.

The next Obama tax on the horizon is the Value Added Tax (VAT) mentioned by Federal Reserve Chairman Paul Volcker. It is actually a national sales tax added incrementally on all products during various stages of manufacturing or production. If enacted it would most likely replace individual state's sales taxes. Every American would be paying the VAT, which would be better than the current system where half of our population pays no income taxes at all. The problem would be that the sales tax now collected and spent by the individual states would end, and they would all look to the federal government for their share of the revenue. In other words, the states are transferring more of their sovereignty and, therefore, more of their power to the federal government. In effect, Obama is now trying to nationalize the states. Almost every country that has implemented a VAT has gradually increased the rate over the years. Denmark started at 10% and is now at 25%. Italy started at 12% and ended (maybe) at 20%. Germany is now 19%, but began at 10%. If the VAT was not combined with the already existing income tax then it might work if controlled, but you and I know that is not how government works. I had a business in Canada where I paid what they call a "Harmonized Sales Tax" of 15% on everything from groceries to attorney bills. In addition to this HST Canadians pay an average of about 50% in income taxes. Like I tell my sons and daughters, "do not under any circumstances vote for any tax increase of any kind on anything because the government will just spend it and come back for more."

CRIMINAL SUFFRAGE

Conservatives, Republicans, and Tea Partiers all express optimism for the 2010 and 2012 elections because of the polls showing disapproval of Obama's job performance, especially after Obamacare passed. They need to rethink their euphoria. Whether they believe that Obama is a radical fascist intent on becoming a dictator or not, does not mean he is not a radical fascist intent on becoming America's first dictator. Dictators do not become dictators by advertising their intentions. If Obama is nothing else, he is a good Alinsky-bred community organizer. While Republicans are busy debating and campaigning, Democrats are rigging the elections. I've already written about Project Vote, Universal Voter Registration, registering felons, the Census scams, and amnesty for illegals. If these efforts fall short then Democrats have redundant, shelf-ready hit-men ready to fill the gap. The first is George Soros' "Secretary of State Project."

The Secretary of State in each of the 50 states is the final arbiter of who votes; which votes are counted and which are tossed. Remember Katherine Harris, the Secretary of State for Florida during the 2000 election? She was there to make sure the ballot count was honest. Project Vote and other Democrat operatives were sure their dirty tricks would put Algore over the top, but Ms. Harris stopped them. George Soros, Rob Stein, and their "Democracy Alliance" swore they would suffer no more honest elections, so they formed the Secretary of State Project (SoSP) to get Democrats elected in states with recent close elections. In 2006 they pumped cash to the Democrats running for Secretary of State in Ohio, Colorado, Nevada, Minnesota, Iowa, Michigan, and New Mexico. They won 5 of the 7 races, losing only in Michigan and Colorado. In Ohio 12 of the 18 donors giving the maximum of $10,000 to elect Jennifer Brunner did not even live in Ohio. Democrat Mark Ritchie, a community organizer and ACORN supporter, won in Minnesota. According to SoSP, "cleansing the dead and fictional characters from voter rolls should be avoided until embarrassing media reports emerge, and anyone who demands that a voter produce photo identification before pulling the lever is a racist, democracy-hating Fascist."

Brunner made sure Ohio went for Obama in 2008 by allowing same- day registration and same- day voting, and trying to invalidate a million absentee ballots issued by John McCain. Brunner refused to provide 200,000 voter-registration forms to county election boards because the driver's license or Social Security information did not match exactly. In Minnesota, Ritchie warmed George Soros' heart by not only giving McCain the middle-finger salute, but knocking incumbent Senator Norm Coleman off and electing Al Franken(stein). For his beloved Obama he simply refused to even look at 261,000 duplicate registrations, and 63,000 non-existent or invalid registration addresses. Norm Coleman's 725 vote lead did not make Ritchie happy at all so, after 8 months "recalculating," his buddy Franken won by 312 dead people, I mean votes.

Flushed with their success in Ohio and Minnesota and near-success in other states, George and the boys at SoSP next took their carpet-bags of cash to Montana, Oregon, West Virginia, and Missouri. They won in all four states. That makes 9 out of 11 fence-sitting states that probably won't be on the fence in 2010. Add those to the blue states where SoSP doesn't have to spend a penny like Massachusetts, New York, Delaware, and Illinois, and it looks like a blue, blue 2010.

In the highly unlikely case of a Republican even coming close to winning a targeted election, the Democrats have the ultimate weapon, physical and electronic manipulation of the voting results. I've already mentioned the ballot-jamming and ballot boxes found floating in San Francisco Bay. Making bogus ballots appear out of thin air, or making them disappear, requires only seconds after locating a weak-link in the physical movement of ballots prior to the counting process. After completion of the counting process the tabulation is even easier to skew. The Democrat party virtually owns Simi Valley, Google, and the Geekdoms in every state. Imbedded software programs are near impossible to identify and delete. Some are "ghost" programs that will perform the vote fraud and then disappear, leaving no trace or trail of having ever existed. I could write a book on this, but it would put you to sleep. Does your constitutional right to vote, and your right to have that vote mean something, still exist? If you live in Dixville Notch, New Hampshire, and vote with the other 20 registered voters then probably, yes; elsewhere, maybe, maybe not.

Joel Mowbray wrote an interesting column on Feb 3, 2010, entitled "Will Ohio Democrats Try to Rig the Census?" It's a scary story. I'll give you a brief overview.

Ohio's Democrat Governor, Ted Strickland, appointed his Democrat State Treasurer, Kevin Boyce, to head Ohio's "Complete Count Committee" which is to have the final authority on the 2010 U.S. Census Bureau counting of Ohio's population. Given our recent history of close elections, the implications are staggering. Ohio, like Michigan and a few other rust belt states, has been losing House representation lately. An exaggerated count could prevent this, plus retain an Electoral College vote, as well as tipping maybe 3 or 4 other swing seats from Republican to Democrat by using the doctored census figures to boost the power of gerrymandering.

The opportunities for a rigged count are too many to cover here, but I'll list a few. Every census form mailed out is strictly on the honor system. Virtually no verification is performed on any of the information written on the forms. If only an average of 10% of the residents is inflated, that will tip the scales. The Complete Count Committee will be given thousands of blank forms at "Be Counted Sites" and any passerby can grab one and fill it out. Last but not least, is that all forms will pass through the tainted head of the Committee head, Kevin Boyce.

Kevin Boyce is vehemently partisan and doesn't hide the fact. His Complete Count Committee is staffed with unqualified, but diehard Democrats, many related to the governor's advisors plus the daughter of the Democrat mayor of Toledo, and the sister of Cincinnati's former Democrat mayor. As State Treasurer, Boyce awarded a lucrative contract to Key Bank for processing of the state's payroll checks only to have Key Bank host a $500 per person fundraiser for Boyce one week later. In democratspeak that's called "coincidence." Boyce has spent over $80,000 of Ohio's tax revenues on monogrammed promotional items all with his name on them. This is just a few of the indictments against one census head in one state. All of them eventually answer to Obama. The original question, "Will Ohio Democrats Try to Rig the 2010 Census?" should be changed to simply, "How <u>Much</u> Will the Ohio Democrats Rig the 2010 Census?"

After reading the GAO's report on the 2010 Decennial Census there is not a doubt that it will be the cornerstone of the Darkside's takeover, and their continued control of America's electoral system. What little remains of our Constitutional mandates to count heads, distribute House of Representatives members fairly among the states, and even the integrity of the Electoral College is now lost to Obama's political machine. You may have thought Obama's plan to have ACORN run the census was dead. No, it is alive and well. It has merely slithered underground without changing course or tactics to take over our republic while using the very constitutional guarantees they hate and are circumventing.

The Census Bureau's budget for the 2010 count is estimated at $13.7 to $14.5 billion. That translates to $25 billion in Obamaspeak. They will spend at least $132 million for ads in 28 languages to make sure they count illegals, so they can be added to the dead and fictitious Democrat voters in 2010 and 2012. They wasted $2.5 million on the Superbowl ad telling us there was a census coming up. Comparing Obama's spending to a drunken sailor is unfair because sailors don't spend money they don't have.

Universal suffrage has wreaked more havoc than any natural disaster or terrorism, and will destroy the U.S. just as effectively as a nuclear holocaust. Universal suffrage is the root disease that has infected us with the likes of Harry Reid, Nancy Pelosi, Barney Frank, John Kerry, and the epidemic disease, "Obamitis." Obama won in 2008 by getting 53% of the vote compared to McCain's 46%. So, just 4% would have changed the results. After my thorough investigation I have concluded that approximately 9% of the vote count was criminally shifted to Obama. Are you still optimistic about 2010 and 2012?

Our founding fathers considered the right to vote to be priceless and the foundation of our republic. Suffrage is the only conduit of the citizen to make his voice heard among many. But, the founders never imagined the scale of corruption that would be ushered in by the Obama crime syndicate. They were only human and set up the best controls available at the time. Obama's mob is systematically dismantling the best man-made systems ever put in place by men greater than he. Technology is part of it, but mostly it is good old fashioned corruption and deceit.

At the time of the constitutional debates and the writing of the 57 Federalist Papers there were few political pimps, despots, or American-hating Obama types around. We had just emerged from our revolution to win our independence from England. The loyalists had been shipped to Canada, the West Indies, or England and mostly the patriots, farmers, storekeepers, and mechanics were left. The founders felt little need to list the credentials required to participate in elections. They were confident that most citizens had sacrificed to achieve their liberties and would continue to promote the new society's lofty goals. But now, as Obama's racist pastor exclaimed, "The chickens have come home to roost." Our electorate is comprised of the illegals, the immorals, welfare slobs, racists, terrorists, the dead, and the non-existent, all backed-up by Obama's failsafe, can't-lose technology straight from Silicon Valley.

Think about it. Is it conducive to the preservation of our unique republic to give equal weight to the vote of a veteran who served his country, came back to the U.S., and retired after 30 years at a factory, raised 3 good kids, has no criminal record, attends church, and pays all local, state, and federal taxes; to the vote of a slob who resides in a dumpster, panhandles and shoplifts for wine money, signs up for every welfare program, never paid taxes, eats at the local soup kitchen, and is in and out of drug rehab? The second voter is Obama's stereotypical target voter and the reason why his ACORN army is out knocking on dumpsters to rouse new voters, and also why the Census Bureau and Elections Commission is gearing-up for the largest fraud in suffrage history.

For a glimpse of America's near future with Obama's brand of suffrage just look at South Africa today. It was once a prosperous, stable, bustling nation founded by Dutch and English settlers with a minority of blacks within its borders. So successful was South Africa that they had to import labor. Blacks poured in and prospered to the extent that there were more black millionaires in South Africa than all of the other black nations <u>combined</u>. Blacks from many of the adjacent African countries could see the prosperity of South Africa and began pouring into the country. These uninvited intruders and the exploding birthrate soon meant blacks greatly outnumbered the white founders. Marxist-inspired slackers like Nelson Mandela saw revolution was easier than working for a living, so the African National Congress (ANC) was born. Desmond Tutu (Jeremiah Wright's counterpart) said God was on the downtrodden blacks' side. Then, the bleeding hearts in Europe and the U.S. got involved and apartheid became the chant worldwide. Prince Buthelezi of the Zulus sided with the whites. He knew that blacks in South Africa enjoyed a quality of life like nowhere else. But, that wasn't enough. Of course, universal suffrage resulted in "one man, one vote, one time" and the blacks scrambled into the unearned seats of power.

South Africa today is a disaster. Gangs, crime, rape, murder, drugs, unemployment, illiteracy, and hopelessness abound. Walk the streets of Pretoria or Cape Town and see the boarded-up businesses, slums where neighborhoods once thrived, broken windows blanketing once elegant high-rises, and groups of depraved blacks loitering in doorways with trash swirling through the alleys and streets amid uncollected piles of garbage replete with scurrying rats. Welcome to Obama's vision of future America.

BIGGER BROTHER

In the late 80's and early 90's my wife and I attended veteran's events all over the U.S., and also promoted gun shows in Georgia, Alabama, and Tennessee. We came across many people that feared black helicopters and government intrusion of all types. They suspected FEMA was the agency designated to round-up all the anti-government types and intern them in camps scattered throughout the U.S. They said the small colored stickers on the back of road signs were coded to show the route to each camp. The killing of innocents at Waco, Ruby Ridge, and other lesser known government murders reinforced these beliefs. Clinton's 8 years kept these fears fired-up too, when he and the Brady bunch went after semi-automatic rifles calling them, erroneously, "assault weapons." When George Bush took over the paranoia subsided, especially when the so-called assault weapon ban was allowed to sun-set. When the terrorists struck on 9/11 the fear was shifted from the government to the Muslims, and most conservatives supported the Patriot Act, even though it allowed more intrusion into our private lives.

When Obama started campaigning for the Presidency the fear started coming back long before he was even elected. The Trilateral Commission, Bilderbergers, Council on Foreign Relations, and Masons were no longer the bad guys. Many feared that "Big Brother" from George Orwell's "1984" might become "Bigger Brother" if a spooky person like Obama got elected. Conservative, gun-owning, family-oriented Americans, who believe as did our founders that less government means more freedom, started monitoring Obama early. Unlike the radical leftists, white guilters, and the "PeopleofWalmart", they knew their history and listened to and read about Obama's radical intentions to "fundamentally transform" America. Their fears were not born of black helicopters or baseless paranoia. They were listening to Obama from day one of his campaign. They reasoned there was no logical reason that a lazy, dope-smoking, inexperienced, unknown upstart that hated everything America stood for should be elected. They watched as he took in up to $150 million dollars in one month from suspicious sources, and then caught up to and passed Hillary Clinton in the polls. John McCain was not their first choice, but Palin helped. When Obama was elected they girded their loins and figured it would be tough, but maybe we would make it. Then they saw his czars, homos in the military, stem cells from dead babies, GM, Chrysler, Obamacare, and so on. It seemed everyday he was attacking and tearing down part of America. He was on a mission. Anybody that grew up in the United States or served in the military sensed that what Obama was doing was not what a President should be doing. They knew that what Obama was doing was different than the incompetence of Jimmy Carter or the philandering and dirty tricks of Bill Clinton. This was a socialist, or worse, that had the Congress and the media under his spell, and was doing an end run around all obstacles in his path. Anyone with the ability to analyze and project Obama's actions can see that we are headed straight for totalitarianism. Who can stand in Obama's way in his headlong rush? He has Congress, agencies, the court system, the media, thugs, unions, financial power, large corporations, executive orders, the military, FBI, all of them. All we have are 50 million armed citizens.

Bigger Brother is a whole lot more sophisticated this time around. Every cell phone has a GPS so they know exactly where every citizen is located. I went on Google Earth years ago and thought it was cool that you could zoom down and see rooftops and the surrounding terrain. The other day I went to Google and zoomed down to my store, and there were little camera icons on the highway in front. So I clicked on them and could turn 360 degrees and see every detail of my business. I could even read what I had placed on my flashing sign out front. That means someone from Google was at my store with a 360 Imax-type camera recently. Years ago you could do this with larger cities, but now they have this ability for rural areas, too. Big Brother has definitely gotten bigger.

You've probably heard the saying, "Just because you are paranoid doesn't mean somebody's not watching you." You don't have to be paranoid anymore because they are watching you, and they do know your every move. I was personally involved in electronic eavesdropping on Castro during the Cuban Crisis. I was also involved in watching the Stasi in East Germany, and running a few errands into East Berlin. That's all ancient history and outdated methodology now. Today, the NSA's Project Echelon filters billions of your emails, faxes, phone conversations, Twitters, and texts every single day. They can access fiber optic cables deep underground and listen to you whisper miles away. My store is located in a hunting and trout fishing area so we issue many hunting and fishing licenses. Many people are reluctant to tell us their social security numbers. You should be cautious, of course, because of identity theft, but your social security number is meaningless to the government. They know everything about you, and you can hide nothing from them. Just as cookies are lodged inside your computers communicating with another distant computer, so can the government or an agent of the government extract information from your desktop or laptop any time they choose. CCTV cameras monitor your every move in and out of public life, and the products you buy may have embedded chips. Every credit and debit card transaction you make, every check you write, and everything you buy and sell is recorded somewhere. Even if all this total invasion of privacy was during a Sarah Palin Presidency you should be worried. Under an Obama Presidency, you should be very worried.

Obama and the Darkside have many other insidious operations underway and on the way to a neighborhood near you. Some of these you will hear about or read about in his controlled media. They will be in the form of laws passed in Congress or rulings by the court system, which is now overwhelmingly skewed to the left. At least half of the left's promulgations will come from the governmental agencies and executive orders, which do not require bipartisan approval at all. Yet other intrusions on our freedoms will come from non-governmental organizations like the offspring of ACORN, SEIU, NEA, or LULAC who also are indirectly controlled by Obama. He and the Darkside see the darkness at the end of the long tunnel of light, and they are not about to let anyone stop them from extinguishing the last flicker of freedom. Obama is not nationalizing banks and industries or consolidating and concentrating power in the hands of himself and a few others only to turn this dictatorial power over to a Republican president.

LAMENTABLE AMERICA

Growing up in the 60's, I often asked myself why any American born and raised in the United States would want to tear down the most unique republic that has ever existed. That led to asking myself what caused someone to adopt that sort of mentality; that kind of desire to bring down a nation that they could plainly see was the best there ever was. Always being a student of history, I finally settled in my mind that if I had to choose one word that led to this kind of behavior it was "prosperity." This was not genius on my part. After all, you must first be sufficiently prosperous to build-up enough wealth worthy of being torn down. I still feel this way today, except that I would not simply say that prosperity leads to destructive behavior, but that those that inherited their wealth are much more likely to revolt against that wealth, than those that worked and earned their own prosperity. The latter person appreciates prosperity because he knew life before his era of prosperity, and he wants to keep it and not return to a less prosperous time in his life. The person who inherits prosperity has no memory of pre-prosperity or the effort required to achieve it. Therefore, he has no appreciation for his improved status. This group fits the Ayers/Alinski mentalities, who want to take theirs and everyone else's wealth and redistribute it to lazy people. The idea that prosperity and peace eventually leads to conflict and war, and vice-versa, is close to the following prose written by George Puttenham in 1589 in "The Art of English Prosie":

"Peace makes plentie, plentie make pride,
Pride breeds quarrel, and quarrel brings warre:
Warre brings spoile, and spoile povertie,
Povertie pacience, and pacience peace:
So peace brings warre and warre brings peace."

When I returned to the states in 1966 from overseas service I was just happy to be in college and not having people shooting at me. The University of South Florida admitted me on final academic warning only because I was a returning vet, and the only way I could afford school was on the GI Bill. The few friends I connected with were returning vets, also. The majority of the students were there to get an education, graduate with a good GPA, and get a good job. A growing minority were there to have fun, drink, party, and become involved in leftist activity. Students on the right, the conservative ones, appreciate and understand that they were born and live in the most exceptional nation on earth and, while it's okay to tweak it now and then, only a fool would want to rip it apart. In socialist or communist countries the government doesn't suffer demonstrations the same way democracies do. In Iran they get beaten, arrested, or shot. In China they get run-over by tanks. In Venezuela they simply vanish. Only in developed, free nations like America do we permit malcontents to march and demonstrate even though they want to tear apart a great nation, and redistribute our earned wealth to the non-producers.

The radicals back in the 60's were the SDS (Students for a Democratic Society) and Weathermen. I thought these groups disappeared into oblivion until I saw an article on National Day of Action to Defend Education held on March 4, 2010. Almost every SDS chapter and socialist, communist, or subversive group in the country was represented. Back in the 60's only the students were demonstrating, having sit-ins, and blocking the entrance to buildings. On March 4th the professors made-up a large part of the demonstrations. The reasons are simple. Obama's deteriorating economy is putting the squeeze on teaching salaries and student grants, scholarships, and loans. Unlike back in my era, both groups are radicalized this time with teachers getting paid far more than they are worth, and many students getting a subsidized education which they do not pay for or appreciate. Both teachers and students today suffer from my "prosperity syndrome," and if we do not arrest this movement toward lawlessness and laziness it will add immeasurably to our already serious problems.

America today is proof that a nation can be too successful for its own good. When two generations forget or have no memory of times when effort was a prerequisite to achievement or prosperity, then they are indeed thankless individuals. When someone like Obama comes along and stirs the pot by making them feel ashamed about folks that have less than they do then they are given a cause, a reason to make themselves feel better about their undeserved life. What Obama and his legions are really doing is attempting to resurrect an economic system that has failed every time it has been tried. Of course, Obama will give it a new coat of paint, and call it something other than Nazi or communist. He will make us feel dirty just because we are Americans.

For at least six millennia nations have been birthed, rose up, became prosperous, and then died. Can and will the United States be the first to be the exception to this unbroken 6000 year-old chain of failures?

There are very good reasons why the United States has survived and prospered for almost a quarter-millennia. Our founders were exceptionally intelligent men, well read and versed in the history of the world, and the rise and fall of empires. They knew why and how empires were created, prospered, became apathetic and corrupt and ceased to exist. They deliberated, argued, debated, and finally reduced to writing the rules and laws that, if implemented and enforced, should last a lifetime. They even made provision for future changes to the laws by a supermajority of the people. The Constitution, Bill of Rights, and all other documents and promulgations from our early pathfinders created the most unique nation on earth. It was only when the Darkside started tampering with our sacred laws out of personal aggrandizement and greed that America started morphing into something unrecognizable by our founders. With the 2008 election of Obama this tampering has become full-blown total destruction of all that was dear to America, to be replaced by a sinister and evil empire favoring the few elitists overseeing its destruction.

The only reason that the United States is still around is inertia. First, Bill Clinton, and now, Obama, were and are both bent on destroying everything standing in this country. They will probably succeed, but they and their comrades found that it is a tad more problematic than expected. What I call inertia is the millions of Americans in the rural areas, small cities, counties, and states that just keep on doing what their fathers and grandfathers did before them, trying to live the American dream. Clinton and Obama have found it hard to wipe out the dreams and ambitions of families who have taught their kids about the honorable past of this nation, and encouraged them to perpetuate that good life through hard work. Even now, with half of all Americans working, paying taxes, and supporting the other half who pay no taxes, the former still can't just join the latter and chuck it all away just because Obama tries to make them ashamed of their success. Obama is finding it hard to convince these Americans to just give up, lie down, and join the losers and malcontents.

Whether it's abortion, homosexuality, pornography, racism, or other issues, we Americans, like Neville Chamberlain of pre-war England, think that retreating a little, surrendering just a bit will satisfy the Darkside. They even believe we can learn to live with the small loss of our values and the morals given up. But, the Darkside always comes back for more and more and more. Pretty soon we are changed, we have nothing left; we have become them without even being aware of our transformation. Look at America today; we are pitiful. Our educators are paid 10 times more than back in the 1950's when we had the best education system in the world, and our kids are dumber. Our politicians are all millionaires who rule over a fat, apathetic, filthy serfdom. We punish hard work and entrepreneurs, and reward laziness and corruption. We have replaced Ben Franklin's "a penny saved is a penny earned" with "spend like there is no tomorrow." Animals are treated like Gods, and we vote to federally fund the killing of 4500 human babies every day just in the United States. I could go on and on, but the bottom line is that if we are to survive, our lamentations must turn into action because Obama has worsened our condition from acute to critical.

The United States is perhaps the least prepared of all nations to withstand the coming privations wrought by

Obama. The depression era survivors and the WWII veterans and workers have seen the bad times, but their generation is virtually gone, and the last remnants are dying at the rate of 1200 per day. Their offspring grew-up in relative comfort and many became the "beat" generation of the 60's. Of the 3.5 million who served in Viet Nam only about 10% ever saw combat. The current generation has not been taught history, and few have ever missed a meal. As a group, we are totally unprepared for external invasion of a foreign power, or internal strife emanating from our own government. Look how quickly we pushed the snuffing-out of three-thousand lives on 9/11 behind us. Physically and mentally Americans are not ready for the shock and awe awaiting them. Physically, they are too fat to waddle to the TV and back to the couch if their remote control batteries die. And, the fit ones are too occupied with MP3's, Viagra, or too busy smoking a joint to prepare for future contingencies. Democrat social welfare programs like SSI, food stamps, extended unemployment compensation, and disability have bred two generations of slothful dependents who live day to day totally at the mercy of government. The Democrats devised this progressive strategy beginning with Woodrow Wilson and continuing through today. Their plan was to create as many de facto or real dependents of the government as possible; make them ignorant, and they would vote for the party that made them beneficiaries of government largesse. Obama is the recipient of this steady, plodding socialism. With an ever-shrinking upper and middle class, and an expanding peasant class, along with uncontrolled suffrage, and, presto! We have Hitler-lite.

PERSONAL LAMENTATIONS

Back in 1988 I remember seeing a book titled something like "888 Reasons Why the World Will End In 1988." Then Y2K came along. I was a large gun show promoter at the time so we combined the Y2K shows with the gun shows and had a banner year in 1999. The combination of the anticipated world's computers crashing, and Clinton's Presidency produced crowds buying guns and everything else, from generators to 5 gallon tubs of hard red winter wheat. Now, we have dire predictions for the year 2012. Nostradamus, the Mayan Calendar, and other predictors are saying that the magnetic poles will flip-flop and all kinds of natural catastrophes will occur. I stay out of the prophesying and predicting business. Doomsday books and articles have been around since Gutenberg invented the printing press. Most empires have ended not by the hand of God or natural disaster, but by the greed of mankind. In my studied opinion, the light that is America grows dim, and will default to perpetual darkness before 2012, but will have nothing to do with Nostradamus or the Mayan Calendar. America has been great to me, but my time is fading and my concern is for my loved ones. I have been a CPA for 41 years, but also a restaurateur, rancher, developer, aerospace technician, combat medic, land speculator, gun show promoter, general store owner, and the only American big game outfitter in Newfoundland, Canada. I've also run for U.S. Congress, worked with (not for) the CIA, and spent time in the jungles of Laos with Phoumano Nosavan. I personally brought back the remains of POW/MIA Major Edward Hudgens, USAF. At the same time I returned the only live American to be repatriated from the secret war in Laos; the son of an Air America pilot who was shot down near Savanakhet, and had been enslaved by the Pathet Lao for 15 years (I appeared before the Senate Select Committee on POW/MIA's in 1989 regarding these events). More important than all my experiences is being married for 35 years to the greatest wife in the world and blessed with my two sons, one daughter, and six grandchildren. My concern for them and the survival of our Republic that they live in is the impetus for this book.

My wife's father, Roy Gilbert, and his only brother, William, were both captured during the Battle of the Bulge in 1945. William was held in a Stalag while Roy was marched in sub-freezing cold 215 miles from Neuengamme to Sanbostel, Germany, which was a sub-camp of Belsen death-camp. He told me the SS killed 20,000 Jews with machine guns in the 3 days before he was liberated by the British. He came home, attended the University of Georgia where he earned his degree in pharmacy, and owned Gilbert Drugs on the circle in downtown Sebring, Florida, until his death in 2006. The reunited government of Germany sent him a check for $9000 because he was one of the few Americans that could prove he was held in a death camp. Roy didn't need the money, but felt the "Krauts" owed somebody for their barbarism. He also told me that his generation saw the best of America. If Roy can still say that after the hell he went through then America must be a pretty exceptional place. To lose America after the sacrifices of thousands of men like Roy over the last 234 years means their lives meant nothing. To me, it means my uncle Woody died for nothing in the 82nd Airborne drop over Arnhem, Holland, in Operation Market Garden in 1944. It means my Uncle Sherman's survival at the Chosin Reservoir in Korea is not important. It means my dad and two other uncles who fought in WWII served for nothing. It means my first cousin Jimmy Martin, my Aunt Karen's only son, died with the other 17 Rangers in Mogadishu, Somalia, for not a thing. Fighting and dying for our country has been the physical expression of my family's love for America. None of us were career soldiers and not one of us found war to our liking. Jefferson said, "The tree of liberty must be refreshed from time to time with the blood of patriots and tyrants." We have shed that patriot's blood and our soldiers are still spilling their life essence today in foreign lands. For what? Obama is choking the life out of the tree of liberty faster than the blood of patriots can refresh it. He cares not a damn how many of our men are killed or maimed. How and why did America elect a be-bopping hustler like Obama to lead our troops and country?

In poll after poll Americans answer "economy" when asked, "What is the most important issue when you go to the polls?" How often have you heard politicians, pundits, and ordinary people on the street say things like "Obama is spending my grandchildren's money" or "My great-grandchildren are going to have to repay the national debt?" This is simple ignorance because our national debt cannot, and will not, ever be repaid by anyone. With only half of

Americans paying any taxes, and our national debt soon to be $15 trillion there is no way to repay the debt. Obama is rushing to expand the proletariat who pay no taxes and will succumb to control more humbly. So, our ability to finance our current existence will take precedence over paying off an old debt. More importantly, is economics and our grandkid's hypothetically repaying the national debt really the most important issue in the lives of Americans? Is that the most terrible tragedy of all the plagues being heaped upon us by Obama? Rather than worry about your grandson repaying the national debt, aren't you more worried about the YMCA in your grandson's neighborhood being replaced by a NAMBLA Youth Center, where "fisting" cartoons are shown while milk and smores are being served? Shouldn't you be more concerned about conserving our traditional values and religion, and preventing the sterility of a "Brave New World" from being foisted upon us? If Americans value the economy and money over morality and exceptionalism then they will lose both. By that, I mean your income in the United States depends on our capitalist, free-enterprise system surviving. Capitalism can exist only in an atmosphere of freedom. And freedom can exist only if the morality of the people allows it to exist. So, if we lose our traditional American values, then we will also lose any opportunity to improve our economic status or exercise our entrepreneurial talents. Strive to preserve the heart and soul of America, and the economy and your income will take care of themselves.

THE FINAL SOLUTION

Hitler's "final solution" was the systematic mass extermination of Jews, dissidents, handicapped, homosexuals, insane, amputees, Jehovah's Witnesses, communists, retarded, and non-Aryans. Just as all these groups thought it inconceivable that their cultured, modern, highly civilized society could ever evolve into barbaric genocide, so do Americans in 2010 laugh at such prospects happening here. Keep in mind that all genocide has occurred during tumultuous chaos that ensues prior, during, or immediately following regime change from a free to a non-free society. Right now we are experiencing the initial pangs of assault from a person whose deep-seated hatreds and totalitarian plans for the United States are boundless.

Many conservatives are rerunning videos and recordings of Obama's speeches during the campaign, and showing us that he told us exactly what he was going to do to "fundamentally change" America. Those same conservatives tell us that nobody was listening. That's not true. Probably 40% of the 53% of the people that voted for Obama understood most of what he was saying. The blacks knew he was black, the special interests knew he was pro-abortion, pro-homosexual, pro-union, pro-illegals, pro-welfare, pro-enviro-wackos, pro-lawyer, pro-Muslim, pro-socialist, pro-media, pro-Democrat, and anti-everything American. The other 13% that voted for him were composed of those suffering under white guilt, and those that were just not parsing his every word. "Fundamentally" changing the most powerful empire ever to exist on a small planet is no small undertaking. Unraveling 234 years of layer upon layer of the footprints and legacies of the 7 generations of Americans preceding us won't be endured peacefully. Forcing unwanted and unwarranted degradation, hopelessness, and Godlessness on 50 million of our 310 million inhabitants will not come without resistance.

Since childhood, Obama has been dreaming and postulating what seemed impossible a short few years ago; reclaiming the rightful throne of the black man from the white Satan, and punishing the progeny of those who held his race in bondage. From Hawaii to Indonesia, to California to New York, to Chicago to New York, and finally, back to Chicago again, he met new and ever angrier miscreants who stoked his racist hatred. He loved and felt at home in Chicago like no other place he had lived. Chicago was half-black, one-third brown, and the rest white. But, race was not the only attraction. There was a Democrat machine like no other in the United States. Obama ingratiated himself with Harold Washington's conglomeration of socialists, communists, Muslims, and aging radicals. In Chicago he slowly formulated the proper mix of persuasion, money, methodology, and religion to meld his radical ideas with the Cloward-Pivens strategy and accomplish, in fact, what the 60's radicals could never quite get off the ground.

You should already know the basics of how Obama went from community organizer, to Illinois State Senate, to U.S. Senate, to President in a whirlwind. He brought many of his closest Chicago mobsters with him, but has added many more as he and his fascist advisors verify their radical credentials. Obama now has most of his people in place, and a chronological plan for implementation of his takeover of America. He is still in the dismembering stage of his plan, and will not proceed to the reassembling level for awhile. Of course, sometimes these two are, of necessity, simultaneous. Rest assured that revolution is coming. Obama and his radicals know that this may indeed be their first and last chance to cause the upheaval that he, Alinsky, Ayers, and the Cloward-Piven's crowd have been working on for 50 years. This cannot be just another Presidency that turned left like Clinton, only to turn right again under Bush. This must be the final battle, the one that sweeps away the evil capitalists and finally gives America back to the downtrodden, the disadvantaged, the non-participants in the American dream, especially the black victims of slavery. I will tell some of what is going to transpire over the next few years, but not chronologically, since even Obama must deal with uncertainty.

DIGGING AMERICA'S GRAVE

Obama's hatred of America and everything she stands for is total. He hates the capitalist, the white majority, the Christians, the constraints of republicanism, and our military power (until he controls their hearts and minds). He looks upon all these institutions as the enemy and is attacking them simultaneously on all fronts to dilute their influence, and increase his dominance over them. Through acts of a collaborative Congress, executive orders, agency directives, and even simple memorandums, Obama is reducing capitalists to a controllable few. The white majority will be a majority in name only because its wealth will be sucked out of it, and redistributed to Obama's chosen legions of blacks and browns, and its numbers will be splintered among white guilters, unions, leftists, perverts, and the disillusioned. The edicts of Christianity upon which our republic was founded are undergoing banishment in all quarters, and will soon find sanctuary only behind the doors of the church (maybe). Our republic already resembles a populist democracy which Jefferson and the other foresighted founders warned us against. Our military is small, scattered, tired, and soon to be devoid of commanders capable of independent thought.

If you study Obama's life you will conclude that he is not a brainiac. Neither was Lenin, Stalin, Hitler, or Mao. He is not even a charismatic speaker like these four dictators. To become a successful totalitarian dictator you merely need to follow the rules already written by Sun Tsu, Machiavelli, Marx, Lenin, Hitler, Trotsky, and Mao and update them with current strategies unique to America like Cloward-Piven and Alinsky. Creating a representative republic, on the other hand, is so complicated and unique that there is none under construction in the world at the moment, and probably never will be ever again. Republics are constantly under attack by those wanting a larger share of the pie. Defending them is a full-time job. Special interests always want to tweak the system to favor them or their friends. The underpinning of a republic is shared power, and human nature shies away from sharing power; preferring to concentrate power in the hands of a few, or even one. Once this consolidation of power commences it is seldom halted or reversed because the losses to the majority being consumed are permanent, and become gains to the predatory cabal extracting the rights of the largely unsuspecting majority until the balance of power shifts forever.

The most visible and current example of power concentration of a once relatively free nation into a fascist/communist/totalitarian state is Venezuela. Hugo Chavez is a short, chunky, ugly, little community organizer with the charisma of a toad. But, he is succeeding in his Hitlerian quest to be dictator-for-life, and has passed the point where anybody can stop him. I compare his rise to Hitler's since both came to power in accordance with the election laws of their country, and then altered the laws repeatedly until the opposition found itself without the power to return the nation to representative government. Many will say that Venezuela is a small country while America is huge, wealthy, and powerful and has checks and balances to prevent such a take-over. Really?

The Bolivarian Republic of Venezuela has a population of about 26.5 million people with a large middle class (shrinking), and derives most of its revenue from oil (CITGO). It has five branches of government: Executive, Legislative, Judicial, Electoral, and Citizen. Of course, Chavez owns the executive branch. The legislative branch consists of 167 seats and Chavez' party controls all 167 seats. The other three branches rubber-stamp whatever Chavez wants. The United States has a large middle class (shrinking) with a $15 trillion dollar economy (Obama already nationalized $4 trillion of it). Obama controls our executive and legislative branches, and probably 80% of our nationwide judiciary. Presently, the Supreme Court has four good conservatives. They hear only cases involving constitutionality. Most judicial decisions that drive our nation to the left, and are antithetical to our capitalist, family-dependent society emanate from one of the Judicial Circuit Courts, Federal Appellate Courts, or lower courts. So, both Chavez and Obama already have dictatorial control of their respective governments. Are they similar in backgrounds, personality, and belief systems?

While in college Chavez and other left-wing students developed "Bolivarianism" which was a Pan-American philosophy based on the teachings of Karl Marx, Vladimir Lenin, and Leon Trotsky. Before, during, and after college Obama befriended Frank Davis, Bill Ayers, Louis Farrakhan,

Edward Said, Khalid al-Mansour, and a whole host of radical Marxists and Jihadists too numerous to mention. Both Chavez and Obama claim to be Christian because no non-Christian can hope to be elected President in either country. In 1998 Chavez ran on a platform of "laying the foundation for a new republic" to replace the existing one. Obama ran on a platform of "hope and change," and promised to "fundamentally change" the way things were run in government. Besides adopting foreign philosophies like Marx and Lenin, Chavez blended his beliefs with South American communists like Salvador Allende, Fidel Castro, and Che Guevara. Chavez even said Jesus was the world's first and greatest socialist. Obama likewise studied Marx and other communists, but combined it with the teachings of Alinsky, Cloward-Pivens, Davis and others. Then, he too was baptized a "media Christian" by radical black theologian Jeremiah Wright. Both Chavez and Obama are ardent followers of Noam Chomsky, a socialist, dissident, and anarchist who presently teaches at Harvard. Chomsky hates Israel, hates our war on drugs, hates capitalism, hates our foreign aid to fight communism, hates our use of atomic bombs to end WWII, and the list goes on. I found not one difference between his beliefs and Obama's or Chavez's. Chavez has organized "Bolivarian Circles" where a few hundred residents meet and decide how to spend the welfare stipend allotted to them by the government. This by-passes representative republicanism in favor of participatory democratic populism. Obama uses the $787 billion "stimulus," agency budgets, AmeriCorps, and literally hundreds of other programs to target his voting groups, and withhold dollars from those that are not included in his constituency. So, the "little people" of both countries are made to feel their supreme leader cares about them and they work to maintain this charade.

Chavez consolidated his power as fast as he could do so without arousing too much suspicion. Sometimes he took one step, sometimes three. He first changed the constitution to allow him to succeed himself, then changed it to a two term limit, and finally to serve indefinitely. He converted the bicameral National Assembly to a unicameral legislature for easier control. He has forcibly shut-down all media opposition and expropriated most industries. What he wants, he gets. Like Chavez, Obama is hell-bent on rapid consolidation of power, destruction of capitalism, redistribution of wealth, and cementing his voter support. He is not concerned that many of his tactics raise eyebrows when they see him nationalizing the automobile industry, nationalizing health care, doling our taxpayer-funded payoffs to politicians, or unilaterally disarming America. Republicans offer little hope for Americans watching Obama's march to socialism. Both Chavez and Obama know the value of saturating the media with their presence, and both dominate the airwaves, print, and web. Chavez even has his own weekly TV show where he takes calls from citizens. Chavez recently started Twittering. In the U.S., not a leaf falls from a tree without Obama being photographed with that leaf. Both of these dictators appeal to the poor and downtrodden, but neither has helped them much. This is not a real problem for either of them because the media in both countries is run by the state, and has so poisoned the opposition that the poor have nowhere else to go for help. The poor at the bottom of the economic rung are the only portion of the population that is expanding. Once the dependent poor outnumber the upper and middle class Obama will have won just as Chavez has won his permanent place in Venezuela as dictator.

AMERICA'S HARDENED HEARTS

Most of you have seen "The Ten Commandents" starring Charlton Heston. Moses wanted to take the Israelites out of Egypt and into the Promised Land but Pharaoh said no. Jehovah sent the 10 plagues one at a time, and Moses asked Pharaoh after each to let his people go, and was each time refused. The plagues in succession were 1. Blood in the water, 2. Frogs, 3. Lice, 4. Flies, 5. Death of Livestock, 6. Boils, 7. Hail, 8. Locusts, 9. Darkness during daylight and 10. Death of Firstborn. After seeing each of these plagues come one after the other, which one would convince you to let the Israelites go? When someone comes to you and foretells terrible calamities coming your way at specific times, and you see things that have never happened before, one after the other, when do you decide to do something about stopping them? Pharaoh let all 10 plagues come upon Egypt including the death of his own son during the last plague. The Bible and the movie both said that Pharaoh would not let the Israelites go because his heart was "hardened." To me, this means that Pharaoh's logic and common sense abandoned him. He wasn't thinking clearly or he would have saved his country and his son's life by capitulating earlier to Moses' demands.

When I was first involved in the pro-life movement I thought that educating apathetic people of the realities of killing unborn children would wake them up. I thought they just didn't know what was happening because they weren't paying attention. When "Silent Scream" came out and people could see what happens when babies are murdered inside the womb, I thought there would be an awakening. I thought pictures of hundreds of white buckets with tiny legs, arms, and heads hanging out the sides of the pails outside a dumpster behind an abortion clinic would shock people. Guess what? People don't care. After Roe vs. Wade people thought they had a new right. Ted Kennedy aside, "back-alley" abortions never happened. They were an invention of Planned Parenthood and the others who were looking to make millions from abortion. But, once our court system said it was okay to kill our young, the abortion clinics immediately were filled. Many would have been appalled at the thought of killing their young in 1972, but after January 22, 1973, they acted like they had a great weight lifted from their conscience. None other than the Supreme Court had told us that this was not murder, this was not anyone's fault, this was a legal, normal right of all Americans, and they should avail themselves of it when needed and feel no guilt. Roe vs. Wade hardened many hearts.

Another plague that swept over our land was homosexuals. Christians have always been taught that homosexuals are an abomination, but that it is not their mission to hurt them. When possible they should witness to them, but that is all. For thousands of years we have co-existed with homosexuals among us, but not really a part of us. Now they have special rights that supersede our own and gain more every day. They practice sickening sexual acts, but we don't react. They started AIDS and we couldn't begin to cure it because it was against the law to identify the chain of people infecting each other. They said they were not ashamed of their homosexuality, but wouldn't disclose who they had sex with. If what they do to each other is so wonderful then why not be proud to identify their lovers? With Clinton, and now Obama, homosexuals are infiltrating every part of America. They are helping to destroy the family unit which is the basic building block of America. Without the family unit America is dead. I have a sign at my store that reads "No homophobes here, no heterophobes hear?" I had this made because I am sick and tired of hearing the word "homophobes." This is a blatant attempt by homosexuals to control the argument, and force you to be PC which I will never be. I don't fear homosexuals; I loathe them and pity them. In balance, many of my favorite songs are by Elton John and Queen. Elton even shares a penthouse level with my wife's cousin and they get along great.

Today in the United States and the world we have seen the hearts of men hardened so that their words and actions make no sense. Their behavior is destructive to themselves and others. I am not saying that everything that is happening today has not happened before. Since Adam and Eve's time we have killed each other, fornicated, and committed every atrocity known to man. For six millennia now, we have sunk to new lows and climbed back up, only to sink again and get up again. This time it's different. The United States is the only cohesion this planet has, and it is under siege like never before. When it is gone the world will devolve into chaos on every continent. Things that you cannot imagine will start happening immediately upon our demise. Stronger nations will slaughter smaller ones. The more numerous ethnic and religious groups within nations will butcher the lesser ones. Democracies will be replaced by totalitarian regimes. Nuclear nations will threaten to annihilate non-nuclear ones. Russia may attack Canada and Alaska. Obama has already said he would not use nuclear weapons, so what do you think he would do if Russia just landed and occupied Alaska? Japan has the second largest economy in the world, but no military. So, China would just threaten Japan with imminent invasion, and they would have no choice but surrender. Central and South America would be consolidated into probably 5 countries (at the most) within 5 years. Africa has always been a killing field, and with no United States to maintain order, the Muslims will exterminate the Christians, and the stronger tribes will butcher the weaker ones. Civilization will largely cease to exist. The disintegration of the United States will open up the 194 other sovereign nations to a frenzy of cannibalism not unlike a feast of feeding sharks. The world will be bathed in blood.

For two and a quarter centuries we have survived wars, natural disasters, and internal strife. The forces that held us together are really not so numerous. Christianity, with its foundation in the teachings of Jesus Christ, taught us to love our fellow man, follow the Golden Rule, be charitable, and not harbor hatred for our fellow man. Our citizens committed every sin in the Bible, but the majority of us did the best we could to obey the Christian Ten Commandments. All of our school books were based on Christianity, so we learned early the rules that had worked for our parents and their parents. Our nuclear families held our nation together too, since it was the basic unit upon which all society was built. When wars came, the men went off to fight, and the women stayed behind to maintain the home and children. The family unit was the centerpiece of America. The family was part of a community, which was part of a city, which formed a part of a state. The central government took care of those things which involved more than one state, such as the common defense and treaties with other nations. The rule of law established the guidelines within which the people must operate as a society. This included the Constitution and all the various laws of the federal, state, and local governments.

Our republican form of government, with three branches limited by a system of checks and balances, worked better than anything man had ever conceived. An ocean on two sides of our coasts, and non-belligerent nations on the other two, provided the United States with time to grow stabile.

We have covered most of the reasons why our nation held together during trying times. The forces tearing us apart are more numerous, and approaching the point of overpowering those that heretofore held us together. How many plagues will the American people endure before they wake up from their malaise, and see that Obama's plagues are dooming them to perpetual serfdom, and that Obama's "fundamental changes" have exceeded "failsafe?" Their roundtrip ticket for traveling back to a Constitutional Republic has been canceled.

AMERICA'S ROAD TO SERFDOM

Astute readers will know that the title of this section comes from F. A. Hayek's, "The Road to Serfdom." Hayek was a Nobel Prize economist from Austria, but lived most of his life in Germany, England, and the United States. He personally witnessed the rise of socialism in Germany, Italy, and Russia, and saw them transformed into Nazism, Fascism, and Communism respectively. He wrote his book because he saw the same tendencies toward socialism happening in the United States. He died in 1992 before he saw the results of Clinton's 8 years, and the even more accelerated transformations under Obama. Hayek's observations are true, factual, and timeless, and those Americans that can still read had better listen-up before they find themselves in the stalags and gulags. I will try and extrapolate Hayek's observations and thoughts, to Obama's actions to date, and his future plans to pave our own road to serfdom.

Pre-war Germany did not move directly from democracy to Nazism, but rather had socialism as a facilitating middle economic system between the two. After WWI Germany was in debt and had huge reparations to pay, and a world-wide depression on top of that. So, before Hitler entered the picture, the progressives and socialist reformers had already been at work establishing social programs of income redistribution, housing subsidies, and worker benefits.

Germans had eagerly accepted government programs to plan and organize their economic system to avoid a repeat of the past hard times. The people responsible for instituting the socialist changes to level out the extremes of cyclical economics were mostly sincere in their efforts to better the lives of ordinary people. Unfortunately, once socialist programs become established, they are like a snowball rolling down a hill, or the start of a nuclear reaction; they can't be stopped. Examples in the U.S. are Social Security, Medicare, welfare, food stamps, and environmental laws. The programs keep multiplying and each one grows like a cancer. There is no one willing to step out and halt the progression. In a representative republic like ours, no politician can risk opposing an established social program if he wants to be reelected. So, while we may have begun with high ideals in helping our fellow man, we end up starting something that cannot be stopped. While Obama and his central core of fascists are inexorably following their roadmap to totalitarianism, most of the folks facilitating his efforts are doing so because they sincerely think they are leveling the playing field for their fellow man. In other words, these people largely hate the historical atrocities committed under Nazis and Communists, but they are performing the labor and laying the groundwork whose fruits will bear the very tyranny they abhor. Most of the Democrats in Congress today are not desirous of totalitarianism, but do want to have majorities in both houses and control of the judiciary, media, the financial and industrial sectors, and the voters. They are enjoying the seat of power and reluctant to even show a spirit of compromise out of fear the Republicans will capitalize on it. The recent healthcare bill was a good example. Obama won out over Democrats that didn't really like the bill, but failure would have meant a chink in the Democrat armor, and a lack of unity which may have spelled doom for the party. The longer they stay in power, the harder it is for even the few good ones to break the chains that bind them to Obama.

Obama started off as a community organizer and is now a nationwide community organizer. Before Obama can concentrate his power over the masses he must first conquer his greatest enemy: our republican form of government. The idea of our founding fathers was to disburse political power among the people and the three branches of government, which had check-and-balance control over each other. Obama already has effective control over the three branches. His objective now is to transfer the power of the individual citizen to the larger society in the form of government bureaucracies. To do this, all Obama has to do is convince the majority of Americans that they will be better served by removing the power over their lives from private organizations to public ones. Although you will not find Obama ever saying the word "nationalization," it best describes the act of Obama taking over a private enterprise of individuals, and promoting it as good for the masses. Few people realize or bother to care that the power of the government entity created in this way is infinitely more powerful than the previous entities in the hands of individuals. In other words, the sum is greater than the parts. For example, Bill Gates is a multi-billionaire, but he can't make you use his software or even force you to buy a computer. But, a low-paid government bureaucrat with the coercive powers given to him by the state can force you to do as he pleases, or impose punitive persuasions as necessary to get the desired results. You may owe a friend $10 and choose to never repay him. Choose to never pay the $10 to the IRS and it is possible their tactical response team will show up at your house in black boots carrying MP-5's. The disbursed power of individuals in society is less than when that power is combined into a government bureaucracy. We have over 100 million people working at jobs in the United States. Most of them can choose to work wherever they want. The military, many government workers, and now GM and Chrysler workers, cannot exercise this choice. As Obama takes-over either direct or indirect control of private enterprise, the workers will lose their rights to move freely among and between their places of employment. They will willingly accept these restrictions at the outset in return for job security. Later, they will discover they have sentenced themselves to a prison from which there is no escape. As Hayek put it, "when economic power is centralized as an instrument of political power, it creates a degree of dependence scarcely distinguishable from slavery. It has been well said that, in a country where the sole employer is the state, opposition means death by slow starvation."

The basic principles of free enterprise and laissez faire capitalism in western civilizations emanated from the

Renaissance period where the freedom to exchange ideas and experiment with different concepts were born. This period of enlightenment, in turn, grew from Christianity, which taught respect for the individual man and his freedom to develop his particular talents. Before, there had been only kings and rulers over masses of serfs or slaves. Unfortunately, the great success of the freedom of ideas, and the entrepreneurial investors also paved the way for its downfall. Earlier, in another section of this book, I said that prosperity leads to discontent and insurrection against the establishment by those that did not earn or share in that prosperity. In the United States, prosperous whites looked back at their black, and now brown, brethren, and saw they had not progressed equally with the whites in any of the measurements used by society, and decided to artificially level the field by affirmative action, welfare, and now, income redistribution. The white guilt fed upon its self and once started, didn't know where to stop. The more blacks were given, the more they became victims, and the more was expected. This all led inexorably to a permanent black underclass, and the election of the most dangerous threat to America's survival. Similar to white guilt, the economically prosperous in the United States satiated their guilt by welfare and income redistribution programs that also knew no limits, and have expanded today into something bordering on democratic socialism. From Social Security to unemployment compensation that never ends, we never give-up trying to make it so nobody ever stubs their toes or has a bad day. The United States has become a micro-managed nanny-state. As somebody said, "What has always made the state a hell on earth has been precisely that man has tried to make it his heaven." As mentioned earlier, most of the individuals and groups working to artificially create equality throughout society do so from a humanitarian bent. Unknown to most of them is that the very process they perform to replace private rights with public rights destroys freedom by taking it from one to give to the other. After a certain point is reached, the transference of rights is irreversible. Democratic socialism is an oxymoron. You can have democracy or socialism, but not both, since they are mutually exclusive.

Laissez-faire capitalism is not a perfect economic system because mankind is not perfect. Greed, dishonesty, and unfair advantage will always rear its ugly head when financial gain is involved. Therefore, some government controls are necessary for the good of society. The partnership of capitalism and minimal regulation has allowed the United States to become the financial superpower of the world. When industry pollutes a river or makes an unsafe product, then government has a right to step in and correct the problem. Government can prevent fraud, assure competition, and dissuade monopolies. Competition among private companies is the best regulator of commerce. So, when government interferes with competition by their planning functions, they destroy private incentives. Capitalism may be the boldest, most aggressive form of economic endeavor, but it is also the most fragile when government gets involved. If Obama's Cap-and-Trade legislation passes, or even if his energy department imposes regulations that punish fossil fuel power plants, and reward solar and wind plants, it will upset the competitive balance and skew upward the competitive advantage of the latter. This will be true in all sectors of the economy where Obama and his operatives exceed government's historically limited regulation of private enterprise.

While western capitalism got its start from Christianity and the Renaissance, socialism began after the French Revolution when Louis IVX lost his head (literally), and the reformers wanted to spread the wealth to the people rather than go back to a system of monarchies and noblemen. Like Obama and Hugo Chavez today, the early socialists were anxious to install their perfect, ultimate, government whether the people liked it or not. One of the earlier French bureaucrats, Saint-Simon, predicted that those who did not obey his proposed planning boards would be "treated as cattle." Alexis de Tocqueville was a French political thinker and wrote "Democracy in America" after two tours to the United States. After seeing the constant turmoil of Europe with its mixtures of kings and changing governments, he pronounced that "America is great because America is good." He also said that "Democracy extends the sphere of individual freedom and democracy attaches all possible value to each man, while socialism makes each man a mere agent, a mere number." He concluded that democracy and socialism have nothing in common except one word: equality. While democracy seeks equality in liberty, socialism seeks equality in restraint and servitude. To make socialism more palatable to the masses, its proponents created a new meaning of the word "freedom." Before, it had meant freedom from tyranny. The new meaning was freedom from the changing economic woes that the old freedom did not guarantee. By redistributing the wealth of a few among the many, each was assured a piece of the pie. The promise of the proponents of socialism, and the hope of its adherents, is that their piece of the pie under socialism will be larger than they would have received in a competitive democracy. It never quite turns out that way except for the elite. Few people realize that the percentage of wealthy citizens is approximately the same under democracies, socialism, or communism; about 8%. The real difference is that democracies have a large middle class while the other two do not. Not many people today know that the ruling elite of the old Union of Soviet Socialist Republic (USSR), during its 70 years of existence, had approximately the same number of privileged, upper-class citizens as did the United States during the same period. The difference was that there was no middle-class in the USSR. So, Obama and his elite, who are rushing all of us into socialism, will not lose their power when we have all been relegated to unidentifiable serfs. In fact, they will have all moved up multiple rungs of the ladder, since they will no longer be answerable to the people for their actions, and can issue edicts with abandon.

Obama has embarked Americans on all kinds of socialist voyages without telling any of us where we are going or what will happen to us when we get there. He has kept everybody divided and diverted by race and income level, and the masses have gotten onboard like blind people and taken us with them. He has nationalized companies, taken virtual control of others, given us a national debt that can never be repaid, and acts like a dictator in all respects but name, while we stumble around and look to others for rescue. Many Americans console themselves with the comfort that we are still a democracy because Obama and our leaders are still elected by the people. But, just because power is conferred by a right of suffrage does not mean that it is not arbitrary if that power is not limited by some means. Also, as discussed in other sections, Obama is deriving much of the black and Hispanic vote from overt racism, and skewing the numbers through census and voter registration fraud. Obama has achieved much of his legislative triumphs and programs because he told us our system was in imminent danger of collapse. That was part of his strategy in moving us from the "fear" to the "dependency" stage of the fatal sequence. Americans have always answered the call and sacrificed even their life in times of war. Obama knew this, and asked us to approve his programs as if we were fighting a war, and needed to sacrifice now to secure our future. What we have done is permanently extinguish our liberty and freedom in return for a short-term promise that will be unfulfilled. In the end, the 40% of Americans that say they could live with a socialist government will find a permanent Fascist government instead.

If and when Obama is successful in converting the most powerful capitalist representative republic on earth into a fascist state, it will not only be the most complicated coup in history, but a one-time, one-way event never to be repeated or undone. As he progresses closer and closer to Fascism, more and more of the current players in the Congress, and many of the lesser bureaucrats, will fall by the wayside. This happened in Russia, Italy, Germany, and other countries that went from free to totalitarian, because many of the original liberals or socialists who voted for the very programs that led to fascism did not have the stomach for the later ruthlessness required. The original socialist parties of these countries were inhibited by their democratic ideals, and refused to perform their new, harsher responsibilities in instituting the draconian cruelty that always accompanies Fascism and Nazism. For this reason, Obama has surrounded himself from the outset with his rogues, demons, and useful idiots and is adding numbers to these daily. These groups comprise his central planners, bureaucrats, and enforcers. But, currently, we still surreptitiously refer to the United States as a republic, and until we have passed the point of no return on the road to fascism, Obama still depends on a core constituency for support. The people that voted Obama into power are little different than those that allowed Hitler and Mussolini to come to power in a democratic election, only to later convert the existing socialism into Nazism and fascism. The main difference is that Hitler and Mussolini had homogenous populations of Italian and German poor who looked to them for economic salvation. Obama has the advantage of race in the blacks and Hispanics, and the disadvantage of a large white population that is reasonably educated, but has also been subjected to 60 years of drugs, white guilt, and media brainwashing. So, Obama's core constituency is primarily the lowest denominator of humanity in this country. The blacks follow Obama because they are pure racist. Nothing else matters to 99% of them. Some may be pro-life, against homosexuality, or doubt global warming, but black rules the day. They take their marching orders from the black elites like the Black Congressional Caucus, Jeremiah Wright, and 10,000 black preachers. The Hispanics take their cue from their Hispanic elites and the 150 radical pro-illegal immigrant groups, who have successfully tied the fate of illegal's to the fate of Obama. The white guilters, radical leftists, and media-believing whites, round out Obama's solid supporters. Obama has already lost some of the white guilters because of his radical turn left, so he is busy shoring-up this loss with gains in other areas. He can ignore the blacks since racism has permanently locked them in, but he must also lock in the Hispanics by passing an amnesty bill or, at the very least, not enforcing Arizona-type immigration laws. That alone will increase his support from the 67% in 2008 to over 90% in the next election. The AmeriCorps, student loans programs, and others will generate more of the youth vote. Juggling the census figures, legalizing the convicted felon vote, and stuffing the ballot boxes with fictitious voters and dead people, will help. As a coup de grace, Obama will call on his geek squad to electronically invent the needed votes to put him and his people over the top in just enough districts to look convincing. Finally, Obama must weld together the above coherent body of supporters by the creation of a boogieman. All totalitarian dictators ever to take power united the masses by pointing-out or fabricating a threat to whatever is held dear by them. Appealing to this common human weakness worked for Hitler when he selected the Jews, and for Lenin when he pointed to the kulaks as the large landowners (8 acres) causing the peasants to be poor. The common enemy can be internal or external, but the boogieman is usually a negative threat because it produces more intense feeling among the dumb and poor. In other words, engineered hatred of a group engenders more response than a positive future promise of reward. Obama has his choice in the United States since he has had a chip on his shoulder all his life. He has already targeted bankers, Wall Street, Christians, make-believe white racists, pro-lifers, and gun owners. My personal opinion is that Obama will opt for the dramatic and ignite a mega-event that will incite violence and rage. His useful idiots have dossiers on thousands of Muslims and their active cells operating in the U.S. All Obama would have to do is inform Eric Holder to do nothing to stop a group of cells from hitting half of our oil refineries to throw the entire country into absolute chaos, so that he could declare martial law and become a virtual overnight dictator. My reasoning is that Obama is not a patient man, and he is literally filled with hatred and rage, and sees our Constitutional republic with its deliberative institutions as slowing him down and impeding his sprint to fascism.

The people that actually promulgate and enforce Obama's Fascist pogroms will all be willing to do immoral things. The supreme rule of fascist philosophy is pragmatism; the end always justifies the means. No individual will long remain a part of Obama's regime who will not carry out absolutely anything for the good of the collective society. Ruby Ridge, Waco,and other murders-by-government events were pulled-off by the same FBI that Obama now owns. None of these multiple murders of innocents caused rioting and looting because the victims were portrayed by the media as enemies of society. Obama knows he can duplicate these atrocities if his propaganda is calculated to elicit the correct public response. He knows he can count on the media in this effort. Often the media acts autonomously in both recognizing and attacking enemies of Obama. This was true when they went after Sarah Palin, the Tea Partiers, Joe the Plumber, and others. All of Obama's mentors, friends, and associates have been radical leftist, willing to serve the higher entity which Obama identifies as his chosen constituency described above. Since taking office, Obama has hand-picked his agency heads, czars, and subalterns specifically suited for the job he wants them to perform. This doesn't mean they are skilled or educated in the particular job to be performed, but rather unquestionably loyal and committed to execute Obama's instructions. Van Jones was placed in the "Greens Jobs" Czar slot not because he knows anything about green jobs, but because he was a communist and loyal to a fault to Obama. Most of Obama's inner circle were brought from

Chicago, and know where all the bodies are buried there, so they all share the criminal's code of silence. When called upon for the brutal suppression of dissent, deception, espionage, lies, and covering-up evidence, they are dependable unto death. They have already been conditioned to perform any act, no matter how brutal or inhumane, and treat it no differently than a routine matter. Whether it be lying under oath to a Congressional committee, or planning sabotage that kills thousands, or blame right-wing white separatists for planning a "subversive" event, Obama's elite or their thugs will perform their orders with no remorse. All of Obama's confidants owe their careers and lives to him. Just as there were 53 murders of witnesses to Clinton's crimes during his years as Governor and President (including Vince Foster), and none of those murders were ever pursued, so is the secrecy within Obama's inner circle so secure that nothing will leak out even if a media still existed in the United States. To Kool-Aid drinkers, and even most conservatives, this all sounds conspiratorial, but my wife and I were married in North Little Rock, Arkansas, and witnessed first-hand the intrigue of the Little Rock "players" that produced Bill Clinton, who, like Obama, rose from obscurity to "serve" two terms as President. Our dumbed-down society will know someday that deception and obfuscation are the tools-in-trade of all totalitarians during their "Trojan Horse" period that precedes their rise to power. Obama has specialists in all fields to perform any task from small to large. He has already called on unions of teachers to march on Springfield, Illinois, to demand increased pension funding, and SEIU thugs to harass and beat-up Tea Partiers. With his unions, AmeriCorps, federal workers, ACORN surrogates, teachers, leftist radicals, and federal agency swat teams, he can literally have a civilian army on call anytime to act as his "Minutemen" in time of need.

Bill Clinton taught Obama a valuable lesson; presidential deniability. As President, you can say and do anything, lie about it, and nobody can touch you or make anything stick. Liberals like to call Ronald Reagan the "Teflon President," but that meant only that the leftist media failed to make any of their frequent scurrilous attacks stick to him. Clinton was favored by the media, but they absolutely drool over Obama. Regardless of what Obama does the media will cover it up. The media does the same service for any of Obama's henchmen. Not only do they cover for Obama's criminals, but they unilaterally pursue, degrade, and defame Tea Party folks, Christians, and conservatives, without even requiring input from Obama. For the first time in the United States, truth is concealed from the populace, and may never again see the light of day. Bias was the term used for the media prior to the election of Obama, but since November 5, 2008, the media is truly the unpaid propaganda organ of Obama's fascist regime. Disinformation and propaganda are even more critical to Obama than they were to Hitler because Hitler had over a decade to work his magic in changing socialism to Nazism. Obama has less time to convert a huge, semi-socialist republic to fascism. Obama has a head-start in that the media was on his side before he had a side. Since America is a reasonably educated country, the propaganda must be fine-tuned and targeted, because there are still large numbers of Americans intelligent enough to see through some deceptions. Even Obama-ites will not automatically obey his new policies because they are foreign to them, and they will not know the end goals that Obama is asking them to strive for. So, the media must help Obama convince the masses that the ends he is trying to achieve are indeed their own, and justify the means necessary to get there. To teach the people a new set of words to adopt and define would take precious time, and Obama doesn't have that much time. So, like his totalitarians before him, he will simply use the words already familiar to the masses, but change the definitions and convince them that the meanings are the same, but they just didn't understand or recognize the true definitions previously learned. Perversion of our language is critical to Obama's subversion of the U.S. The word "freedom" is a word American's have always cherished because they interpret it as a right enjoyed by individuals. Obama must change the basic right of freedom from an individual right to a collective right, or a right of a group to have freedom. This concept of "group freedom" will be repeated to blacks, Hispanics, homosexuals, earth-worshippers, unions, and tree-huggers first, who have mostly already accepted the group concept anyway. The lukewarm citizens will need more convincing. The collective freedoms replacing individual freedoms are really not a freedom of the masses at all, but rather the transference of individual freedom to the unlimited freedom of the totalitarian regime to do as they please with the population.

Before, during, and after Obama's fascist regime is in place, any dissent from individuals or groups must be attacked timely and efficiently. You have already seen this tactic in play even before Obama took office. As Rush and others have often pointed out, the left has a playbook which is distributed daily if not hourly. When they reply to a remark or event they all respond with the same words and phrases simultaneously all over the country. And, the response may come from Obama himself, Baghdad Bob, a media anchor, an agency head, the SEIU, or all of the above. By blitzing the airways and internet with a blizzard of overkill rhetoric, the regime kills the issue before it gets a toehold. This overwhelming preemptive response forces the conservatives to go from offense to defense, and waste time until the Darkside has won. Any deviation from socialist dogma previous to its permanent installation cannot be tolerated by Obama since even a small doubt may grow into a major problem for him. No public or private criticism of the regime, however small, can be tolerated even when it seemingly has no political significance. For example, during Hitler's conditioning of the Germans to hate the Jews, even Albert Einstein's Theory of Relativity was labeled a "Semitic attack on the foundation of Christian and Nordic physics." The 40% of Americans that responded favorably to the poll asking their opinion of socialism should think twice about what they like, or they may get their wish. They probably have no idea of the level of scrutiny exercised by the socialist or fascist state. They should read "1984," "Brave New World," or read about Lenin's and Stalin's Russia before they wish for socialism. As you will see later in this section, even upper-level bureaucrats in totalitarian regimes are subject to period purging to make sure the regime remains "pure" and committed to the dictator.

When America was first settled in the 17th century, we brought with us a unique set of Anglo-Saxon qualities that set us apart from all other nations. We prided ourselves on independence and self-reliance. Succeed or fail, we were on our own, and liked it that way. Whether settling in the city, or heading to the Indian-infested west, we would rather take the gamble on succeeding than work for the king or nobleman. We didn't bother our neighbors, and we didn't want them to bother us. We were free to pick-and-choose who we wanted to associate with, and those we didn't want to befriend. We were also wary of power and authority because, along with those two words, came shackles and control of our lives. Yes, we Americans enjoyed the freedom and liberty denied to everyone else in the world. Then, why have we been voluntarily surrendering our freedom and independence, bit-by-bit, for the past 100 years? Because, for over 100 years, progressives and socialists have been busy trying to make Americans feel guilty about their prosperity and wanting them to redistribute the wealth earned from the sweat of their own brows. We have been under attack by our own pseudo-educators to forget individualism and become a "team" player. Forget competition or wanting to be first in anything; because it might be damaging to those that don't finish first. We were made to feel guilty that others were left behind. Leveling the playing field, and equality for all, was paramount to performance of the individual. The civil rights movement caused much of this because blacks were portrayed as incompetent victims who needed patronizing and hand-outs, and we felt bad because we succeeded and they didn't. Rather than elevate them up to our level of society, these "progressives" wanted us to lower our living standards to the level of the "unfortunates." The bottom line is that Americans have already, slowly but steadily, given up their independence and self-reliance, and received assurance from society that their sacrifice has made them a better person. The trouble is, the transference of rights and wealth feeds upon itself, and enough is never enough.

The main attraction of socialism and the most often repeated promise from the bureaucratic socialists is security. There are two types of security promised by the socialists to make it palatable to the masses. The first is the basic sustenance of life which includes food, clothing, shelter, and a safety net for old age or unforeseen calamity. This security can be possible even with a democratic form of government if it doesn't exceed limits. In fact, the United States has already reached this level of security. Nobody in the United States today can starve or have to sleep in the streets if he doesn't want to. Regardless if a person is on the skids due to drugs, alcohol, or laziness, our charitable or public systems will care for them indefinitely. The second type of security is more dangerous to a democratic system, and that is the guaranteeing of no-risk in income production. Since the early 20th century we have passed legislation limiting competition or stabilizing prices. Each time we meddle with the free market we help one segment at the expense of another. Often, politics is involved, so it is a case of which industries' lobbyists is more highly paid or influential. In the United States this process has left us with a tax code of over 70,000 pages and subsidies for all sorts of products that make no sense at all. All of this activity has had as its goal the elimination of risk. Risk is at the very heart of the capitalist economic system, so when risk is eliminated the core of our free enterprise system is missing, and makes the transition to socialism easier. When risk and competition disappear from America we will officially have socialism. The recent health care and financial reform bills have removed risk from our society in huge ways, and along with a multitude of other Obama initiatives, will usher in socialism, not incrementally, but almost overnight.

We can never diminish the influence of the leftist elites running our universities today, and the effect of their anti-capitalist ranting for the past 50 years. It has had deleterious effects on the students who have been subjected to their teachings. Virtually all of them are dyed in the wool socialist or communist now. Yes, Wall Street is still alive, but Obama's financial reform bill will place it on life-support until he pulls the plug. The college professors have been telling their students that managing and overseeing 100 employees is preferable to owning the business and owning the 100 employees, since the former is more akin to socialism while the latter is capitalism. While these left-over 60's leftist are extolling the virtues of the security of socialism at the expense of freedom, they should be teaching that freedom can be had only if they are prepared to make severe material sacrifices to preserve it. As Ben Franklin stated, "Those who would give up essential liberty to purchase a little temporary safety deserve neither liberty nor safety."

I included this section on serfdom because Obama has purchased a one-way ticket for America to end up there on the fastest mode of transportation possible. As of this moment, I see no national conservative leader that can take charge, energize our morale, and guide us in our battle to survive. I see the unencumbered march of Obama's hordes and they smell the blood of success in their nostrils for the first time. Maybe I'm the only one that can see it, but the end of this revolutionary takeover shall not be reached without the deaths of millions of Americans. There is a small and closing window of opportunity to stop it before it reaches critical mass.

THE COMING DEMICIDE

I wrote this section in the hope that it does not come to pass. But, I know it will. Never has Santayana's quote, "Those who do not remember the past are condemned to repeat it," meant more. America is fast approaching a point in time when a freedom-loving people must decide between freedom and tyranny. There is no doubt among thinking people that Barack Obama is racing toward a totalitarian state. I am fully aware that most of you have been told that Obama is steering us to socialism. If you think Obama will reach socialism and stop, then you do not know his philosophy, his ideology, his mentors, his cadre of facilitators, or the efforts already in place and those coming soon. Although Obama is moving toward socialism, and I label him a fascist, he and his closest associates are Marxist-Leninist. They look at the socialist state that would come into being with the overthrow of capitalism as nothing more than an intermediary dictatorship of the proletariat through which the transition to the final stage of communism would be prepared. And stripped of its feudal or capitalist exploiters, and thus its agents of war, communism would mean enlightened cooperation among all people as each works according to his ability and receives according to his need. The state then would wither away, and the masses would live in true, everlasting peace and freedom. If Obama would do a little reading and research he would discover that instead of "everlasting peace" over 200,000,000 innocent children, women, and men were brutally murdered by communists just in the 20th century, and never arrived at Marx's promised "freedom." Besides, don't be naïve and assume Obama is ignorant of the brutal history of communism. The vast majority of his friends since childhood have been communists, and he has studied the subject and history thoroughly. To continue pursuing his course after knowledge of its bloody consequences only reinforces the axiom that the pursuit of power is paramount to all other human drives, and "power corrupts and absolute power corrupts absolutely."

In previous sections of this book I have shown you how the road to socialism and beyond was under construction by thousands of radical groups and individuals before Obama rose to national prominence. These groups know that the leap from republicanism to socialism is long and contentious, but once gained can then morph into totalitarianism at a faster pace. Bill Clinton attempted to push the country farther left than he actually did, but was sidetracked by personal failures (Lewinski, bimbos, napkins, FBI files, etc.). Obama has surrounded himself with like-minded radicals, and has jolted the nation permanently to the left in less than 15 months. The changes cannot be reversed by the historical political process. For the reasons described in other parts of this book, control of the three branches of government shall remain in the hands of Obama and the Democrats. Henceforth, Obama needs only a little more time to tighten his grip on even the smallest vestiges of conservative influences remaining. Simultaneous with solidifying his hold on the political power from the national level down to the smallest political entity, he will be decimating Christian influence wherever he finds it. Wherever morality, patriotism, or American sovereignty exists, Obama's lieutenants will be there to destroy or diminish them into obscurity. You have surely seen school children on YouTube chanting "Obama, um-um-um." You will see it a lot more in the near future because all totalitarian regimes must indoctrinate the youth as they assuredly must eliminate the elderly, since they are not only a burden on society, but all remembrances of the former freedoms need to be erased.

There is always an incorrigible remnant of citizens in a nation undergoing radical conversion to totalitarianism. This remnant can only be cleansed from a society by murder. Don't be shocked or have the slightest doubt that this murdering of the recalcitrant patriots of the United States will start soon. This is not my amateurish attempt at prophesy, or an unsubstantiated prediction. The radical left of the United States has been poisoning minds and multiplying their operations throughout the country for 60 years. Good examples are the media and education. Democracies cannot exist without a free press and we have lost ours. I have named and described just a few of the thousands of well-funded organizations hell-bent and single-goal driven to demolish America and all it stands for. They elected one of their own, Obama, to lead them and both leader and followers know that it is now or never. Like the suicide terrorists, they are all willing to die for the cause, but they prefer that we die for our cause: America. To that end, they have history on their side. I will give a few examples. Much of my source information is from "Death by Government" and "Statistics of Demicide" by R. J. Rummel.

I asked my 32 year old son, Rhett, to guess what caused the most deaths in the 20th century. His first guess was influenza and his second was war. My guess was the Black Plague. The answer is "demicide," the murder of any person or people by a government, including genocide, politicide, and mass murder. This does not mean one nation attacking another nation. Nor does it mean combatants and collateral deaths caused during wartime. It is the premeditated murder of a group within the nation by the government. I have limited my discourse to the 20th century because any period prior to that lacks creditable source data and is less appropriate to the current era. Rummel spent years in research, wrote 24 books, and used the most scientifically accurate methodology and analysis to arrive at his conservative numbers. I include this section because history is no longer taught in the U.S. and two generations now know only a world of Twitter, cell phones, and Viagra. Demicide has not taken a vacation; it simply has never crossed the oceans and visited the United States. It will.

For those of us who still care, we are astounded at the geometric increase in technology. I remember in 1962 working on "magnetic donuts," and/or "gates," and voice filters which are now ancient history. I remember our mechanical Burrough's calculators were the size of large TV sets, and a simple calculation took one minute and sounded like it was tearing itself apart. I was amazed while working on the Dynasoar Space Project in 1963 when those mechanical monsters were replaced by totally electronic Freidan calculators. Now, this technology is on the head of a pin. Our societies have evolved, knowledge has grown exponentially, science advances more in one day than it used to in 100 years, and technology is a blur. Only our collective violence against each other has not evolved. The degree of violence today has not changed since Cain slew Abel. Only the mega-numbers of humans available for murdering have changed. With a world population of at least 6.8 billion people, death by natural causes is proving insufficient to limit them to a size manageable by the growing oligarchy of totalitarian power-seekers. At least one-third must be eliminated to conserve natural resources and facilitate control over the remaining populace. These are my words, not Rummels.

Rummel says that today all collective violence resulting in demicide is generally organized violence between collective "oughts." We who share similar interests about how society ought to be structured, about the best policies of government, or how to improve our lot tend to seek out others with similar interests and organize into groups. These groups can be based on ideological, theological, nationalistic, or racial interests. The violence between the groups results from either altruistic or fraternal differences on what "ought" to be. The poor think they "ought" to be wealthy. The illegal immigrants think we "ought" to give them amnesty. Blacks think they "ought" to get reparations for past injustices. Homosexuals think they "ought" to have access to little boys. Obama thinks he "ought" to have the power to bypass pesky Constitutional prerogatives. And so on. Violence always is the result when collective groups cannot adjudicate their "oughts" peacefully. As social animals, we all try to balance our three spheres: fundamental needs (protectiveness, self-assertiveness), morality (superego and self-esteem), and our will (that which we would like to do). The most common threats to this balance come from class distinction, morality issues, race, and religion. When the collective imbalance reaches a tipping point, either real or perceived, collective violence will ensue. There is no reason to think this will not be eternal in mankind's future.

Rummel discusses two types of societies. The first is the "spontaneous" society where exchange power dominates; interests are divided and cross-pressured by the diversity of groups such as clubs, associations, churches, universities, leagues, institutions, fraternal groups, and special interest organizations. Across these multifold and intersecting groups people are in different positions of power and form many different conflict helices. In the spontaneous society the government is only one of the many pyramids of power. In other words, people are diverse in their personal, business, and social life such that a small upheaval in one sector of the society does not affect all of them. Violence in one area of a spontaneous society will most likely remain a local event. A democracy is a form of spontaneous society.

The other type of society is termed "antifield." This is where coercion reigns, where the government totally controls all meaningful aspects of society; a "them" verses "us" scenario. Here, government inhibits and prohibits any pyramids of power other than themselves and overlapping groups who would otherwise mediate, moderate, or contain violence are non-existent. When even a small instance of violence occurs in any sector, the government reacts quickly and violently in suppressing it to set a harsh example. An example of an antifield society is totalitarianism. Below you will see a table showing all of the countries of the world who committed demicide during the 20th century. This table is from R.J. Rummull's book, "The Statistics of Demicide." I will discuss some of them in the order that they appear in the table.

20th Centry Mortacracies

Democide Level Mortacracies	Years	Democide (000)	Total (000)
Deke-Megamurderer	1900-87		219,634
China(PRC)	1949-87	76,702	
U.S.S.R.	1917-87	61,911	
Colonialism		50,000	
Germany	1933-45	20,946	
China (KMT)	1928-49	10,075	
Megamurderer	1900-87		19,180
Japan	1936-45	5,964	
China (Mao Soviets)	1923-48	3,468	
Cambodia	1975-79	2,035	
Turkey	1909-18	1,883	
Vietnam	1945-87	1,670	
Poland	1945-48	1,585	
Pakistan	1958-87	1,503	
Yugoslavia (Tito)	1944-87	1,072	
Megamurder?	1900-87		44,145
North Korea	1948-87	1,663	
Mexico	1900-20	1,417	
Russia	1900-17	1,065	
Centi-Kilomurderers	1900-87		14,918
Top 5	1900-87	4,074	
China(Warlords)	1917-49	910	
Turkey (Ataturk)	1919-23	878	
United Kingdom	1900-87	816	
Portugal (Dictatorship)	1926-82	741	
Indonesia	1965-87	729	
Other	1900-00	10,844	
Lesser Murderers	1900-87		2,792
World Total	1900-87		260,669
World Total	1987-99		1,331
World Total	1900-99		262,000

China started off the 20th century with a mixture of a dying Dynasty and warlords ruling their own small kingdoms. General Yuan Shih-k'ai was looked to as a unifying force and tried to establish a central government, but his death in 1916 ended any hope of unity. Anarchy reigned supreme until two elements rose to power. One was the Kuomintang under Sun Yat-sen whose vision for China was national unity, self-determination, and democracy. The other was Mao Tse-tung's communists. They actually joined forces and fought together against the warlords until Mao started taking his orders directly from Moscow. They went their separate ways after a bloody coup in 1927 when Chiang Kai-shek assumed command after the death of Sun Yat-sen. For the next 22 years the two would have negotiations, truces, and sometimes even resumed joint operations against the warlords. The Chinese people just wanted to work their rice paddies and raise their families, but it was impossible to avoid the constant battles between the communists, nationalists (Chiang Kai-shek), and the warlords. As if that was not deadly enough, the Japanese invaded China in 1937 and made it a four-party war. As usual, the people not involved suffered the most. After the United States defeated Japan in 1945 it allowed the communists and nationalist to turn on each other in a massive civil war that involved millions of troops, militia, peasant laborers, massacres, and terror. This continued until 1949 when the communists, with the support of Russia, drove Chiang Kai-shek to flee to Taiwan and form the offshore Republic of China.

The long struggle from 1900 to 1949 killed 8,963,000 civilians and combatants. But my interest here is demicide, not war dead, or even the civilians that were killed collaterally. Rummel's best estimate is that a minimum of 910,000 civilians were sought out and murdered just by the warlords. The nationalists murdered another 10,075,000 through cruel recruitment, starvation, retribution, famine, and intentional acts such as the dynamiting of the Yellow River dikes that drowned or otherwise killed 440,000 people in just a few days. The Chinese Communists executed counterrevolutionaries, nationalist sympathizers, and political opponents. Like Stalin and Hitler, they also had systematic purges of the Army, executing as many as 10,000 in a single day. To gain followers, Mao would redistribute land to the peasants and execute landlords in front of the peasants. This was done only until he solidified power in 1949, when he took the land back away from the peasants and executed them. When Mao officially proclaimed victory on October 1, 1949, for his Peoples Republic of China he had murdered 3,466,000 Chinese people. This was only phase one of Mao's demicide.

Once in power, the Chinese communist launched numerous movements to systematically destroy the traditional Chinese social and political system, and replace it with a totally socialist, top to bottom "dictatorship of the proletariat." In the beginning, they used Stalin's Soviet Union as their model including Soviet advisors to construct their own Chinese Gulags. Their ideology was strictly Marxist-Leninism as interpreted by Mao Tse-tung. Like Obama today, Mao seemed to be everywhere at once; working on land reform, suppressing anti-communist guerrillas, designing a new marriage contract for peasants, purging religion but calling it "reforming," killing counterrevolutionaries, fighting the anti-rightist movements, and suppressing the "Five Black Categories," (landlords, rich farmers, anti-revolutionists, bad influencers, right-wingers). In a speech to his party cadre in 1958 Mao said:

"What's so unusual about Emperor Shih Huang of the Chin Dynasty? He had buried alive 460 scholars only, but we have buried alive 46,000 scholars. In the course of our repression of counter-revolutionary elements, haven't we put to death a number of the counter-revolutionary scholars? I had an argument with the democratic personages. They say we are behaving worse than Emperor Shih Huang of the Chin Dynasty. That's definitely not correct. We are 100 times ahead of Emperor Shih of the Chin Dynasty in repression of counter-revolutionary scholars.[8]"

Mao's "Great Leap Forward" and collectivization produced a famine in the early 1960's that in effect murdered 27,000,000 people by starvation. In the mid-60's Mao had a struggle with a more moderate, pragmatically oriented faction that resulted in the "cultural revolution" and the murders of another 1,613,000 innocent lives. Soon after, Mao died and the pragmatists regained power and moderated

China's communism until the Tianamen Square demonstrations, and the subsequent massacres of 1989. From the beginning of the Chinese communist activities around 1923 to the end of the 20th century the communists murdered 76,702,000 people. When you combine the communists with the nationalist and warlords there were 87,687,000 Chinese slaughtered, not counting the millions killed in actual warfare. Just the democide by the Chinese communists alone far exceeds, by a factor of two, the total number of humans killed in all of the international, civil, revolutionary, and guerrilla wars in the 20th century. This is the pragmatic, historical end result of raw totalitarian power that Obama and the Democrats seem so happy to have finally been able to initiate embryonically by criminal means in what was the representative republic of the United States.

The actual acts of murder behind the democide in China are numerous. The innocent, unarmed people were worked to death to create tank traps, drowned in an intentionally created flood, starved to death because their food was stolen by an official to sell in the black market, killed because they demonstrated against the government, murdered in the process of rape, bayoneted as drill for soldiers, executed because they were allegedly pro or anti nationalist, communist, Japanese, or loyal to a particular warlord, shot because they didn't bow low enough, buried alive for objecting to a soldier's looting their house, beaten to death as a landlord or rich peasant, and on and on. The underlying causes are just as numerous: dehumanization, segregation, group polarization, racism, a subject majority, hegemonic drive, threat to the power structure, "outsider" minorities, ethnic / racial / religious stratification, primitiveness, retribution, development, scapegoatism, ideology, cultural clash, war/revolution, among others. The reason for mass murder are many for the warlords and nationalist, but not for the communists. The single cause of democide for the communist is simply adherence to the totalitarian Marxism-Leninism ideology. The Soviet Union murdered a few million less than the Chinese communists simply because they had less population to murder.

The Communist Party of the Soviet Union murdered approximately 61,911,000 people in the 20th century. Of these, about 54,769,000 were its own citizens, and the rest were unarmed citizens of nearby countries. This does not include combat deaths in wartime. When the communists started killing en masse it became more mechanical, ruthless and routine. It mattered not if the murdered were the elderly or sick, young or old, women or men, infants or toddlers, or sick or infirmed. These people were guilty of absolutely nothing.

When the murders began there was often a reason or justification given to the subalterns. Later, as it became more routine and acceptable to the subordinates, no reason was necessary or expected by the underlings doing the actual killing. Initially, the reason given might be that the bourgeoisie or upper class were greedy and the enemies of the state. The aristocracy held large tracts of land, while the peasants grubbed-out a meager existence on rented parcels. Therefore, the large landowners and aristocrats must die to redistribute the land to the poor. After a few years, the communists started running out of wealthy landowners, so they moved down a notch and started on the kulaks; former peasants who had managed over the years to accumulate eight to ten acres of land that enabled them to both feed their families and sell some of their produce. Unlike the aristocracy, the kulaks had risen in stature through hard work, and had resisted efforts to move to collective farms and work side-by-side with the peasants. From 1930 to 1937 over 6,500,000 of them were executed, starved, herded into gulags, and never heard from again.

Simultaneously with murdering their own people, the communists killed people based on their race or ethnicity. They murdered Germans, Kalmyks, Greeks from the southern Black Sea area and, of course, the numerous, poor Ukrainians. Always, the communists killed anyone that differed politically, such as the Trotskyites, Mensheviks, and social revolutionaries. Not only card-carrying opposition party members were killed, but also their wives, sons, daughters, mothers, fathers, cousins, and even friends. When the politician fled and could not be located, the assassins would eliminate the entire family of the fugitive. When the Soviet Union enveloped all of its neighbors after WWII and occupied their lands, the Red Army started systematically murdering the citizens. This was not war. This was not combat. The people were merely living where they had always lived. These were the Balts, East Germans, Hungarians, Czechs, Poles, Rumanians, Romanians, and

Bosnians. Some were killed for their religion, any religion, since Lenin considered religion the enemy of the state. As Pol Pot would do many years later in Cambodia, the communists systematically murdered potential opposition such as teachers, writers, churchmen, city officials, and community leaders.

Although the word, egalitarian, is usually associated with equality of people, the murdering of absolutely innocent people also became egalitarian in that all people were murdered for all and any reason. There is no class distinction, no political affiliation, no ethnicity, no race, no nationality, no skill or intellect, and no level of authority that would make anyone immune from being murdered. No one ever felt totally secured, even upper echelon Communist Party members. Once a person was arrested for suspicion of counter-revolutionary thought, or for speaking against the state, there was no escape. If they denied the charge, they would be tortured, sign a confession, and be killed. If they confessed, they would sign a confession and be killed. Once a person was in the system there was no escape except death.

The Don Cossacks were a freedom-loving, semi-independent ethnic group of Russians with a tradition of military acumen and horsemanship. Since the communists prefer for their subjects to accept and obey orders like cattle, the Don Cossacks were slated for extermination. By 1919 the communists had killed over 400,000 of them. During 1932 and 1933 over 5,000,000 Ukrainian peasants were murdered, and in just the year of 1949 from 50,000 to 60,000 Estonians were murdered. Even the officers and enlisted soldiers of the Red Army were not immune from demicide. Just in the period from 1937 to 1938, known as the "Great Terror," almost one million Communist Party members were executed.

The murders became so random and common that reasons were not given nor asked for when the orders to kill were handed down. Vladmir Petrov was a political operative and spy in Australia when he defected. In testimony before the Royal Australian Commission on Espionage about his work during the years of 1936 to 1938 he said:

> *"I handled hundreds of signals to all parts of the Soviet Union which were couched in the following forms:*
> *'To N.K.V.D. Frunze. You are charged with the task of exterminating 10,000 enemies of the people. Report results by signal.—Yezhov.'*
>
> *And in due course the reply would come back:*
> *'In reply to yours of such-and-such date, the following enemies of the Soviet people have been shot.'"*

Alexander Solzhenitsyn, who later received the Nobel Prize for Literature, was sentenced to serve 8 years in the gulags and describes the Great Terror of 1936-38 as follows:

> *"The real law underlying the arrests of those years was the assignment of quotas, the norms set, the planned allocations. Every city, every district, every military unit was assigned a specific quota of arrests to be carried out by a stipulated time. From then on everything else depended on the ingenuity of the Security operations personnel."*

Often, the N.K.V.D. simply ran out of plausible reasons to kill. In the beginning they would try to arrest people with a semblance of guilt, such as the wife of a man whose father was descended from a White Russian or Don Cossack. As time went on, and they exhausted the supply of citizens with even the most remote connection to counter-revolutionary activities, they began to use ingenuous methods to fulfill their quota of murders. They began to literally arrest and shoot people who crossed the street at locations other than intersections. When wives and friends would visit jails or prison to visit loved ones, they would meet with execution instead. A teenager fishing in a Moscow river without Party permission would be murdered. People caught failing to pay rapt attention to one of Stalin's speeches, or not stopping to give proper recognition to Lenin's image, might be slated for execution.

Rummel was right in suggesting that Americans have no concept of mindless, wanton murder on the wholesale scale that has occurred in every part of the world except North America. And kindly don't even bring up the killing of Indians and the lynching of blacks in the U.S., or I will rattle off to you the savage butchery of the American Indian tribes and the current black violent crime rate that is nearly 8 times that of whites. Our discussion here is demicide, not crime or combat between two divergent groups wanting the same piece of property, or a race that can't seem to contain its violence.

If Americans are aware of any democide at all, it is the Holocaust, because Jews have done a good job of keeping us informed of Hitler's attempt to exterminate every Jew in the world. He did manage to kill an estimated 5,291,000 of them. But, few of us know that Jews were not only rounded-up and shipped to death camps to be gassed, but Hitler also sent units of specialized squads to follow his armies in their offensive movements across Europe and Russia. These units had as their sole mission to round-up Jews and shoot them on the spot without further ado. I truly think that if this country continues lurching toward totalitarianism, and adopts the radical mindset of racists like Louis Farrakhan and Jeremiah Wright, then Jews and Christians may find themselves in the cross-hairs again. Trying to understand the incomprehensible hatred within Obama and many of his closest friends is as futile as understanding Hitler's.

> *"Hitler told Himmler that it was not enough for the Jews simply to die; they must die in agony. What was the best way to prolong their agony? Himmler turned the problem over to his advisers, who concluded that a slow, agonizing death could be brought about by placing Jewish prisoners in freight cars in which the floors were coated with...quicklime...which produced excruciating burns. The advisers estimated that it would take four days for the prisoners to die, and for that whole time the freight cars could be left standing on some forgotten siding.... Finally it was decided that the freight cars should be used in addition to the extermination camps."*
> ----Robert Payne, *The Life and Death of Adolf Hitler*

Hitler and the Nazis murdered 20,946,000 men, women, handicapped, critics, homosexuals, Jews, Slavs, Unionists, Jehovah Witnesses, Serbs, Germans, Czechs, Italians, Poles, French, Ukrainians, and many others. Included among them were over one-million children under the age of 18. This does not include civilian and military combat or war-related deaths during WWII. They were murdered as hostages, in reprisal raids, by forced labor, by euthanasia, from exposure, in medical experiments, by terror bombing, by "ferret-out and kill" expeditions, and in concentration and death camps.

Of the 20,946,000 people murdered by the Nazis 5,219,000 were Jews. Who were the other 15,727,000 people? After the Nazis' blitzkrieg of Poland and after all resistance had ceased, the murder of civilians began. The Nazis rounded-up intellectuals, and anyone in a leadership position, and in many cases simply executed them. While in most cases these were men. If a female occupied a leadership role, then sex had no bearing on the decision to execute or not. The Nazis murdered over 2,400,000 non-combatant Poles. Above, I told you about the 5 million Ukrainians murdered by their own government in 1937-38, but their trials were far from over. During Operation Barbarossa, as the Nazis were pushing the Russian Red Army eastward, they stopped long enough to kill 3,000,000 more innocent Ukrainians plus 1,593,000 unarmed Russians, and 1,400,000 Byelorussians.

Totalitarian governments, whether they are Nazis, or communists, or Obama's fascists, do not limit their murders to those outside their inner circles. In 1934 Ernst Rohm, head of the "Brown Shirts" (Nazi SA's or Sturmabteilung) who had been with Hitler from the very beginning, were vying for power with the SS (Schutzstaffel) under Himmler. Rohm was a known homosexual and too busy with his love-life to notice that he was increasingly falling out of favor with Hitler. During June and July of 1934, the SS systematically killed Rohm and thousands of his Brown Shirts. After the assassination attempt on Hitler's life in 1944, Hitler ordered the execution of over 5000 German officers including Rommel, the "Desert Fox." Actually, throughout Hitler's reign people were murdered daily and included critics, pacifists, conscientious objectors, campus rebels, dissidents, and others. They were executed, disappeared, or were sent to concentration camps and never seen again. In all, the Nazis killed at least 288,000 ethnic Germans not counting Jews, homosexuals, and those forcibly euthanized.

We are all familiar with the term "zero tolerance" when applied to illegal drug possession. It was more serious to the Nazis when dealing with occupied territories or partisan resistance. As they conquered cities and villages in Russia and the rest of Europe and the Balkans, they would of necessity leave a unit of an occupying force to hold the ground and maintain supply lines and communication. These units would be as small as possible because soldiers were needed at the front. Therefore, zero tolerance was allowed of the citizens who caused problems or were part of the local resistance. Whenever guerilla units were organized, the Nazis had a simple rule; for every Nazi soldier killed, one hundred civilians were lined up and shot immediately, and fifty for every wounded Nazi. If problems continued, the numbers would increase to 200 or 300 for every soldier killed or wounded. Although the Germans kept accurate records of the Jews murdered in the camps, the numbers in occupied countries required much research by Rummel. In just three towns in Yugoslavia the murders were: Kraguyevats-8000, Kraljevo-1,755 and Jajinci-80,000.

Although the murders by the Nazis in the occupied territories were not comparable to the death camps, they did add up to huge numbers. From an official German war diary dated December 16, 1942, comes the following:

"In Belgrade, 8 arrests, 60 Mihailovich (the guerrilla Chetnik leader) supporters shot;" December 27, 1942: "In Belgrade, 11 arrests, 250 Mihailovich supporters shot as retaliation."

Rummel further notes that a German placard from Belgrade announced that the Nazis shot fifty hostages in retaliation for the dynamiting of a bridge. On 25th of May 1943, the Nazis shot 150 hostages in Kraljevo; in October they shot 150 hostages in Belgrade; fifty hostages in Belgrade in August 1943; 150 Serbs at Cacak in October, and so on. In Greece, as another example, the Nazis may have burned and destroyed as many as 1,600 villages, each with populations of 500 to 1000 people, no doubt massacring many of the inhabitants beforehand. Overall, the Nazis thus slaughtered hundreds of thousands in Yugoslavia, Czechoslovakia, Greece, and France; and millions overall in Poland and the Soviet Union. Rummel concludes:

"But many other regimes have also killed opponents and critics, or used reprisals to maintain power. What

distinguished the Nazis above virtually all others was their staggering genocide: people were machine gunned in batches, shot in the head at the edge of trenches, burned alive while crowded into churches, gassed in vans or fake shower rooms, starved or frozen to death, worked to death in camps, or beaten or tortured to death simply because of their race, religion, handicap, or sexual preference.

Most Nazis were absolute racists, especially among the top echelon; they believed utterly in the superiority of the "Aryan" race. They had no doubt that they were the pinnacle of racial evolution, that eugenically they were the best. So science proved, as many German and non-German scientists told them. And therefore they could not allow inferior groups to pollute their racial strain. Inferior races were like diseased appendixes that had to be surgically removed for the health of the body. Therefore they must exterminate the Jew and Gypsy. So also must they liquidate the homosexual and handicapped. So eventually they must also eliminate the Slavs, after exploiting their slave labor. Slavs were not only biologically inferior, but also inhabited territory that Germany needed for the superior race to expand and grow.

But then the Nazi program ran into the problem of numbers. Exterminating millions of Jews would be hard enough. But the Slavs numbered in the tens of millions. Therefore they envisioned a two-part approach: reduce their number through execution, starvation, and disease. And then after the war that the Nazis would of course win, deport the remaining 30,000,000 or 40,000,000 Slavs to Siberia.

These genocides cost the lives of probably 16,315,000 people. Most likely the Nazis wiped out 5,291,000 Jews, 258,000 Gypsies, 10,547,000 Slavs, and 220,000 homosexuals. They also "euthanized" 173,500 handicapped Germans. Then in repression, terrorism, reprisals, and other cold-blooded killings done to impose and maintain their rule throughout Europe, the Nazis murdered more millions including French, Dutch, Serbs, Slovenes, Czechs, and others. In total, they likely annihilated 20,946,000 human beings."

The democide under the heading of colonialism in the above table refers mostly to the deaths of forced laborers in the exploitation of natural resources by Europeans in Africa. More specifically, it was Belgium's King Leopold imposing industrial socialism on the Congo Free State. Understand that this was not the country of Belgium's colonialism, but rather the personal property of Leopold himself. Other countries with colonial operations in Africa and Asia were England, France, Germany, Italy, Netherlands, Portugal, and Spain.

Referring to the table again, the megamurderers who killed under 10 million each still killed a total of over 23 million, and the centi-kilomurderers and lesser murderers killed another 18 million. You can't really point out any of the murderous groups as any worse than the others because when the killing is so brutal and intentional and huge, the differences in methodology are insignificant. The Japanese murdered 5,964,000 in their rampage across China, Manchuria, Malaya, Korea, Philippines, Indonesia, Burma, and so on throughout Asia. Keep in mind this omits totally the people killed in combat. The fascist regime of Japan thought they were a superior race as did Hitler's Aryans. Just as Obama's Muslim friends today teach their children that Jews are ignorant monkeys, so too did Japanese children receive indoctrination that they were a superior race. Jap democide was due to a morally bankrupt political and military strategy, military expediency and custom and national culture. Over 3 million of the near 6 million victims of Jap democide were in China. Perhaps this was because they had so much land to cover and so many more opportunities to kill. The "Rape of Nanking" is one of the best documented atrocities among the many because of the actual orders to the Japanese troops to rape and murder over 200,000 Chinese women and their children.

Pol Pot is not as well known as Hitler or Mao, but his Khmer Rouge murdered 2,035,000 Cambodians in less than 3 years. Had he stayed in power longer he would have surpassed the communists and Nazis, or at least run out of people to murder. The Khmer Rouge were fanatical communists who wanted to establish the most advanced and purist form of agrarian communism in the world. With military victory over the lon Nol government in 1976 and absolute power thus in their hands, they hastily proceeded to construct their utopia. No actual or potential opponent was allowed to stand in their way. No violation of their draconian rules could go unpunished. No independent thoughts or groups could be allowed. No independent movement or property or enterprise was permitted. All Cambodians were as bricks in the hands of these supreme social engineers, and human lives counted for little. In proportion to its population, Cambodia underwent a human catastrophe unparalleled in this century. Out of a 1970 population of probably near 7,100,000 Cambodia probably lost slightly less than 4,000,000 people to war, rebellion, man-made famine, genocide, politicide, and mass murder. Pol Pot delegated the killing to boys as young as 7 years old, and once they became adept at killing they were efficient and couldn't stop themselves. Before the Vietnamese ran him out of Cambodia he had over 20,000 "killing fields," most of which can still be seen today doting the countryside. A witness to just one of these murders writes:

> *"It was . . . of Tan Samay, a high schoolteacher from Battambang. The Khmer Rouge accused him of incompetence. The only thing taught the children at the village was how to cultivate the soil. Maybe Tan Samay was trying to teach them other things, too, and that was his downfall. His pupils hanged him. A noose was passed around his neck; then the rope was passed over the branch of a tree. Half a dozen children between eight and ten years old held the loose end of the rope, pulling it sharply three or four times, dropping it in between. All the while they were shouting, "Unfit teacher! Unfit teacher!" until Tan Samay was dead. The worst was that the children took obvious pleasure in killing."*

Ataturk and his Young Turks of the Islamic country of Turkey deserves the infamy of executing the 20th century's first full scale ethnic and religious cleansing during WWI. In the highest levels of government, the Young Turks made a command decision to exterminate every Armenian in the country, whether a front-line soldier, or pregnant woman, famous professor or high bishop, important businessman, or ardent patriot, all 2,000,000 of them. When the Young Turks lost power to the Nationalist government the new leaders continued the demicide against the Greeks and the remaining or returning Armenians. From 1900 to 1923 the

Turkish regimes killed from 3,500,000 to 4,300,000 Armenians, Greeks, Nestorians, and others, all Christians.

According to Rummel, the democide committed by the Vietnamese was the toughest to sort out and isolate since there were six separate wars over a 43 year period. He determined that over 3,800,000 Vietnamese lost their lives, and of these, 1,760,000 were murdered for non-war reasons. The lion's share of the murders were committed by the communist North Vietnamese devoted to eliminating non-communist nationalists, anti-communist, and those who were pro-French prior to 1956. With the backing of Soviet communists and Chinese communists, the North Vietnamese communists just kept murdering peasants and landowners right on through the periods of the Viet Minh, French, South Vietnamese, Americans, Koreans, Australians, Chinese, and Cambodians until they all gave up and went home. After the Viet Nam War was over the pitiful South Vietnamese were put into re-education camps and the demicide continued. The peaceful Hmong people of the hill country who worked with us and the loyal ARVN troops who trusted us were murdered for that trust when we went home and left them behind. The politicians that sent us to war in Viet Nam never missed a meal and enjoyed the good life right on through our 15 year involvement. For 58,000 of our best young men they ended their good lives on that bloody ground for absolutely nothing. Obama hates whites and he hates the soldiers, and he is without a patriotic bone in his body, yet he sends boys to their death every day in Iraq and Afghanistan just as was done during Viet Nam. My best advice to our soldiers serving in these two countries is to get out now because one American's life exceeds the value of the combined population of these two Muslim countries.

Poland's demicide total of 1,585,000 is probably not caused by what you think, or at least was not what I thought. When you watch a documentary on WWII it is always about the war itself, and not about what happened after the war ended. After Hitler's Operation Barbarossa against the Russians failed, and the Russian Red Army started pushing the Wehrmacht back to Germany, approximately 5,000,000 Reichdeutsch (ethnic Germans) fled west also with the army rather than face the wrath of the Russians. Another 10,000,000 Reichdeutsch had relocated during the war to Germany's conquered lands or other

European countries for safety, or to populate conquered lands with Aryans. Within a few years of the war's end all 15,000,000 civilians would be forcibly ejected from Poland, the Baltic States, Memel (East Prussia), Czechoslovakia, Hungary, Rumania, Yugoslavia, and the Netherlands. Recall that after WWII the USSR enveloped almost all of these countries including East Germany. This forced repatriation was cruel and many were executed, starved, or simply locked-up and left to die. The orders from the USSR was to treat the Germans no better than the German POW's were being treated, and they were all destined to die, although they are not in these numbers since they are considered casualties of war. At any rate, Poland alone under the communists murdered 1,585,000 Germans in the four years after the war's end.

In 1971 the self-appointed President of Pakistan and Commander-in-Chief of the Army, General Agha Mohammed Yahya Khan, and his top generals prepared a careful and systematic military, economic, and political operation to take control in East Pakistan (now Bangladesh). They planned to murder its Bengali intellectual, cultural, and political elite. They also planned to indiscriminately murder hundreds of thousands of its Hindus and drive the rest into India. And, they planned to destroy its economic base to insure that it would be subordinate to West Pakistan for at least a generation to come. This despicable and cutthroat plan was outright genocide. After a well organized military buildup in East Pakistan, the military launched its campaign. No more than 267 days later they had succeeded in killing perhaps 1,500,000 people, created 10,000,000 refugees who had fled to India, provoked a war with India, incited a counter-genocide of 150,000 non-Bengalis, and lost East Pakistan. Pakistan initiated this murderous campaign for two reasons: to exercise their power to annex land and to expel non-Muslims (Hindus).

During the Second World War in Yugoslavia, the Nazis, Chetniks, Croatian Ustashi, and the communist Partisans and successor Tito regime, committed massive democide. The Croatians alone may have murdered some 655,000 people, the greater majority of them Serbs. Can you blame the Serbs for taking revenge during Bill Clinton's war? Croatia was a puppet state of Nazi Germany and murdered Jews, Gypsies, and Serbs, perhaps as many as 1,088,000, but some of these are omitted since they were war-related. The Tito regime itself killed in cold blood some 500,000 people, mainly "collaborators," "anti-communists," rival guerrillas, Ustashi, and critics. And after the war it probably killed even more people, now also including the rich, landlords, bourgeoisie, clerics, and in the later 1940s, even pro-Soviet communists. From 1944 to 1987 Marshall Tito was guilty of murdering 1,072,000 human non-combatants.

I have touched briefly on 240 million of the 262 million innocent people that have been murdered in the 20th century. Giving you details of the remaining 22 million would be redundant. Since Obama took office we have all become familiar with the term "trillion," and many people have tried to help us visualize just how much a trillion is by giving us examples such as stacking $100 bills from here to the moon to equal one-trillion dollars. Well, dollars are inanimate objects, but humans are not. To give you a perspective of the incredible number of murders by government in the 20th century: if all the bodies of the murdered were laid head to toe and each was presumed to be just 5 feet in height then they would circle the earth 10 times. You have heard of the cruelty of war, but this demicide, this wanton murder, has killed 6 times more people than all those killed in combat in all the foreign and internal wars of the 20th century. It is as if we had a major nuclear war, but with its dead spread over a century. It seems Americans can tell us who won "Dancing with the Stars," but they don't have any idea that 262 million unarmed, innocent, helpless men, women, and children have been shot, beaten, tortured, knifed, burned, starved, frozen, crushed, worked to death, buried alive, drowned, hung, bombed, or killed in a hundred other ways. Hollywood stars can demonstrate against the execution of a Black Panther who murdered two L.A. police officers, but totally ignore the rape, butcher, and murders of 500,000 Black Sudanese Christians. The old saying "what you don't know won't hurt you" is just another definition of ignorance, and ignorance of what Obama and his Ayers/Alinsky philosophy will do to you will hurt you.

As the table shows, the vast majority of wholesale murders were committed by communists against the innocent. Next came the Nazis and fascists. Then, the millions murdered for religious and ethnic reasons. The United States has always had a certain number of communists, Nazis, socialists, Fabians, and other ideologies and, of course, we have literally hundreds of different religions and ethnic beliefs. Why haven't we seen democide committed by our government? The answer lies in the fact that none of our domestic totalitarian ideologies have been able to dominate here due to the dispersion of power that our founders designed into our Constitutional Republic. The shared power of our three branches of government: executive, legislative and judicial have prevented the concentration of power, and prevented one from dominating the others. Our natural competitive instinct in life is to win, to gain power over our adversaries. In politics and government this power feeds on itself, and if nothing comes along to check it, the power will become total and lead to the killing of others who are perceived to be an obstacle. Our two party system, in unity with our suffrage rights, have allowed us to remove from office people who we think are not doing a good job of representing us. Our system of checks and balances, codified laws, established institutions, and a free, countervailing press have all rested on the rock of our Constitution and guided us through 234 years of domestic freedom and peace, while the rest of the world has murdered 262 million citizens just in the 20th century. This equilibrium is now facing its greatest threat and if not stopped, will sweep us into the same cycle of murder suffered by most of the other nations of the world.

The major shift in the equilibrium of power began when it was decided by the radical left within the Democrat party that the power of the party was more important than the survival of the nation. The Democrats and Republicans have always competed for political power, but neither used extreme measures, and if they did, either the authority of the judiciary or the press would step in and correct the imbalance. Beginning in the 1960's the radical elements of the Democrat Party, such as the SDS and Weatherman Underground, started subverting the traditional paths to political office and looking for ways to permanently give the Democrats an edge. Cloward and Pivens, George Soros, and the myriad of radical leftist groups combined their criminal strategies described in other sections of this book to subvert our democratic processes. This movement culminated in capturing the educational system, the media, and even the validity of our vote. With the election of Obama and a

Democrat Congress the permanent end of democracy may be at hand. Obama sees the permanent end of democracy as a good thing because, since his teens, he has been brainwashed by his atheist and communist mentors into seeing American democracy as a racist shackle around the ankles of blacks. Similar to the imprinting of young birds discovered by ornithologists, Obama has been imprinted with the idea that only totalitarian power can bring about the equality of his race. Rather than look around the world at the plight of the blacks, and see that the former slaves in America have been blessed with special privileges unknown in Africa or other black-dominated areas, he laments about what he doesn't have, rather than the bounties of the black existence in the United States. In trying to make his own heaven on earth for his perceived underclass he will create instead a hell on earth for the rest of us. But, like the imprinted bird, there is no hope of changing Obama or his followers. They have set on autopilot their course for the destruction of America and her democracy. I sometimes find it comical and ridiculous when I see Republicans pleading with Obama to compromise, or work on a bi-partisan idea for the good of the American people. Obama has no interest in fairness or bi-partisanship. He has tasted power and it tastes good.

In a letter to Bishop Creighton, Lord Acton wrote, "Power tends to corrupt, absolute power corrupts absolutely." I didn't include this section on demicide to gross you out, but to make you realize that war is not the biggest killer of humans. Neither is flu, hurricanes, earthquakes, or tsunamis. It is the frenzied power vested in a single individual over his fellow man that leads to murder for the sake of murder. The more power a government has, the more it can act arbitrarily according to the whims and desires of the elite. The more power, the more it will make war on others and murder it's foreign and domestic subjects. The more constrained the power of governments, the more it is diffused, checked and balanced, the less it will aggress on others and commit democide. At the extremes of power, totalitarian communist, Nazi, and fascist governments slaughter their people by the tens of millions, while many democracies can barely bring themselves to execute even serial murderers. Approximately one-fourth of the world's population is under the governance of democracies, and yet they have not had a war among themselves, not even one. The democracies represent an oasis of peace, an island of virtual tranquility among a sea of turbulence and death. There is not one case of any democracy ever killing its own citizens en masse.

Peaceful democracies are not modern phenomena. Wherever power is shared and disbursed, war is unlikely. From the time of the Greek democracies, through the forest democracies of medieval Switzerland, to the modern democracies, they did not and do not fight each other. France, Germany, England, Spain, Holland, Portugal, and others were warring constantly under monarchies and later, Hitler. But, once they became democracies the fighting ended, and they even united in the European Common Market. But, as horrible as war is, its avoidance is not the greatest benefit that democracy bestows upon its citizens. Democracy limits concentrated power, and therefore it prevents the larger massacres in cold blood of those helpless people it controls.

Napoleon said it is not men who make things happen, but "man." By this, he meant that it is always a single individual in history that is behind every significant event. Nothing monumental ever is the result of a collective thought or action, but rather a single person initiates the process. Sometimes we forget that the murders in China are not China's fault but, Mao Tse-tung, not Russia's fault, but Vladimir Lenin's and Joseph Stalin's, not Japan's, but Tojo Hideki, and not Yugoslavia's, but Josip Broz Tito's. God gave mankind free will including the free will to destroy himself and all those around him as did Hitler. That is why every American should be concerned when school children chant the name of Obama, when the media treats Obama like a bronze god, when Obama takes over private companies, when Obama usurps the Constitution, and circumvents established law without anyone objecting. He hangs Mao Tse-tung's Christmas ornaments on his White House tree and nobody remarks about it. I don't even hang a Ronald Reagan ornament on my tree, and he didn't murder 76 million people as did Mao. Humans, even the most intelligent ones, are constantly searching for someone to lead them. I'm not a cultural anthropologist, but it seems that this is almost instinctual with humans because a leader takes over the tiring function of having to make decisions in life. It is so much easier just to follow orders rather than considering and weighing the pros and cons, and taking the risks of making an error. This must be at least partially correct, otherwise how can we explain the election of a person who is still a blank, yet is leader of the greatest nation that ever was.? I have met many people who voted for Obama only because they listened to the Bush-bashing media day in and day out for eight years. In effect, they allowed the media to tell them whom to believe and follow. For those of you who are enlightened and watch only Fox News, listen to conservative talk radio, and go to the intelligent conservative blogs and honest, non-partisan websites, and wonder how Obama and his operatives can get away with their outlandish, anti-American crimes, you must remember that most Americans watch, read and listen to the totalitarian propaganda of the perverted media surrounding the majority of Americans today. Watching and listening to Democrats and leftists today, I can understand how the whole of pre-war Germany got swept-up into Nazism, and didn't realize their nightmare until 60,000,000 innocent lives had been snuffed out.

I cannot help but think that Obama has studied democracy, republicanism, communism, fascism, Nazism, and the other ism's and knows that only democracies offer the free exchange of ideas and a life without constant war or mass murder of its citizens. But, knowledge of right and wrong matters not if the lust for power is so consuming as to obviate the course of right. I have on occasion told my wife that I'm happy to have lost my race for election to Congress in 1988 because I do not consider myself beyond the grasp of greed and power, and I would probably have succumbed to the sins of office as have almost 100% of those serving in Congress. I am not aware of a single Congressional officeholder that has not partaken of monetary or personal gain after a few years in office. Obama will choose the path of power because he is just one of many examples of positive knowledge gained but discarded in favor of power.

Obama's race and his use of racism to appeal to both blacks and Hispanics add a new dimension and danger to his seat of power. The many books written by Rummel over the period of a quarter century are magnificent in depth and data accumulated, but did not delve into the complicating factor of race on the scale practiced by Obama. Rummel's democracies are composed of free people, spontaneous, diverse, and pluralistic. They have many, often opposing, interests pushing them one way or another. They belong to independent and overlapping occupational, religious, recreational, and political subgroups, each involving its own interests. They are moved by the separate and even antagonistic desires of different age, sex, ethnic, racial, and regional strata. The freedom of the democracies creates a social field in which forces point in many different directions, and in which individual interests, the engine of social behavior, are often cross-pressured. This pluralism worked well in the United States allowing neither political party to hold dictatorial power for very long because when power became concentrated, the press or another of the countervailing influences arose to dilute the power. With the help of the united actions of purely racist groups like the Congressional Black Caucus and the NAACP, Obama got almost 99% of the black vote based only on the color of his skin. His surrogate community organizers and activists have succeeded in transference of this racism to the Hispanics who gave him 67% of their vote in 2008, but may shadow the blacks in future elections and give him 99% like the blacks. Add this 27% of the electorate to the other white votes mentioned earlier in other sections of this book in addition to voter fraud, deceit, and criminal rigging of elections, and we may already have a dictator without calling him such.

Among R. J. Rummel's 24 books perhaps his greatest contribution to inform the world of the startling inhumanity of man was his "Death by Government." He ends the book with the following statement:

> *"After eight-years and almost daily reading and recording of men, women, and children by the tens of millions being tortured or beaten to death, hung, shot, and buried alive, burned or starved to death, stabbed or chopped into pieces, and murdered in all the other ways creative and imaginative human beings can devise, I have never been so happy to conclude a project. I have not found it easy to read time and time again about the horrors innocent people have been forced to suffer. What has kept me at this was the belief, as preliminary research seemed to suggest, that there was a positive solution to all this killing and a clear course of political action and policy to end it. And the*

results verify this. The problem is Power. The solution is democracy. The course of action is to foster freedom."

No academic knows more about the senseless slaughtering of the innocents on this planet, and the easy solution to stop it than Rummel. He is 77 years old and has dedicated his life to informing you and me about the butchery that has been going on daily, and yet hidden from our view. You knew about the 6 million Jews, but did you know about the other 256 million unarmed, non-combatants murdered? Now that you know, do you care, and will you do something about it? No, you won't. Will Robert Mugabe stop butchering his own black people, and stop killing the white farmers of Zimbabwe who founded and developed Rhodesia before the blacks multiplied and took it over? Will he cease being the sole supplier of uranium to Iran? No. Will Kim Jong Il open the gates of his death camps, or stop supplying young girls to his officer corps? No. Will Hugo Chavez cease his forced socialism in preparation for changing Venezuela into a gulag like Cuba? No. Will President Omar al-Bashir of Sudan stop his Sudanese Arab Muslims from murdering anymore than the 500,000 black Christians they have already killed in Dafur? No. Will Mahmoud Ahmadinejad and Sayyid Ali Khamenei of Iran grow tomatoes in their centrifuges instead of enriching uranium, and embrace Binyamin Netanyahu instead of threatening death to all Jews? No. Will Than Shwe of Myanmar release Aung San Suu Kyi and stop murdering his own people? No. Will Isayas Afewerki of Eritrea stop helping terrorists and murdering people? No. Will Cuba give up communism, and murdering and imprisoning people, despite the asinine opinions of the black idiots at the Congressional Black Caucus? No. Will Muammar al-Qaddafi of Libya, Gurbanguly Berdymuhammedov of Turkmenistan, Hu Jintao of China and King Abdullah of Saudi Arabia stop the persecution and allow freedom for their people? No, because we get too much oil and other benefits from them. Most importantly, will Obama and his Darkside see the bloodbath that must accompany his lust for power, and finally see what he is doing to the very people that gave him the honor and privilege only granted to 44 men in the history of the planet? Sadly, no again. If the slaughter of 262 million people doesn't change minds then they will never change. That should speak volumes to you about the power of power. In his "A Vindication of Natural Society" Edmund Burke said, "Power gradually extirpates for the mind every humane and gentle virtue." After a life devoted to democide, Rummel said, "Power kills, absolute power kills absolutely."

Americans reading this book will wonder why in the hell I included this section on the mass murder by governments of their own citizens. I understand why they feel this way. Murder to us has always meant a drive-by shooting or a drug deal gone bad. Or, it was Albert DeSalvo, the Boston Strangler, killing 13 people, or Jack the Ripper killing six prostitutes. Also, before Rummul dedicated his life to demicide, it was as he describes it, a "black hole" in our textbooks and even in college teaching and research studies. How can we discuss an issue like mass murder if we have no statistics or verifiable material from the crime scene? The reason for lack of data is that the communist and other totalitarian regimes that commit most of the murders, seldom want anyone to know of their crimes. They write the history, and omit what they are ashamed of. Probably the most reluctance on the part of Americans comes from the fact that mass murder is disgusting to us and since we don't do it, why worry about it. It's like showing pictures of black lungs to a smoker. We know smoking is bad, but don't show me proof. I have color photos of hundreds of dead aborted babies outside a dumpster in Los Angeles. Twenty years ago I thought showing it would wake people up to what abortion is. Most would just turn their head away. Rummel has spent much of his life on this study of death in the hopes that people will see that the solution to demicide is freedom and democracy. But, is anyone listening? Obama is moving us ever closer to the mid-stage of socialism, and he will then move even faster to a form of fascism or Marxism-Leninism. That is when the murdering will begin. Will Americans listen to my warning? Probably not. Sarah Palin and others warned us of coming "Death Panels" if the Health Care bill was passed. It passed anyway and yes, there will be a committee that decides who lives and who dies. So, the warning from Santayana will be ignored once again as it always has in the past.

WHY OBAMA MUST MURDER YOU

Having been to the Cambodian refugee camps in Thailand where the people are still mortared, raped, and mistreated by communist infiltrators and their Thai hosts, I saw a connection between the trusting, docile, beautiful Cambodian people and the ignorant, trusting Americans who voted for "hope and change," but will get Golgotha instead.

That Obama is rushing the United States into socialism there is no doubt except by those too dumb or numb to see it. Even most conservatives see Obama as just another progressive in the order of Woodrow Wilson or Teddy Roosevelt. Like Obama, Pol Pot did not believe in evolutionary socialism, but rather revolutionary socialism to bring about radical transformation in Cambodia. Instead of incrementally introducing government-owned means of production and eliminating all private endeavors and individualism, he simply selected those not apt to adapt to socialism, and put a gun to the heads of those who wore glasses, or had no calluses, or wore nice clothing. As the murdered bodies filled up one field he would just move on to another field and fill it up, too. Soon, there were over 20,000 "killing fields" chock full of innocent women, children, and men randomly selected by young boys and girls to be shot because they didn't look agrarian enough. Throughout the 20th century the introduction of socialism into free societies has always involved killing fields.

The United States has been a capitalist, free enterprise, representative republic since before our official founding in 1776. We have always been free to produce what we want, and consume what we desire with few or no restrictions. If you want a red Mustang with a Shelby-Cobra package and a dealer tries to force you to buy a Yugo instead, you would probably say a few expletives and take your business elsewhere. If identical flat-screen TV's are $50 less at Wal-Mart than Target, you shop at the former. If nobody has what you want you keep your money and go home. Most often you will find that red Mustang because profit-driven capitalists want to make the products that you demand so that they can stay in business and pay their bills. Those producers that react best to the demands of consumers prosper if they continue to combine their ambition and ability with opportunity and a little luck.

Under socialism, producers are insulated from the consumers. They produce products and services only in conformance with directives from the state apparatchik. Individual consumer input would interfere with proscribed production goals of the statists. The central "planners" do not appreciate individuals tampering with their rigid system of selecting, producing, and allocating goods and services to the "community." Rather than tinker with their master planning, the statist finds it more effective to use negative incentives to punish those that are displeased with the decisions of the state. They punish the uncooperative ones by accusing them of "parasitism," or "hoarding," or "black marketeering," and similar "crimes" of socialism. These crimes do not exist in free-market capitalism because the marketplace always adjusts itself to correct imbalances. Thus, the socialist state by its very nature must be operated like a large prison and all of its citizens are lifers, trapped behind the prison walls with their families until death overtakes them. Needless to say, as this socialist system is being rapidly forced upon an unwilling populace, many people who remember the lost days of capitalism and freedom will misbehave, and attempt a forced return to a better time in their lives. The state cannot arrest these people and send them off to prison because they are already serving their life sentences behind the ribbon-wire of state socialism. So, if a socialist state is to succeed, then the regime must at the outset be prepared to set aside one of their assembly-lines dedicated solely to the murdering of those citizens unwilling to appreciate the benefits of the socialist state.

I am a pessimist by nature which makes me a happy person. In explanation, I always expect the worst outcome when anticipating a future occurrence, which makes me work harder to produce the best outcome. Most often the worst does not happen and therefore, I am usually happy. I don't see this happy scenario playing out with Obama's head-long rush to rip asunder the only superpower with one-quarter of the earth's GDP, and resurrect a socialist or fascist state in its place without employing killing fields.

Socialism usually denotes an economic system where the means of production and distribution is owned by the state. But, there are so many more tangible and intangible human needs and qualities that are changed right along with a change in the economic system. Obama is not merely drastically altering our economic system, but forcing every repulsive and disgusting form of behavior upon us that has historically been abhorred by Americans. One of his first acts in office was to push for homosexuals in the military, and it will assuredly happen. You may not see it in the Obama-controlled media, but pro-homosexual activists are busy right now in every state integrating themselves into every part of your family's lives. Obama has always been pro-active in abortion, infanticide, and embryonic stem cell harvesting, and he has moved on all these to reward his donors. Planned Parenthood is already creating their own construction boom in anticipation of more babies to kill. Forced abortions are just around the corner, and girls will have planned abortions to sell their stem cells just as blood is donated today by alcoholics to support their habit. If you think our education system is horrendous now, wait until Obama and his Education Secretary, Arne Duncan, teach your son "fisting" and the finer anal stimulation techniques. Of course, Christianity and socialism mix like oil and water, so the former must be beaten into submission. Witness the increasing inclusion of Muslims and Earth-based religions, and the exclusion of Christians in all areas of our military. All of the other social aspects of life will be regimented and conformed so as not to conflict with the "greater good" of the state.

While Obama and his surrogates are making the behavioral changes necessary for citizens to blend with the new socialist United States, he is moving just as fast in "fundamentally transforming" our economic system. Bush gave him the $700 billion TARP fund to reward and punish the financial sector in accordance with his socialist goals. Congress gave him a $787 billion slush fund to advance these same goals by micro-directing money to politicians and supporters to tighten his grip. He is half-way toward passing his Cap and Trade bill which will give him control of the energy sector, flood the welfare rolls, and reduce GDP by $3 trillion. He stealthily stole the $60 billion student loan program, while endearing a million students to his cause through their indebtedness to him. He fired the head of GM and then nationalized both GM and Chrysler, while simultaneously repaying the unions for their election support. When Congress couldn't pass "Card Check" Obama recess- appointed Craig Becker to the NLRB who will use "back alley" means to force Card Check on companies.

Obama's Corporation for National and Community Service will total at least 2.5 million propagandized Obama robots that will be called on to do his bidding in the future. By 2012 there will be a total of 2.5 million highly-paid federal employees who will owe their jobs and lives to Obama. Obama's criminal voting schemes, rigged census, and amnesty for illegals will guarantee reelection for him and his select. Obama's crown achievement was the so-called Healthcare Reform Bill that will give Obama control of $3 trillion of our $15 trillion economy. The above are just what the overt portion of the Obama media and a little digging discovered. Imagine what Obama and his agents are doing covertly behind closed doors and late at night to imprison you and me in our own country.

Obama accomplished all of the above and more in just 15 months. Republicans and conservatives made a lot of noise, but not a lot of difference. The Tea Parties came to life all over the country and hope to make a difference starting this year, but their influence will be diminished by the Obama attack machine. Most Americans are still locked into the thought that this is just another political cycle, and common sense will prevail to bring us back from the brink. But, the overt and covert activities of the Darkside described in other parts of this book are increasing in numbers and intensity. There's a whole lot more coming your way. Obama knows many Americans have their breaking point. When they have taken all they can take of his radicalism, then fear will turn to anger. He not only knows this, but is preparing to meet force with greater force. That is when the killing fields will start filling up.

SUM

In this book I have given you a peek at the tip of one needle in a haystack of needles. If you care about America then you will have to find and examine the rest of the needles yourself. If you and 50 million Americans do not do this we will not survive as a free nation. I simply cannot tell you in a single book how devious, corrupt, and life-changing are the mind-boggling attacks on your freedoms now underway by the Darkside and its perverted leader, Barack Hussein Obama. This charlatan was birthed by a dysfunctional atheist-socialist; fathered by a philandering alcoholic; mentored by communists; schooled and befriended by radicals; packaged with pseudo-Christianity; elected by perverts, malcontents, racists and fools, and has set about dismantling capitalism, Christianity, and freedom in the United States of America, and replacing it with a fascist empire the likes of which Hitler only dreamed. What has taken 234 years to perfect, 1,350,000 lives to defend, and countless patriots to construct, has required less than two years to irreversibly seal its doom. In those few short months Obama has nationalized General Motors, Chrysler, Freddie Mac, and Fannie Mae, the $3 trillion dollar health industry, and the $60 billion dollar student loan program; taken virtual control of Wall Street and the financial industry; bankrupted our Treasury; created a permanent unemployed underclass; exacerbated our racial divide; exploded welfare; institutionalized abortion and infanticide; perverted our military; decimated our energy industry, and installed corrupt leftist radicals in all levels of government. Much, much worse is yet to come.

Hitler came to power in early 1933 and made his hatred of Jews clearly known to everyone. The Nazis did not commence routine killing of Jews until December 1941. Most Jews had over 8 years to affect their escape from Germany and avoid the concentration camps and gas chambers. Why did most of them stay and die? Just as the airline passengers on 9/11 could not comprehend a hijacker using a 747 as a guided suicide-missile, the Jews could not fathom civilized Germany systematically murdering 20,946,000 helpless people. But they did. Why can't Americans see the empirical proof of R.J. Rummel's conclusions that, as a democracy morphs into a socialist state, and then into a more totalitarian one, people are going to die; a lot of people are going to die. Why can't people see that Obama hates and wants to destroy America? Your response may be that you want to see more proof. I'm sure the Jews wanted to see more proof too, right up to December 1941. Theologian and Pastor Martin Niemoller of Lippstadt, Germany, also wanted to see more evidence of Hitler's intentions. He was in his office wondering how to confront Hitler's claim of supremacy of the state over religion when the Gestapo solved his dilemma by arresting him in 1938, and throwing him in Dachau concentration camp. Propaganda Minister Joseph Goebbels tried to have him executed twice, but Niemoller had received the Iron Cross as a submariner in WWI so appeals for his life to be spared worked, barely. Finally, just before he was scheduled to be executed for a third time in April 1945, the camp was liberated by the Allies. He gave a speech on January 6, 1946, to the Confessing Church in Frankfurt where he said:

"First, they came for the communists, and I did not speak out because I was not a communist,
Then, they came for the trade unionists, and I did not speak out because I was not a trade unionist,
Then, they came for the Jews, and I did not speak out because I was not a Jew.
Then, they came for me, and there was no one left to speak out"

There is always a short period of time early in the rise of a totalitarian despot when a unified effort by citizens can thwart the evil before it passes the point of no return. That time in America is either fast approaching, has already arrived, or has past us by and it is too late.

A lot of authors have made a lot of money writing "doomsday" books. Predictions have included natural disasters, famine, war, financial crisis, and Biblical Armageddon. Prognosticating our coming holocaust is mere hindsight now, since the debris of Obama's cataclysmic devastation is already littering our American landscape. You are in the eye of a hurricane and the calm may have left you unscathed so far, but the sidewall winds of the Darkside will soon leave not one American untouched. On social issues, Obama instituted tax-funded abortions, homosexuals among our soldiers, and harvesting stem cells from dead babies. Perhaps these decisions left you still in the calm of the eye because you are neither a soldier nor an unborn child. Over 10 million have lost their jobs under Obama. You may still have a job so your winds remain calm. Nationalizing auto companies and giving them to his UAW donors is okay with you also, since you drive a Ford and don't work for the auto unions. Obama allowed witches to have their own Wiccan altar at the Air Force Academy, and allowed Muslims to deny Billy Graham's son a chance to speak at the National Day of Prayer. But, you can still attend your neighborhood church, so those are not your concerns either. You heard a lot of "renting of garments" and "gnashing of teeth" over nationalized health care, but you still have your same health insurance for awhile. So calm still prevails in your part of the hurricane. Soon, Obama will control Wall Street and private businesses with his financial reform legislation. But, you don't trade stock and you are not a business owner. Next, Obama will give amnesty to 16,000,000 illegal aliens. But, you don't live in a border state so the effect will be minimal, probably. Maybe, you even pick-up one of those illegal aliens now and then to mow your lawn because they are cheaper than professional lawn maintenance people. Come the next election, the criminalizing of the census and mass Democrat voter fraud will keep Obama in power. Since he is already in power, maybe that doesn't bother you either. Cap and Trade, Global Warming, nationalizing the internet, making permanent a 20% unemployment rate, expanding the already bloated welfare system, Value Added Tax, and $7 gas prices are coming your way, too. Meanwhile, Obama's 37 "czars" are covertly issuing unilateral promulgations and rules that are snaking through every facet of your personal and business life to limit your freedom and make you a ward of the state. Which issue, which depravation, which freedom, which violation of your unalienable rights will wake you from your slumber? What will you do about it when you do awaken? Will you awaken in time?

I have shown you how our adventurous pioneers escaped tyranny and carved out a bare existence on the Atlantic coast; how they rose from bondage to freedom and expanded West until they occupied three and a half million square miles and then added Alaska and Hawaii; how they fought foreign wars and how 619,000 whites died to set 4,000,000 blacks free. And, I showed you the Darkside; how the blacks re-enslaved themselves by self-subjugation to the devil's pact between the black elites and liberal whites; how that same evil union corrupted the morals of Americans with abortion, homosexuality, a dumbed-down education system, and criminal politics. In the Black Imbroglio section I've shown that slavery is not unique to any race, and that if white flagellation does not cease then whites will forfeit their inheritance earned by them from 234 years of exceptionalism. I've introduced you to a man more dangerous to world stability than Hitler, Stalin, and Mao combined - Barack Hussein Obama. I've told you of his dark past, his black presence, and his bleak future plans to punish white Americans for their audacity of success, and bind them down with fascism so they can never rise again. I've given you a minute glimpse of the radical groups who methodically dismantled and corrupted America's foundations brick by brick in the hopes that someday a "messiah" would arrive and carry their work to fruition. This Darkside rallied around Clinton, but the Republican sweep of Congress in 1994 slowed their progressive creep. With the arrival of Obama in 2008 already partnered with an adoring media, the Darkside turned the reins over to their new leader, and for the first time could smell the blood of victory.

I have borrowed Hayek's own words to show you how easily democracies allow socialism to enter under the guise of charity, but grow into a behemoth of perpetual welfare. You have seen that socialism is merely a midway rest stop on the way to totalitarianism. This has been the result because love for mankind has never been the reason for implementing socialism in the 20th century. The pursuit of power has always been the pragmatic goal of the Darkside. And, power kills while absolute power kills absolutely. Finally, I've asked you if the murder of 262,000,000 unarmed, helpless, innocent children, women, and men by the totalitarian governments that rose out of the quagmire of socialism just in the 20th century is enough proof to make you fight to preserve our democracy. Democracy has proven to be the only form of government that does not murder its own people, and it is the only hope for you and your loved ones to survive.

We now have the knowledge to comply with Santayana's admonition to avoid the mistakes of the past to prevent recurrence in the future. From the exhaustive research and writings of Hayek and Rummel, and a thousand others, we now know and appreciate that our founding documents written by our founding fathers gave us the most perfect set of governance formulas ever conceived by man without the direct intervention of God. The United States Constitution with its 27 Amendments actually did originate from the hand of God because all the 10 Commandments given to Moses are intrinsic. We are discovering to our detriment that mere knowledge of the most perfect man-made form of governance is not enough. The innate evil in the hearts of men requires that constant vigilance be maintained to guard against contamination of our sacred documents. To the consternation of the guardians of America's heritage we have allowed Presidents starting with Woodrow Wilson and progressing through FDR, Johnson, Carter, Clinton, and Obama to each advance their own ultra-liberal perceptions of public charity, welfare, civil rights, egalitarianism, and political correctness. The same ultra-liberal perceptions have crept into our judiciary, educational system, media, and institutions until our original Constitutional constraints have been abrogated and bastardized beyond recognition. Many of these liberal violations of our Constitution had already occurred prior to Bush 43 entering office in 2000. And, while they did not deteriorate our democracy at the same speed under his tenure, neither did they regress back to earlier Constitutional models. They just slowed down a little. Now, we face a radical President and his formidable Darkside, both with the pent-up madness of the ages to relegate our sacred Constitution, and 234 years of codified laws and traditions to the trash heap of history. While those patriots among us were overseas fighting foreign tyrants, we failed to see our own homegrown invaders desecrating our homeland from within. We failed our founding fathers in not holding sacred Thomas Jefferson's warning that "The Tree of Liberty Must be Refreshed from Time to Time with the Blood of Patriots and Tyrants."

I doubt that enough Americans are even aware of the seriousness of Obama's ambitions, or his timeline in killing democracy to make a stand against him and his Darkside. Like all totalitarians, only he, and a few of his rogues and demons, are privy to his master plan of sucking the life out of what they perceive as a racist America as revenge for slavery. No, not even "Dingy" Harry Reid or "Plastic Face" Pelosi think Obama is anything more that their ticket to retain power. Obama got 53% of the vote in 2008. Have enough of those voters opened their eyes? Will they now see the errors of their ways? If enough have opened their eyes, is defeat still inevitable given that the Darkside has so corrupted our suffrage rights, criminalized the census data, and legalized illegals? Will people admit they were deaf, dumb, and blind in 2008 during Obama's campaign? Obama has always loathed the military. He has no roots in America, not even slave blood. He has contributed nothing to make this a free nation. He has never worked for a paycheck. He has never owned a business, never had to make a payroll, never worried about a budget. His mentors are Frank Davis, Saul Alinski, Jeremiah Wright, and Louis Farrakhan, all terrorists who hate America. America is the oldest of the democratic republics because almost all of our Presidents (except Clinton) loved their country, displayed strength of character, made significant accomplishments, or served with valor in the military. Obama has done absolutely nothing of importance in his entire life. We cannot see his certificate of live birth. We cannot see copies of his grade transcripts from Punahou, Occidental, Columbia, or Harvard. He admits in his books that he stayed high on alcohol, marijuana and cocaine, partied continually, and hung-out with radical Muslims and communists. Every single one of his cabinet officers, department heads, and czars is a radical leftist, socialist, or communist; all of them. Obama has physically bowed on numerous occasions to the heads of lesser nations, some of them communist, and apologized profusely for America's exceptional status among the powers of the world. He has let it be known that America is not a Christian nation, has reclassified terrorists as "man-made disasters", and treats Israel as an enemy state. He has decided to unilaterally dismantle our nuclear weapons, and reduce our military budget during this time of greatest danger. Does anyone think it strange that Obama hangs a Christmas ornament displaying an image of Mao Tse-tung, or refuses to salute our flag, or fail to mention Christ or Jesus at the White House Prayer Breakfast?

    Obama rose to power from the Chicago mob and was financed by Jihadist's Muslims. The motley coalition that elected him was composed of racist blacks, welfare

Hispanics, homosexuals, criminal unions, abortionists, socialists, communists, Muslims, welfare recipients, brain-challenged environmentalists, perverts, and most importantly and sadly, the ignorant hordes of white voters dumbed-down by 50 years of propaganda from a super-biased, slobbering media. A democracy simply can't exist without a free media and, while Clinton was their darling in the 90's, Obama's treatment was and still is an absolute love fest. During the 2008 campaign Obama was their messiah, and McCain and Palin their Satan. The treatment of Sarah Palin reminded me of the Bible's description of the perverts coming to sodomize the angels in Sodom and Gomorrah. From David Letterman, to Saturday Night Live, to all broadcast TV and newspapers, the media attacked Palin and her entire family relentlessly. The viciousness, pure hatred and vile attacks on Palin and her family is indicative of the black hearts and wrath felt for anyone not sharing the filthy, diseased, perverted minds of Obama's demonic hordes. Like Satan, Obama knows he has but a short time on earth to wreak havoc and desolation upon the soil of the hated white tormentors of his race.

In his pursuit of a rapid transition from democracy, to socialism, to fascism, Obama knows that one of his greatest adversaries is Christianity. America was given birth by Judeo-Christian ideals, and will wither and die without them. The ACLU, atheists, agnostics, earth-worshippers, Satanists, and the leftist judiciary have made every effort to remove all public vestiges of Christianity possible, so that democracy will be so weakened as to allow either pure socialism or fascism to flourish. Obama has taken the lead in this crusade. Unlike Islam, Shintoism, Buddhism, and other non-Christian religions, Christendom places great importance on individual freedom and the rights of men. Islam treats women as subhuman because it is based on murder, deceit, and sex. I realize you may think I've been hard on homosexuals in previous sections, but Christianity is the only religion where they have been safe from prosecution and persecution in modern times. Witness the genocide of homosexuals by the Nazis and the current Islamic laws against homosexuals. Christians abhor their deviant practices and want them to repent or keep to themselves, but do not believe in harming them. Obama embraces homosexuals for the same reason he snuggles-up to Planned Parenthood and unions - money and votes. When homosexuals, abortionists, unions, teachers, or any other group loses its usefulness, Obama will excise them as Hitler did the homosexuals, unions, pastors, and former political associates.

In Obama's socialist/fascist mind, power sharing with God is antithetical to his statist beliefs. We Christians believe God is supreme, while Obama sees man as the Supreme Being. If Obama believed in God, then belief in His Ten Commandments would naturally follow as would reverence for the Constitution, and other documents emanating from natural law. This would create an irreconcilable conflict with his political dogma. Belief in God simply has never co-existed with a Nazi, fascist, or communist government. Murder of innocents, from abortion to demicide, is an integral part of these systems, and cannot occur under true Christianity. Hearts have become hardened, and politics have become implacable in 2010 America, and will worsen under Obama's relentless crusades against Christianity. In my opinion, you cannot be a liberal, progressive, leftist, radical, socialist, communist, or Democrat today, and simultaneously believe in an omnipotent, living, loving, wrathful, jealous, vengeful, God. This was not true of a minority of Democrats just a few years ago. Like the court system and society in general, the Democrats have veered sharply left. As Rush says, "There are no more Blue Dogs left." Nancy Pelosi, the devout Catholic, and Harry Reid, the Mormon, see no contradiction between their worship of God, and the crushing of tiny skulls and vacuuming out the brains of His creation. By the way, I do not believe in a theocracy as a workable form of government in our secular and pluralistic country. I do know that a representative republic like the United States cannot exist without being anchored within a Judeo-Christian belief system. A good example is countries with both Muslims and Christians. Where the Muslims dominate, Christians are murdered, or, at the very least, persecuted. Where Christians dominate, Muslims enjoy the same rights as all citizens. When even minority Muslims try to bully a half-hearted Christian majority there are problems similar to what is happening all over Europe now. They let the situation get out of hand by bowing to the Muslims too often, and fail to realize Muslims have multiplied like cancer cells. This is happening in the United States also, and if not checked will get out of control. Muslims will never coexist peacefully with any other belief system due to their intolerance. Separation from a religion that is based on murder, war, and sex is the lone solution. Christians look at all men as children of God regardless of color or belief. Muslims look upon people as infidels if they are not Muslim, and subject to death if they do not convert to Islam. Recently, Muslims succeeded in blocking Franklin Graham from speaking at the National Day of Prayer. Their complaint was that Christians dominated the program. Could it be that Christians also founded the whole damn country, and all that Muslims really want to do is eventually get rid of all religions except Islam as they have done in every Muslim country? Judeo-Christianity founded America and it is America's rock. To say that Islam is equal to Christianity in America is to say that wrong is the same as right and elevates relativism to a science. Like it or not, if Muslims or the atheist-based groups of the Darkside succeed in their present, long-running campaign to minimize Christianity in both the public and private lives of Americans, then the United States will devolve into anarchy and chaos, which in turn will destabilize the entire planet and result in demicide exceeding that of the 20th century.

Over a billion people have called themselves Americans in the seven generations since our nation was founded. Of that billion, only 44 of them have been honored to be President of the United States. What a privilege; what an honor. Instead of marveling at the great opportunity of rescuing the nation that selected 1 of these 44 from a 13% black minority, Obama assembled the most perverted rabble of miscreants ever to descend on Washington, and assigned to each of them a specific part of our life to dismember. You have read about some of them in my "rogues" and "demons" section. A book could be written about each one of these freaks and their weird, twisted beliefs, actions, and behavior. There is not a single one that could be labeled a morally normal person. They are all the sewer dregs and vermin of a sick society. Fiscally, they are socialists, Nazis, communists, and fascists, believe in confiscatory taxation, and wealth redistribution. Morally, they are lesbians, homosexuals, cross-dressers, transsexuals, transvestites, sado-masochists, bisexuals, pedophiles, and practitioners of bestiality, multiple-partner sex, and fisting. Of course, rather than keep these abnormalities to themselves they share their perversion whenever possible, especially if part of their job description is instruction of others or education. There could be no other reason for hiring these misfits than to create, multiply, and begat a society in their own sleazy image. In fashioning their vision of heaven on earth they will bequeath to us and our progeny a lasting hell. They could all mimic the characters that you might see in a triple-X rated mutant porno flick, but these semi-humanoid curs have been hand-selected from the black abyss by Obama to rain terror and excise the remaining remnants of good that is still evident in parts of a once great nation. Not even one of them possesses any character, skill, or attribute remotely reminiscent of the American spirit of exceptionalism. They are Obama's assassins, snipers, and hit men come to surgically remove the healthy tissue of heritage and traditions of a once-proud nation, and graft in their place the cancerous implants of the Darkside to metastasize throughout the body of America until only disease remains.

Uniting the perverted brains of the Darkside's rogues and demons with the brawn of their useful idiots, Obama's multitudes of grim reapers have descended on America's fruited plains like a swarm of locusts. I have told you just a little of the devastation of the past and present. Unlike some clairvoyant authors, I can only conjecture what the future will bring after having symbiotically dwelled in Obama's brain for the past year. I know that unemployment will rise, terrorism will increase, government will become more oppressive, gas prices will creep up, and welfare in its various forms will expand. Federal employees, union membership, and AmeriCorps programs will recruit and hire millions more to their ranks. All of this must come to pass based on Obama's performance to date, and his critical path methodology to achieve power. Gold will continue to rise because increasingly, people know that the truth about our economy is a stranger most rare to Obama. Financial markets are going to crash and burn again in 2010 or early in 2011. Every American is in debt. Every state is in debt and broke. The United States is drowning in a sea of debt and can never begin to repay it. So, they will keep printing dollars until inflation explodes. People in foreign nations are saddled with enormous personal debt. Their countries are in debt and can never repay it. The world population in general and the American people in particular, have spent too much, too long. We, the American people, are always accountable, eventually, for our personal extravagance, but the politicians under orders of Obama have robbed the Treasury like Robin Hood, and it is bare. This economic ruin must also come to pass, and is integral to Obama's blueprint for power.

Illegal aliens will increasingly divide Americans because they are taking jobs that will never return to unemployed Americans, and Obama needs their votes. Actually, whether Obama's amnesty is enacted by Congress matters little because the illegals will not go home. They will vote like American citizens, thanks to voter fraud. They will have jobs and they will enjoy life in our America as if they were citizens. The only American right and privilege that most illegal's will forego is paying taxes. Violence, especially in the Southwest, will spiral out of control. With the increase in unemployment, elevated terrorism, illegal aliens, and the normal level of black violence, fear of traveling, and fear even in previously safe communities will be an impetus for people to stay at home, become more survival conscious and spend less on frills. This will further contract the economy. The oil spill, Cap and Trade, and Obama's destructive energy policies will transfer more power to Obama, increase cost of living, and increase unemployment. Quasi-government insiders like Algore will gain stature, wealth, and power, also.

As Rush Limbaugh says, "Please do not doubt me," when I say irrevocably that Obama and his Darkside have not demonstrated, rioted, murdered, planned extensively, and sometimes given their lives to crash and burn the giant among giants, the United States of America, only to see their sacrifices go up in flames . You have read what I've written about Cloward-Pivens, Alinsky, Ayers, and the thousands of radicals and revolutionaries working toward this goal. Well, multiply what you've read by a thousand times and that is what I didn't have room in this book to tell you about. This many radicals, this many years, this many causes will not have been spent in vain, so says Obama and the Darkside. To fail after coming this far, getting this close only to turn it all over again to the Republicans who will dilute Obamacare, and reverse all the other gains of the Darkside in the fiscal and moral arenas, is the death knell of the Darkside and it will not stand. Obama's Darkside legions are not only the sleaziest reprobates on the planet morally and fiscally, but they are willing to give their lives and fortunes (your fortune too) to prevent loss of the 60 years spent in corrupting our nation. To them, it would be like telling homosexuals to go back in the closet; like telling Planned Parenthood to stop their construction of new abortion mills; like telling the black elites there will never be another black President, since this one was a disaster. They know there is a battle looming. Eleven states are preparing lawsuits to dismantle Obamacare. The same number of states is enacting stiff illegal immigration laws to match Arizona's. The Darkside knows these and many more battles are ahead to unravel their progress and stop further destruction of the "Big Satan." Obama and the Darkside will pull out all the stops and stop at nothing in their quest of our doom. As Samuel Jackson's character said in Jurassic Park, "Hang onto your butt."

Keep in mind that Obama's ultimate goal is to be America's first fascist President or dictator. This can be accomplished in a few ways. He may choose to take the route of populism, like Hitler and Hugo Chavez, and thereby gain the popular support of the people and politicians in order to change the term limits, and retain power indefinitely. I realize that our Constitution would have to be amended to allow more than two terms, but this prohibition could be quickly remedied if Obama enjoyed sufficient popular support of the people. You may think this is a distant possibility, but do you recall the unknown black community organizer that we still know nothing about who raised $668 million dollars, had no experience, lied like a rug, beat the Democrat front-runner, and easily defeated a war hero to become President?

The most likely path that Obama will follow is a crisis strategy. In other words, create panic, fear, and confusion among all the people, and they will readily accept any leader that promises to quickly end their pain and give them peace and security. This scenario is probably much easier than most people imagine. If terrorists (maybe with the help of Obama) were to blow-up just 11 of our complicated, yet delicate oil refineries, we would lose 50% of our fuel production overnight. Gas would be rationed and shoot to $20 per gallon. Food deliveries would cease. Doctor's appointments could not be kept. Businesses would fail for lack of customers. And, power plants would shut-down for half-days. In other words, America would come to a dead stop. Neighbors would be at each other's throats, and crime would be rampant. If it happened during the winter thousands would freeze to death. The National Guard would be stationed on every street corner, and marshal law would be declared. Obama would be in charge and have immediate dictatorial powers. What and who would make him return those powers? There are many other scenarios to quickly bring the United States to its knees. Americans are a law-abiding nation. We have a history of obeying what we are told to do. We have always trusted our national leaders to protect us, not treat us like cattle awaiting slaughter. The average, coddled American would say, "Hey, that's unconstitutional, you can't do that." When Obama's reply is "Yes, I can" what are you going to do about it? Like the 9/11 airline passengers who had never imagined such a thing as a "suicide hijacker," we have never faced a renegade President who has proclaimed himself Caesar. Think about it, because it may just happen.

With our current economic crises, Jihadists within and without our borders trying to kill us, and an increasingly angry and restless citizenry, it would require only a minor interruption in the lives of Americans to foment chaos. The vast majority of Americans have never missed a meal or done without cable TV. They are fat, lazy, and dependent. At least half of them would surrender their freedom and the control of their own lives for just a promise to relieve them of a simple misery or discomfort. With almost half of all Americans not paying any income tax, most of them have already virtually surrendered their freedom to the government, anyway. Controlling the other half or most of them is Obama's real problem. These are business owners, independents, workers and earners, thinkers, and most don't like Obama. The majority of them are gun owners, know their American history, and are not so easily fooled by Obama's tele-prompters and stuttered incompetence. If Obama can control a sufficiently large majority, he will not have to concern himself immediately with these malcontents, since we are still a voting democracy and 51% is all that is needed.

The timing of the aforementioned created crisis is dependent on the anticipated outcome of the 2010 mid-term elections and the margin of victory. If Democrats retain control of Congress then Obama would not need a crisis, since he would have two more years in which he and his Darkside could do even more damage than they wreaked in the first two years. If 2010 is a close election, and the Republicans hold a small lead in either or both houses, then Obama may still not need a created crisis if he feels fence-sitting Republican Senators like Lindsey Graham, Scott Brown, Susan Collins, Charles Grassley, or Olympia Snowe can be bought-off, and a few house members can be coerced to vote with the Democrats. Under either of these hypotheses Obama's departments, agencies, and czars, complimented by executive orders to overcome and bypass obstinate Republicans, can actually legislate as if they were still the majority in Congress. Obama's veto power can stop the Republicans from passing any legislation. Every agency is passing major quasi-laws as I write this. A good example of this is the FCC takeover of the internet by redefining it as a telephone communication service. As I mentioned earlier, who is going to tell Obama and his creeps that he can't do that? We have some good Republicans, and they can get noisy, but noisy doesn't change anything.

Now, for the third and more dangerous scenario. If Obama is certain that the Democrats are facing a huge loss of seats which will effectively halt the Darkside's siege of America, and even seriously dampen his ability to legislate from his cabinet, czars, and agencies, he must act or all will be lost and revert back to the Republicans. I'm sure Obama has an off-the-shelf plan ready to meet this contingency. It will be either the aforementioned oil refinery attack, a "man-caused disaster" (terrorism), a financial meltdown, an internet cyber attack, or even an electromagnetic pulse weapon. Whatever crisis Obama pulls from his bag of tricks it must be of sufficient magnitude to throw the entire country into panic and shut-down business-as-usual in the United States. What would you do if your food was running low, you couldn't drive to work, your baby had no formula, you were out of a life-dependent drug, the power was out so your dialysis machine wouldn't operate or, heavens forbid, you couldn't watch Oprah? While you may be a good traditional American, don't forget that many are second generation apathetic slobs who will sell their soul for security. Not only will they sell their soul, but they will sell you out also. You never really know a person's valor until they face a crisis.

This is why soldiers often become closer to their "band of brothers" than they do to their own families.

Once Obama has his crisis, he will do as Rahm Emanuel said, "Never let a crisis go to waste." One of his first acts will be to place all of his "useful idiots" strategically around the country. The active duty military and National Guard will be deployed, also. To prevent riots and disorder Obama will issue an order for all citizens to turn-in their personal weapons for "safe-keeping" until the crisis is over and order is restored. Of course, they will never be returned. Once most of the gun owners have surrendered their weapons, the orders will go out to hunt down and forcibly confiscate the remainder. No doubt, in some cases, they will take them from their "cold dead fingers." With no means of self-defense, unarmed citizens will become government subjects with no ability to defend their families against government tyranny. For Americans, **"It's Over."**

For arguments sake, let us assume Obama finds it unnecessary to create a crisis. Our demise will then be incremental. In other words, the end results will be the same, only it will take a little longer. You have seen the dizzying array of Obama's style of governing over his first year and a half in office. Your kids can't watch a cartoon show, and I can't watch Fox News, without seeing his face and hearing his teleprompter voice. He is a man on a mission. He's not too bright, but he is a community organizer who never stopped organizing. He has pushed the envelope many times by nationalizing General Motors, passing Obamacare, refusing to prosecute ACORN or the New Black Panthers, and other questionable, suspicious, or extra-Constitutional actions. After each time, what is left of our independent media squawks about it, but nothing is done and it passes. He learned early in his Presidency that he could get away with about anything he wanted because we are really a country without an independent press or opposition with the power to do anything. He is Commander-in-Chief of the military, owns the FBI, ATF, IRS, U.S. Marshalls Service, CIA, 8 million robotic union thugs, and 2.5 million federal workers.

When elected Republicans or conservatives outside government speak against Obama's actions, they are attacked from every quarter by politicians, talk show hosts, blogs, and even cartoonists. Tea Partiers are shadowed by

SEIU thugs and vocally and physically ambushed. If the Darkside has no real event to rail about they invent one; like the black Congressmen who said racial epithets were voiced at them during the Obamacare debacle. If you shut-up and cooperate, Obama will send you a check, whether it's unemployment compensation or food stamps. If you want to be a trouble-maker, you will get nothing in your mailbox, and you will be put on a list for future reference. Obama's ascendancy to Washington has more resembled an invasion of Rome by the Visigoths, than by a 21st century American political party. It's as if we are an occupied nation, rather than a four or eight year stint by one of our democratically elected parties. We have Craig Becker at the NLRB acting as if Card Check was a reality even though Congress refused to pass it. We see Eric The Red's legions of lawyers hovering over Islamic terrorists, protecting them like revered military heroes, even though some of them helped kill Americans on 9/11. Think about all the millions of federal employees busy altering and creating everything from explicit homosexual films for your kids, to appointing death panels to determine who lives and who dies. Now, imagine what our country will look like after 4 or 8 years of these daily doses of radical changes in your life; all of them inching down the path toward serfdom. Actually, it won't take 8 years or even 4 years. If he and the Darkside retain their Congressional majority after the 2010 elections, it should be smooth sailing thereafter. By that, I mean that he will probably go on to win in 2012, 2014, and so on. Why do I feel this way? Because you have seen a small part of the hundreds of radical groups working 24 hours a day to rig the census, stuff the ballot boxes, allow illegals to stay and vote even without an amnesty bill, and you have been numbed and are beyond shock by the blitzkrieg that Obama has ushered into our lives. No nation, not even the United States can stand up to this relentless punishment.

Recently, a Gallup Poll showed that Obama has an approval rating of 50%. That means he wins, and I'll tell you why. After all my research, which included a report from the Heritage Foundation, I conclude that in the 2008 elections the criminal fraud accounted for an average of 3% to 9% voting advantage for the Democrats. By the time the 2010 elections are held the Democrats will have had two more full years to practice their art of vote-rigging since they are in control of the country. If the Gallup Poll holds at 50% that means Obama and his Democrats will get 53% to 59% of the vote. Theoretically, Obama's popularity could drop to near 41% and he could still get reelected. And remember the vote-rigging in 2008 did not include the fraud that will be introduced into the vote count by George Soros and his "Secretary of State Project" in 2010, or the Obama "Geek Squad" who will be in charge of the electronic vote counting.

Mark Levin, Glenn Beck, Sean Hannity, and others greater than I have told you how to take this gift from God, this United States of America, and wrest it back from the demonic grip of those who never really earned the right, the privilege of being called Americans. There are so many true Americans like Michelle Malkin, Thomas Sowell, Rush Limbaugh, Walter E. Williams, Mark Steyn, and Herman Cain who work to exhaustion every day trying to arouse Americans to the imminent threat, posed by this pretender, to the Presidency. Like me, they are not casual observers to the irreversible harm done not only to our economy, but to the moral fiber that binds together this last bastion of morality on earth. They know that the United States is the linchpin holding together an already wobbling world that will spin uncontrollably off its axis when we are no more. These conservative Americans witnessed first the acquiescence of the media, followed soon by actual conjoining with the Darkside, to spew out proselytism and prevarication to deny time-strapped working Americans the traditional privilege of a reliable news source. They, along with Fox News and internet conservatives, are now our only source of accurate news. It all reminds me of the Iron Curtain around the USSR and stories of captive, freedom-loving people secretly listening in their basements to American-funded "Radio Free Europe" on their tiny germanium diode crystal radios. While in Berlin in the early 60's I remember seeing the multitude of wreaths on the West side of the Berlin Wall, each marking the spot where the East German "Geckos" murdered another freedom-loving escapee fleeing to West Berlin. When Obama and the Darkside commence their desolation of America in earnest, where will we flee to? We don't even have a Berlin Wall to tunnel under or float over in a hot air balloon, and no West Berlin either. How about Canada? I've owned a home and business in Canada and Canadians are already in a socialist state under siege by Muslims, and its citizens seem robotic like in the "Stepford Wives," so I want no part of Canada. Mexico is filth, murder, drugs, and also empty because all the Mexicans are here with us. No, we have nowhere to flee.

So, we have a life-changing decision to make. We either accept the life of a serf under totalitarianism, or we take back the America bequeathed to us by the greatest flesh and blood humans ever to set foot on this planet, our founding fathers. Mark Levin, Sean Hannity, and especially Glenn Beck have expended much effort on how to rally Americans to wake-up and just see what we have, and be pro-active in keeping it. They are telling you not to just sit in front of your TV, don't just call in to Rush and criticize Republicans when they all vote against the socialists, but the legislation still passes anyway because they are the minority. I know it's a tough call. You have a job, a family, and a life to live. One of the reasons that the Darkside is winning is that they do not work for a living, or have a traditional family to love and cherish. They are rich college professors paid with our tax money and tax-funded grants, with ample time on their hands to rouse their equally leftist students to march and demonstrate for socialism. They are pseudo-educators teaching from kindergarten to senior high school level that can't read or write, but like to have their custom license plates with "EDUCATOR" on them, and dream of having sex with their students. They are the 99% of black racists who are unmarried with three kids by three different fathers, or drug dealers, or rappers, or affirmative action recipients who crossed the "Peter Principle" line the moment they started work. They are Hollywood stars with Hollywooden brains who tell us to wipe with one square of toilet paper while they have solar collectors on just one of their 12 homes, drive three Hummers, burn enough Jet A-1 in their Gulfstreams to heat 50 homes, and use enough electricity in their Beverly Hills mansions to power a small city. They are the UAW workers of Obama Motors with Cadillac insurance plans who are paid $74 per hour only because their union gave Obama $61 million, while the private auto workers make half of their pay and produce better cars. They are the miscreants in Obama's government who make 20% more than the same job in private industry, and spend their time and our tax money devising ever more schemes to rape America. They are the tort lawyers who suck the life blood out of private industry, doctors, small businesses, and hard-working Americans, with their frivolous balderdash adjudicated by a judiciary that climbed out of the same slime pit. They are the ignorant whites with eyes that do not see, and ears that do not hear, but deep in the recesses of their parched brain they do recall being told that all whites are racists, and salvation can come only through a messiah that shall rise from a city called Chicago and bring absolution from his Imam, Jeremiah Wright. They are the sub-species of carnivorous gargoyles who call themselves Planned Parenthood, but rip God's children out of their liquid environment before their tiny screams can be heard, and deny the child bearing the child her God-given right to be a parent. They are the media who were the clarions of democracy, the voices of the oppressed, and the speakers for those that could not speak, but who have become the mouth of the false prophet, the forked tongue of socialism, and the lips spitting-out a brand of racism never seen in America. Finally, they are the 47% of Americans who do not pay income taxes, but drive on the same highways, eat the same food, live in the same homes, and enjoy the same freedoms as us taxpayers, yet clamor for more welfare, more benefits, more food stamps, more of everything, while we who pay taxes are told to wait at the end of the line.

My family and I will do our part in supporting the conservatives and Republicans in trying to take America back from the precipice where Obama has placed it. Unfortunately, win or lose, we all face an America that will never be the same as the America we grew up in. If we lose and Obama wins, he will have enslaved us all, white, black, brown, and yellow in an irrevocable totalitarian gulag. As in all totalitarian states, there will be the winners and losers which means they just take turns dying because the winners always become losers later.

If we win, we are left with the debris of Obama which is considerable. If we somehow patch together the slimmest of majorities in enough states in 2010 to win Congress, we still will not have achieved the desirable position of deadlock. Obama will still control Washington and still be legislating vociferously through the agencies, rogues, demons, useful idiots, and executive orders. Any legislation sponsored and passed by Republicans can be vetoed. Republicans will physically occupy, but they will not govern. Obama will simply ignore them as he goes about business as usual. Even the Senate's Constitutional mandate to advise and consent to judiciary nominations can be circumvented by recess appointments. Since protocol and tradition will be a forgotten courtesy, all of the waiting nominations will be recess appointed the minute Congress recesses. If just one of the four conservative justices of the Supreme Court leaves, or is assassinated by the Darkside, then Obama will own the Supreme Court, also.

The lop-sided deadlock in the Congress, while Obama continues shredding the Constitution, will be depressing to watch, but is not the whole problem faced by conservatives. There will be a seething anger and resentment throughout the fruited plains, and extending to the purple mountain majesty of our West. Every one of the 40 million blacks will hate whites for denying their demi-God his rightful throne in ruling over America in the unencumbered style to which he had become accustomed. Being of an innate, violent nature, they will spend this hatred often, and with no aforethought on the nearest white. In other words, there will be black anger and blacks will riot, as usual, and steal things.

Since Obama's politics have served to divide rather than unite, the browns will follow the blacks in seeing whites as the enemy. So, the Hispanics will be madder than ever at Arizona, Republicans, and white people. They still want the Southwest states back, but will take free healthcare, free college, welfare, food stamps and freedom to commit crimes, until we give them the titles to the states. Browns represent about 46,000,000 people, and they have been united by the radical Hispanic groups under the Obama/Darkside tutelage. The 24% that voted Republican in 2008 have mostly fled and joined the Democrats. They also will be rioting and demanding things from whites.

On top of the race and anger we will still be a bankrupt nation facing huge and growing unfunded mandates like Social Security, Medicare, and Medicaid on a federal level, and huge and growing unfunded mandates in the form of pensions, on a state level. Obamacare will still be adding $1 trillion each year to our deficit. Our national debt will be $15 trillion late in 2010 and shoot like a star after that. This does not include the financial crash coming late in 2010 or early in 2011, which will happen. Unemployment will go up as all our problems come crashing down on our heads. Americans will be damn sick and tired of crooked, thieving politicians, but half will still love Obama, and half will hate his guts. Domestic chaos will reign rampant for the first time in our history.

I have not discussed concerns outside our borders, but other countries will not be innocent bystanders while our chaos is occupying our attention. Obama told the world that we are unilaterally reducing our nukes in the future with no corresponding, verifiable reduction required of other countries. That will not happen for years, so we still have about 6000 armed nuclear weapons. But...we will not use them according to the messiah. Ronald Reagan's policy of peace through strength and mutual assured destruction worked just fine, and that is why Obama has abrogated it. He wants chaos and chaos it will be.

The United States has been the world's policemen since WWII. I am personally sorry we got involved in Vietnam and Somalia because both were a waste of young American lives for absolutely no good results. Like the cowardly idiot John Kerry, at first I was for the wars in Iraq and Afghanistan, and now I'm against them. Going after the Taliban for killing 3000 Americans on 9/11 seemed the only right thing to do. After killing most of the Taliban and putting Hamid Karzai in power, we should have left even though Bin Laden was still in a cave. Now, Obama and his anti-war crowd are getting more of our best soldiers killed for nothing. When, and if, we leave Afghanistan, it will revert back to al Qaida or the Taliban quickly. That's what Muslims do, have sex and kill each other. One American soldier is not worth the whole damn Muslim population. We should have left Iraq, too, no later than the hanging of Sadam. It also will revert to constant internal war. In fact, the suicide bombers and car bombs have picked-up lately, so you can imagine what will happen after we are gone. Iran feeds both these nations with arms and bodies, so killing will be perpetual.

I'm sure that Muslims killing Muslims does not surprise you. What will surprise you will be what happens when the internal chaos of the United States forces us to suspend our role as the cops of the world. Hugo Chavez's Venezuela is getting hit with a 30.4% inflation rate. They are short of food, oil exports are down, and he is busy nationalizing all the industries he can without appearing too anxious to lock-in his planned dictatorship. He desperately needs a distraction, a boogieman. If he can be certain that the U.S. would not stick its nose in his business, he would love to attack Columbia and Guyana to acquire their land and resources for Venezuela. He has, for years, supplied rebels with arms and equipment in Columbia, but that hasn't gone too well because the U.S. Special Forces keep killing them. We now retain SEALS or Army Special Forces in 92 of the 195 countries of the world. If we recalled them back to the states, or Obama told them to stand down, countries like Venezuela with ambitious wannabe dictators like Chavez would have a field day.

Venezuela is not the only country that would like to stop looking over its shoulder to see if the U.S. is watching every time they want to do something that is not quite kosher. North Korea is shipping technology and equipment through other countries with a final destination of Iran to speed-up Iran's development of nuclear weapons. Unfortunately, the irksome United States keeps intercepting their shipments and confiscating everything. Mostly this is the result of the CIA and Mossad cooperating to stop Iran's little hairy guy from blowing up the little Satan. With Obama's well-known dislike of Israel, compounded by chaos in the U.S., the likelihood of nuclear technology getting through to Iran improves greatly, and the invasion of Israel by Islamic countries is guaranteed.

If the chaos in the U.S. reaches critical mass and forces the U.S. to devote all of our time to domestic problems, you will then see that the world will erupt like Mount Krakatoa. Besides Venezuela invading Columbia and Guyana, you will witness North Korea attacking South Korea. Like the Banzai attacks during the 1950-53 Korean War, you will see the huge army of the North Koreans streaming across the 38th parallel by the hundreds of thousands, and maybe even use a few nukes to soften-up the South. The 20,000 or so American troops stationed in South Korea cannot withstand the numbers of the North, so they will die or be taken prisoner.

Of course, the relaxing of our vigilance will precipitate our known enemies in the terrorist groups to hit us hard and hit us often. Hezbollah, al Qaida, Hamas, and Islamic Jihadists inside our borders and outside, will take immediate advantage of our weakness. That's when Americans will find out that the nice Muslim guy next door really doesn't love them all that much.

Once the chaos starts in the United States it will feed on itself. Like a nuclear reaction, once the electrons start bumping into each other causing others to bump into even more electrons, it can't be stopped. Illegal aliens, both already here, and those still in Mexico, will see their opportunity of a lifetime. With our weakened defenses and lack of border protection, Mexicans will flood north like a tidal wave. They will be whipped-up by La Raza and the other 123 radical Hispanic groups. They will be told that it is now or never to retake the Southwest U.S. that was wrongly taken from them. When this happens, and the active duty military and National Guard troops that can be spared are dispatched to the Southwest, then other areas of concern will come into play. Let me throw you a real curve ball that would have been unthinkable before Obama brought us hope and change. If our country is in the midst of a racial/civil war, then what would be our response to Russia crossing the Bering Strait from the Chukotka Peninsula to the Seward Peninsula, and assaulting Alaska with 50 divisions of Spetznaz and regulars? They would quickly bulldoze over Elmendorf and Eielson Air Force Bases and the 8897 soldiers at Forts Greely, Wainwright, and Richardson, and subdue the rest of Alaska within hours. If Obama was still in charge we would not retaliate with nuclear weapons. The most logical outcome would be for him and Hillary Clinton to sit down with their Russian counterparts, and negotiate a compromise. Russia would drill for oil in ANWAR and anyplace else oil is discovered, occupy the Prudhoe Oil Fields, and take over the other natural resources and our citizens could keep their homes and live in colonial Russia Alaska. Don't laugh too hard at this scenario. Neither you nor I can predict the amazing events that will unfold with our United States no longer a superpower and keeper of the peace on the planet. Once the walls of our Jericho start crumbling, and reach national anarchy, we will be powerless to stop it. With no leader commanding enough of a following to make a difference, it will be every man for himself, and every group for themselves. Order will be non-existent. People will do battle over food and fuel. Even loved ones will turn on each other if things get bad enough. All Obama wanted to do is start the ball rolling on socialism by playing

Robin Hood, and then become dictator. Even Obama didn't figure that the snowball couldn't be stopped once it got under way.

Will the above happen, or am I crazy? Obama has come to divide our people and our nation. He has done a good job. The blacks and browns increasingly hate the whites. These two races plus the left represents about 50% of the population. The other 50%, which represents most of the patriotic, family-oriented, hard-working, tax-paying Americans, despise what Obama has done to our country. Both sides are rigid and uncompromising and ready for a fight. You be the judge as to the possibility of a civil war. As for me and my loved ones, I plan on something happening very nearly as I have conjectured. I now know the illogical, fanatical, suicidal, almost satanic, hatred that the Darkside feels for the "establishment," which is me and the other conservative Americans. We are the wall that separates them from nirvana; we are the ones that block Jihadist from their 72 virgins; we are the weakening membrane between the Darkside and the dark they have been striving to reach for 60 years at the end of our tunnel of light. If you doubt the depth of hatred felt in the twisted minds of the Darkside you need only listen to their many virulent spokesmen or even surrogates, like Chris Matthews, who was considered just another boring liberal before Obama made stuff run down his leg upon just hearing the voice of the chosen one. Have you ever seen a President before with such a huge chip on his shoulder, who resents anyone questioning his actions on the rare occasions that his state-owned media asks real questions? If you have self-doubts about whether Obama is an aberration, just listen to him and mentally visualize George Bush speaking the same words. Obama gets praise for saying things that George Bush would be vilified for saying. It is as if half of all Americans do not see, hear, or understand just how permanently profound are the changes being made by Obama to the United States. We all know the media kisses-up to him but who, besides the conservatives and Republicans, even seems to care how outlandish are his actions and statements? Have you heard the body count listed daily for Iraq and Afghanistan since Obama became Commander-in-Chief? I remember the count during Bush's years. What if Bush had taken $787 billion and slowly doled it out billion by billion to only his supporters and friends?

Would not the media be waiting with baited breath to quote the amount, the FOB's (friend of Bush) who received it, and the gall of the man for his blatant corruption? When is the last time you saw Cindy Sheehan or Code Pink protesting Obama's wars even though our soldiers are dying every day in Afghanistan? Picture media reaction to Bush labeling a Cambridge cop and his whole police force "stupid." Bush was ostracized for Katrina even though he warned people to evacuate a day before the hurricane hit, while Obama waited 7 days before even mentioning the oil spill in the Gulf, and the media was silent. What if Bush had a Mao Tse-Tung Christmas ornament on his tree at the White House? Can you even hazard a guess of what the media and Democrats would do if Bush used the same sleight-of-hand trickery to pass a pro-life bill that Obama, Pelosi, and Reid used to pass Obamacare?

Has this book failed or succeeded in demonstrating to you that your 44th President is the most bazaar aberration ever chosen to govern 310 million people? Obviously, I didn't vote for him, and I have always prided myself on thinking out of the box, but I still can't fathom the depth of our collective ignorance in seemingly doing the opposite of what is logical and reasonable. I worry that even after reading this book Americans will still not understand that we are not facing minor changes in our life. We and our loved ones are soon to be residents of Sodom and Gomorrah facing Armageddon. I know exactly why Obama is the way he is, but how do I warn the American people? I had a "Huck Finn" childhood, an adventurous adulthood and ended up with an "everything" wife and an all-American family. Obama began life with dysfunctional parents, graduated in his teens to a communist mentor, hated his skin color, stayed drugged or drunk by his own admission and learned that scamming the system rather than honest effort was the preferred route to success. Unlike me, he didn't have loving parents, tree-houses, Boy Scouts, rabbit hunting, scads of uncles, aunts and cousins, 4th of July picnics, family reunions, family vacations, the innocence of youth, military service and the million and one experiences of growing up in the greatest country there ever was. Just as an adult who suffered sexual, physical or mental abuse as a child is permanently scarred, so has Obama suffered permanent mental disfigurement from his perverted beginnings to his present demented view of the world. He can no more become an American than I could become a narcissistic racist like him. What is important to Americans is that they understand that his whole being, his life's grand achievement, is to punish every white American for living the dream that he never had. Reaching the pinnacle of power as President of the United States does not atone for the perceived injustices done to Obama in his twisted mind. More and more must be done to the American people because no amount of punishment will ever be enough. If Americans do not grasp the seriousness of Obama's immediate threat to their existence then we will all go down together.

The United States and indeed the entire world are in dire straits. It will never return to the "good ole days." But, for the sake of our loved ones we all would like to survive what's coming. The gist of what I have told you above is that there is no way the United States can avoid catastrophic upheaval. The debt is not going away, the Mexicans are not going home, and the 99% of blacks will always be racist and dependent. We have no country to flee to. Our government is totally corrupt. We are a nation divided by race. We are a nation divided by those that work and those that don't and won't. Even if we survive as a nation, the world has become a hostile environment where other nations will be circling like vultures looking for weakness.

The population of the United States is about 310 million people. In the 2008 Presidential election there were 129,392,711 total votes cast. Obama got 69,456,897 votes (52.9%) and McCain got 59,934,814 votes (45.7%). That means Obama got 9,522,083 more votes than McCain. If the recent polls can be trusted, Obama is now at about 50%, which means he has lost about 3.7 million voters (assuming the number of voters remains constant) who now realize he is a socialist or worse. I don't think he can win many of these voters back. If this holds and the Darkside adds even 1% (I estimate 5%) through fraud and manipulation, instead of the 3% to 9% added in 2008, then Obama, and probably a Democrat Congress, will stay in power until at least 2016, which is far beyond the time that the United States will still exist as a free nation if indeed it exists at all. This means there are about 65 million Americans that probably do not like, and will not vote for Obama. Since Obama's constituency we know consists of 99% of the blacks who vote by color only, and a minimum 75% of the Hispanics, and a large number of ignorant whites, we can deduce that a large percentage of Obama's voters are among the lower class economically. This does not include what I call Obamaites who are the affluent, radical, leftist core of the drive to socialism. The 65 million that will vote Republican represent the lower-middle to upper scale economically.

These 65 million anti-Obama Americans are mostly the salt of the earth and the only, best, and last hope of the United States, and probably the planet, to survive. How does 65 million Americans with morals and good intentions, but not enough votes, beat 65 million racists and socialists of the Darkside who will cheat and even block voting precincts to win? The answer is, we probably can't win at the polls, given what I've told you of the Darkside's ongoing corruption. Your government has now declared war on you, and will use your tax money to crush all resistance. I'm not telling you to not vote, or not fight against the corruption, or not support your candidates. I'm saying after all is said and done, the evil will probably triumph.

What I call the Darkside, Newt Gingrich calls the secular-socialist machine. Like me, Newt sees the systematic obliteration of anything Christian, and the enhanced, federalized Chicago machine politics, steamrolling over Americans like the tanks in the Chinese Tiananmen Square massacre. But, he doesn't go far enough. Obama is a strange mix of racist, Islamisist, Black Liberation Theology, and fascist. European-type socialism here would fall short of the revenge preached by his mentors that must be exacted from white America.

What to do? We are an army of 65 million with no hope of a peaceful recovery of our precious America by the traditional political process. We could try a national boycott. Sixty-five million mostly affluent consumers supporting, or not supporting, targeted causes could literally shut-down any part of the private or public sector overnight. But, who will lead it? When the countervailing forces of SEIU thugs, and even the FBI and IRS confront us, will we be prepared for the violence that surely will ensue? How many of our 65 million are willing to refresh the tree of liberty with their own blood or the blood of their sons and daughters?

Another, even fainter hope is that our military would wake-up and see what is happening. After all, they are merely us with uniforms and guns. The vast majority of them are young, good men with morals and belief systems similar to ours. They are our kids, brothers, and fathers. If they were living in our homes, instead of stationed here or in Iraq or Afghanistan, they would join us. But they are not. They are mostly scattered at bases around the world, and represent the lower ranks of enlisted men or officers. They have all signed oaths agreeing to fire on civilians of the United States during insurrections. If called on to do so, most of them would not be in their area of residence so they would be asked to fire on strangers they do not know. So, they would most likely comply with the orders of their superiors, because soldiers are taught to obey orders. Like Clinton, Obama has selected the higher echelon military commanders that reflect his hegemony, and will unquestionably obey his directives. Consequently, I feel a military coup to save this country is highly unlikely.

Our last and final hope is the selfsame one described by Thomas Jefferson in a letter to James Madison in 1787 when he wrote, "I prefer the tumult of liberty to the quiet of servitude. Even this evil is productive of good. It prevents the degeneracy of government and nourishes a general attention to the public affairs." Jefferson was not referring to foreign conflict. He, like all of our founders, felt that when our own government became oppressive, the people had the God given unalienable right to preserve their liberty with force of arms. It has taken 234 years, but the time has sadly come for our founder's intended purpose for bequeathing to all of us the only Amendment in our Constitution that forcibly protects and defends all the other Amendments, the 2nd Amendment. It is all that stands between free Americans, and the servitude of the Darkside.

I have reviewed all the claims of both pro and anti-2nd Amendment sides as to the number of gun owners presently in the United States. I conclude there are 75 million owners of 275 million guns in the United States. Over 60 million of these gun owners are us. The other 15 million are Obama people. The United States has a total military compliment of 3,385,400 soldiers consisting of 1,473,900 active duty, 1,458,500 reserve and 453,000 paramilitary. Women comprise approximately 503,000 of the total. These soldiers are our fathers, sons, brothers, daughters, sisters, and mothers. Since the majority of the troops abhor what Obama is doing to our country, they will balk en masse if pushed too far by the Darkside. Some may fire on civilians initially, as stated above, but this will not last when they see the cruelty of the Darkside. All totalitarians participating in the murders of the 262 million innocents in the 20th century required soldiers to do the actual murdering. Obama presently lacks this commitment from our soldiers. It is conceivable he could use deceptive Hitlerian propaganda to deceive some of our soldiers, but most will remain loyal to their families. Discounting 10 million civilians on our side as half-hearted, fair-weather supporters, but not fighters, we still have left 50 million Americans that are willing to give more to their country than rhetoric. Estimating that 500,000 soldiers will be loyal to the Darkside means our American militia is over 100 times larger than Obama's palace guard of loyal military.

Our 50 million armed militia is already strategically placed in every neighborhood, city, county, and state. We are everywhere. We outnumber all the standing armies of all the nations on earth combined. We are veterans of Vietnam, Grenada, Panama, Persian Gulf, Bosnia, Afghanistan, and Iraq. We are the farmers, good old boys and girls, unemployed construction workers (thanks to our perverts in Washington), coal miners, roughnecks, union members, hunters and fishermen, pilots, NRA members, IT geeks, truckers and, yes, we even work for the Darkside (but they won't know who we are until it's time). We listen to country and western and Rock and Roll. We homeschool, or complain when the Darkside teaches filth to our kids. We own small businesses, play the stock market, still celebrate Christmas for Jesus, have never been racist like the Darkside, and know our history despite the attempt to hide it from us by our PC "educators." No amount of sophisticated weaponry can stand against us. We don't have to infiltrate enemy bases or spy on their enclaves, because we already surround them and have friends on the inside. We don't need to be indoctrinated on our mission, because we inherited that knowledge at birth, and it was reinforced by our parents and God's Word. The fear of our power does not have to be broadcast to the Darkside; they have already seen and heard it in the words of Janet Napolitano and Eric Holder. They know we are the only force that can check their cancer. They have called us "domestic terrorists" and say we are the real threat, while they euphemistically rename the real terrorists "man-caused disasters" in deference to their terrorist-in-chief. No, we are not the terrorists, but we are the only threat to their cowardly usurpation of our sovereign republic. How disgusting are these interlopers who want to tear asunder the land of the free and home of the brave, but prefer to act the poltroon rather than come out in the daylight.

In the coming days ahead, the Darkside will be searching, wanting, looking, for a way to disarm America. They will not attempt this coup d' etat by political means. Too many Democrats fear the clout of the gun vote. It will be by deception through a ruse such as a staged act of terrorism, or similar Darkside-engineered event. Believe neither this nor anything coming from the mouths of these derelicts ever again. Begin now to prepare for the times that will try our souls. List everything you require for life and secure it immediately; food, fuel, generator, water source, recreation, communication, transportation, medicine, guns, ammunition, heat source, entertainment, and special needs. Make preparations to survive for a period of six months, depending only on what you have, with nothing from the outside. Don't be paranoid, but be paranoid. Even before the Darkside swept in with Obama, intelligence gathering, whether by physical or electronic means, has become universal and intrusive even in the most remote locations. When the confiscation comes, your neighbor whom you confided in may be the one who informs the Darkside that you buried a weapon in the woods. Know your enemies better than you know your friends.

I will not lead this battle, but I will do my part. Don't wait for a leader because leaderless people are the ones who put Obama in power. Unite with trusted loved ones and friends, and these will grow into larger groups and natural leaders will develop from within. Start today to make lists of those you trust and what each member can contribute to the group. One may own a service station, one may be a doctor, one may own a grocery store, one may be a mechanic, and one may be a gun smith. Have meetings, assign tasks, establish communications and rehearse action plans. Stay alert, keep abreast of events, and do not be deceived. Just as Satan promised the whole world to Jesus, so will the Darkside promise the world to you. Our inspired founding fathers warned us over and over that this day was coming.

They loved you like you love your family, and that is why they bequeathed to you the 2nd Amendment to preserve our heritage for posterity. The rest is up to you.

If you fail, then... **"It's Over."**

POSTSCRIPT

If the preceding 425 pages failed to get my message across to you then I want to leave you with a few final thoughts. Unlike the Darkside, the authors of our founding documents did not think they were God. They bequeathed to us what they knew to be the most perfect system of governance conceived of man, but they did not claim infallibility. The founders all had well-stocked libraries, and studied the histories of all previous civilizations to aid in creating one that would avoid past pitfalls of failed governments. In almost every society studied, they saw that time and time again tyranny would always rear its ugly head after the passing of time. Thomas Jefferson, George Mason, John Adams, and most of the other founders, later expressed warnings in their correspondence that imperfect humans would periodically appear to question the power-sharing concepts of our constitutional republic, and attempt to create an imbalance. They instructed us to be ever vigilant and quash these attempts in their embryonic stage before they grew to unmanageable size. If this failed, and a breach of the proscribed checks and balances threatened the equilibrium of our republic, then they gave us permission to use the 2nd Amendment as a last resort, and a corresponding individual right to own the weapons to effect this right. The 2nd Amendment has nothing to do with hunting or defense against foreign powers. Its sole purpose was defense against the tyranny of our own government.

Only once, in over two and a quarter centuries, has the equilibrium of power been so concentrated amongst one group in controlling our federal government that force of arms was attempted to put an end to the tyranny of the majority. The Confederate States had all freely joined the union of states, and legally had the right to freely and peacefully leave that union when it became intolerable. The Confederate States fully expected the Union to "let my people go", so they formed their own country and went about establishing their own Constitution and infrastructure. They, more than ever, revered George Washington, Thomas Jefferson and the other founders. Most had come from the South anyway. The South hated slavery because it was unprofitable and unsustainable, but had been initiated by the North until the Yankee hypocrites found religion. The

South even initiated the beginnings of the repatriation of the slaves back to Africa. But, like Moses and the Israelites, the Union refused to let them leave and the result was the wanton killing of 618,000 Americans. So, the result of the Civil War was more a case of refreshing the tree of liberty with the blood of patriots, than the blood of tyrants. Afterwards, the tyrants were still in control, and our nation has been declining since that unfortunate event. If American patriots are not more successful this second time around there will be no third attempt.

Must an estimated 50 million patriotic Americans actually fight to restore America to its former greatness? Unfortunately, yes. The Civil War not only failed to wrest control from the northern despots and put our nation back on track, but served to entrench their tyranny which later morphed into the Darkside of today. The most radical Marxist magazine still in circulation in America is "The Nation" which was founded by northeastern abolitionist, E.L. Godkin, in 1865. All of the liberal/progressive, utopian, and yes, unworkable, changes to our near-perfect system of governance came from the northeast liberals, all Republicans, and oozed like slime westward. Later, like changelings, the Republicans became Democrats. Slowly at first, but inexorably, the "soft-socialism," disguised as charity, began to creep across our country. Woodrow Wilson got the ball rolling in 1913 with the income tax and Federal Reserve System. After FDR passed Social Security, and Johnson installed Medicare and Medicaid, socialism was here to stay. Had these and other social mandates been managed properly, we could have still survived as a regulated capitalist nation after 2008. If we had let AIG, Bear-Stearns, GM, the UAW, and others take the hit and fail as they deserved, we would have been a viable half-socialist, half-capitalist superpower, a little leaner and meaner but wiser and alive. Instead, Obama swept into power during this "Perfect Storm" and has set in motion not only full-blown socialism and dead capitalism, but a one-way, express route to fascism.

Concurrent with the progressivism came the social changes that have been equally detrimental to America. Homosexuality, drugs, abortion, pornography, immorality, loose mores, instant gratification, apathy, less patriotism, dumbed-down education, nanny statism, universal political corruption, political correctness, racial divisiveness, and most important, destruction of the family. The steady march of progressivism and decline of social values continued unabated from 1865 until today. Over 145 years of putrefaction of society has overloaded even our almost perfect system until it can no longer self-cleanse itself. Had we installed some automatic virus scanning device like our computers of today, to ascertain the degree of deviation from our founder's thoughts and documents, and made corrections periodically, then perhaps we could have stopped our decline. This didn't happen, the cancerous Darkside has burrowed too deep, and there is no political solution to turn back the clock and return America to its heyday. By hesitating and not periodically cleansing our nation, we have sacrificed many of those that would be standing by our side right now instead of standing with the Darkside. We stood by for too many years and didn't say anything, while our friends and children were led by the hand and indoctrinated into all the many enticements of the Darkside enumerated above.

This book opened with the "Fatal Sequence" explaining why all democracies collapse from loose fiscal policies when the majority always votes for the candidate who promises the most benefits from the public treasury. This is always followed by a dictatorship. In 2010 we will elect all 435 House Members and 36 Senators. Billions will flow to the candidates from lobbyists, special interests, and corporations and hundreds of billions will flow back to them as gifts from our treasury. And, as foretold, this never ending circle of power, votes, and money has caused chronic overspending and fiscal collapse. We hear about term limits and fraud, but 90% of the most nefarious members in Congress will again get re-elected.

The 2010 elections are the last hurrah for the Republicans. Regardless of the outcome, Obama's solid race-based black and brown voting blocs coupled with the perverted, hard-core left will never dip seriously below 50%. Given the rampant voter fraud already discussed and the coming gerrymandering from the census chicanery he can never again be beaten. So, Republicans, Tea Parties and conservatives base all their hopes on taking control of the House and Senate in 2010. First, they must offer more of our bankrupt treasury largesse to the voters than is offered by their Democrat opponents because voters have been conditioned to always expect more of everything. This will actually succeed in some majority white districts, but never in the black, brown, liberal, or union controlled areas who vote only Democrat. Since optimism burns deep in the hearts of conservatives, let us assume Republicans take control of both Houses. How will they erase 100 years of progressivism and two years of Obama's Kamikaze attacks on every part of our republic? Pray tell me which rights, safety nets, privileges, tenures, grants, programs, contracts and awards bequeathed to the slobbering citizenry by the Darkside will now be removed by the pusillanimous Republicans? How do we locate, capture, detain and transport 20 million illegal aliens back to Mexico? Remember, they are all unregistered Democrats. Are we going to force Obama and the UAW to sell their GM and Chrysler stock, and who will buy it knowing the exorbitant UAW contracts that go with it? Will we allow the pensions of the teachers, police, firemen and public workers unions to go belly-up, or print trillions of dollars to keep them solvent? What is the Republican plan to force the 48% of Americans who pay no income tax to start paying their fair share? They are registered Democrats. For that to happen we must provide millions of real jobs that will never exist in our lifetime. Will Republicans finally get rid of the behemoth NEA when Ronald Reagan couldn't do it when it was much smaller?

How can Republicans reverse and rehabilitate two generations of morally bankrupt zombies who have known only the drug culture, pornography, alcohol, depression, welfare, and victim status? Who will fire 95% of tenured university faculties who are grossly overpaid and actively inculcating socialist and communist dogma into our youth? Allowing these people to continue despoiling our children will assure a perpetual crop of America-haters. How can Republicans hope to re-educate the 40% of Americans that think socialism is a good idea, and show them how we are exceptional and how capitalism has made us the greatest people on earth? Do Republicans have the guts to deny benefits to millions of veterans, and 20 million food stamp and welfare recipients who continue to receive illegitimate windfalls? Will they remove the 1.25 million excess, overpaid, unneeded and underworked federal employees?

How will Republicans reduce the trillion dollar budget deficits coming in perpetuity, or ever hope to pay the $15 trillion national debt that is assuredly shooting to $20 trillion and more soon? When the Bush tax cuts expire at the end of 2010 federal revenue will dive, unemployment will rocket, and the projected deficit will balloon in 2011. How can they possibly do anything about the EPA adopting the rejected Kyoto Treaty regulations, or the FCC taking control of our internet? What can Republicans do about the NLRB forcing "card check" on companies, or the other agencies and czars continuing to seize our freedoms since Obama will still be President and have executive power? Republicans can never reverse Obamacare or the Financial Reform Act. These two acts alone will give Obama the power to eventually control half of our economy given his recent history of expanding presidential enumerated powers.

Will the Republicans overseeing a broke Washington refuse to bail out 50 broke states? What will Republicans have gained by winning Congress? They will be surrounded, hounded, challenged, thwarted, and harassed by Obama, his rogues, demons and useful idiots, the leftist court system, ACLU, environmentalists, ACORN, SEIU, unions, radical special interests, and two and a half million federal workers who owe their loyalty to Obama. There will be 46 million Hispanics and 40 million blacks who will be angry that Republicans pose a threat to their paladin, Barack. Stirring the simmering anger will be relentless attacks by Obama's protectors, the media. Hamas, Hezbollah, al Qaida, and other jihadists who have been filtering into every state and training faithfully, will also be angry that their preferred President has lost total power and will strike. They have learned much from the amateurish attempts of a few and will not repeat the mistakes of the past. While the Republican Congress stagnates amongst chaos and anarchy, Russia is no longer on life support, and China has spent her surpluses on arms, oil, gold, and influence. Iran, North Korea, Venezuela, Turkey, Syria, and more see our weakness and lose their fear. They will attack Israel because Obama has left them all alone. We also are alone. Like us, Europe is soft, spoiled, fat, white, and exists on the pensions and largesse of a bygone era. We are Atlas holding up the earth on feet of clay. Only the inertia from our past glory and fading preeminence as a superpower keeps us afloat. When we fall nobody will pick us up. Instead, they will pick our bones.

When I ran for Congress back in 1988 I exhorted my apathetic, would-be constituents to "Get serious or get used to it!" Even then, between the administrations of Reagan and Bush "41", I was concerned about the direction of our nation. Today, in this era of Obama, there are more "Take back America" books than I care to mention. They all wax eloquent and enrich their authors, but all will fail to restore America because they all depend on a discerning electorate, honest elections, the reasonableness of men, or the rule of law. These ploys did not work with King George III, Hitler, Tojo, Stalin, or Mao and they will not work in 2010 to wrest back America from the clutches of the Darkside Democrats. We are past socialism and heading rapidly toward Godless totalitarianism. Can you honestly look at the dysfunctional, pitiful excuse of what's left of our heritage from our founders and say that the miniscule changes and tweaks of even a saint like Sarah Palin will reverse 100 years of debasement by the Darkside? Do you really think that even a total takeover by Republicans will return this nation to a moral Constitutional Republic? If so, then you are not serious and you and your loved ones must get used to chaos and servitude, or worse.

Many of you will discount my denouement that our only recourse for a return to a Constitutional Republic is use of force. Why do you doubt Thomas Jefferson's admonition that the tree of liberty must occasionally be refreshed with the blood of patriots and tyrants? Do you brush-off his warning as mere hyperbole? By denying Jefferson's words you are saying that politics and persuasion will reverse our long slide into the abyss. Do you not know the unbounded power of evil and intransigence in the hearts of Obama and the Darkside? Have you not seen what 100 years of creeping progressivism has wrought upon our republic? It is no longer creeping and it is no longer simple Wilsonian progressivism. Under Obama it has mutated at an accelerated rate and is now beyond reversing. Only forceful upheaval can hope to cleanse the poison and heal the nation by starting fresh. Fear of physical combat is normal, but lack of resolve to resort to it as your last full measure of devotion to your God, your family and your country is a sentence of death. Your opponents in this struggle have this resolve. Do you?

Unlike the 262 million peasants murdered by the Darkside, we are armed, strategically positioned in every state, and there are 50 million of us. I can't tell you the hour or even the day, but the season is upon us.

GOD BLESS.

About The Author

Ron Martin is married with three grown children and six grand children. He was a CIA contractor during the Cuban Crisis and in Berlin, aerospace technician on Gemini, Apollo, Posidon and Dynasoar, pilot, candidate for U.S. Congress, Army combat medic, CPA, rancher, gun and knife show promoter, land developer and home builder, only American big game outfitter in Newfoundland, Canada, general store owner, went on two missions to Laos and brought back remains of one MIA and repatriated the son of a downed Air America Pilot. He currently lives in the North Georgia Mountains with Dianne, his wife of 35 Years.